TAYLOR SWIFT

The Brightest Star

The Life, Loves and Music

of a Global Sensation

An unauthorised biography

Michael Francis Taylor

NEW HAVEN PUBLISHING LTD

Published 2021
First Edition
NEW HAVEN PUBLISHING LTD
www.newhavenpublishingltd.com
newhavenpublishing@gmail.com

Cover picture
Taylor Swift at the premiere of the movie *Easy A*. Hollywood, CA, September
13th 2010 (© *Shutterstock*)

Cover design © Pete Cunliffe
pcunliffe@blueyonder.co.uk

Contents

Introduction

"I write songs about my life, When my life changes, so will my music. It's as simple as that. I tell stories"

What does it take to be called America's Sweetheart? To date, there have probably been only a dozen or so. The names Shirley Temple, Mary Tyler Moore, Meg Ryan, Sandra Bullock, and Julia Roberts spring to mind, actors each and every one; surprisingly, very few have been music artists until now. So, what does it take to be given such an endearing title?

With girl-next-door looks, energetic personalities, and clean-living lifestyles seemingly essential criteria, there have been many wannabes who appear to fit the bill, but then fail to meet expectations. In a world where the excessive pressures and pitfalls of stardom can derail the most lovable of characters, reputations can be shattered in the blink of an eye, falling easy prey to the media hawks looking for those gossip-fed headlines that can damage careers, sometimes irreparably.

Not so Taylor Swift, whose incredible rise to fame, from small-town childhood to global superstardom, has been achieved by simply staying true to herself, remaining an inspiration and source of motivation for her legion of Swiftie fans around the world, and continuing to be the genuine role model, in every sense of the word. In 2013, *Vanity Fair* dubbed her "the girliest girl in America."

In a recording career of a little over fifteen years, Taylor has not only helped shape country music, but successfully made the crossover to mainstream pop without completely taking off her cowboy boots, evidenced in some of her subsequent writing. Along the way she has amassed a catalogue of nine critically-acclaimed albums with total sales of over $50 million, had dozens of hit singles, including many chart-toppers, and continues to break records for her music, videos and live performances. The sum of all this has made her one of the world's most successful artists.

And it's not hard to see why. As a songwriter she matures with each and every album, with beautiful melodies and autobiographical lyrics showing an insight that truly exceeds her young age. Her words can be either romantic love letters or vengeful put-downs for being betrayed, and along the way a succession of real-life lovers have all been subjects of her insightful writing, leaving her millions of eager followers poring through her lyrics like detectives looking for leads. She has hatched her very own Swiftian universe, the likes of which have seldom been seen before in any genre.

Then there's that soft and sweet vocal range which still shows hints of a Tennessee twang, but also has the knack of making words sound like what they mean.

As a live performer, Taylor has complete control of the stage, and to watch her interact with her fans is to see a hugely intelligent and creative mind in overdrive, with dazzling visual displays, both vibrant and intimate, which have her audiences in raptures, hanging on to every spoken word, and mouthing each and every lyric. And they, too, continue to break records for a chance to experience it.

For many young women around the world, she is also a leading style icon and continues to be a trend-setter, her choice always coinciding with the aesthetic look and feel of her most recent album. Since barely leaving school, she has graced the front cover of some of the world's leading music and fashion magazines, and in her many media interviews she often relates how she owes her incredible success to her parents. Although playing down their role, they are one of the key factors in their daughter's mercurial rise to stardom.

Then there are her selfless, less well known charitable efforts which continue to help those in need and inspire others to do the same through their action. Her heart is as big as her career.

Taylor has not only matured as an artist; she has blossomed into a deeply caring and sensitive woman, with the added strength to stand up to those who would do her wrong. Like many artists, certain events in her career conspire to add fuel to the media fire, but Taylor deals with all of them the only way she knows how. Along the way, she has made the music industry sit up and listen with her ongoing crusade for artists' rights.

The 2020 release of her eighth album *folklore,* in the midst of a global pandemic, took everyone completely by surprise, showcasing a whole new musical direction, lyrically more sophisticated than all that had gone before, and, with its subdued tone and vivid imagery, led to the music world fraternity comparing her songcraft to the likes of such luminaries as Joni Mitchell, Neil Young and Bruce Springsteen. It served to prove that Taylor was now among the few artists who were willing to put their careers on the line and experiment with a radical change of musical style. To show it wasn't just a passing whim, within just five months Taylor went one incredible step further by releasing a similar album which also garnered excellent reviews.

It had been a bold move for Taylor, dubbed "pandemic art" by a few, but hailed by many as being some of her finest work to date.

Without any doubt, Taylor Swift has proved to the world she is one of the greatest songwriters of her generation, and one of the most popular artists of the century. Now seen as more of a Badass Superstar than her country's sweetheart, she'll forever be the sweetheart, inspiration, and companion to Swiftie fans around the world, and with her creative energy at an all-time peak, she will no doubt continue to surprise and astound for decades to come.

So, this is the story of that incredible road to success, the good times and times not so good, the euphoria, depression, and the heartbreak, and, above all, the creation of a wonderful musical legacy by one so very young.

Michael Francis Taylor

June 2021

About This Book

To say at this moment in time that Taylor Swift is perhaps the most famous, the most photographed, and the most celebrated artist in the world, is perhaps an understatement. Despite being one of the most private artists in show business when it comes to her personal life, and rightly so, she is also, by choice, immediately accessible and forthcoming when it comes to talking about her career in music.

This is my attempt to chart that incredible career, with the focus being on her music, but at the same time highlighting those events in her life which, without question, have had a marked influence on her songwriting. With that in mind, it takes the form of both a mini biography and a critical review of her entire career to date.

All soundbites, reviews and interviews have been judiciously chosen for their succinctness and to give a clearer understanding to the narrative. They are included here under Fair Use guidelines, and source material is duly credited in the final section. Deep appreciation goes out to all concerned.

To say I am a fan of Taylor is also an understatement. Finding out more and more about her background and rise to fame has not in the least taken anything away from my opinion that she is something very special.

Sadly, I am no musician, nor do I profess to be a music critic, but, with a little indulgence, I have chosen to rate the songs. Music will always be subjective, and I have taken the view that we should all be able to take from Taylor's songs what is meaningful to us at the time. No doubt my favourites will be some of your least favourites, and vice versa. So, please, from one Swiftie to another, no brickbats.

This book has been a labour of love, and the one person I would like to thank is Taylor herself, whose incredible talent, energy and charisma continue to amaze me, and I relish the thought of what the future has in store for this brightest of stars.

Author's note

While every effort has been made to trace and contact the owners of copyright material reproduced herein and secure permissions, the publishers would like to apologise for any omissions and will be pleased to incorporate missing acknowledgements in any future edition of this book.

Abbreviations

AC   Billboard Adult Contemporary
ACA   American Country Awards
ACM   Academy of Country Music
AMA   American Music Associations
AP   Associated Press
BBC   British Broadcast Corporation
BMI   Broadcast Music Inc.
CMA   Country Music Association Awards
CMT   Country Music Television
GAC   Great American Country
MTV   Music Television
NPR   National Public Radio
RIAA   Record Industry Association of America

Song ratings

1 star - disappointing
2 stars - average
3 stars - good
4 stars - very good
5 stars - outstanding

Acknowledgements

To Teddie Dahlin at New Haven Publishing, for her continuing faith in me.
To Sarah Healey, for once again making my writing that little bit more legible.
To Peter Cunliffe, for continuing to do an amazing job with his cover designs.
To Angela, for not complaining when there were so many other things I should be doing.

By the same author

Harry Chapin - The Music Behind the Man (New Haven 2019)
Songs from the Vineyard - The Music of Carly Simon (New Haven 2020)

14-year-old Taylor Swift at a photo shoot for Abercrombie & Fitch's
Rising Stars Campaign 2003   (© Bruce Weber/Vanity Fair)

A Crazy Kid with Tangled Hair

"I was brought up with a strong woman in my life, and I think that had a lot to do with me not wanting to do anything half way."

The Swifts and the Finlays

Their young daughter should be looking forward to a career in finance, or so Taylor's parents believed. And it was not hard to see why. Her father, Scott Kingsley Swift, "a descendent of three bank presidents", was a marketing specialist working for the large financial company Merrill Lynch. One of three sons, Scott was a native of the affluent Philadelphia suburb of Bryn Mawr, Pennsylvania, born on March 5th 1952 to Archie Dean Swift (1914-1998) and his second wife, Rose Baldi Douglas (1920-1994).

Scott studied business and graduated with a first-class degree from the University of Delaware in 1974. Following in the footsteps of his father and grandfather, he entered the world of finance and became a successful stockbroker, eventually setting up Swift Group, an investment banking firm offering well-founded financial advice under the Merrill Lynch umbrella. He eventually rose up the ladder of success to become the company's first vice-president. His professionalism was noted by lecturer Scott McCain at a business convention:

"I learned three important points about Scott Swift. First, he is a remarkable professional - managing millions of dollars for powerful and important clients. He's an example of a pro who creates 'the Ultimate Customer Experience.' Second, he's one of the most creative and imaginative people I've ever met…His ideas are simultaneously simple and profound. Finally, and most important, he is a true 'connector.' By that I mean that he connects with people in a highly meaningful manner. When he told me that I could change the world, I just knew he really meant it!"

Taylor's mother, Andrea Gardner Swift, also had a successful career in finance, and before becoming a homemaker worked as a marketing executive for an advertising agency. Like Scott, she was a highly-driven professional with a gritted determination to succeed in what was then an almost entirely male sector. Taylor once commented in a televised interview that, before meeting Scott, her mother was financially independent and had "a career of her own and lived alone." The strong independence her mother had would go a long way to shaping Taylor's own outlook on life and her chosen career.

Like Scott, Andrea was also a native of the Keystone State, born on January 10th 1958. Her father was Ohio-born Robert Bruce Finlay (1920-2003), and after graduating from the University of Virginia, he began a successful career in engineering, culminating in becoming president of the Texas-based Raymond Construction Company.

11

Andrea's mother was Marjorie Finlay, born in Memphis, Tennessee, in 1928. Her parents were Missouri-born Elmer Henry Moehlenkamp (1897-1972) and Arkansan Cora Lee Morrow (c1901-1962). Raised in St Charles, Missouri, Marjorie was an alumna of the prestigious Lindenwood College, and, having developed a wonderful coloratura soprano voice, set her sights on achieving a career in opera. At the age of 21 she earned her Bachelor of Music and became a member of the renowned Mu Phi Epsilon, an international professional musical fraternity.

The following year, whilst working as a receptionist for a St Louis bank, Marjorie won a talent contest on the ABC radio show *Music with the Girls*, and was given the opportunity to tour with the show for the next 15 months. After that she honed her vocal skills by attending the Berkshire Music Center in Tanglewood, Massachusetts, and also studying music in New York.

Robert and Marjorie were married on March 22nd 1952 in Palm Beach, Florida, and shortly afterward moved to Havana, Cuba, where Robert's engineering office was based. Due to the growing political unrest there, they later relocated to Puerto Rico. Whilst Richard's engineering acumen flourished, especially in the oil business, Marjorie's amazing voice soon gave her celebrity status, performing concerts at local clubs and hotels, and, even with only a slender grasp of Spanish, she became the regular host of a top-rated variety show called the *El Show Pan-Americano*.

Richard's work would also see the family spending months in Southeast Asia. Finally returning to the States, they settled into their new home in Houston, Texas. By this time Andrea was about ten years old and had her education at the Memorial High School before going on to graduate from the University of Houston.

This was the nomadic world in which Andrea spent her childhood, watching her mother grace many concert halls, with lead roles that embraced both opera and musicals.

Taylor would share memories of her celebrated maternal grandmother: "I have these gorgeous, glamorous pictures of her in black-and-white. She was just so beautiful. Wherever my grandfather would go for his engineering job, my grandmother would go and perform and sing opera. She was in all these musicals in Singapore and all these gorgeous places where my mom grew up. My mom had these amazing stories of growing up overseas." In another interview, she recalled: "I can remember her singing, the thrill of it. She was one of my first inspirations."

A girl with a boy's name

It was while on a business trip to her hometown in Harris County, Texas, that Scott first met Andrea, and they struck up a whirlwind romance that led to them getting married in Houston on February 20th 1988. Scott was a few weeks shy of his 36th birthday; Andrea had just turned 30. They set up home in the small town of West

Reading in Berks County, Pennsylvania, about midway between Philadelphia and Harrisburg.

Their first child, Taylor Alison Swift, came into the world at Reading Hospital on Wednesday, December 13th 1989, under the star sign of Sagittarius. Her ancestry included English, Scottish, Welsh, Irish, German, and even a little Italian. Although seen as unfortunate for some, the number 13 would bear significance in Taylor's future career. She explained: "I was thirteen when I got my first record deal and my Twitter name is taylorswift13. My first single, 'Tim McGraw', had a 13-second intro, and every time something good happens, 13 is involved. If I ever get a tattoo, it will be 13."

With such a solid family foundation cemented in the world of finance, it was no wonder that Taylor's parents visualised their daughter following in their footsteps one day. With that in mind, they gave her the gender-neutral name of Taylor (after singer James Taylor, a favourite artist) in the belief that it would look favourable on her résumé and help her get a good start in a business career. Taylor explained their logic: "She named me Taylor so that if anybody saw on a business card the name, Taylor, they wouldn't know if it was a girl or a guy if they were thinking of hiring me."

Right from the word go, there seemed to be something very special about baby Taylor, and even the paediatrician at the hospital told her mother: "She's a really good-natured baby, but she knows exactly what she wants and how to get it!" Given time, Andrea would come to see just exactly what the doctor meant.

Taylor was born with blonde corkscrew curls and a captivating smile. Her distinctive Sagittarian personality would later reveal opposite traits - honest and intellectual, spontaneous and fun, making friends easily and being an excellent conversationist; but at the same time could be judgemental, reckless, superficial, and have a habit of taking risks and worrying about it later.

Much of Taylor's early childhood was spent on the family's 11-acre farm in rural Cumru Township. It had belonged to Scott's father in the past, and, although her parents were no farmers, Andrea ran a small business selling Christmas trees every December. For young Taylor, it provided the perfect setting, and she described it as "the most magical, wonderful place in the world."

Being able to let her imagination run wild would go a long way to foster both her creative and emotional development. Scott and Andrea identified with this. They saw something in Taylor that was indeed special, and they began to nurture it. Without them letting her indulge her dreams and fantasies in the picturesque surroundings, her life could have turned out so differently, and Taylor Swift could very well have found herself working in an office.

Taylor owed a lot of it to Andrea, and explained to the *Ottawa Citizen*: "My mom decided to stay at home to raise me. She totally raised me to be logical and practical. I was brought up with a strong woman in my life and I think that had a lot to do with me not wanting to do anything half way."

13

At the age of three, Taylor had a sibling. Austin Kingsley Swift was born on March 4th 1993, and, within a couple of years, Andrea decided to put any idea of continuing a career on hold to become a full-time mother. Like his sister, Austin would eventually embrace the arts, becoming a successful actor after graduating from the University of Notre Dame in 2015.

Taylor would never forget her mother's sacrifice, and later told the GAC cable channel: "I really look up to that. She had me when she was thirty. She had a complete career of her own and was supporting herself."

By the time Austin was born, Taylor had started attending nursery school and then pre-school at the Catholic Alvernia Montessori School in Reading, which was run by Bernardine Franciscan nuns. Interviewed for the hometown paper, the *Reading Eagle,* Head Sister Ann Marie Coll remembered young Taylor: "She was kind of shy but not too shy, and she always liked to sing. When she was in grade school, she came back and played guitar for the children."

Indeed, by the age of three, Taylor had certainly found her voice and was trying to find an audience she could sing to. During the long summer holidays the family would retreat to their recently-bought holiday home at picturesque Stone Harbor on the Jersey Shore. For Taylor it was a paradise, and later she described it to *Philadelphia Style* magazine (the *Philly*): "I was there every summer, all summer, for the majority of my childhood. It was such an amazing place to grow up. There were so many places to explore…I could not have had a cooler childhood."

Even at the age of two, Taylor was caught on camera trying to sing 'Unchained Melody', and her performances were not confined to her home. In a later interview for *Marie Claire*, Taylor recalled those early summer days on the beach and how she attracted an audience with her singing: "My parents have videos of me on the beach at, like, three, going up to people and singing *Lion King* songs for them. I was literally going from towel to towel, saying, 'Hi, I'm Taylor, I'm going to sing "I Just Can't Wait to Be King" for you now'."

Taylor was inspired by watching Disney movies, and although captivated by the magic of the stories, it was the music that attracted the most attention. She would learn the lyrics to the songs in no time at all, and even for those she might forget, she would just make up her own words instead.

Nothing was going to stop her singing. At this tender age, she was already developing a musical mind. In an interview with CMT News, she remarked: "So I think that was my first real comprehension of the fact that music was what I remember the most from a movie. Not exactly the plotline as much as the music."

The family were also regular church goers and would attend Sunday services and send their children to Sunday School. It was while singing along to the hymns that Taylor had the chance to hear her grandmother Marjorie's wonderful voice, no doubt outshining everyone else in the building.

Like most girls her age, she could be mischievous, but instead of waiting for her parents to tell her off, she did it herself, as she later revealed to the *Daily Mail*: "When I was naughty as a kid, I used to send myself to my own room. My mom

14

says that she was afraid to punish me sometimes because I was so hard on myself when I did something wrong. I haven't changed much since then."

As Taylor blossomed into a young girl, her parents began to recognise similarities between their daughter and her charismatic grandmother. At the many parties she would have at her house, Marjorie would captivate everyone with both her persona and her voice. That gravitas was what Taylor later identified as having the "IT factor", which made her grandmother different from everyone else. It made Taylor want to be the same.

Taylor was also becoming a great observer of people, as Andrea recalled: "From day one, Taylor was always trying to figure out how other people thought and what they were doing and why they were doing it. That was probably an early telltale sign that she had the makings of a songwriter."

Meanwhile, Taylor was experiencing all the delights of living on a farm. The family owned several Quarter horses and a Shetland pony, and horse riding soon became a popular pastime, as did hitching a ride on the tractor. There were also several cats on the farm, and their mouse-hunting exploits and the demise of their prey became the subject of some of young Taylor's sadder short stories. In the run up to Christmas, she was also given the important but less glamorous job of collecting praying mantis egg pods off the trees, lest they infest someone's house. Not all farm life was idyllic.

A love affair for words and music

Although the suggestion of her five-year-old daughter having a career as a child model was quickly dismissed by Andrea, and for all the right reasons, Taylor was able to follow what would be a more artistic path. Exuding confidence and charming everyone with her innate ability to engage in conversation made her parents realise just how special their daughter was becoming. Writing had now become more of an obsession.

Taylor not only read poems, she studied their structure and then replicated it with her own rhymes. She was now displaying an extraordinary creative talent. Whilst still at primary school, she was given an assignment to write a two-sentence essay, and to her teacher's amazement ended up handing in a two-page composition.

At the age of six, Taylor's parents bought their daughter her first album, LeAnn Rimes' *Blue*. LeAnn was already one of the biggest country artists of all time and was only 13 years old. For Taylor, it proved to be a significant moment in her musical education. How different it might have been if she had been given an album by Madonna or Mariah Carey! LeAnn had a majestic voice, but it was the words that captivated Taylor. These songs were telling stories.

As her parents were not really great country music fans, it was left to their young daughter to fully embrace the kind of music that had seldom been played around the house. She later told *The Guardian*: "LeAnn Rimes was my first impression of country music. I got her first album when I was six. I just really loved how she could be making music and having a career at such a young age." Thanks to the

Mississippi-born songstress, Taylor now had her first music idol, and the seeds were being sown for her own musical career, a career that in just a matter of a few years would shake the music world by its very foundations.

It was an epiphany for Taylor, and from that moment she listened to other country artists, both young and old, and found a deep connection between the little rhyming couplets and poems she was creating in her mind and the storytelling lyrics of these established artists - often romantic, sometimes heartbreakingly sad, but always captivating. Other female artists that inspired her at the time were the Dixie Chicks, Dolly Parton, and even the venerable Patsy Cline.

At the age of eight, Taylor was lucky enough to get to see LeAnn Rimes in concert at Atlantic City, and later told the *Philly*: "I was totally freaked out. Seeing this person who was my hero…it was crazy."

But despite her newfound love for music, Taylor still had no aspirations to make it her career. With her school friends wanting to grow up to become either astronauts or ballerinas, she just wanted to be like her father, although she didn't know what a stockbroker did, and later quipped: "My dad is so passionate about what he does, like in the way I'm passionate about music. He's so gung-ho for his job, and I saw how happy it made him, and I just thought, like, 'I can broke stocks'."

No ordinary child

In 1996, Taylor began her primary education at the nationally-recognised Wyndcroft School, a private co-ed establishment in Pottstown, some 30 miles away. In a school renowned for its first-class academic excellence, Taylor became a star pupil, especially in English. No one noticed this ability more than her teachers. Even at this tender age, Taylor was now writing pages of long poems when most of the students could barely muster a line or two. This was a clear indication that they were seeing a budding writer, maybe a future author. What they didn't appreciate was how she was honing that skill to become a great lyricist.

One of her tutors recalled: "She was incredibly quick-witted. She would come up with these complex ideas that you just wouldn't expect from someone her age and it would leave people open-mouthed. She was always making up her own stories to entertain the class. She wasn't a show-off, but she was just genuinely excited to be learning…I had no idea that Taylor would become a singer, but I knew she would probably be famous for something. It would be an injustice if she hadn't been - she just stood out from the rest…This was no ordinary child."

While at Wyndcroft, Taylor also excelled in music, and by her final year in fourth grade, she could play the recorder to a high standard, sing two-part harmonies, and read music in the treble clef. But it was with the written word that she left everybody astounded. A tutor revealed: "Even as early as first grade, she was using positional phrases unheard of from kids that age, and by fourth, she was standing out as smart."

16

When hearing about a national poetry competition for children, she jumped at the chance. She had already written some wonderful deep and meaningful poems, but decided to make it more light-hearted. As an avid reader of the fantastical rhymes of Dr Seuss, she came up with her own three-page piece called 'Monster in the Closet'.

There's a monster in my closet and I don't know what to do!
Have you ever seen him?
Has he ever pounced on you?
I wonder what he looks like!
Is he purple with red eyes?
I wonder what he likes to eat.
What about his size!!
Tonight I'm gonna catch him!
I'll set a real big trap!
Then I'll train him really well.
He'll answer when I clap!

When I looked up in that closet, there was nothing there but stuff.
I know that monster's in there!
I heard him huff and puff!
Could it be he wants to eat me?
Maybe I'm his favorite tray.
And if he comes to get me,
I'll scream loudly, "Go away!!"
If he's nice, I'll name him "Happy."
If he's bad I'll name him "Grouch."
I suspect that he is leaving, but if not. . .I'll kick him out!
   © Taylor Swift

Looking back, she told the *Washington Post* about the hard work that went into it: "I picked the most gimmicky one I had to submit. I didn't want to get too dark on them. Poetry was my favourite thing. I loved putting things down on paper. It was so fascinating for me...[I was] trying to figure out the perfect combination of words, with the perfect amount of syllables and the perfect rhyme to make it completely pop off the page."

Winning the competition brought a surge in her passion for reading books. One of her early favourites was Shel Silverstein's *The Giving Tree*, and its message of showing kindness to others. Any stories that had a moral to them were readily embraced, as she explained to her fans later: "If those are the first things you start reading, it can really affect your character. Being good to other people was the main concept I really loved in books." Another favourite was the humorous series of

Amelia Bedelia books that depict a housekeeper who takes her instructions too literally.

Taylor's thirst for stories was never more evident than with Andrea, who later reflected on the ritual of reading her bedtime stories and realising that each time it was igniting another creative spark in her daughter's young mind. In a later interview with Katie Couric for a Grammys Special, Taylor recalled: "I think I fell in love with words before I fell in love with music. All I wanted to do was talk, and all I wanted to do was to hear stories. I would drive my mom insane…"

In her final year, Taylor was desperate to get a lead role in a school play as it required a solo singing part. Finding out the character had to be male, she wore a fake moustache, drew black eyebrows, and put her curly hair under a hat to get the part. For her teacher, it showed how dedicated she had become when it came to the arts.

Meanwhile, Taylor had discovered new musical heroines in Faith Hill and Shania Twain. It was Shania, dubbed the Queen of Country Pop, who left the greatest impression. Here was a star who not only sang great songs - she wrote them too. In a later interview for *Time* magazine, Taylor recalled her admiration: "She came out, and she was just so strong and so independent and wrote all her own songs. That meant so much to me, even as a 10-year-old. Just knowing that the stories she was telling in those songs - those were her stories."

Whilst still in fourth grade, Taylor's musical tastes expanded to include the very latest artists who were making the pop charts, and for a time she flirted with the likes of the Spice Girls, Hanson and the Backstreet Boys, not so much for their music, but for their choreography. However, while emulating all their moves with her friends, her greatest love remained firmly embedded in country.

A Small Girl with a Big Voice

"My parents raised me to never feel like I was entitled to success. That you have to work for it. You have to work so hard for it. And sometimes then, you don't even get where you need to go"

New house, new school

With music now well and truly a firm fixture for Taylor, she had the chance to perform too, and found that school plays and local productions were the perfect stage to show people what she could do. Although chosen for small parts, she relished the opportunity to dress up, rehearse, and perform for an audience, and in return receive their applause. As she got taller, the parts would get bigger.

Taylor's grasp of the English language went far beyond her tender years, and, in her own words, she had the knack to "create stories and fairy tales out of everyday life." Growing up on Christmas Tree Farm had much to do with this. In a later interview for *Vogue*, she recalled: "I had the most magical childhood, running free and going anywhere I wanted to in my head. It had cemented in me this unnatural level of excitement about fall and then the holiday season. My friends are so sick of me talking about autumn coming. There're like, 'What are you, an elf?'"

However, rural life on the farm had not been idyllic for her parents. For Scott, in particular, it had been hard to make the adjustment from his city-based financial work by day, to living like "country bumpkins" in the evening. But for Taylor and her younger brother, it was the perfect environment. Not only was she embracing country music, she was becoming a bona fide country girl in both character and appearance. Working on the farm had indeed given her the opportunity to run wild, have straw in her hair, and dirt under her fingernails. In her own words, she recalled those joyous days when she could be "a crazy kid with tangled hair."

Sometime in 1999 the Swifts sold their farm and moved to nearby Wyomissing to live in a large white six-bedroom detached mansion on Grandview Boulevard in an upmarket part of town. It was an unsettling time for both Taylor and Austin, who were leaving their friends behind.

Taylor was enrolled at nearby West Reading Elementary School, but, almost from the start, found it difficult to fit in. It was a school that straddled two postcode boundaries and catered for a cross section of kids who came from both the poorest and wealthiest parts of town, and there were the customary "cliques" of girls who would make her unpopular through their jealousy of her comfortable home life and constant good grades.

In a classroom where rich and poor kids collided, Taylor's life of luxury at home made her feel isolated at school, and in a later interview for *Rolling Stone*, she confessed: "I didn't have friends. No one talked to me...I didn't know anybody." For a kind-hearted girl who craved friendship, these were going to be tough years to come.

To deflect the criticism, Taylor tried her hand at sporting activities, and although being tall for her age could be a physical advantage, she soon realised she wasn't cut out for sport. She later noted that "it mattered what kind of designer handbag you brought to school." Not only that, country music just wasn't fashionable for West Reading teenage girls.

This experience would have a lasting effect. As a result, she would later turn her feelings into words, and her words into songs.

In the book *Taylor Swift: The Rise of the Nashville Teen,* one of her former classmates confessed: "We treated Taylor like crap, but you know why? We were absolutely downright jealous. Her star shone so brightly, it eclipsed the rest of us and made us feel inferior."

But there was a way to escape the loneliness. Another little milestone in Taylor's story came when she watched in fascination a production of Roald Dahl's *Charlie and the Chocolate Factory* that was staged by the local actors' association called the Berks County Youth Theatre Academy (BYTA), for which Andrea soon had her signed up. Taylor found an instant connection with the more friendly, albeit fiercely ambitious, fellow students.

In a matter of days, she had auditioned for *Annie,* their next production, and although she gained only a small part it gave her experience and added confidence. It was at this first audition that Taylor first met Kaylin Politzer, and they became the best of friends. Kaylin noted how "awkward and clunky" Taylor was in her dance movements.

With other like-minded wannabe actors sharing the stage, there was also the inevitable competition, and Taylor realised that to succeed she had to keep focused and be prepared to up her game. That growing self-belief, and no doubt her advantage in height, helped her gain lead roles in future productions as Maria in *The Sound of Music,* and Sandy in *Grease.*

In a later interview with the GAC channel, Taylor recalled how her voice at this stage had developed a noticeable country twang: "It just came out sounding country. It was all I had listened to, so I guess it was just kind of natural. I decided [there and then] country music was what I needed to be doing."

Around this time Taylor started taking singing and acting lessons. One of her earliest supporters was the theatre company director Kirk Cremer, who also ran the local TheatreKids Live! - a sort of *Saturday Night Live*-inspired comedy group that put on weekly shows in the rehearsal building, with each performer paid $200 for a three-month season. Cremer also gave Taylor private voice lessons, and for her role as Sandy in *Grease* tried unsuccessfully to remove her noticeable Southern twang. In fact, her distinctive voice would prove another advantage in securing lead roles.

During the summer break, Cremer persuaded Taylor's parents to allow her to join Kaylin, and two other girls who had displayed extra potential, in a group he had put together called Broadway in Training, which held auditions in New York for roles in Broadway and other productions.

Cremer also acted as their unofficial manager, finding auditions through a manager website and arranging for some professional photo headshots to be taken of the girls. He also helped them select their audition songs and prepare monologues. In an interview for *Inquirer Entertainment*, Taylor recalled that time: "I went to several auditions in New York. I was always going there for vocal and acting lessons...and for auditions, where we would stand in line in a long hallway with a lot of people...I never lost my passion for the theatre."

The competition was hard, but Taylor and Kaylin finally secured parts in a movie, began rehearsing, and then had the disappointment of seeing it cancelled due to lack of funding. Apart from the four girls getting a chance for a one-off performance at Disney World's Magic Kingdom, nothing much came from the venture, and the decision was made to disband the group.

Taylor continued to be chosen for lead roles, which led to a certain amount of envy among other performers and remarks from some disgruntled parents. After what was described as a "phenomenal" performance in the lead role of Kim in a Berks County production of *Bye Bye Birdie*, Taylor began to realise that music, not musical theatre, was the way she wanted to go.

Speaking to the *Reading Eagle*, she later commented: "My interest [in musical theatre] soon drew me back to country music. I was infatuated with the sound, with the storytelling. I could relate to it. I can't really tell you why. With me it's instinctual. Ever since I discovered their music, I wanted to do country music. I wanted to sing country music. Didn't matter if I lived in Pennsylvania. Didn't matter if everybody at my school was like, 'You? Play country music? Why do you like country music? You're so weird'."

Finding her audience

Although becoming a little disillusioned with theatre, Taylor did enjoy the after-show parties for parents and kids alike, and it was there she first discovered a karaoke machine. It was like being given a golden ticket by Willy Wonka. Now she could try and emulate her favourite singers and sing her favourite songs. On one of these occasions, Cremer's mother Sandy Wielder watched Taylor sing and was so impressed she suggested to her son that she believed Taylor would do better following a career in country music rather than becoming an actor. She just seemed to be a natural.

It was all Taylor wanted to hear, and it signalled the beginning of her journey to stardom. As luck would have it, Andrea readily agreed with the advice, and over the next few months drove her daughter to various venues to let her sing, with appearances at open-mic nights and karaoke competitions. It wasn't too long before Taylor was becoming quite a hometown celebrity, and many thought she was destined for bigger things.

One person who saw this as a genuine prospect was Kirk Cremer's brother, Ronnie, who not only was a director of the youth academy, but was also a guitar teacher, manager and music producer. After seeking advice from Andrea, he leased space at a local mall to showcase his young protégé singing with karaoke backing tracks.

The more Taylor performed, the easier it became. Speaking to *Elle* magazine, she said: "Every time you play another show, it gets better and better. But when I first started singing in front of crowds...it was a little scary at first. Anything you've just started doing is going to be scary." Taylor was able to mask her initial insecurity and display nothing but confidence.

Taylor recalled for CMT News: "Every single weekend, I would go to festivals and fairs and karaoke contests - any place I could get up on stage. The cool thing about this is that my parents have never pushed me. It's always been [my] desire and love to do this. If I had been pushed, if I didn't love this, I would probably not have been able to get this far."

One of her regular karaoke venues was a roadhouse just out of town owned by former country star Pat Garrett. She would turn up and sing every weekend, leaving her parents feeling a little embarrassed by it. In an interview for CMT News, she recalled: "I started out singing karaoke in his roadhouse - his little bar - when I was ten years old. He'll vouch that I was in there every single week saying, 'I'm just going to come back if you don't let me win one.' I was kind of like an annoying fly around that place. I just would not leave them alone. What they would do is have these karaoke contests. And if you won, you got to open for, like, Charlie Daniels or George Jones. I would go until I won."

During one of the karaoke performances someone came up to Andrea and told her straight that this was what her daughter should be doing for a living. But by now, Andrea needed no convincing. She watched how Taylor sang with supreme confidence, belting out one of her favourite country songs as if it was something she had been born to do. And then she saw the audience's response. This was her precious little girl, not yet a teenager, making people take real good notice of her. It was a moment to be both proud and blessed.

 Taylor was clearly getting herself a name as a performer, but it also led to more friction with the other members of the theatre group. Before long, BYTA closed for good.

Meanwhile, after winning a local talent competition, Cremer was so impressed by Taylor's performance that he arranged for her to be the opening act for the legendary Charlie Daniels Band at the Strausstown Amphitheater. Unfortunately, her booking was for mid-morning, hours before the main act, and there was hardly anyone there to watch her perform. Amends were soon made when Cremer got her a slot at the Bloomsbury Fair, a large outdoor event that attracted hundreds of people. With a little backing band provided, Taylor nervously performed two songs. It went well, and, with each successive performance, her confidence grew. She now looked for bigger audiences.

A magical land called Nashville

Opportunity soon came when she was invited to sing the national anthem for the local baseball team, the Reading Phillies, in front of a sizeable crowd. However, if this failed to quench her thirst, she had her sights set on bigger things. That chance came on April 5th 2002 when, through her father's connections with the marketing manager of the local basketball team, the Philadelphia 76ers, she was invited to sing the national anthem in front of some 20,000 fans. Wearing a red headband and a top covered in tiny American flags, she belted out the song and received a wild ovation. In her own words, it was "an awesome experience," made even more so when she encountered someone she recognised as she was leaving: "Jaz-Z was sitting court-side and he gave me a high-five after I sang…I bragged about that for, like, a year straight." It was indeed one of the proudest moments of her early career. Here was one of the biggest names in music congratulating her, and it must have felt like she was walking on air.

Taylor's parents were blown away by their daughter's talent and encouraged and supported her along her journey. In an interview for *The Independent*, Taylor recalled something her mother had once told her: "You can do whatever you want in life - as long as you work hard to get there. You have to work hard for every single baby step that you take that is closer to what you want - and we will support that until you change your mind and do something else. And when you want to do something else, we will be your cheerleaders in that too."

Heartfelt words from Taylor's mother, whose tenacity was matched by her commitment to do right by her daughter and let nothing stand in her way. It was not by coincidence that Taylor would inherit those traits, which helped her through some difficult times in the years to come.

Kirk Cremer was so amazed with how Taylor was building up her confidence that he felt it was the right time for her to record some tracks for a demo cd. Having the use of a studio owned by older brother Ronnie, Taylor recorded four cover versions - LeAnn Rimes' 'One Way Ticket', the Dixie Chicks' 'There's Your Trouble', Dolly Parton's 'Here You Come Again', and Olivia Newton-John's 'Hopelessly Devoted to You'.

Ronnie Cremer recalled that first meeting: "The first time I heard of Taylor, my brother had a theatre company. They would have parties after the show, and they would do karaoke. My mom would attend these. I only met Taylor face-to-face in 2002. I had a shop up in Leesport. It was a computer shop, and that's where I had my little studio. My brother brought Taylor and her mom and her brother over and introduced me, and said, 'Would you be interested in recording a demo?' It was a couple of cover songs. I recorded the demo for her. It wasn't a great demo, but it was a demo."

Everything was seemingly fitting into place. One evening Taylor happened to be watching a program called *Behind the Music* on VH1, showcasing the career of Faith Hill, one of Taylor's country music favourites. It was only then that she learned that the Mississippi-born singer, like LeAnn Rimes, had also been discovered in Nashville. It was a singular moment. From that day on, Taylor was even more determined to go to what was dubbed "Music City, USA" and be discovered like two of her idols.

In an article for the *Daily Telegraph*, she recalled: "I got it into my head that there was this magical land called Nashville where dreams come true and that's where I needed to go. I began absolutely non-stop tormenting my parents, begging them on a daily basis to move there."

In a later interview for *Rolling Stone*, she spoke about how three of her music heroes had inspired her in different ways: "I saw that Shania Twain brought this independence, this crossover appeal; I saw that Faith Hill brought this classic old-school glamour and beauty and grace; and I saw the Dixie Chicks brought this complete 'We *don't* care what you think' quirkiness. I loved what all of those women were able to do and what they were able to bring to country music."

Mom to the rescue

Taylor continued to look forward to the long summer vacations at Stone Harbor. "It was really cool living on the bay, and we have so many stories about it," she told the *Philly*. Her parents gave her the large attic space above the garage, almost an entire floor that comprised three rooms. For any of her vacation friends invited back to her "clubhouse", it must have seemed like this girl had her own apartment. She explained how she made a filing system of club members: "I would write on tiles I found. I painted the whole room different colours and used to spend all day in there just doing nothing but sitting in my little club. Because it was mine."

While on vacation, Taylor's mind was constantly on the son of her parents' friends who happened to live next to their holiday home. He was the same age as Taylor and spent many summer days around the Swift house. "I swore I would marry him one day," she recalled. Hoping against hope that he would ask her out, it never happened. Instead, he told her he had his eyes set on other girls. Although Taylor's young heart was crushed by the rejection, it led to her writing one of her very first songs, 'Invisible'. She recalled: "I felt, well, invisible. Obviously. So, I wrote that song about it."

As sad as the experience was for Taylor, she continued to put her heart and soul into performing during the summer breaks. With her guitar playing now reaching an acceptable standard, she played longer acoustic sets. If she ran out of songs to perform, she would just make some up on the spot and carry on.

While staying at Stone Harbor, Taylor found the perfect spot to serenade friends and strangers at Harry's seafood restaurant, where she became known as "the little girl with the big voice." Another venue was the Coffee Talk café where she would play "for hours and hours."

From the age of eleven Taylor had a good friend called Britany Maack and they did everything together until Britany moved away. She would later write a song called 'Me and Britany' in which her friend moves away to Memphis to be with a boy and then becomes a movie star, instead of Taylor moving to Nashville to become a singer. In reality, Britany never moved to Memphis, and they remained close friends for many years to come.

It was while sharing a holiday at Stone Harbor in August 2002 that Taylor and Britany managed to get their names in the local press, all thanks to Andrea. In a *Reading Eagle* headline that read *Wyomissing mother makes ocean rescue*, the paper reported how she had taken her daughter Taylor and her friend Britany for a wave-jumping ride on a three-person watercraft. The ocean was quite rough that day, and as they approached the mouth of Hereford Inlet, she saw a 28-foot boat perched precariously on a sandbar. With other boats too big to get close, Andrea put the two girls ashore and headed back to rescue most of the 12 people on board, two at a time. Fortunately, the grounded boat soon freed itself and those left on board took her to safety. Back on shore, one of those rescued was a 70-year-old woman who thanked Andrea, calling her a Godsend. On being asked if she was a *Baywatch*-type rescue service, Andrea replied, "No, I'm just a mom out for a ride."

Not all Taylor's heroes were singers.

While on vacation, Taylor also found time to lock herself away and write a 350-page semi-autobiographical novel entitled *A Girl Named Girl*, basically about a mother who wants a son but instead has a girl. In an interview for *Vogue*, she recalled: "We lived on this basin where all this magical stuff would happen... One summer, there was a shark that washed up on our dock. I ended up writing a novel that summer because I wouldn't go in the water. I locked myself in the den and wrote a book."

In a later YouTube Presents interview she recalled: "I'd write different chapters of this book and send them back to my friends. And I'd write them into this book under different names but totally describe their personalities."

Meanwhile, Taylor never let up on her determination to go to Nashville, and her relentless pleading to her parents continued until she finally wore them down. They would not be moving there, at least for the moment, but it was decided that she could go there and see for herself what "Music City, USA" was all about, and how the music people there would react to the demo she had made.

It was the chance Taylor had been dreaming of for most of her life. Success, she hoped, lay just around the corner, or, more realistically, a 780-mile, 11-hour drive away.

Nashville Calling

"The whole process of songwriting starts out in a very lonely place for me ... I sit down to write a song because I'm feeling a very intense emotion, usually an intense form of pain"

Music Row

Taylor's mother-inspired tenacity and "I'll show em" determination had finally paid off. During the school break in March 2001, Andrea took Taylor and Austin and drove all the way to Nashville to see if anyone down famous Music Row would listen to her daughter's demo. In an interview with *Teen Superstar*, Andrea explained how it was all up to Taylor now: "I made it really clear. Okay, if this is something you want, you've got to do it...I'm not a stage mom. I didn't sign up to dive into the music business, so I would walk to the front door and wait for her. She went to every place on Music Row."

Music Row was the nucleus of the business side of country music, and if record deals were to be made there was no better place to begin. Taylor thought it would simply be a matter of someone hearing her voice to make it a done deal - she was that supremely confident: "I was like, 'if I want to sing music, I'm going to need a record deal.' So, I'm going to get a record deal. I really thought it was easy." The truth is, she knew how popular she was back in her hometown in Pennsylvania, and naïvely believed her talent would be recognised here, even at such a young age.

With her photo on the cover and contact details on the back of each cd case, there was also the simple message "Call me". It seemed a little pretentious, but this was Taylor Swift, starting as she was meaning to go on in life. As her mother drove her down Music Row, she would stop by some of the industry's biggest label offices and Taylor would then run inside and hand a demo in at the reception, saying something like, "Hi, I'm Taylor, I'm eleven and I want a record deal. Call me." It was as simple as that, just as if she was back on the beach announcing herself to an unsuspecting audience.

On the long journey home, Taylor was both excited about the experience and anxious about what would happen next. Her mother too was growing more apprehensive. She saw how her daughter's hometown success was being covered by the local paper, leading to her being teased, bullied and even shunned at school, just for being, in their eyes, so different. It seemed like individuality for young girls in Wyomissing was never an option.

Each time the phone rang, Taylor's excitement mounted, only for it to be dashed. Eventually, just one of the record labels replied, telling her that this wasn't the right time, but urging her to keep on trying. Disappointed as she was, it made her think more clearly. There must be hundreds of young wannabes, like her, going through the same motions and having their dreams shattered time and time again: "I thought, you don't just make it in Nashville. I've really got to work on something that would make me different."

She gave it some thought. It was one thing to have a voice and the confidence to sing, and to sing well, but what about having the ability to play an instrument?

Taylor would be going to Nashville again, but in the meantime she resolved to add the word musician to her résumé. In the summer of 2002, she began having proper guitar lessons. Her parents had bought her one when she was just eight, but at that tender age she found it almost impossible to play and frustratedly abandoned it for several years. She related the story of what happened next: "When I was about 12 this magical twist of fate [happened]. I was doing my homework [when the tech fixing my computer] looked over and saw the guitar in the corner. And he said, 'Do you play guitar?' I said, 'Oh. No. I tried, but…' He said, 'Do you want me to teach you a few chords?' and I said, 'Uh, yeah. YES!'"

The technician was none other than Ronnie Cremer, the local musician who had made the demo cd for her. In a later interview for the *New York Daily News*, he revealed a different version of events, saying that he was first approached by both Andrea and his brother Kirk and asked if he would be interested in giving Taylor guitar lessons, as she was eager to learn country music. Although preferring rock music himself, he readily agreed and went to the house, giving Taylor three-hour lessons on two evenings a week at $32 an hour.

According to Cremer, it was months before he even got to look at a computer that needed repairing. He recalled how the lessons began at a slow pace, beginning with teaching her basic chords: "We started with G, D, E, A. Where she had problems were the more difficult chords, the F's and the B's. F is really hard on the fingers, so I would teach her things like, 'Ok, if you want to play a song in F, play it in D and put the capo on the third capo.' So, you notice when she plays, she still moves that capo around a lot."

With the added help of a computer program, Cremer taught Taylor the basics of song structure: "In all honesty, I thought she was a pretty good student. I said, 'Here's your chorus. Here's your verse. Move these around, and look what you've got. You can write one verse, one chorus, and then you've got a song.' That just clicked to her, and made sense."

Taylor was determined to become a musician and give herself the slight edge on her would-be competitors. What followed were months and months of practice. Andrea recalled: "She was driven beyond anything I had ever witnessed."

That determination was in evidence when she also wanted to learn to play a 12-string guitar. Her school teacher had already told her that her hands were too small to play one. Andrea told *Entertainment Weekly*: "She saw a 12-string guitar and thought it was the coolest thing. Of course, we immediately said, 'Oh no, absolutely not, your fingers are too small - not till you're much older will you be able to play the 12-string guitar.' Well, that was all it took. Don't ever say 'never' or 'can't do' to Taylor. She started playing it four hours a day - six on the weekends. She would get calluses on her fingers and they would crack and bleed, and we would tape them up and she'd just keep on playing."

Taylor recalled: "At first, it seemed really hard and then I realised that if I put my mind to something that it was really mind over matter and maybe my fingers weren't long enough or developed enough to play it, but I played it. It's really exciting to see that. I'm like, 'Ha, guitar teacher!'" In her own words, she asserted: "Anytime someone tells me that I can't do something, I want to do it more."

One of the first songs she learned to play on the guitar was the Dixie Chicks' 'Cowboy Take Me Away'. Cremer, with guidance from Andrea, also helped Taylor design her very first website, with the heading: "TAYLOR SWIFT is a name that you will surely hear quite a bit on the country music scene in the near future. This talented 12-year-old singer and stage performer has an amazing natural country sound. Her delivery of songs, solid stage presence and ability to capture an audience combine to make Taylor an incredible young artist. It's no surprise that she already has a long list of performing credentials which include musical theatre as well as country music."

Taylor's newfound confidence knew no bounds.

"I want to touch people with my songs"

Meanwhile, school was playing its part in Taylor's development, but not in a normal way. To begin with she looked different. At five feet ten she was already taller than most of the students her age, and her curly hair was something to be mocked by the more popular straight-haired girls. Many of them were already into party-going, drinking, and dating boys, but not Taylor. Even when she did try and fit in, it often backfired. Her passion was writing and music, and with the imposed isolation through her being seen as "uncool", she would find some kind of sanctuary in hiding away and writing songs.

She recalled in *Style* magazine: "I first started writing songs because I didn't really have anyone else to talk to. As sad as that sounds, I was going through this really hard time at school where I didn't have any friends. Songwriting for me just started out as therapy. When you're dealing with something like loneliness or confusion or rejection or frustration, those emotions are so jumbled up in your head."

Now on the threshold of becoming a teenager, she had already written a few songs. The first was 'Lucky You', about a girl who dares to be different, and a song in which she recalls she sounded like a chipmunk. But there would be many others, including 'American Boy', 'The Outside', and 'Crazier', which were probably written around the age of 12-13.

In an interview for the *Daily Mail,* Taylor revealed: "When I first started writing songs, I was pretty lonely. I was about twelve and at school in Pennsylvania. I wasn't popular and didn't have many friends, and never knew where to sit at lunch. But songwriting became a release. I'd think, 'Ok, three more classes to go and then

I can write about this', so it became a reward. I didn't know how to articulate my feelings, but I'd strum my guitar and the words would come out. It allowed me to understand better the way I felt and get through it."

Although not experiencing teenage romance herself, she observed her classmates, and in her writing often placed herself as someone more experienced in break-ups and make-ups than she actually was, as she explained to CMT: "I found that I was alone a lot of the time, kind of on the outside looking into their discussions, and the things they were saying to each other. I started developing this really keen sense of observation - of how to watch people and see what they did. From that sense, I was able to write songs about relationships when I was thirteen but not in relationships."

The one person guaranteed to lift her spirits when she was down was her mother, and the two of them often "ran away" from all the problems she was facing and went on adventurous day trips together. She told *The Boot*, "I was really not cool enough for anyone but my parents at that phase. I had no friends! My mom was the one person that I could turn to."

In September 2002, Taylor won the audition to sing 'America the Beautiful' at the US Open Tennis tournament in New York. Jumping at the chance, she later explained to *Rolling Stone*: "It occurred to me that the National Anthem was the best way to get in front of a large group of people if you don't have a record deal, so I started singing everywhere I possibly could…I figured out if you could sing that one song, you could get in front of 20,000 people without even having a record deal. So, I sang that song many, many, many, many times…"

As luck would have it, watching her sing that day was Dan Dymtrow, a New York talent manager who was also part of Britney Spears' management team. Making enquiries about Taylor, Dymtrow had the entertainment director of the tournament send him her demo of cover songs. When he made contact with the Swift family, Taylor's father agreed to send him a home video of her performing. In an interview for *Wood & Steel* magazine, Taylor recalled: "My dad put together this typical 'dad video' type of thing, with the cat chewing the [guitar] neck and stuff like that."

Dymtrow was still impressed by what he saw, and in January 2003 invited Taylor to come to his New York office with her parents and play for him. After performing some songs with her 12-string, Taylor entered into a management agreement a couple of months later, although the terms were never made clear.

To give her a more marketable image, Dymtrow first had her auditioning for Abercrombie & Fitch's Rising Stars campaign to be published in *Vanity Fair*. Taylor was among others chosen as a potential future star. In the photo shoot, Taylor was shown wearing denim jeans and a white top, holding a guitar, and, by wiping a tear from her eye with a handkerchief, portraying a girl whose heart had just been broken. Maybe not the image Taylor wanted to show, but, no doubt, it was the coolest thing she had ever done.

It was not hard to imagine that when the students at Taylor's school saw the picture in the popular magazine (published in July 2004), this "uncool" outsider suddenly became the coolest kid in town. In the accompanying text, Taylor goes on to say: "I love the stories that you hear in country ballads. I sometimes write about teenage love, but I am presently a 14-year-old girl without a boyfriend. Sometimes I worry that I must be wearing some kind of guy repellent, but then I realise that I'm just discovering what I am as a person... Right now, music is the most important thing in my life, and I want to touch people with my songs."

RCA and the move to Nashville

Sometime in the spring of 2003, Taylor's parents hired local producer and music engineer Steve "Mr Mig" Migliore to record a few demos of her self-written songs to show to record labels. The songs included 'American Boy', 'Lucky You', and 'Smokey Black Nights'. Migliore was well known and respected in the industry, and with Taylor making a strong, positive impression, he began to put word out to his industry connections that here was a young girl with a remarkable talent.

But there would be no instant success working with Dymtrow. Taylor took what was handed to her, including a slot as an admin assistant with a clipboard at the annual CMA Music Festival in Nashville. She was also signed up to contribute her self-penned song 'Outside' to a compilation album *Chicks with Attitudes,* promoted by the Maybelline cosmetics firm (released in July 2004). She also took part on *Good Morning America* for a feature called *Nashville Dreams*.

Dymtrow realised just how much Taylor wanted a record deal, and he began taking her to regular meetings with record labels in Nashville. While Taylor was practising songs, she began having rare moments of doubt in her ability and confessed to herself in her journal: "I don't know if I can do this. I want it so bad but I get so scared of what might not happen. When I miss notes, I dive bomb and the whole thing goes crashing down. I just have to breathe in...breathe out...breathe in... relax. Nashville is not going to kill me. I can handle it. I'm okay. I'll be fine. I'm young. I'm talented. They'll see it in me. I'll be okay. I've got to hang on. Can't worry. I'm only 13. I'm bound to make mistakes, right? Oh, this is a lot to handle."

It wasn't long before they struck lucky. On Thursday, June 19th 2003, they dropped by the RCA office on Music Row, and after a meeting with executives in which Taylor played them a few songs, they said they would call her on Monday. They then went to Capitol Records for a similar meeting. Taylor noted in her journal: "They totally flipped out over me! They even said I was the most talented 13-year-old they had ever seen! ... Well, I appreciate the compliments, but they followed it up with 'I'd just hate to see you jump into this right now and have a short-lived career.' They very politely agreed that country is directed to 35-year-olds. Radio just doesn't play teens. That's where I'm going to prove them wrong..."

On June 24th Taylor's manager called the Swift home to give them some news. Andrea passed the phone over to Taylor, and with Scott listening in from work,

Dymtrow said: "Well, we got follow-ups on all of the labels and they think you need a couple of years to grow so they can put you on the radio...except for RCA, who want to sign you! Congratulations!" Taylor went crazy with excitement. Dymtrow told her the label was offering what was known as an artist development deal. In essence, a "demo deal", as it's also known, is a contract that promises to develop the skills and public profile of the artist. In exchange for the support, the label receives a right to future high royalties or other desirable rights.

Taylor explained how she saw it in later interviews for *Teen Superstar* and NBC: "A development deal is an in-between record deal. It's like a guy saying that he wants to date you but not be your boyfriend. They don't want to sign you to an actual record deal and put an album out on you. They want to watch your progress for a year."

Taylor was over the moon. It was the first step to having a real recording contract, but being a non-commercial commitment, she knew nothing was guaranteed. But this was RCA, one of the biggest labels in the country, and home to stars like Christina Aguilera, Britney Spears and the Foo Fighters. Not only that, they were prepared to give her sponsorship money and recording time. But it was not unusual for labels to wait for artists to turn eighteen before offering a recording contract. To Taylor, four years seemed a lifetime away.

However, this was the chance she had been looking for all her life, and no one knew this more than her parents. It was now up to them to give their daughter all the help and support they could, even if it meant moving to Nashville. And, of course, that's exactly what they did.

Taylor explained what she felt about her parents' expectations at this time: "They didn't put me under pressure at all. It wasn't like, 'This is your one shot, so make it happen.' They presented it as a move to a nicer community. If I made something out of it, great. But if that didn't happen, that's ok, too."

"Maybe I'm just not bad enough"

In an interview for *Women's Health*, Andrea said: "It was never about 'I want to be famous.' Taylor never uttered those words. It was about moving to a place where she could write, with people she could learn from."

Scott Swift needed little convincing. He asked local country singer Pat Garrett for advice about the music business. Garrett was sure to remind him what a gifted and ultra-confident daughter he had. In an interview for CBS News, the veteran musician recalled: "Her dad showed me a notebook she had, and in this ring notebook the only thing she had was her signature, practising her autograph. She has an insatiable drive."

With that added assurance, Scott soon got the ball rolling and arranged to have his business transferred to the Nashville office of Merrill Lynch. In an interview for *Blender* magazine, Taylor was fully aware of her parents' sacrifice: "My father had a job he could do from anywhere. My parents moved across the country so I

31

could pursue a dream." It was a sacrifice that Scott and Andrea tried to play down, as Taylor explained to *Self* magazine: "I knew I was the reason they were moving. But they tried to put no pressure on me. They were like, 'Well, we need a change of scenery anyway,' and, 'I love how friendly people in Tennessee are.'" Even Andrea admitted, "I never wanted to make that move about her 'making it'."

During the summer of 2003, Dymtrow, having been part of Britney Spears' management team, managed to get Taylor enrolled in Britney's performing arts camp for ten days. The summer camp ran as a charity, mostly for kids from low-income families, but Taylor's parents were able to get her a place by making a sizeable donation.

Returning to school, Taylor was still finding it hard to fit in. In October, she wrote in her journal: "I really have decided that school is a big disappointment. It's only cool when you're popular. I'm not. It's cool when you have a boyfriend. It's cool when everybody likes you. I don't have that... I guess I'm not just good enough for people my own age, or maybe I'm not bad enough?"

Meanwhile, Andrea was house-hunting in Nashville, and eventually chose one along Old Hickory Lane in rural Hendersonville, about half an hour from the centre of town. It was a popular residence for the stars, and had been home for the likes of Johnny Cash and Roy Orbison. Their new home would be a beautiful lakeside house, and it took little persuasion for Scott to fall in love with it too when he saw the Sea Rays powerboats moored at the dock.

By the spring of 2004, the family had moved in, and Taylor and Austin were enrolled at Hendersonville High School. For Austin, it would take time to adjust to his new surroundings, having left all his friends behind in Wyomissing. But for Taylor, it was a welcome change from her old school, with her fellow students showing no envy toward her at all; in fact, many of them had grown up with country music in their blood.

On the very first day she found a best friend in Abigail Anderson, a girl who, like herself, had felt like an outsider. Minnesotan Abigail was a champion swimmer and like Taylor had never felt that she fitted in. With the two of them exchanging past stories of lack of romance and unrequited love, they quickly bonded, and, as she later told the *Los Angeles Times*, they "kind of came to the conclusion in ninth grade that we were never going to be popular, so we should just stick together and have fun and not take ourselves too seriously."

Signing with Sony/ATV

Almost as soon as she settled in class, Taylor was asked to take part in a school talent contest, and after performing her song 'Beautiful Eyes' with her 12-string guitar in front of the whole school, she was given a standing ovation. That same day she went with Andrea to the RCA office to let them see her perform 'Beautiful Eyes' and 'Angelina', only to find out that from now on they would have to pay for any demos to be made. After that, they went to the RCA café. That evening,

Taylor scribbled in her journal: "The people who played were really good, and I want to write with a girl named Liz Rose who played."

Taylor's innate talent as a songwriter soon became known around the wider Nashville circuit. The music publishing company Sony/ATV Tree soon heard about her and offered her a contract as a songwriter for other artists. In May 2004, she became their youngest ever signing at the age of 14.

Taylor knew that this was a road test and she would have to raise her game to impress the older and well-established writers. Fortunately, they soon recognised just how good she was - a genuine gifted and committed songwriter, eager to both learn and share ideas. Among those she would be working with were Brett James, Mac McAnally, Troy Verges and brothers Bret and Brad Warren.

The highest praise came from company boss Troy Tomlinson, recognising her as "among the few artists who are born with a gift that just rolls out of her. I still marvel at how this young girl with limited life experiences at that point could write such lyrics and melodies. She was born with it, that gift."

For Taylor, it would be like going to songwriting college, but in the meantime she still had to knuckle down and do schoolwork during the day. In that, she excelled, especially in Science and English, and reading books like *To Kill a Mockingbird* only helped to enrich her creativity. But songwriting was always in the back of her mind, even in class. She recalled: "If we had random notebook checks, my teachers might find biology notes…biology notes…then suddenly a bunch of lyrics." Other students would spot her humming a new melody and then recording it on her cell phone. She may have been ticked off by teachers for lack of attention, but, unlike at her previous school, her classmates only offered their genuine friendship and inspiration, relishing a chance to sing with her and watch her perform.

Incredible for an artist so young, Taylor already had a teenage fan club, but she was also attracting the attention of boys. First there was Drew Dunlap, who she dated for about a year and even wore a necklace with his name on. Brandon Borello was a senior when he dated Taylor, who was still a freshman, and their relationship ended amicably when he left for college. Taylor would reportedly write several songs about him, including 'Our Song', and later co-write 'Tim McGraw' as a parting gift. Classmate and semi-professional wrestler Drew Hardwick was another who Taylor had a "huge crush" on, but it would remain unrequited, and whatever feelings she had for him only became apparent to him in a seminal song she later released called 'Teardrops on My Guitar'. By then it was all too late.

Writing with Liz

All this newfound social activity going on in her life helped foster a more positive frame of mind, one of the key assets to becoming a successful songwriter. It was perhaps through a twist of fate that Taylor would be paired up with established songwriter Liz Rose, but it would prove to be another milestone in Taylor's career.

The two of them first met on April 20th, the same day Taylor had sung in the school concert.

In a 2020 interview for *Music Week*, Liz recalled the day she first met Taylor: "I played a writers' room at a record label and she was there. She heard a couple of my songs and liked them and asked if I would write with her. That's what I've learned in this business: you're never too big to write with a new artist. So, I said yes. We had a great time the first time we wrote and we just kept writing and kept writing! It was a lot of fun. There's nothing like writing with her."

Born Elizabeth Wagner in Dallas, Texas, in 1957, Liz was the youngest of six children and grew up with a wide taste of music. She fell into songwriting after moving to Nashville with her husband and family. In need of a job, she started off in music publishing and co-writing songs for artists. Her first big break came with 'Songs About Rain', a #12 Billboard hit for country singer Gary Allan in 2003.

Asked whether she thought back then that Taylor would be a huge star, Liz replied: "You don't think that, but I did know that she was going to do something special. With her drive and her talent, I knew that she was going to do something, absolutely. She's always been a songwriter that wanted to figure out how to get her music out there. And the best way to do that was write the songs and be an artist; then you get your songs out to the fans."

In a 2019 interview for the *Dallas Observer*, she recalled: "There aren't many like Taylor. I write with a lot of people, but I've never experienced what it's like being in the same room with her. It is the only time I've ever really experienced that." Liz had a knack for accessing Taylor's innermost feelings, as she told *Music Row* magazine: "Whoever I'm in the room with, I pick their brain and make them spill their guts. I'm there to help artists say what they want to say."

Unbeknown to either of them, Liz would become one of Taylor's key collaborators and share the credit on some of her early hit singles, as well as co-writing what is, arguably, one of the artist's greatest songs. Talking to *Blender* magazine, Liz attempted to play down her contributions: "Basically, I was just her editor. She'd write about what happened in school that day. She had such a clear vision of what she was trying to say. And she's come in with the most incredible hooks."

The two writers would complement each other extremely well. The first song they did together was 'Never Mind', a typical Taylor story about liking a guy but never telling him for fear he might not feel the same, and then losing him as a friend. Another one written around this time was a paean to unrequited love, 'Teardrops on My Guitar', destined to become her breakthrough hit.

In an interview for the *Washington Post*, Taylor explained: "You can draw inspiration from anything. If you're a good storyteller, you can take a dirty look somebody gives you, or a guy you used to have flirtations with starts dating a new girl, or somebody you're casually talking to says something that makes you so mad - you can create an entire scenario around that. You don't have to date people or be married to people to write songs about them."

34

Then there was the song 'Tim McGraw'. Taylor had huge respect for McGraw, one of the biggest names on the country music scene, the winner of two Grammys, and, along with his wife Faith Hill, dubbed the celebrated King and Queen of Country Music. But this was not an intentional tribute to the great artist. Its origins began with Taylor's boyfriend Brandon Borello, her first great love, and the imminent but amicable ending of their relationship. She began putting a melody together during class, and when she got home quickly put the basic structure of the song together. She just needed the right words to capture both the sadness and sweetness of first love. For that, she looked to Liz Rose for help.

Originally titled 'When You Think of Tim McGraw', it takes the form of a hopeful letter in which she tells him to think of her every time he hears a song by the legendary artist. In an interview for CMT News, Taylor recalled: "I wrote the song in my freshman year of high school. I got the idea in math class. I was just sitting there, and I started humming this melody. I kind of related it to this situation I was in. I was dating a guy who was about to go off to college. I knew we were going to break up. So, I started thinking about all the things that I knew would remind him of me. Surprisingly, the first thing that came to mind was that my favourite country artist is Tim McGraw."

Speaking to *Entertainment Weekly,* she explained: "It was reminiscent, and it was thinking about a relationship you had and then lost. I think one of the most powerful human emotions is what should have been and wasn't…That was a really good song to start out on, just because a lot of people can relate to wanting what you can't have."

Taylor and Liz had just written their first hit together, but, according to Liz, losing Brandon was still having a deep personal effect on Taylor, and, following the initial recording, the song was shelved for months. Eventually, it would be chosen as the first track on her debut album, the first single taken from it, and her very first chart entry.

The two of them now began collaborating in earnest, and they composed seven more songs that would make it onto the album. However, any talk of even having an album was still very much in the future.

The Big Break

"Basically, there are two types of people - people who see me as an artist and judge me by my music. The other people judge me by a number - my age, which means nothing"

Turning her back on RCA

Just when Taylor was on a high with her songwriting, news came that was potentially devastating to her career. After what she thought to be such a promising start, RCA had second thoughts about the development deal. They liked her singing, but were not overly struck by her songwriting. They now planned to keep her in development for at least another year, and then have her record music written by other songwriters.

It was a crushing blow, especially when she thought she had been ready for a number of years. In an interview for the *Daily Telegraph*, she recalled: "Basically, there were three things that were going to happen. They were going to drop me, shelve me - that's like putting me in cold storage - or give me a record deal. The only one of those you want is a record deal."

Speaking later to GAC, she explained: "I didn't want to just be another girl singer. I wanted there to be something that set me apart. And I knew that had to be my writing. Also, it was a big, big record label with big superstars, and I felt like I needed my own direction and the kind of attention that a little label will give you. I just did not want it to happen with the method of, 'Let's throw this up against the wall and see if it sticks, and if doesn't, we'll just walk away.' I wanted a record label that needed me, that absolutely counted on me to succeed. I love that pressure… Basically, there are two types of people - people who see me as an artist and judge me by my music. The other people judge me by a number - my age, which means nothing."

It was not a decision to take lightly, but Taylor's unwavering determination to realise her dream gave her little choice. At the age of 14 she took a bold move and turned her back on one of the biggest record labels in the land. She might never be given another chance, she knew that, but this was Taylor Swift, showing a maturity seldom seen in one so young and having the courage to make such a massive decision all by herself. She told *Entertainment Weekly*: "It's not a really popular thing to do in Nashville, to walk away from a major record deal - but that's what I did."

In the end, there would only be one loser. Unbeknown to Clive Davis, the newly-crowned chairman of RCA Records, he had just let a mountain of gold dust slip through his fingers.

To understand RCA's decision is to better understand the shifting music landscape of the noughties. It was not exactly a golden age for country music.

Teenagers were no longer buying into it in significant numbers, and the music coming out of Nashville was seen in some circles to be floundering and heavily reliant on its ageing fanbase. Rock and pop were still the predominant genres and the next generation of teenagers were embracing them for all they were worth. Very few country artists were willing or even able to make the crossover, and it needed a shot of adrenalin to revive its popularity in terms of the all-important sales figures and remain a major player in the music industry, and not become just a niche market.

In the meantime, Taylor continued writing for Sony, but, at the same time, went in search of a label that would believe in her ability as both singer and songwriter.

The man who made her queen

For Taylor, it was time to kickstart her career. She told the *Daily Telegraph*: "I had so many songs I wanted people to hear, [so] I did not want to be on a record label that wanted me to cut other people's stuff. That wasn't where I wanted to be…I genuinely felt that I was running out of time. I wanted to capture these years of my life on an album while they still represented what I was going through."

She came up with the idea to showcase her talent and invite all the Nashville contacts she had made over the last few months, including a few publicists and record executives. For a suitable venue, she booked a slot at none other than the legendary Bluebird Café at 4014 Hillsboro Pike in Nashville. The 100-seat music club had opened in 1982 as a focal point for starting the careers of a number of artists. Garth Brooks had been spotted there in 1987 and shortly afterward signed by Capitol. Situated on a quiet street, with a small stage and a no-talking rule while artists performed, it was a place that took music seriously. Taylor could not have chosen a more perfect spot to showcase her music, and she was confident she could pull it off: "I figured, if they didn't believe in me then, they weren't ever going to believe in me."

On November 4th 2004, just a month shy of her 15th birthday, Taylor took to the stage with her guitar. In all her life, she had never been this nervous, but this was no rundown roadhouse, and those watching were waiting patiently to see this young girl perform. Adorned in typical country music attire - denim jeans and pretty blouse - she stepped onto the stage and sat on a stool. Adjusting the microphone, she pushed her long corkscrew hair away from her face, and introduced herself, "Hi, I'm Taylor Swift."

Among those watching that evening was Scott Borchetta, one of the youngest and brightest label bosses in Nashville. Born in Burbank, California in 1962, his father had been involved in record promotions for several LA labels. After playing in a number of local rock bands at the age of 16, he moved with his family to Nashville, where his father started his own independent record company. Borchetta's love of music continued to grow and for a while he played bass guitar and toured in a country band, while also helping his father in the mail room promoting country singles.

All the time he was learning about the mechanics of the music industry, and he spent three years working in the promotional department at MTM Records. After trying his hand as an independent promoter, he worked for several record labels, including the Nashville offices of MCA and Universal Music. Under the latter's umbrella, he became executive of the new record label, DreamWorks Nashville.

As Taylor was about to begin her acoustic set, in the back of her mind she wondered if there might be a label boss out there in the audience who would make her dream a reality. Whether it had been written in her Sagittarian stars or not, history was about to be made that evening.

Taylor had met Borchetta once before, very briefly, at the DreamWorks office on Music Row. He had certainly heard how good this young artist was, perhaps the reason he was here now to see it for himself. The first song he heard was 'Teardrops on My Guitar'. Talking to GAC, he recalled: "Is this going to hit me? And it absolutely did. I was just smitten on the spot. It was like a lightning bolt."

Andrea was in the audience that night and could see for herself the look on Borchetta's face as her daughter had everyone in awe with an astonishing performance: "I looked across the room and I saw this person just watching her play, absolutely immersed in her music. I thought to myself 'I don't know who that is, but I hope that's the guy who ends up working with her.'" Taylor knew she had made a good impression on Borchetta: "Out of all the people in the room, he was the only one who had his eyes closed and was totally into the music."

The day after the Bluebird performance, Taylor wrote in her journal: "This last week was crazy, ok. So, Capitol Records doesn't think I'm ready right now, and I could get a deal right now with them, but not the deal I would want. So, on the other hand, there's Scott Borchetta, who we met at Universal. And you know, I really loved all the stuff he said in the meeting, and he stayed for the whole Bluebird Show, and he's so passionate about the project. I think that's the way we're gonna go. I want to surround myself with passionate people..."

There was no doubt about it in Borchetta's mind - here was a super-confident and remarkably gifted young artist who was destined to have a big future. He knew then he had to sign her to his new label. Looking around, he could see that there were like-minded music people in the room, so he had to act fast. Rather than approach her after the show finished, he desperately tried to contact her with voicemails. When he finally got a reply a few days later, he suggested to Taylor that they meet up again at his office, rather than pitch what he had in mind over the phone.

At the meeting in Nashville shortly after, he explained that he was eager to sign her to a record deal, and, as Universal was about to shut down their Nashville office, he was taking that as an opportunity to start a label of his own. He said, if she wanted, he could introduce her to executives at Universal, but that he'd rather have her as an artist on his future label, if she was willing to wait. He shared her vision and agreed that she could record her own songs.

Taylor took some time to be convinced. This was a label that didn't even exist, with a man who had nothing but a dream in his head. It was a huge risk for an unknown singer, but there was something about him that appealed to her: "You can tell when someone really gets you. The best part of getting a record deal was it wasn't just a record deal; it was the right deal for me. I'm with people I believe in and they believe in me."

While it would be a risk for Taylor, it was also a risk that faced Borchetta. He had been in the business for two decades, and in that time had earned a solid reputation, but signing Taylor would mean having to overcome some well-ingrained traditions in country music. It was becoming increasingly uncool for youngsters to buy a country album, with the market now aimed chiefly at an older generation, and many female listeners tended to prefer male artists anyway. According to another record executive, by signing Taylor, Borchetta would be breaking two rules - she was a teenager *and* she was female.

Here were two independently-minded people willing to take such risks. Call it chemistry, but they did seem to have a kindred spirit. She had someone who could make her dreams come true; while he had found a music sensation, a talent unlike anyone else out there, and, once signed, was convinced she would become a huge star: "I was smitten. I couldn't get up in the morning and not have her on my record label."

Borchetta knew that within a few months he could establish the label as a joint venture with his friend and major investor, country singer Toby Keith. Hopefully, Taylor would be his first signing and become the centrepiece of a roster of artists.

Ten days after the meeting with the Swifts, he got a message from Taylor that simply read, "I'm waiting for you."

Signing with Big Machine

After the Christmas break in January 2005, Taylor began her second semester at Hendersonville High. On January 21st, she was invited to perform at the NAMM (National Association of Music Merchants) trade show for the world-famous company Taylor's Guitars, held in Anaheim, California. Taking the stage with her guitar, and dressed in blue jeans and red blouse, she sat on a bar stool and performed an acoustic version of 'Beautiful Eyes', a self-penned song written back in 2003, and one that would be released on an EP three years later.

In the meantime, her songwriting continued in earnest, with both solo efforts and collaborations with other writers, including Liz Stone.

Taylor had every reason to be proud of herself. Indebted to her parents for their continuing support and sacrifices made along the way, this teenage girl had come this far due to her self-belief and gritted determination to succeed and overcome all obstacles that threatened to shatter her ambitions. She had faced ridicule and bullying at school with dignity; had been mocked for just being different; had persuaded her family to move nearly 700 miles to pursue her dream; and even walked away from one of the biggest record labels in the country. With an exceptional talent, dogged hard work, solid professionalism, and amazing charisma, the main driving force that had made this all happen was 15-year-old Taylor Swift.

Later in January 2005, and again in March, Taylor met up with Borchetta to discuss the record deal. Within months of Universal closing down their Nashville operation, he was hard at work setting up his new label. It would be called Big Machine, named after an album by the band Velvet Revolver.

Taylor showed no ill-feeling toward the labels that had overlooked or simply neglected her in the past; she understood their reasoning, as she explained to CMT News: "They were afraid to put out a 13-year-old. They were afraid to put out a 14-year-old. They were afraid to put out a 15-year-old. Then they were nervous about putting out a 16-year-old. And I'm sure if I hadn't signed with Scott Borchetta, everybody would be afraid to put out a 17-year-old."

Taylor's father was smart enough to be one of the minor investors, purchasing a 3% stake for an estimated $120,000, which also enabled him to keep a closer eye on how the label was handling his daughter's career. Taylor later recalled Scott Swift's role in her success: "My dad believed in me, even when I didn't. He always knew I could do this. I'm sure that everyone in Reading remembers how much he talked about me. I thought that was sweet, but really, I just wasn't as sure it would happen. So, I just love my dad for believing in his little girl."

On July 12th, just before signing with Big Machine, Taylor's parents fired her manager Dan Dymtrow, who then sued them for unjustly ending his contract and causing him to lose the apparent 5-10% of her music revenue. Since he was fired before Taylor's career had actually taken off, it meant he would get nothing. But as Taylor was still classed as a minor, Dymtrow was unable to get the required court approval for the contract. According to court records, her parents paid him $10,000 for his services for the past two years.

Big Machine Records was finally launched on September 1st 2005. Borchetta's bold mission statement for his new venture would be to put "the music first and the artist first", and made the point of expressing that "it's the music business, not the business of music."

A month after beginning tenth grade, Taylor signed the contract at a special ceremony held at the Country Music Hall of Fame in Nashville. Remembering all the practice that Taylor had put into signing her name, this would be one of the most important times in her career. As she put pen to paper, she remarked how it looked like a wedding contract. Borchetta jokingly replied, but with a serious face, "No, it's more binding."

Almost straight away, work began on putting an album together, and Taylor felt comfortable about the type of songs chosen to form the backdrop of the album. She told *Entertainment Weekly*: "There was no reason why country music shouldn't relate to someone my age if someone my age was writing it." For *Billboard* magazine she made the point: "I was writing about the same things that I'm writing about now, of course - boys. And I've always been fascinated by the way that people treat each other and the way that they interact. Stuff like that just really, really fascinates me and always has."

Enter Nathan Chapman

Although Borchetta brought in a team of producers to work on the album, Taylor had only one person in mind. She had first met Nathan Chapman, through Liz Rose, while he was making demos in a little shack behind the Sony/ATV offices: "I'd always go in there and play him some new songs, and the next week he would have this awesome track, on which he played every instrument, and it sounded like a record. We did this for a period of a year or two before I got my record deal." Chapman was a graduate of Lee University in Tennessee, with a major in English, and as his parents were Christian singers, he was no stranger to the music industry, and in time became an accomplished multi-instrumentalist. Although wanting to be an English professor, he found his degree helped him with his songwriting. Creativity ran in the family, as his wife was also a songwriter and country music artist.

With production credits going back nearly two years, Chapman was yet to work on an album, having only done demos in the past. Because of that, Borchetta was sceptical about hiring him, especially someone lacking experience with using the kind of technology required to make a first-class studio album. In the end, Taylor got her man, as she told CMT News: "I got to record with a whole bunch of really awesome producers in Nashville, but none of them sounded the way it did with Nathan…the right chemistry hit."

Originally, Chapman was brought in to produce just a few of the songs, but would end up producing all but one of the eleven tracks over the next four months.

It was no longer just a dream. For the first time in her career, Taylor Swift was now standing in a recording studio about to record the first song for her first album. With what she considered the right man at the helm, they went straight to work. But Taylor was no stranger herself to the recording process, and felt she could contribute a lot to the production. She recalled later: "When I write a song, I hear how it is supposed to sound in my head. I can hear the production. I can hear what the drums are doing, what the mandolin is doing, what the bass is doing, when I'm writing that song. So usually, when we go to the studio, all I have to do is sit down with Nathan for ten minutes and say, 'This is how I want this to sound,' and he brings it all to life."

During the early stages of production, Taylor had a meeting with Borchetta to discuss which of her songs would make the album, and she played the angst-ridden 'Tim McGraw' to him on a ukulele. According to Taylor, he said to her, "Do you realise what you just wrote? - That's your first single." What she considered to be her most important song was also to be the opening track, and the fact that it mentioned the country music legend by name would no doubt nurture curiosity and encourage sales.

Taylor would be working on the recordings every weekday after school throughout the fall. Production took place in four or five separate Nashville studios, with Taylor playing her 12-string guitar and Chapman on a variety of instruments, including electric and acoustic guitars, banjo, bass, drums, and mandolin. Among the session musicians brought in were Gary Brunette on electric guitar, Mike Brignardello and Tim Marks on bass, Tony Harrell on keyboards, Nick Buda and Shannon Forrest on drums, Bruce Bouton on Dobro, and Ilya Toshinsky on acoustic guitar and banjo.

Taylor's impatience to get the album out soon got the better of her, and she now embraced social media to promote its imminent release and launch an online publicity crusade. She set up her own page on MySpace, at the time the largest networking site in the country, and some of her first blogs included film clips of her at home, thanks to her parents buying her a video camera. Whatever free time she had was used on MySpace to connect with her growing number of fans - soon to be dubbed Swifties - who in no time at all would be counted in their millions.

Speaking to *Billboard*, Taylor recalled how important social media was in the early days: "I spent so much time on MySpace. It's the best way to figure out what your fans and what your friends and these people that helped you get where you are, what they're going through and what they want to hear from you, what they're liking, what they're not."

This personal approach to viral marketing had seldom been seen in country music. Not only did Taylor want to be in control of her career and the music she was making, she also needed to be in control of how her followers saw her. This one platform, and others that followed over the years, would become just as important to Taylor as the music she was making, and over the next few weeks she would see an explosion in the number of hits on her page. By streaming some of her songs online prior to their release, she not only gauged their popularity, but was able to interact with her growing fanbase, who were eager to know all about her, and about the songs and their subject matter.

On June 9th Taylor performed at the celebrated CMA Music Festival held at LP Field in Nashville and debuted the songs 'Tim McGraw' and 'Picture to Burn'. Ten days later, the 'Tim McGraw' single was released, soon followed by the music video on July 22nd.

Three months later, on October 24th 2006, the eponymous album *Taylor Swift* was finally released. In the liner notes, she paid a heartfelt tribute to her fans: "I love everyone who's inspired me to write a song, whether you know it or not. I love anyone who has ever turned the volume up when my song comes on the radio, anyone who has bought this album. Anyone who can sing along to my songs when I play them live. Anyone who's ever requested my song on the radio, or even remembered my name. If you ever see me in public, I want to meet you. I will thank you myself. You have let me into your life, and I will never be able to thank you enough for that. I love YOU, and I love God for putting you in my life…"

With a cheeky postscript, she added: "To all the boys who thought they were cool and break my heart, guess what? Here are 14 songs written about you. HA."

For this, and a number of albums to follow, Taylor would introduce her now-legendary "Easter Eggs" - hidden messages within the printed lyrics or liner notes that gave clues to the background or subject matter of the song. As a marketing ploy, it was sheer genius.

TAYLOR SWIFT
Label: Big Machine Records
Recorded - The Castles Studio-A, Franklin TN, Quad Studios-A,
  Sound Cottage, Sound Emporium & Darkhorse Recording, Nashville TN
Produced - Nathan Chapman, Robert Ellis Orrall & Chad Carlson
Released - October 24th 2006
Singles - 5
Chart peak positions
  Hot 200 #5; UK #81; Australia #33; Canada #13
RIAA Certification - 7 x Platinum
Selected awards and nominations
2008 ACM Awards - Album of the Year (nominated)

Tim McGraw ****
(Taylor Swift - Liz Rose)
1st Single
Recorded - Quad Studios-A & Sound Cottage, Nashville TN
Produced - Nathan Chapman
Released - June 19 2006
Chart peak positions
  Hot 100 #40; Hot Country Songs #6; Canada Country #10
RIAA Certification - 2 x Platinum
Selected awards and nominations
2006 CMT Online Awards - #1 Streamed Video from a New Artist (nominated)
2007 BMI Awards - Award-Winning Song (won)
2007 CMT Music Awards - Breakthrough Video of the Year (won)

What had its origins in a freshman algebra class would eventually go on to become Taylor's first-ever published song. It was written as her parting gift for high school senior Brandon Borello, believing that they would break up their relationship before he left for college (although it has been linked to earlier boyfriend Drew Dunlap). After parting, it was her hope that listening to a Tim McGraw song would bring back memories for them of their time spent together.

She wrote later: "After school I went downtown, sat down at the piano, and wrote this with Liz Rose in fifteen minutes. It may be the best fifteen minutes I've ever experienced. It deals with the haunting power of music and how hearing a song years after it was first popular can have such an emotional appeal."

The hidden lyric clue here is "Can't Tell Me Nothin", the name of one of McGraw's songs on his 2004 album *Live Like You Were Dying,*

The bittersweet song, full of vivid imagery, serves as a fitting introduction to the world of Taylor Swift and is a rollercoaster ride of emotions; one minute full of romance, funny the next, and then heartbreakingly sad at the end. In this one song, the essence of Taylor's songwriting style is laid out for all to see, and rubber-stamps her as being no flash-in-the-pan starlet, but a serious, down-to-earth artist with a natural gift for telling stories about teenage love and all its complexities. The perfect beginning to what will be an award-winning debut album - and the critics loved it.

The accompanying music video, made by top director Trey Fanjoy, features actor Clayton Collins as Taylor's love interest, chosen by her due to his similarity to Brandon. It was filmed at the former home of Johnny Cash, which was destroyed by fire the following year. It had its premiere on Great American Country channel on July 22nd 2006 and would win Fanjoy the award for Breakthrough Video of the Year at the CMT's the following year.

Taylor would later perform the song in front of Tim and his wife, Faith Hill, at the ACM Awards in 2007, and then sing it with them during the Nashville leg of her *Reputation* Tour in 2018.

Rolling Stone - "Her writing style was plainspoken and straightforward but succeeded in illustrating detailed scenes that evoked universal emotions ... All of this filled in the finer details of a story that's simply about longing for an old flame"; **Vulture** - "Even as a teenager, Swift was savvy enough to know that country fans love nothing more than listening to songs about listening to country music."

Picture to Burn ***
(Taylor Swift - Liz Rose)
4th Single
Recorded - The Castles Studio-A, Franklin TN; Sound Cottage &
  Sound Emporium, Nashville TN
Produced - Nathan Chapman
Released - February 3 2008
Chart peak positions
  Hot 100 #28; Hot Country Songs #3; Canada #48; Canada Country #1
RIAA certification - 2 x Platinum
Selected awards and nominations
2008 Nashville Music Awards - Country Performance Activity Award (won)
2009 BMI Awards - Award Winning Song (won)
2009 BMI Awards - Publisher of the Year (won)

Unlike the romanticism of the opening track, here we have Taylor venting her anger in typical teenage fashion. She wrote later: "It's about a guy I liked who didn't like me back, and I got really mad, you know?" The lyrics describe him as "just another picture to burn" and how she plans to seek revenge. It was claimed to have been about Jordan Alford, who she "almost" dated around the summer of 2005. Before performing the song in concert, it usually came with a friendly warning: "I always try to tell the audience that I really do try to be a nice person...but if you break my heart, hurt my feelings, or are really mean to me, I'm going to write a song about you..."

According to the *Daily Mail*, Alford was in the same year as Taylor at high school and they went out before he dated fellow classmate Chelsea, who later became his wife. Chelsea described how she and Taylor "exchanged a few words over a locker fight…we were just being girly, snarky", and how everyone in the school who had listened to the album tried to figure out who each of the songs were about: "She really does write her own songs, so I guess if you date her you have to know you're going to get a song written about you. In our case, back in school nobody thought she was actually going to go anywhere."

Chelsea also remembered how Taylor was in class: "She'd be writing, rather than paying attention at all. She was different, she wasn't super-popular, she kind of did her own thing. A normal, high school girl kind of thing."

In an interview for CMT, Taylor said: "I think girls can relate to the song because it's about just being mad - and it's okay to be mad after a breakup, or after something goes wrong with a relationship. It's just, like completely brutally honest."

The accompanying music video was again directed by Trey Fanjoy, her fourth in a row, and shows Taylor fantasising about exacting revenge on her ex-boyfriend as she sees him with another woman. For the comical video, Taylor chose football player Justin Sandy to portray her ex as he had a "classic and suspiciously perfect demeanour" and looked like a "real-life Ken." Also appearing are her backing band, as well as real-life best friend Abigail Anderson in a cameo role. Shot over two days at two locations in Nashville, and using pyrotechnics for the first time, the video premiered on March 14th 2008 on AOL's The Boot.

The song's lyric hint is "Date Nice Boys".

Vulture - "Swift's breakup songs rarely get more acidic than they do in this country hit"; **About.com** - "Swift takes no prisoners in her quest to make a former flame feel her wrath for doing her wrong."

Teardrops on My Guitar *****
(Taylor Swift - Liz Rose)
2nd Single
Recorded - Sound Cottage, Nashville TN
Produced - Nathan Chapman
Released - February 19 2017
Chart peak positions
 Hot 100 #13; AC #5; Adult Top 40 #6; Mainstream Top 40 # 7; Hot Country
 Songs #2; UK #51; Canada #45; Canada Country #6
RIAA Certification - 3 x Platinum
Selected awards and nominations
2008 BMI Country Awards - Song of the Year (won)
2008 Nashville Music Awards - Recurrent Country Performance Activity Award (won)
2008 MTV Music Awards (video) - Best New Artist (nominated)
2009 BMI Pop Awards - Award-Winning Song (won)

A sad tale of unrequited love and one of Taylor's most popular songs, written with Liz Stone about her ninth grade crush on friend and classmate Drew Hardwick, who sat beside her at Hendersonville High. It would be one of the very few songs in which she actually mentions the subject's name in the lyric.

Hardwick never realised her feelings about him, but, as a friend, would talk to her about another girl he liked. Taylor was like a smitten kitten, pretending to be happy for him, while deep inside she was crushed. It was an unrequited love that would last for several years. Even on the release of the album, he remained unaware of her intentions, and only when he heard the single did the penny drop. Two years later, after attempting to contact her several times, he eventually turned up at her house, maybe believing those feelings she had were still there. Of course, she rejected him.

This is a heartbreakingly beautiful song with Taylor playing her tear-drenched 12-string guitar to perfection. It was even offered to the Dixie Chicks to record, even substituting the word "you" for "Drew", but thankfully they passed on it, leaving Taylor's version both unique and definitive.

Introducing an acoustic performance of the song, Taylor told her fans: "This is a song that I wrote about a guy who went to school with me, and I was that 'friend,' you know, that girl who's your friend. And, you know, he had this awesome girlfriend who he would tell me about every single day. And, you know, I was that girl that he would go to and be, like, 'what should I get her for Valentine's Day? I have to make this Valentine's Day so awesome! It's her birthday, what should I do? What would the perfect gift for a girl be?' And of course, I'd give him, like, the most awesome ideas, awesome plans, like, *I* would want them!"

This endearing song became her second and breakthrough single, remaining on the Hot 100 chart for a year, just missing out on the number one spot on the Hot Country chart, breaking into the Top Ten on the mainstream and adult pop charts, and ultimately selling some three million digital copies. Critics were mixed on whether the song could be classified as country music, due to its pop music production. But that mattered little to Taylor; maybe an earlier indication that her music roots would not be entirely fixed in Nashville.

The lyric hint is "He Will Never Know".

For the music video, Taylor again turned to Fanjoy. Although some of her team believed it should be shot in a prior era or in a big city setting, Taylor chose Nashville again to keep the song's integrity. It follows her unrequited love for her friend who falls in love with another girl, and features actor and singer Tyler Hilton, who had appeared in the tv series *One Tree Hill* and the movie *Walk the Line*. Taylor saw how he closely resembled the real-life Hardwick, and invited him to play the role after he had performed at one of her concerts. The video was shot in January 2007 at Hume-Fogg High School, replicating Hendersonville High where her flirtations with Hardwick had taken place. The drama room was transformed to look like a bedroom, depicted in some of the scenes.

Billboard - "The straightforward conversional quality in her lyrics is like hearing the love-lorn confessions of a dear friend"; **About.com** - "Remove the twang of soft country guitar and [the song] is the best teen-pop ballad for quite some time"; **NPR** - "What differentiates Swift from other teen pop stars is that her songs impart viscerally what it feels like to be a teenager, when hyper-real emotions can still be conveyed with timidity"; **Pitchfork** - "The ease in which Teardrops translated to straight pop showed that her deft melodic touch and conversional way with deeply felt emotions could scale to the widest possible audience"; **Vulture** - "An evocative portrait of high-school heartbreak, equal parts mundane …and melodramatic".

A Place in This World ***
(Taylor Swift - Liz Rose - Robert Ellis Orrall - Angelo Petraglia)
Recorded - The Castles Studio-A, Franklin TN, Sound Cottage, Nashville TN
Produced - Robert Ellis Orrall & Nathan Chapman
Released - October 24th 2006

A song about the uncertainty of what the future holds, and accepting that if it doesn't work out, life will still go on. This was going to be the original title for the album. Taylor recalls: "I wrote this song when I was thirteen and had just moved to Nashville. It was tough trying to find out how I was going to get where I wanted to go. I knew where I wanted to be, but I just didn't know how to get there. I'm really happy this is on the album, because I feel like I finally figured it out." The lyric hint is "Found It".

Written on January 21st 2004, along with 'I'm Only Me When I'm With You' and the unreleased track 'What Do You Say', it was finally completed at Sony with the help of Liz Stone and two other writers, including Robert Ellis Orrall, who helped produce the album.

Rolling Stone - "Apprentice work from the debut, when she was still learning the ropes as a country songwriter. Yet, the seeds of greatness are already there"; **Vulture** - "This one feels like it missed its chance to be the theme tune for an ABC Family show".

Cold as You ***
(Taylor Swift - Liz Rose)
Recorded - Dark Horse Recording, Franklin TN & The Love Shack,
  Nashville TN
Produced - Nathan Chapman
Released - October 24th 2006

A song about her experiences with an emotionally unavailable guy. Taylor explains: "I wrote this song with Liz, and I think the lyrics to this song are some of the best we've ever written. It's about that moment where you realise someone isn't at all who you thought they were, and that you've been trying to make excuses for someone who doesn't deserve them. And that some people are just never going to love you." Where William Shakespeare famously compares his lover to a summer's day, Taylor compares her guy to a cold, rainy day. Some commentators say that this could be about the same guy as the one in 'Picture to Burn'.

In an interview for *Rolling Stone*, Taylor cites this as her favourite song on the album: "The hook is 'I've never been anywhere cold as you'. I love a line where afterward you're just like 'burn'." The song sees the beginning of Taylor's habit of making the fifth track on each of her albums an "emotionally vulnerable" ballad.

The lyric hint in the album's booklet is capitalised letters that spell "Time to Let Go".

Vulture - "A dead-serious breakup song that proved the teenage Swift …could produce barbs sharper than most adults".

The Outside ****
(Taylor Swift)
Recorded - The Tracking Room & The Love Shack, Nashville TN
Produced - Robert Ellis Orrall, Nathan Chapman
Released - October 24th 2006

Taylor puts some demons of her earlier years to rest with this insight into loneliness. It was one of the first self-penned songs she wrote when she was just 12 years old. At that time, she was feeling like a complete outcast at school (West Reading Elementary), and although she was writing about relationships, she was not experiencing one herself.

In an interview for *Entertainment Weekly*, she revealed: "I would look at other people and try to observe what they were going through…in the case of 'The Outside', I was writing exactly what I saw. I was writing from pain … Some days I woke up not knowing if anyone was going to talk to me that day…You can choose to let it drag you down, or you can find ways to rise above it. I came to the conclusion that even though people hadn't always been there for me, music had. It's strange to think how different my life would be right now if now if I had been one of the cool kids."

The way Taylor composed the song made it relatable to anyone who was going through the same emotions, and it would remain a hallmark of her songwriting for years to come. The song had originally been included on Maybelline's 2004 compilation cd sampler, *Chicks with Attitude.*

The lyric hint is "You Are Not Alone".

Rolling Stone - "Still a rookie. Still learning"; **Vulture** - "Though the lyrics edge into self-pity at times, this is still probably the best song written by a 12-year-old since Mozart's Symphony No. 7 in D Major"; **NME** - "The Outside speaks of the feeling of being a misfit growing up".

Tied Together with a Smile ****
(Taylor Swift - Liz Rose)
Produced - Nathan Chapman
Released - October 24th 2006

A tender song about insecurity, what Taylor believed was the biggest enemy of teenage girls, and one that focuses on bulimia nervosa, an eating disorder. For *Entertainment Weekly*, she told the story behind the song: "I wrote about one of my friends, who is this beauty queen, pageant princess - a gorgeous popular girl in high school…I wrote that song the day I found out she had an eating disorder. It completely blew my mind and this one was tough to write, because I wasn't just telling some sad story - this one was real."

Speaking to *Glamour* magazine, she confessed: "This is one of the moments when your heart kind of stops. How can somebody that seems so strong have such a horrible, horrible weakness? Something that is killing her."

Apparently, Taylor played the song for the girl when she asked who it was about, and believed she never suffered from it again. Taylor also played it for Borchetta for the first time while waiting to sign to his new label.

To all readers out there - Seek help, no one deserves to be alone…

Rolling Stone - "An unsung highlight of the debut - a teen pep talk about self-esteem"; **Vulture** - "This early ballad about a friend with bulimia sees Swift and Rose experimenting with metaphor. Most of them work".

Stay Beautiful ***
(Taylor Swift - Liz Rose)
Produced - Nathan Chapman

Released - October 24th 2006

Another heartfelt song about a high school crush for a boy who eventually moves away before she gets the chance to tell him her feelings. She mentions his name is Cory, giving it that added personal touch. Taylor recalled: "You don't have to date someone to write a song about them. This is a song I wrote about a guy I never dated! ... a guy I thought was cute, and never really talked to him much, but something about him inspired this song, just watching him." In a Target commercial for her third album *Speak Now*, Taylor finally revealed the inspiration for the song: "It all started with my first crush in fourth grade: Cory Robertson. He liked a cool girl. He had straight hair. Little did he know I was a country singer."

The lyric hint is "Shake n Bake".

Rolling Stone – "An early stab at a take-the-high-road breakup song": **Vulture** - "[Chapman] brings a sprightly arrangement to Swift's ode to an achingly good-looking man"; **NME** - "This twanging debut cut is dedicated to the high school crush that Swift never worked up the courage to ask out".

Should've Said No **
(Taylor Swift)
5th Single
Recorded - Darkhorse Recording, Franklin TN
Produced - Nathan Chapman
Released - May 18 2008
Charts peak positions
  Hot 100 #33; Hot Country Songs #1; Canada #67; Canada Country #5
RIAA Certification - Platinum
Selected awards and nominations
2009 BMI Awards - Publisher of the Year (winner)
2009 BMI Awards - Award-Winning Song (winner)

The final single off the album became Taylor's second Hot Country chart topper (after 'Our Song'), and was also the last song written for the album, apparently just two days before the mastering was scheduled, and then only completed overnight. She explained: "Basically, it's about a guy who cheated on me and shouldn't have because I write songs" (reputedly classmate Sam Armstrong, who later tweeted he had once dated her).

Having already thought of the line that became the song's title, she went on to write the chorus in just five minutes, and much of the lyric in the finished song is based on what she had actually said to him at the time. She commented later: "Just being a human being, I've realised that before every big problem you create for yourself, before every huge mess you have to clean up, there was a crucial moment where you could've said no."

Apparently in 2018, Armstrong claimed via Twitter that he and Taylor "were cool and dated again after the incident."

In one of her early cryptic clues, Taylor capitalised certain letters to spell out repeatedly the name SAM. Unlike the anger of 'Picture to Burn', Taylor reflects that there is a kind of "ok, you've messed up, but I still love you" message here. A number of critics rated this song and 'Picture to Burn' as the two most striking tracks on the album.

An eye-catching performance at the 2008 ACM Music Awards was later used for a music video.

49

Vulture - "What this early single lacks in nuance makes up for in backbone".

Mary's Song (Oh My My My) ****
(Taylor Swift - Liz Rose - Brian Maher)
Produced - Nathan Chapman
Released - October 24th 2006

A sentimental song about childhood love. Taylor looks at the older generation and takes inspiration from her long-time next-door neighbours, and how one night they related how they first met. Originally titled 'Oh My My My', it was probably written after moving with the family to Hendersonville.

Taylor said: "They'd been married forever and they came over one night for dinner, and were just so cute. They were talking about how they fell in love and got married, and how they met when they were just little kids. I thought it was so sweet, because you can go to the grocery store and read the tabloids and see who's breaking up and cheating on each other (or just listen to some of my songs!). But it was really comforting to know that all I had to do was go home and look next door to see a perfect example of forever."

The track was co-written by Liz Rose and songwriter Brian Dean Maher, who would later go on to co-author 'Small Town USA', the country chart-topper for Justin Moore.

The lyric hint is "Sometimes Love is Forever".

Vulture - "A young person's vision of lifelong love".

Our Song ***
(Taylor Swift)
3rd Single
Recorded - Quad Studios-A & Sound Cottage, Nashville TN
Produced - Nathan Chapman
Released - September 9 2007
Chart peak positions
 Hot 100 #16; Hot Country Songs #1; Mainstream Top 40 #18; Canada #30; Canada
 Country #1
RIAA Certification - 4 x Platinum
Selected awards and nominations
2008 CMT Music Awards - Video of the Year (won)
2008 CMT Music Awards - Female Video of the Year (won)
2008 CMT Online Music Awards - #1 Streamed Music Video (nominated)

The record-breaking third single and the last of Taylor's three self-penned songs on the album. It was written in about 20 minutes before having to perform it in a ninth grade talent show at Hendersonville High: "I wrote it about this guy I was dating, and how we didn't have a song. So, I went ahead and wrote one." Again, some commentators believe it's about her crush on Drew Hardwick, but it's more likely to have been inspired by her two-week relationship with Brandon Borello. Taylor recalled in an interview for the website The Boot: "I was thinking, 'I've gotta write a song that's gonna relate to everyone in the talent show, and it's gotta be upbeat'."

Originally, she had no intention of putting it on the album, but with its upbeat melody and the story about a young couple who use the events in their lives in place of a regular song, it proved to be a great success with the other students.

50

On her website, Taylor recalled: "I just sat down one day with my guitar and got in a groove, and went with it. I like to write about how music affects people, and this was fun to write because it's about a couple who don't have a song. I like the banjo and you really can't go wrong with banjo. I wanted it to be last on the album, because the last line of the chorus is 'play it again'. Let's hope people take it as a hint to go ahead and play the album again!"

She told GAC: "I think there's just some sort of magic in the way the track sounds like it's bouncing."

When it became her first Hot Country chart topper the week before Christmas 2007, remaining there for six weeks, it was the largest leap on the chart since Tim McGraw's 'Just to See You Smile' in 1998, making her the youngest solo writer and singer to have a number one country song.

The lyric hint is "Live N Love".

The award-winning music video, directed by Trey Fanjoy, features Taylor singing in various settings. Taylor recalled Fanjoy's ideas for the video after listening to the song: "She had this idea for a front porch performance and then a field of flowers for another performance, then a black-and-white performance shot. It all came together in her head. She was able to translate that so well onto film." The video had its premiere on CMT on September 14th 2007 and would go on to win awards.

Country Universe - "There's a youthful exuberance and enthusiasm to it, capturing the need to make mundane things bigger than they really are just because that's how they seem when you're a teenager"; **Vulture** - "Even at this early stage, Swift had a knack for matching her biggest melodic hooks to sentences that would make them soar".

I'm Only Me When I'm With You **
(Taylor Swift - Robert Ellis Orrall - Angelo (Petraglia)
Taylor Swift Deluxe Edition bonus track
Recorded - Abtrax Recording, Nashville TN
Produced - Robert Ellis Orrall & Angelo Petraglia
Released - November 6 2007
Chart peak position
 Hot 100 Bubbling Under #15
RIAA Certification - Platinum

Laid-back song about Taylor's friendship with Abigail Anderson, and how they feel free to be themselves when they are together. A video featuring Abigail and some of Taylor's family and other friends was released on March 3rd 2008 and later debuted on Taylor's YouTube channel. The song was written on January 21st 2004, along with 'A Place in the World'.

Remarkably, a platinum-selling record.

Vulture - "As if to reassure nervous country fans, the fiddle goes absolutely nuts".

Invisible ****
(Taylor Swift)
Taylor Swift Deluxe Edition bonus track
Produced - Nathan Chapman & Scott Borchetta
Released - November 6 2007

Chart peak position
 Hot 100 Bubbling Under #3
 RIAA Certification - Gold

Taylor recalled this gentle ballad is "about the son of my parents' friends. They were always at my house and their son was my age, and he would always tell me about other girls he liked. I felt, well, invisible. Obviously. So, I wrote that song about it, and it was a bonus track on my first album." Reputedly written one summer while on vacation at Stone Harbor, some commentators say it could be about her crush on Drew Hardwick, the person who inspired 'Teardrops on My Guitar', who was also on her radar around this time.

Rolling Stone - "A teen ditty about a boy who doesn't realise she's alive, from pretty much the last moment in history that was possible".

I Heart? **

(Taylor Swift)
Taylor Swift Best Buy digital download
Recorded -The Tracking Room, Masterfonics & The Love Shack, Nashville TN
Produced - Robert Ellis Orrall
Released – November 6 2007

A song in which she is searching for reasons for the end of what appears to be a recent stormy relationship and now is unsure of who to love. Originally it was written for a 2003 demo cd, along with 'Your Face' and 'The Outside', the latter of which did make it onto the debut album. When released as a promotional single in June 2008, it served as a stopgap to tide fans over until the release of her next album. Because of that, it was not heavily promoted.

Vulture - "Swift code switches like a champ on this charmingly shallow country song".

A Perfectly Good Heart **

(Taylor Swift - Brett James - Troy Verges)
Taylor Swift Deluxe Edition bonus track
Executive producer - Scott Borchetta
Produced - Brett James & Troy Verges
Released - June 23 2008

One of Taylor's first break-up songs, describing her first experience of heartbreak and hinting that there will be more to come in the future. The song was co-written with Grammy-award winner Brett James, and country songwriter Troy Verges, twice recipient of awards for Songwriter of the Year.

Vulture - "A pleading breakup song with one killer turn of phrase and not much else".

"A talent to be reckoned with"

Taylor Swift debuted on the Billboard 200 album chart on November 11th 2006, with estimated sales of 40,000 copies. It eventually reached the top spot week-ending January 19th 2008, having spent 63 weeks on the charts, the longest stay in the decade. Eventually it would register a total of 275 weeks before dropping from the chart. As expected, it did even better in Billboard's Top Country Album chart, making number one for a total of 24 non-consecutive weeks.

Another record was broken when Taylor's subsequent EP *Beautiful Eyes* replaced it at number one with *Taylor Swift* dropping to second spot. She became the first artist to hold the top two positions since LeAnn Rimes in 1997. 'Tim McGraw' also remained on the Hot 100 singles chart for 20 weeks.

The album would eventually go on to be one of her best-selling albums, with some seven million copies sold by the end of 2020, giving it platinum certifications seven-fold by the Record Industry Association of America.

PopMatters - "Lyrically, musically, and in terms of the overall presentation, right down to the 'hidden' messages in the lyric sheets, this is country music, Disney style... At 16, Taylor Swift already seems too mature to be considered a child. It's to be hoped that when she finds both her place and her full-grown voice, she's able to find an accommodation between the country tradition and her very obvious pop sensibilities, because *Taylor Swift* [the album] suggests she has much to offer; **AllMusic** - "[Swift's] considerably strong voice straddles that precarious edge that both suggests experience far beyond her years and simultaneously leaves no doubt that she's still got a lot of life to live. It's a fresh, still girlish voice, full of hope and naïveté, but it's also a confident and mature one. That Swift is a talent to be reckoned with is never in doubt"; **Country Standard Time** - "Swift's best efforts come on her deeply personal, self-penned songs...It's an impressive debut that, while she pines about lost love and Tim McGraw, will likely have others singing the praises of Taylor Swift"; **Country Weekly** - *"*The more thoughtful material suggests a talent poised to last well past high school"; **The Toledo Blade** - "[Swift] deftly handles lyrics and subjects in that shadowy area between teenager and womanhood"; **About.com** - "Country music has not seen a phenomenon like Taylor Swift since Shania Twain broke through in a big way back in 1995".

Promoting the album

After returning from New York, Taylor took time out to catch up with family and friends. With her sudden newfound fame there were to be the inevitable changes to her daily life. One of the decisions she now had to face was her continuing education for the following year. She knew it was going to be impossible to return to Hendersonville High and still continue her recording career. Having reached the age of 16, she was no longer legally bound to pursue her education, but she wanted to graduate, and found a way by enrolling in the Aaron Academy, a Christian school in Gallatin, which offered a home-schooling programme by sending assignments by mail. It would still mean hard work juggling studies, music, and seeing her friends, but it was something she was committed to do.

Meanwhile Scott Borchetta had got the promotional wheels in motion. He had already released the single 'Tim McGraw' a month before the album was released, quickly followed by the music video. Now he set his mind to getting country radio stations to add the song to their playlists. Together with Taylor, he began to use social media as a powerful promotional tool.

He explained to *Entertainment Weekly*: "People laughed at me. They said, 'You're starting a new record label and you signed a 15-year-old female country singer - good for you! You have a teenager - there's a lot of those on country radio.' They were looking at me like I had two strikes. But I knew we didn't want to count on country radio…So, we went heavy on tv, putting the video out before the single, and doing a special with GAC, and we went heavy on her MySpace and online stuff. By the time we got to country radio, we said: 'We have you surrounded and you don't even know it'."

It proved to be a breakthrough. With Taylor amassing so many teenage followers on social media, and using it in such an endearing and intimate way, she was just too big for radio programmers to ignore. As a result, they began to play her music more and more, which, in terms of increasing record sales, was priceless.

Taylor's raw energy and confidence were beginning to rub off on her label boss. But now Taylor added a personal touch. Many of the demo discs of the single had been hand-picked and sent out to radio stations by Taylor and Andrea. With each one, Taylor had enclosed a handwritten note and added a whispered good-luck message on each disc. And it worked, her teenage charm having the effect of softening the heart of many a cold DJ.

During the summer of 2006, Taylor and Andrea set off in a rental car on a mission to tour hundreds of radio stations to promote her music. Her manager had once told her: "If you want to sell 500,000 records, then go out there and meet 500,000 people." Andrea did the driving while her daughter slept in the back. Radio programmers loved both her polite outlook and her music; no doubt sweetened by Andrea's specially baked cookies that were brought to the studio. When asked questions in interviews, Taylor would always come back with intelligent and well-thought-out replies, giving her full attention to every detail. She recalled the importance of the tour: "Radio tours for most artists last six weeks. Mine lasted six months. That's because I wanted it to. I wanted to meet every single one of the people that was helping me out."

Although Andrea was in the driving seat for the tour, she remained in the back seat when it came to managing her daughter's affairs. Going forward, Taylor now liked to be firmly in control of every aspect of her career. In an interview for *Harper's Bazaar*, she explained: "When I'm in management meetings and we're deciding my future, those decisions are left up to me. I'm the one who has to go out and fulfil all these obligations, so I should be able to choose which ones I do or not. That's the part of my life where I feel most in control."

Opening for the stars

Taylor was also becoming much sought after to be the opening act for more established artists. It began on June 5th when she was invited to open for Hootie and the Blowfish in Phoenix, Arizona. Later, on October 17th, and with just 48 hours' notice, she was asked to open for country trio Rascal Flatts. They had just lost their support, Eric Church, apparently fired for continuing to play past his allotted stage time, thus forcing them to extend their own set and having to pay venues extra money. In her journal, Taylor wrote: "Oh my God. I am on the Rascal Flatts tour. I got a call yesterday and I screamed louder than I can ever remember screaming before."

Two days later, she opened for them in Omaha, Nebraska, and remained with them for their final eight concerts. Her experience of singing at festivals stood her in good stead, and the fans took her to their hearts as soon as she stepped on stage, dressed in a black knee-length dress, and wearing her good-luck red cowboy boots with imprinted skull and crossbones.

A typical setlist at the time would be 'I'm Only Me When I'm With You', 'Our Song', 'Teardrops on My Guitar', 'Should've Said No', 'Picture to Burn', and 'Tim McGraw'. As she introduced and then performed each song, the audience knew they were watching the next country sensation. When she sang 'Tim McGraw', they held cell phones in the air with the illuminated screens that looked to Taylor like galaxies of stars, perhaps something she had never witnessed before. After the show she also made a point of signing autographs for all of her newfound fans.

The tour ended with two concerts in Las Vegas on December 2nd and 3rd. Taylor was forever grateful to Eric Church for giving her this unexpected opportunity, and even sent him her first gold record with a note that read: "Thanks for playing too long and too loud on the Flatts tour. I sincerely appreciate it." A reply came: "We remember that day well! Honoured to have a page in your story. Love the new record!"

On October 22nd, GAC TV aired a short 23-minute documentary, *Taylor Swift: A Place in This World*, chronicling the singer's journey thus far. Directed by James Rink, the cameras followed Taylor in the recording studio, on the road at the CMA Musical Festival, and on a radio tour, including performances of several tracks from her album and seeing her interact with her fans through her website.

More television appearances quickly followed. On the morning of October 24th, Taylor was in New York getting ready to appear on *Good Morning America* and then the *Megan Mullally Show,* quite a coup for a relatively unknown artist. But there was one other thing she needed to do on this momentous day - the very day her album was being released. She went to a record store and bought a copy of the album, just to see her name come up on the register.

With the release of the debut album and the accompanying lyrics, there was bound to be some backlash from some of those suspecting they had been the subject of one of her songs, and a virtual war of words was about to break out on social media. Although Drew Hardwick was namechecked in 'Teardrops on My Guitar', other references were not as easy to detect. But it was only a matter of time before fans dissected the printed lyrics, seeking easy-to-crack codes to find how who each song was about.

Woe betide anyone who had done her wrong or broken her heart in the past: "If you're horrible to me, I'm going to write a song about you and you're not going to like it. That's how I operate."

In the meantime, Taylor was becoming ever-popular for singing at huge sporting events across the country. In November she was invited to perform 'The Star-Spangled Banner' at both the 2006 Checker Auto Parts 500 in Avondale, and for the NFL on Thanksgiving Day in Kansas City. By now, more established country stars were approaching her to join them on tour, and few came bigger than the legendary George Strait, who invited her to support him on a 20-date arena tour, beginning in January 2007 and ending in Denver at the beginning of March. She recalled: "The Rascal Flatts tour was a perfect match for me. With George Strait, I feel I'm lucky to be in front of a more traditional country audience."

As usual, Taylor gave it her all in every performance and later reflected on what it meant to her: "When you're live, people can see it on your face and they can see what the song means to you. I'll never sing one of my songs with a straight face like it means nothing to me because I wrote these songs and they all mean something to me. When you can look at two people in the front row who are singing the words to your songs, I love that. I love to be able to look at someone and make that contact and nod your head and say thanks for being here."

One person who showed a little concern about Taylor's meteoric rise was Scott Borchetta. In an interview for the *Washington Post*, he recalled: "My fear is that she'll conquer the world by the time she's 19. She'll get to the mountaintop and say, 'This is it?' Because she's just knocking down all of these goals that we didn't even have for the first album... My job at this point is really to protect her and not burn her out."

Starstruck

"Years from now, I'll look back and go 'I didn't know anything back then' [but] I got to immortalise those emotions that when you're so angry, you hate everything. It's like recording your diary over the years - and that's a gift"

Performing coast to coast

Taylor now had time to consider her future and the fear of messing it all up. She told *Vogue* magazine: "I get so ahead of myself. I'm like, 'What am I going to be doing at 30?' But there's no way to know that! So, it's this endless mind-boggling equation that you'll never figure out. I over-analyse myself into being a big bag of worried."

On February 13th 2007, Taylor was in Los Angeles guesting on *The Tonight Show with Jay Leno,* although she did not perform, and two months later played a bittersweet homecoming concert in Reading, close to where she had been born. With a small five-piece band playing banjos and fiddles, she decided not to sing any album tracks lest they cause some personal embarrassment to some of those watching, and instead performed a mixture of traditional country songs and pop favourites, including Eminem's 'Lose Yourself', Beyoncé's 'Irreplaceable', and an emotional version of John Waite's 'Missing You'. Three days later she was in Los Angeles with her small band to open for a Dodgers game.

That same month, Taylor attracted the attention of 34-year-old country star Brad Paisley, who invited her to go on tour with him. Beginning in May, she would be one of his three alternating opening acts, the others being Jack Ingram and Kellie Pickler. Paisley recalled for *Entertainment Weekly* that Taylor "was one that I called my manager when I heard her album and said, 'We have to get her out on tour.' For her to have written that record at 16, it's crazy how good it is. I figured I'd hear it and think, 'Well, it's good for 16' - but it's just flat out good for any age." He also spoke of his admiration for her music in *Blender* magazine: "She is operating at a level I will never reach - already - in the ground-breaking way that she has taken a new audience and said, 'I'm a country singer', and they love it..."

It was during the tour that Taylor formed a special relationship with fellow singer Kellie Pickler, a former pageant queen who had taken part in the talent show *American Idol*. Unlike Taylor, she had suffered a traumatic life, but the one thing they shared was a love of music. The two of them become best friends, with Taylor fondly calling her "the older sister I never had."

Accompanied by Kellie, Taylor attended the fan-voted CMT Music Awards in Nashville on April 16th and won Breakthrough Video of the Year for the song 'Tim McGraw'. Wearing a stunning white dress studded with silver sequins, she accepted the award from the 24-year-old former *American Idol* winner, Carrie

Underwood, now a well-established country star. From that moment on, she would be in a friendly rivalry with Taylor for the top awards in country music.

Totally surprised at winning, Taylor thanked her voters: "I cannot believe this is happening right now. This is for my MySpace people and the fans." Speaking to *The Tennessean* magazine, she said: "I can't explain the feeling. I have never been nominated for anything before, I had won nothing before, literally nothing. To have my name called, I didn't know what that was like. I didn't think I was going to get it…"

Taylor and Kellie shared an even bigger night a month later at the ACM Awards, held in Las Vegas on May 15th. This was the event Taylor had been waiting for ever since receiving the nomination for the category New Female Vocalist of the Year. Not so much for the prestigious award, but for the fact that she had been invited to perform 'Tim McGraw' in front of her music peers, artists that would include her idol LeAnn Rimes, and husband and wife Tim McGraw and Faith Hill. It was a sobering thought as Tim and Faith would be sitting in the front row. But this was Taylor Swift, and alone on the stage with just her trusty guitar, she gave a truly emotional and heartfelt rendition of the song.

After singing, she stepped off the stage and introduced herself to the couple: "Hi, I'm Taylor", before shaking their hands and giving both an affectionate hug. Even though she would not win the award (it went to Carrie Underwood), this was one of those moments she would never forget, and it was all captured on live television for the world to see.

McGraw, of course, was delighted, and in a later radio interview for The Boot said, "It's awesome…except I don't know if I should take it as a compliment or I should just feel old. But I found out she was about 14 and in math class when she wrote that, which made me feel better. She was pretty nervous when we first met, but it was fine. I told her I appreciated it. It's cool to have a song written about you, especially by a teenager. I didn't think any teenagers even knew who I was."

Three days after the ACM Awards, Paisley's tour kicked off in San Francisco and would continue with several breaks for the remainder of the year, ending in Vancouver, Washington State, at the end of January 2008. During that time, Taylor and Kelly appeared as dancers in the music video for Paisley's single 'Online'. The concert portions were shot at the White River Amphitheatre in Auburn, Washington. Although intentionally tongue-in-cheek, it had an underlying message about the danger of people misrepresenting themselves on the internet.

The single peaked at #39 on the Hot 100 and #1 on Hot Country Songs.

Following its release in July, Taylor joined up with the Governor of Tennessee and a local police association to become involved in Delete Online Predators, the first of many charities and good causes she would support in the coming years. Just the following year she would promise to donate $100,000 to the Red Cross to help those affected by the devastating floods in Cedar Rapids, Iowa: "They've stood by me and gave me a solid show. You've got to pay it forward in life…"

At the beginning of June, Taylor was back in Nashville to perform 'Tim McGraw' at the 2007 Reading Writing & Rhythm Benefit Concert, held at the legendary Wildhorse Saloon. Also on the bill were Kellie Pickler, Trent Tomlinson and Mindy Smith. A few days later she appeared at the annual CMA Music Festival, a four-day event held in the city, and once again performed what had become her signature tune. While there, she learned that her album had just been certified platinum, having sold a million copies in just eight months since its release. The platinum plaque was presented to her at a ceremony at the Convention Centre in Nashville.

By July, Taylor had amassed a staggering 20 million hits on her MySpace site. She had plenty to thank her growing army of Swifties for: "I think one of the cool things about this is that MySpace is one of the main reasons why I'm here, along with radio and word of mouth…it's bringing a completely different audience to country music. And I'm so grateful for that." But to Taylor, these were not her fans; she preferred to call them her friends and liked to share as much of their lives as they did of hers. Unlike many celebrities, she was very approachable and confessed to being a natural-born hugger.

Although there was no doubt that Taylor had come of age and was evolving immensely as a songwriter, there were still questions over her continuing need to showcase her fiery outbursts of emotion in her songs. In an interview for MTV: "Years from now, I'll look back and go 'I didn't know anything back then' [but] I got to immortalise those emotions that when you're so angry, you hate everything. It's like recording your diary over the years - and that's a gift."

That same month, Taylor had the honour of being invited by Tim McGraw and Faith Hill to join them for a week on their record-breaking *Soul2Soul* tour. The eight concerts, commencing in Jersey City, culminated in Columbus, Ohio. Two days later, she rejoined Paisley's *Bonfires and Amplifiers* tour at the concert at Raleigh, North Carolina.

Taylor was in Las Vegas in August for a special appearance on the season two finale of NBC's *America's Got Talent*. In the show, Taylor performed 'Teardrops on My Guitar' with 14-year-old finalist Julienne Irwin, and after the wonderful performance, Taylor told host Jerry Springer that Irwin had "such an adorable personality, and that's so much of the battle right there. You know, being so endearing and so, so humble. I think she should just stay as she is. I think she's got it." Irwin, who would go on to have a record deal, told her country music blog: "She could not have embraced me more. She treated me as though we had been friends our entire lives."

With Brad Paisley's tour taking her all the way from Toronto to Tampa over the next four months, Taylor still managed to fit in a few tv appearances and some solo concerts consisting mainly of 16-song sets.

In October, she travelled to New York to appear on the morning chat show *Live with Regis and Kelly* in which she chatted and performed her current single, 'Our Song', with band members Grant Mickelson (guitar), Amos Heller (bass), Emily

Poe (fiddle) and Al Wilson (drums), soon to become permanent members of what would be her regular touring band, The Agency.

She was also honoured by the Nashville Songwriters Association, sharing their Artist of the Year award with veteran country singer Alan Jackson, and becoming their youngest winner. To win such a prestigious award from her songwriting peers at the age of 17 must have seemed a very special honour.

Swiftmus

Meanwhile, Taylor's label was about to release a new record. Back in the spring, Taylor had spent a couple of months in the Nashville studios with producer Nathan recording a special "Swiftmus" album to be released ahead of the festive season. Just shy of 20 minutes long, the six tracks consisted of four Yuletide standards and two new songs, one a collaboration with Nathan Chapman and Liz Rose. Taylor explained the reasoning: "The album has been out for a year, but it's too early to put out the second studio album. But we wanted to give [the fans] more music. So, this was an opportunity to put out two new songs and a bunch of exclusive content…"

Taking those fans completely by surprise, *Sounds of the Season - The Taylor Swift Holiday Collection* was released on October 14th as a limited cd available exclusively at Target stores in the US and also via their website.

SOUNDS OF THE SEASON - THE TAYLOR SWIFT HOLIDAY COLLECTION
Label: Big Machine Records
Recorded - Sound Emporium, Quad Studios, Warner Brothers Studio, & Mastermix,
  Nashville TN
Produced - Nathan Chapman
Released - October 14 2007
Chart peak positions
  Hot 200 #20; Top Country Albums #14; Holiday Albums #1
RIAA Certification - Platinum

Last Christmas **
(George Michael)
Produced - Nathan Chapman
Released - October 14 2007
Chart peak position
  Hot Digital Songs #46
  A cover of the perennial festive song from Wham!'s 1986 album, *Music from the Edge of Heaven*. **Rolling Stone** - "The ache and quaver of her voice fit the George Michael melancholy; this might be the saddest 'Last Christmas' since the original".

Christmases When You Were Mine ****
(Taylor Swift - Liz Rose - Nathan Chapman)
Produced – Nathan Chapman
Released - October 14 2007
Chart peak position
  Hot Country Songs #48

60

Complemented by Chapman's gentle acoustic guitar, this beautiful, melancholic ballad was described by Taylor as "a different spin on a Christmas song. My favourite kind of thing to write about is heartbreak or something like that, and a lot of times in the holidays you're reminiscing about holidays past, maybe with people you're not around anymore, and so this song is really special to me and I hope it's a little bit different…"

A wonderful song that should have graced the charts as a single release and been up for awards. A missed opportunity by the label. **Vulture** - "The clear standout of Swift's Christmas album…If you've ever been alone on Christmas, this is your song".

Santa Baby *
(Joan Ellen Javits - Philip Springer - Tony Springer)
Produced - Nathan Chapman
Released - October 14 2007
Chart peak position
  Hot Country Sings #43

Taylor following in the footsteps of her friend Kellie Pickler, who had released her own version of this Eartha Kitt standard from 1953. **Rolling Stone** - "An oldie about a gold digger wooing Little Saint Nick was perhaps a dubious pick for a singer still in her teens".

Silent Night *
(Joseph Mohr - Franz Xavier Gruber)
Produced - Nathan Chapman
Released - October 14 2007
Chart peak position
  Hot Country Songs #54

A slightly uptempo version and different vocal interpretation of this most famous of Christmas carols played on guitar. **Rolling Stone** - "This bizarre version manages to miss almost every single note in the melody. They sure were in a rush to get this Christmas album out"; **Vulture** - "Points for ambition, but sometimes you just want to hear the old standards the way you remember them".

Christmas Must Be Something More **
(Taylor Swift)
Produced - Nathan Chapman
Released - October 14 2007

Describing the true meaning of Christmas, this was apparently a song Taylor wrote for church when she was about 12 or 13. If so, that would make it her oldest released recording. **Vulture** - "Here the vibe is judgemental in a way that will be familiar to anyone who's ever reread their teenage diary".

White Christmas ***
(Irving Berlin)
Produced - Nathan Chapman
Released - October 14 2007
Chart peak position
  Hot Country Songs #59

No Christmas album would be complete without this classic. Taylor is joined by Heidi Beall on backing vocals. **Vulture** - "This gentle rendition sees Swift's vocals cede centre stage to the mandolin and fiddle".

A number of critics were of the same mind - this should have been a full album - but once again applauded her delivery. **Country Standard Time** - "Swift is such a fine singer, who finds ways to inject sincere emotion into every line she sings"; **AllMusic** - "[The new arrangements were] suitably seasonal but also faithful to her bright-country pop".

Eager to hear new material from Taylor, the fans still bought enough copies to earn it a number one spot on the Billboard Holiday Albums chart, and, with subsequent re-releases, eventually earning it platinum status. The following year it would be re-released on iTunes and Amazon, and again in 2009 for Target, with "Sounds of the Season" dropped from the title.

In late October, Taylor was again called on to sing the national anthem, this time at Citizens Bank Park in Philadelphia at the start of the World Series third game between the Phillies and Tampa Bay Rays.

Another big day came on November 7th with the CMA Awards in Nashville. Accompanied by Andrea, she was presented with the coveted Horizon Award for best new artist, joining past winners that included Carrie Underwood, Garth Brooks, LeAnn Rimes and Keith Urban. During the show, she changed from wearing a long gold dress into a short black sequinned one to perform 'Our Song', currently riding high on the country charts.

That same month, Big Machine released another digital download EP, this time through the Rhapsody online music store. *Rhapsody Originals* consisted of four of Taylor's most popular live radio hits - 'Tim McGraw', 'Teardrops on My Guitar', 'Our Song', and 'Should've Said No'.

In December, Taylor performed at a Christmas for Kids charity event at the legendary Ryman Theater in Nashville, raising funds for otherwise poverty-stricken families to make it a happier time for their children. This was followed by a string of tv appearances promoting her Christmas album, including being a special guest at the annual lighting of the Rockefeller Center Christmas tree in New York. Broadcast live on television, she sang a moving 'Silent Night', dressed in a seasonal white coat and playing her glittering six-string guitar.

At the 50th Grammy Award nominations, held in Los Angeles and broadcast on December 6th, Taylor was one of the artists standing at the podium as Dave Grohl of the Foo Fighters announced her name as one of the nominees for Best New Artist. Looking shocked as her name was called out, Grohl gave her a hug and said, "Don't worry, Taylor, you got in the bag." The award ceremony would be taking place in February.

A week after the Grammy nominations, Taylor celebrated her 18th birthday in style, with a pink-themed party in Nashville organised by her parents and attended by some 200 guests. Speaking to *People* magazine, Andrea said: "This party is our birthday gift to her. She knows the real gifts in life are relationships." Scott Borchetta also recognised this personal milestone for his starlet by gifting her a pink Chevrolet truck. However, before the celebrations even began, the first thing Taylor did that morning was go and register to vote.

On Christmas Day morning, she was in Las Vegas as a special guest on *The Today Show,* performing 'Silent Night' and the wonderful but underrated 'Christmases When You Were Mine'. Two days later, the workaholic singer appeared live on stage in Times Square for her very first *Dick Clark's New Year's Rockin' Eve,* in which she performed a high-octane version of 'Our Song' and a more subdued 'Teardrops on My Guitar'. She then rounded off the year by joining Brad Paisley for the final concert of his tour on the last day of the year.

2007 had been an enormous year for Taylor Swift, with two chart-topping albums, non-stop performances across the country, a string of awards and nominations, and breaking records along the way. Just two years ago she was still in high school; now she was taking the world of country music by storm. Her music and lyrics had been critically acclaimed and her concert appearances celebrated, and artists were falling over one another to have her on their tours. Having already written enough material to fill two more albums, she had fans now waiting with bated breath and poring over her MySpace page for clues to what the new year might bring.

Taylor readily acknowledged that it was this growing army of Swifties that had helped to make her long-cherished dream become reality. In her acceptance speech at the CMA Awards, the singer closed with a gracious tribute to them: "You have changed my life."

Taylor Swift had come of age in more ways than one.

Flawless Fearless

"You have to believe in love stories and prince charmings and happily ever after. That's why I write these songs. Because I think love is fearless"

Crossover appeal

Since signing for Sony/ATV, Taylor had written over 200 songs, both on her own and as collaborations, and some of these had already been recorded for what would be the next studio album. She had told CMT News in December 2006: "I've been very selfish about my songs. I had this dream of this project [her debut album] coming out for so many years now that I just stockpiled. I'm so happy that I did because now we have a second album full of songs and a third album full of songs, and I don't have to lift a finger."

Constant touring by herself and in support of other artists had meant that whatever spare time Taylor had while on the road was spent writing, and only when on vacation and back in Nashville could she team up with other writers and musicians like Liz Rose, Robert Ellis Orrall and John Rich. For the online Songwriting Universe magazine, she related: "I've written a lot of songs myself lately, especially since I've been alone so much on the road. I do love writing on the road - I usually write at a concert venue. I'll find a quiet place in some room at the venue, like the locker room." As a result, eight songs on the new album would be solo efforts.

A little of Brad Paisley's light-hearted but touching writing style had rubbed off on Taylor, as did the vulnerability and honesty of Sheryl Crow's lyrics, especially on her wonderful album *Wildflower*. All the time spent on the road could have taken Taylor in a different direction with the theme of the album, but she stuck to the formula and focused on relationships.

Speaking to the *Oakland Press*, she revealed she did not want to alienate the growing fanbase she had, who were expecting to hear more of her romantic angst-ridden songs: "I really try to write more about what I feel and guys and love because that's what fascinates me more than anything else - love and what it does to us and how we treat people and how they treat us..." Although still not having experienced a deep relationship herself, she felt she had enough pent-up emotion to write the kind of material her fans were expecting to hear.

Ideas for the new studio album began as far back as April 2007, shortly after touring with George Strait had come to an end. With as many as 75 potential songs, she got together with Nathan Chapman in Nashville to whittle them down to the planned 13 tracks, a figure that Taylor regarded as being her lucky number. As well as songs penned some time ago, there were some recent ones, including 'Sparks Fly', 'Fearless', 'I'd Lie', and 'Permanent Marker'. These new songs were showcased at the Gold Country Casino in Las Vegas on May 29th 2007, but it was decided that only 'Fearless' would be selected for the album.

Taylor Swift entered 2008 as somewhat of a paradox - an incredibly successful and much-celebrated artist on the one hand; still an 18-year-old schoolgirl on the other. But what next? Half the new album's songs had already been recorded. The final two recording sessions would take place in Nashville in March and again that summer. Asked to describe the new album for the *Oakland Press*, Taylor said: "It's the same kind of album I made (in 2006) - just two years older. Sound-wise, it's the kind of songs I like to write, which are country songs, but I guess because of the subject matter and because of some of the melodies I love to use, I guess they have crossover appeal."

With the new album still months away from release, something was needed to tide fans over in the meantime, and on January 15th they were treated to some live recordings with the release of *iTunes Live from SoHo*, an exclusive EP available on iTunes, and consisting of special live versions of songs recorded at the Apple store in New York's SoHo. Seven songs were from the debut album, together with a surprisingly faithful version of Rihanna's 2007 single 'Umbrella'. When asked why she had chosen a pure pop song to add to her country repertoire, she simply replied: "You say bizarre, I say interesting." Sufficient sales saw it placed in the Top Ten on Billboard's Alternative Streaming Chart.

Two days later, Taylor was in Burbank making the first of what would be two appearances on *The Ellen de Generes Show*, chatting candidly with the host about her early life and finishing with a performance of 'Our Song'. That same month she supported award-winning country singer Alan Jackson for dates on his successful *Like Red on a Rose* tour.

In February, she parted with a substantial amount of money to buy a huge tour bus from singer Cher and then turned it into her own luxurious pad. Above the entrance was a sign that read, "Never, never, never give up", and inside it was adorned lavishly with all the girly trimmings one would expect, including a velvet couch, a fireplace, and a huge bed over which hung her platinum discs. She commented later: "I think my biggest splurge so far has been my tour bus. If I'm spending money, it's gonna be putting it back into my career."

Toward the end of March, she rejoined Rascal Flatts in Winnipeg on their *Still Feels Good* tour, and continued to perform with them over the next three months, with the final gig in Kansas on June 28th. In between appearances and performances, Taylor continued to write new songs, both at home and while on the road, adding them to those already filed away over the last few months.

In April, Taylor took time out from touring to attend the CMT Music Awards in Nashville. Wearing a short black dress and sporting a black fedora, she performed what seemed to be a soulful rendition of 'Picture to Burn', before casting aside her hat and treating the audience to a signature showstopping performance. That evening she walked away with two awards for Video of the Year and Female Video of the Year for 'Our Song', while her friend Kellie Pickler also won the Breakthrough Award for her video 'I Wonder'.

Two weeks later, Taylor and her band (which now included Paul Sidoti on guitar) performed 'Our Song' and 'Picture to Burn' on *Good Morning America,* and during the show she was presented with her special *Seventeen* magazine cover picture. The following day she sang the latter song on *Live with Regis and Kelly.* Also that month Taylor appeared on the cover of *Blender* magazine, with the introduction: "Meet the boyfriend trashing, radio ruling, girl next door".

Meanwhile, awards kept on coming her way. May brought the ACM Music Awards, held in Las Vegas. With Andrea and her friend Kellie looking on, Taylor appeared on stage wearing just jeans and a dark hooded jumper and began to perform what appeared to be a slow acoustic rendition of 'Should've Said No'. As she reached the first chorus, she threw her guitar to the side of the stage, and then had her outer clothes whipped away by two dancers to reveal a knee-length black dress underneath, before finishing the stunning performance drenched by a cascade of water pouring from above, something that had been rigged by Taylor and the show's producers as a surprise for her fans.

On her MySpace page, the 18-year-old singer wrote: "I've dreamt about that performance since I was in middle school. I've always wanted to perform an angry song and have water rain down from the ceiling and have a little freakout on stage...Oh, and the water was like 40 degrees. So cold."

Before walking away with the award for Top New Female Vocalist, she paid tribute to her mother - "the person that used to go to lunch with her friends and cook dinner for her family and sleep in her bed every night; and she gave that all away and left it all behind to go on the road with her 16-year-old daughter. And then she was sleeping in rental cars and in aeroplanes with her mouth hanging wide open cause she was so tired."

Taylor lost out in the nominations for Album of the Year (won by Miranda Lambert for *Crazy Ex-Girlfriend*) and Top Female Vocalist (won by Carrie Underwood). Thanking her fans on her blog, she wrote: "Honestly, I didn't expect to come away with an award, and I have you to thank for all the things you've done to support me. You're the reason my album is three times platinum. You're the reason the concerts sell out. You're the reason I'm able to be out here in Vegas."

The teaser album

As a teaser for the fans, still awaiting her next studio album, Taylor had her label put out the limited-release EP *Beautiful Eyes,* on January 15th, in an exclusive deal with Wal-Mart which meant it was only available to purchase online from the store's website. Explaining to GAC, she said: "I'm only letting my record company make a small amount of these. The last thing I want any of you to think is that we are putting out too many releases. I'm not going to be doing a bunch of promotion for it, because I don't want there to be confusion about whether it's the second album or not. I've gotten so many e-mails from people asking for new songs, and I thought this might tide them over till the new album comes out in the fall."

With the name taken from a song she had first written for a demo back in 2003, the EP also included three different versions of previous hit singles and two tracks previously released on special editions of the *Taylor Swift* album - 'I'm Only Me When I'm With You' and 'I Heart?'. The accompanying dvd included music videos of 'Beautiful Eyes' and her hit singles, an interview, and a live performance of 'Should've Said No'. Part of the promotion was the claim: "If this disc is any indication of what's to come, she is just warming up. If you haven't already jumped on the bandwagon, you's better do so now while there's still some room left".

BEAUTIFUL EYES
Label - Big Machine Records
Produced - Nathan Chapman, Robert Ellis Orrall & Angel Petraglia
Released - July 15 2008
Chart peak positions
Hot 200 #9; Top Country Albums #1

Beautiful Eyes **
(Taylor Swift)
Recorded - Studio Schmudio & The Play Room, Nashville TN
Produced - Robert Ellis Orrall
Released - July 15 2008

Taylor describes how someone's eyes are a big factor when it comes to attraction. Written back in 2003, supposedly while on vacation with her family in Tahiti, it was performed live at the *Vanity Fair* party in July 2004 and later at the NAMM show in January 2005. In the promotion for the release, the song was described as a "sweet, simple love song [that] doesn't have some of the clever hooks that Swift uses so well as a songwriter; instead, it captures the innocence of young love in an endearing, effervescent package".

The music video shows footage from her 18th birthday party.

Vulture - "A spirited vocal performance in the outro saves the song from feeling like homework".

The album's success took the label by surprise. On the week ending August 2nd, *Beautiful Eyes* replaced the album *Taylor Swift* at the top of the country charts, the first time that an artist had held the top two positions since LeAnn Rimes with *Blue* and *Unchained Melody: The Early Years* in 1997, and it went on to sell over 360,000 copies in the US. As a result, Taylor would include the title track in a number of future concerts.

Sputnik Music - "[Swift's] persona on the EP is her at her most human; she really does sound like she might be the shy girl with the locker next to yours that writes poetry in her free time. If nothing else, this release succeeds in making Swift even more relatable than ever before and accomplishes this not with revenge fantasies but by letting her guard down and revealing that she really is just like the rest of us".

A guy named Joe

The summer of 2008 saw the beginning of what would become an ongoing media circus that threatened to overshadow Taylor's music career, and it was for the simple reason that she had found for herself her first celebrity boyfriend in Joe Jonas. Born in Arizona just four months before Taylor, his mother was a singer and father was a songwriter and musician, as well as a former ordained minister. Raised in a deeply religious Christian environment, Joe was one of four brothers whose clean-living mirrored that of the Osmonds three decades ago. In 2005 Joe and his brothers Nick and Kevin formed a pop/rock band called Jonas Brothers, and as their popularity grew, with regular appearances on the Disney Channel network, they released their debut album *It's About Time* in 2006.

Taylor had once revealed that she was keen to date someone in the music industry. During one of their concerts in Anaheim in July 2008, she was spotted in the crowd by reporters, and, according to the *Atlanta Journal-Constitution*, was seen again at their Atlanta gig the following month, this time dancing along to their music. Just three nights earlier Jonas had been spotted with Taylor's father at her own concert in West Palm Beach, and more recently the two of them had been seen together eating ice cream close to her home in Hendersonville.

Although both denied any romance, the media hounds were on their case, and it soon became obvious that Jonas didn't want them to be seen together in public, which, of course, Taylor took to heart. More fuel was added to the rumours when Taylor was given a cameo role in the brothers' film, *Jonas Brothers: The 3D Concert Experience*, and performed 'Should've Said No' with them.

With Jonas now the centre of media speculation, he was asked by a radio host about the romance. As his beliefs forbade him to lie, he replied: "She's a great girl. I think anybody would love to go on a date with her." When it became Taylor's turn to face the media's bullets, she gave a similar answer: "He's an amazing guy and anybody would be lucky to date him." More than likely, these were well-rehearsed replies the two had agreed on beforehand.

As often is the case, it was their continuous schedules that eventually saw the relationship fizzle out in October. Jonas was rumoured to have ended it with the now-famous 27-second phone call to Taylor, but it also came to light that he was already dating actress and future wife, Camilla Belle, who had appeared in his video for 'Lovebug'.

With news of the split came the usual media frenzy, with one incendiary rumour saying Taylor had fallen pregnant. With both their public images at threat, Taylor was quick to react and declared: "I read a very curious rumour saying I'm pregnant, which is the most impossible thing on the planet. Take my word for it - impossible!"

With the media now focusing on Jonas as the villain in the story, he felt it was time to dispel all the rumours and prevent his squeaky-clean image becoming tainted. In an open letter to his fans, and without mentioning Taylor's name, he wrote: "Several things I will state with all my heart...I never cheated on a girlfriend. It might make someone feel better to assume or imply I have been unfaithful but it is simply not true. Maybe there were reasons for a break-up. Maybe the heart moved on. Perhaps feeling changed. I am truly saddened that anything would potentially cause you to think less... I called to discuss feelings with the other person. Those feelings were obviously not well received. I did not end the conversation. Someone else did. Phone calls can only last as long as the person on the other end of the line is willing to talk."

According to Jonas, he did try making contact again without a response, and concluded: "I wish the best for the other person but could not sit back any longer and leave our fans with a wrong impression of the truth."

Their ongoing story would continue for years to come, with each party contributing in their own way to keep it in the spotlight. But it had been a sobering experience for Taylor. Not only were people writing about her music, there now seemed to be as much interest in her personal life. Although at first it cut deep, with the later heartbreak songs to come, she would be playing it out in a never-ending dance with social media.

For the present, her first response was to do what she did best, and put her feelings into lyrics, and the lyrics into songs.

"That guy's not in my life anymore"

On October 6th Taylor appeared in an episode of *CMT Crossroads,* a music show that paired artists from different genres. Filmed at the Acuff Theatre in Nashville, she joined her mother's favourite band, Def Leppard, to duet and perform each other's songs. Among those were her own 'Picture to Burn', 'Teardrops on My Guitar', and 'Love Story', and the band's 'When Love and Hate Collide' and 'Two Steps Behind'. The show was later released on dvd, bought exclusively from Wal-Mart. Three weeks later, Taylor appeared on the cover of *Billboard* magazine for the first time, with the heading, "Country Teen Queen Takes Her Music Global".

The following month saw a trio of television appearances to promote the imminent release of *Fearless*. In New York on November 10th, Taylor again guested on *Good Morning America*, performing her new song, 'Love Story', with her band. That evening saw her make her first appearance on *The Late Show with David Letterman* for which she sang the new album's title track. Taped earlier in the day, she managed to fly back to Nashville, where, at the stroke of midnight, she made a promotional appearance at Wal-Mart's store in her hometown of Hendersonville to sign copies of the album and thank her delighted fans in person.

The new album was released the following day, with Taylor and her band flying to Los Angeles for a second appearance on *The Ellen De Generes Show,* with performances of 'Love Story' and 'Should've Said No'. During the interview with the host, the obvious question came up about Joe Jonas, and, being shown a photo of them together, she replied: "That guy's not in my life anymore, fortunately... It's all right - I'm cool. You know what, it's like, when I find that person that is right for me, he'll be wonderful. When I look at that person, I'm not even going to remember the boy who broke up with me over the phone in 27 seconds when I was 18."

As a special surprise, the show had Taylor's friend Abigail Anderson flown in for the occasion, and, even as a bigger surprise, had Taylor's "musical crush" Justin Timberlake appear to complete the celebration.

The following day found Taylor back in Nashville for the annual CMA Awards, performing 'Love Story' in an eye-catching long purple dress that perfectly matched the period setting. Nominated in the category of Female Vocalist of the Year, she lost out once again to Carrie Underwood.

On November 23rd Taylor was back in Los Angeles with Andrea for the AMAs, for which she was once again nominated for the fans' Favourite Country Female Artist, along with country greats Carrie Underwood and Reba McIntire. During the show, she sang 'White Horse', one of the outstanding tracks on the new album. For those watching there and at home that night, this was perhaps Taylor's most emotional performance to date. To cap off a great night, she finally walked away with the award she truly deserved, and, in her acceptance speech, thanked her fans for voting: "It's an honour that you even care about the songs I write in my bedroom. You've no idea how much this means to me." That same night, the Jonas Brothers were there to receive the award for Breakthrough Artist of the Year.

Taylor described the story behind choosing the album title in the accompanying booklet: "To me, Fearless is not the absence of fear. It's not being completely unafraid. To me, Fearless is having fears. Fearless is having doubts. Lots of them. To me, Fearless is living in spite of those things that scare you to death. Fearless is falling madly in love again, even though you've been hurt before… Fearless is getting back up and fighting for what you want over and over again…even though every time you've tried before, you've lost. Fearless is having faith that someday things will change. Fearless is having the courage to say goodbye to someone who only hurts you, even if you can't breathe without them…I think loving someone despite what people think is fearless. I think allowing yourself to cry on the bathroom floor is fearless. Letting go is fearless… You have to believe in love stories and prince charmings and happily ever after. That's why I write these songs. Because I think love is fearless."

On November 11th, the world would at last get a revealing look into what all this meant.

FEARLESS
Label - Big Machine Records
Recorded - Various Nashville studios
Produced - Nathan Chapman & Taylor Swift
Released - November 11 2008
Singles - 5
Chart peak positions
  Hot 200 #1; Top Country Albums #1; UK #5; Canada #1; Canada Country #1;
  Australia #2; NZ #1
RIAA Certification - Diamond
Selected awards and nominations
2009 Canadian Country Music Association - Top Selling Album (won)
2009 CMA Awards - Album of the Year (won) ·
2009 ACM Awards - Album of the Year (won)
2009 AMA - Favourite Pop/Rock Album (nominated)
2009 AMA - Favourite Country Album (won)
2009 Teen Choice Awards - Choice Female Album (won)
2010 Canadian Country Music Association - Top Selling Album (won)
2010 Grammy Awards - Album of the Year (won)
2010 Grammy Awards - Best Country Album (won)

70

Fearless ***
(Taylor Swift - Liz Rose - Hillary Lindsey)
5th Single
Produced - Nathan Chapman & Taylor Swift
Released - January 3 2010
Chart peak positions
  Hot 100 #9; Pop 100 #18; Hot Country Songs #10; UK #111; Canada #69;
  Canada Country #7
RIAA Certification - Platinum
Selected awards and nominations
2010 BMI Awards - Award-Winning Songs (won)
2010 BMI Awards - Publisher of the Year (won)

Taylor conceived the song while touring as an opening act. At the time she wasn't dating anyone, but pondered over her idea of the best first date. Explaining her writing process on her label's website, she stated: "I think sometimes when you're writing love songs, you don't write them about what you're going through at the moment, you write about what you wish you had. So, this song is about the best first date I haven't had yet."

The song was co-written with Liz Rose and singer-songwriter Hilary Lindsey, who had composed the Grammy-award-winning 'Jesus, Take the Wheel' for Carrie Underwood in 2006. After completing the song, Taylor explained how she defined the word "fearless" - "It doesn't mean you're completely unafraid and it doesn't mean that you're bulletproof. It means that you have a lot of fears, but you jump anyway."

The song was originally released as a promo single on October 14th 2008, as part of iTunes *Countdown to Fearless* campaign, and was officially released as the final single from the album on January 4th 2010.

The lyric hint is "I Loved You Before I Met You".

The music video, directed by Todd Cassetty, features clips from the *Fearless* tour and behind-the-scenes footage of Taylor and her band. It received its premiere on CMT on February 17th 2010.

The Observer - "Perceptive lyrics about universal truths that can be enjoyed at any age": **Vulture** - "The exuberance of the lyrics is matched in the way she tumbles from line to line into the chorus".

Fifteen ***
(Taylor Swift)
4th Single
Produced - Nathan Chapman & Taylor Swift
Released - August 30 2009
Chart peak positions
  Hot 100 #23; AC #12; Hot Country Songs #7; Adult Top 40 #10; Mainstream
  Top 40 #10; Canada #19; Canada Country #4; Australia #48
RIAA Certification - 2 x Platinum
Selected awards and nominations
2010 BMI Awards - Award-Winning Songs (won)
2010 BMI Awards - Publisher of the Year (won)
2010 Teen Choice Awards - Choice Country Song (won)
2010 MTV Video Music Awards - Best Female Video (nominated)

A ballad written around the age of 15 cautioning fellow teenagers not to fall in love too easily. It related to one of her first experiences of heartbreak at

71

Hendersonville High and was inspired by her best friend Abigail Anderson. Taylor asked her for authorisation to record the song, as it referenced her friend's name: "I started everything with the line 'Abigail gave everything she had to a boy who changed his mind' and wrote everything else from that point, almost backwards. I just decided I really wanted to tell that story about our first year of high school because I felt in my freshman year, I grew up more than any year in my life so far."

When the single debuted on the Billboard Hot 100 in November 2008, it equalled Hanna Montana's (Miley Cyrus) record for the most songs in the chart (seven) by a female artist.

The lyric hint is "I Cried While Recording This".

The music video for the song was directed by Roman White, who also worked on 'You Belong with Me'. He intended to make something different from Taylor's past videos by taking it out of a school setting and having her in a new world revisiting her past, with memories blooming around her like a garden which grows more when she is happy, but dies when she feels negative emotions. Taylor's friend Abigail Anderson portrays herself in the video, with their love interests having been cast from images on e-mails Taylor received.

The video premiered on CMT on October 9th 2009.

Pitchfork - "She serves straight chicken soup for the Teenage Soul with 'Fifteen', half guardian angel and half alarming guidance counsellor to high school freshmen everywhere"; **Rolling Stone** - "Swift is a songwriting savant with an intuitive gift for verse-chorus-bridge architecture": **Vulture** - "She knows the real thing is awkward, occasionally unpleasant, and almost guaranteed to disappoint you…and she knows how fantasies can sustain you when nothing else will"; **NME** - " One of Swift's greatest songwriting moments".

Love Story *****
(Taylor Swift)
1st Single
Recorded - Blackbird Studios, Nashville TN
Produced - Nathan Chapman & Taylor Swift
Released - September 12 2008
Chart peak positions
  Hot 100 #4; AC #2; Adult Top 40 #3; Hot Country Songs #1; Mainstream
  Top 40 #1; UK #2; Canada #4; Canada Country #1; Australia #1; NZ #3
RIAA Certification - 8 x Platinum
Selected awards and nominations
2009 ACM Awards - Video of the Year (nominated)
2009 BMI Country Awards - Song of the Year (won)
2009 BMI Country Awards - Publisher of the Year (won)
2009 CMA Awards - Music Video of the Year (won)
2009 CMT Music Awards - Female Video of the Year (won)
2009 CMT Music Awards - Video of the Year (won)
2010 APRA Awards (Australia) - International Work of the Year (won)
2010 BMI Pop Awards - Award-Winning Song (won)
2010 BMI Pop Awards - Song of the Year (won)

A song about one of Taylor's boyfriends who her family and friends didn't approve of: "I used to be in high school where you see [a boyfriend] every day. Then I was in a situation where it wasn't easy for me, and I wrote this song because I could relate to the whole Romeo and Juliet thing. I was really inspired by that story." With the lyrics written from Juliet's perspective, Taylor replaced the original tragic ending with a happier one.

In an interview for the *Los Angeles Times,* she explained: "It is one of the best love stories ever told, but it's a tragedy. I thought, why can't you...make it a happy ending and put a key change in the song and turn it into a marriage proposal?" On the label's website she said: "When I wrote the ending to this song, I felt like it was the ending every girl wanted to go with her love story. It's the ending that I want. You want a guy who doesn't care what anyone thinks, what anyone says."

According to *The Tennessean* magazine, Taylor was supposed to have composed the song with country songwriter Craig Wiseman, but in their writing session in 2006 he disliked her ideas and they wrote a different song instead. Taylor then went home and finished 'Love Story': "I couldn't stop thinking about the idea. I thought there was something to it. I really liked it."

The song is rumoured to be about either Joe Jonas, as it was recorded in March 2008, just four months before she actually started dating him, or Martin Johnson, the lead singer of punk group Boys Like Girls, who Taylor dated briefly earlier in the year, and who co-wrote her song 'If This Was a Movie'.

The lyric hint is "Someday I'll Find You".

'Love Story' became Taylor's first number one on Billboard's Mainstream Top 40 Airplay chart, marking the highest peak for a country song since Shania Twain's 'You're Still the One' in 1998.

The multi-award-winning music video was directed by Trey Fanjoy. Taylor saw the plot for the video as a timeless scenario, drawing influences from medieval, Renaissance and Regency periods. Six months before the shoot, Taylor watched different actors who could play the "Prince Charming" love interest and a friend recommended Justin Gaston, who had appeared as a contestant on *Nashville Star.* A castle was sought for the setting, and eventually one was found: Castle Gwynn at Arrington, just south of Nashville, which was part of the Tennessee Renaissance Festival and built in 1973.

The video has Taylor meeting Gaston in a present-day university campus while also recalling meeting each other in a past life and falling in love. It was premiered on CMT on September 12th 2008.

American Noise - "Considering that there are few songwriters in country music today who are willing to make symbolism such a prominent part of their writing...The fact that Swift, arguably the genre's biggest star at the moment, has done so here is a breath of fresh air, even if the song does otherwise follow a disappointingly unoriginal pattern"; **Billboard** - "The production has a swirling, dreamy quality, and Swift's vocal is all sweetness and light"; **Vulture** - "Swift employs a key change so powerful it literally rewrites Shakespeare".

Hey Stephen ****
(Taylor Swift)
Recorded - John McBride's Studio, Nashville TN
Produced - Nathan Chapman & Taylor Swift
Released - November 11 2008
Chart peak position
 Hot 100 #94; Hot Country Songs #28

Another song about unrequited love, this time for Stephen Baker Liles of the country band Love and Theft, who had opened a few shows for her. Apparently, she sent him a text when the album was released saying, "Hey, Track 4". He replied with an e-mail, saying "Oh, my God!" and later wrote a song for her called 'Try to Make It Anyway'.

In an interview for the *Philadelphia* magazine, she explained: "This is a guy I had a crush on. I wrote about all these reasons he should be with me instead of other girls...This guy had absolutely no idea I had a crush on him. It's gonna be kind of interesting when he finds out."

The lyric hint is "Love and Theft".

Vulture - "Swift is in the zone as a writer, performer, and producer on this winning deep cut"; **Rolling Stone** - "It begins and ends with her finest humming solos. If she wanted to hum on every song, she could make that work"; **NME** - "It's wonderfully schmaltzy, and comes with a chorus you'll sing full belt".

White Horse *****
(Taylor Swift - Liz Rose)
2nd Single
Produced - Nathan Chapman & Taylor Swift
Released - December 7 2008
Chart peak positions
  Hot 100 #13; Hot Country Songs #2; Country Airplay #2; UK #60;
  Canada #43; Canada Country #5; Australia #41
RIAA Certification - 2 x Platinum
Selected awards and nominations
2009 Nashville Music Awards - Country Performance Activity Award (won)
2010 BMI Awards - Award-Winning Song (won)
2010 BMI Awards - Publisher of the Year (won)
2010 Grammy Awards - Best Female Country Vocal Performance (won)
2010 Grammy Awards - Best Country Song (won)

In Taylor's opinion, this is "the most heartbreaking part of a break-up - that moment when you realise that all the dreams you had, all those visions you had of being with this person, all that disappears. Everything after that moment is moving on." The boyfriend in question was not what she perceived him to be, and the song focuses on that terrible moment when she realises it's over.

Speaking to CMT, she described the background to the song: "When we're little girls, our parents read us storybooks. And we think that Prince Charming's gonna come along, is gonna have a white cape on, is going to put you on a pedestal. And the bad guys wear black and we always know who that guy is. But what we don't realise is that, in reality, the bad guy is wearing jeans. And he's cute. And he's charming, makes you laugh, and you believe him. You think he's the good guy. Then, you realise he's not."

She also gave a similar version to GAC: "This girl falls in love with this guy and he's perfect. He's adorable. He's charming. He's endearing. She falls in love with him. Then, she comes to realise that he's been leading a double life. He was already in a relationship years before he ever met her...You find out that I'm the one that was ruining a relationship without even knowing it...That's always the hardest thing, when someone has you fooled so much that you think they're never gonna hurt you. And then they do. That's when you get the worst heartbreak."

This was one of Taylor's favourite songs, as she described to *Billboard*: "It's one of those songs that I am really proud of on the record because it's so sparse - it's guitar, piano and cello. It talks about falling in love and the fairy tales that you are going to have with this person, and then there is that moment where you realise that it is not going to happen. That moment is the most earth-shattering moment."

Taylor later revealed that she wasn't going to put this song on *Fearless*, but was going to hold it back for the next album, believing there was already enough "sadness" on it. Then she heard that her agency in Los Angeles had set up a meeting with NBC, the makers of the hit show *Grey's Anatomy*, for the possibility of using one of her songs. She played them 'White Horse' on her guitar and they loved it. They recorded it right away, and the episode was aired on September 25th as a two-hour season premiere: "You should've seen tears streaming down my face when I got the phone call that they were going to use that song. I have never been that excited. This is my life's goal, to have a song on *Grey's Anatomy*...It's my longest relationship to date."

The lyric hint is "All I Ever Wanted Was the Truth".

The music video for 'White Horse' was another directed by Trey Fanjoy. With the plot being centred on infidelity, it was decided that, as the video for 'Picture to Burn' had covered that same theme, they would reverse the scenario so Taylor would not be the victim of the infidelity, but instead the one who someone is unfaithful with. Actor Stephen Colletti was chosen to play the love interest, having been noticed for his acting skills on the reality tv series *Laguna Beach: The Real Orange County*. The video was shot in Nashville in January 2009, with heavy rain adding to its gloomy feel, and for the difficult last scene in which Taylor has to cry in front of the film crew, Fanjoy, once an actor herself, coached her effectively through the three-hour shoot.

The video had its premiere on CMT on February 7th 2009.

Vulture - "You'd never call Swift a genre deconstructionist, but her best work digs deeper into romantic tropes than she gets credit for. In just her second album, she and Rose gave us this clear-eyed look at the emptiness of symbolic gestures"; **NME** - "Filled with romantic, fairy-tale imagery, it's run through a realist filter that makes it like the older, more sceptical sister of 'Love Story'."

You Belong with Me ****
(Taylor Swift - Liz Rose)
3rd Single
Released - April 18 2009
Produced - Nathan Chapman & Taylor Swift
Chart peak positions
  Hot 100 #2; AC #1; Hot Country Singles #1; Adult Top 40 #2; Mainstream
  Top 40 #2; UK #30; Canada #3; Canada Country #31; Australia #5; NZ #5
RIAA Certification - 7 x Platinum
Selected awards and nominations
2009 MTV Video Music Awards - Best Female Video (won)
2009 Nashville Music Awards - Country Performance Activity Award (won)
2010 BMI Pop Awards - Award-Winning Song (won)
2010 BMI Pop Awards - Publisher of the Year (won)
2010 ACM Music Awards - Video of the Year nominated)
2010 ACM Music Awards - Song of the Year (nominated)
2010 CMT Music Awards - Female Video of the Year (nominated)

2010 CMT Music Awards - Video of the Year (nominated)
2010 Grammy Awards - Record of the Year (nominated)
2010 Grammy Awards - Song of the Year (nominated)
2010 Grammy Awards - Best Female Pop Performance (nominated)
2010 Nickelodeon Kids' Choice Awards - Favourite Song (won)
2011 BMI Pop Awards - Award-Winning Song (won)
2011 BMI Pop Awards - Publisher of the Year (won)

Taylor was inspired to write the song after overhearing one of her friends (maybe a band member) arguing with his girlfriend on the phone, and noticed she seemed to be giving him a hard time. Taylor then developed a story of what might have happened afterward. She sat with Liz Stone and explained that the story would be that this guy should be with her instead of in what seemed like a toxic relationship. Liz recalled that the song was written at the very end of the recording sessions: "We wrote 'You Belong to Me' in one or two hours. It's amazing to go back to the work tape and listen to it, because you wouldn't believe the nuances that show up in the album version, too. When she's writing something, she's already producing in her head. She hears it all." The lyric hint is "Love Is Blind So You Can't See Me".

'You Belong with Me' also became one of 13 songs from *Fearless* that charted on Billboard 100's Top 40, breaking the record for the most entries from a single album.

The music video was directed by Roman White, with the love interest played by actor Lucas Till, who Taylor had met during the filming of *Hannah Montana: The Movie* in April 2008 and remembered for his "cool look". Shot over two days in Gallatin and Hendersonville, Tennessee, Taylor used a body double for scenes showing her as both protagonist and antagonist. The video premiered on CMT on May 2nd 2009.

NPR - "A trope-heavy teenage underdog romance tale - told with sincerity as to feel suddenly original...100 per cent perfect pop, forecasting Swift's unprecedented crossover"; **The New Yorker** - "The typical Taylor Swift song is gentle but full of insistent hooks; it features Swift's delicate voice, singing about love in all its variations"; **Country Universe** - "The lyrics here sound directly ripped from the cute pink diary...of a self-conscious girl unsure of how else to express herself"; **Vulture** - "Swift had written great songs drawn from life before, but here she gave us a story of high school at its most archetypal: a sensitive underdog facing off with some prissy hot chick, in a battle to see which one of them *really got* a cute boy's jokes".

Breathe (Featuring Colbie Caillat) ****
(*Taylor Swift - Colbie Caillat*)
Recorded - Blackbird Studios & Starsturck Studios, Nashville TN
Produced - Nathan Chapman & Taylor Swift
Released - November 11 2008
Chart peak positions
 Hot 100 #87
RIAA Certification - Gold
Selected awards and nominations
 2010 Grammys - Best Pop Collaboration with Vocals (nominated)

By some recent accounts this song is about Taylor's old friend and ex-band member Emily Poe, who played fiddle and sang backing vocals for her on live

76

performances from July 2006 up to and including the concert at the Grand Ole Opry in January 2008. In an interview for *That's Country*, Taylor explained it was "a song about having to say goodbye to somebody, but it never blames anybody. Sometimes that's the most difficult part. When it's nobody's fault." The song was co-written by Californian singer-songwriter Colbie Caillat, who also sings velvet backing vocals.

Four years Taylor's senior, Colbie had released her debut album *Coco* in July 2007 which would go on to be certified double platinum. She recalled their time working together: "She wanted to write with me, and I flew there [Nashville] and she had this beautiful song started and it's about having to let someone go and say goodbye to a really good friend. And we became friends after that. She is so sweet, so beautiful, so talented, and honestly just a really intelligent young woman. She knows what she is doing and she knows how to handle her career and take charge. I love her."

Emily, who went on to study law at the University of Tennessee, later alleged that she had been booted off Taylor's band without an explanation, but rumours abounded that it was Taylor's management being concerned that their close relationship would damage the singer's reputation.

The song was nominated for a Grammy in the category Best Pop Collaboration, but lost out to none other than Colbie herself for her work on Jason Mraz's 'Lucky'. The lyric hint is "I'm Sorry, I'm Sorry, I'm Sorry".

Vulture - "A rare Swift song about a friend breakup"; **NME** - "A sleepy, acoustic number… it's a largely forgettable tune".

Tell Me Why **
(Taylor Swift - Liz Rose)
Produced - Nathan Chapman & Taylor Swift
Released - November 11 2008
Chart peak positions
 Hot 100 Bubbling Under #1;

A song about a guy Taylor never officially dated, but still managed to infuriate her all the same: "Sometimes it's the hardest thing when you have all these dreams of dating them, and you're getting close, but it doesn't work out…Because he didn't know what he wanted, he would just play all these mind games."

She told AP how the song originated during a writing session with Liz Rose: "I walked into Liz's house, and I said, 'I can't believe what's going on right now, I've got to tell you about this.' I told her all about it. She goes, 'If you could say everything you were thinking to him right now, what would you start with?' So I told her, 'I would say to him "I'm sick and tired of your attitude, I feel like I don't even know you"' and I just started rambling, and she was writing down everything that I was saying, and so, we turned it into a song."
The lyric hint is "Guess I Was Fooled by Your Smile".
Vulture - "One of Swift and Rose's most winning melodies".

You're Not Sorry *****
(Taylor Swift)
Promo single
Produced - Nathan Chapman & Taylor Swift

Released - October 28 2008
Chart peak positions
  Hot 100 #11; Pop 100 #21; Canada #11
RIAA Certification - Platinum

Like 'White Horse', this power ballad is another song written while in an emotional state, and inspired by an ex-boyfriend. In the track notes, Taylor writes: "[The song is about] this guy who turned out to not be who I thought he was. He came across as Prince Charming. Well, it turned out Prince Charming had a lot of secrets that he didn't tell me about." She also revealed that the song was written when she was at a "breaking point" and knew that she "had to walk away."

Some commentators believe it's about cheating ex-classmate Sam Armstrong, the subject of 'Should've Said No' on her first album. In a 2007 article, Taylor said that she wanted to put a song about him on *Fearless* because she wasn't done with being mad about what happened.

Taylor stated the song was "about this guy that kept apologising and kept doing the same thing over and over again and after a while you just have to stand up to that person and say, 'You're not sorry at all. Bye...'." The lyric hint is "She Can Have You".

Rolling Stone - "A dramatic piano-and-strings...showing off how much her voice has deepened between her first two albums"; **The Independent** - "On this sombre ballad, accompanied by a cello and piano, she shuts out an ex who betrayed her trust"; **Vulture** - "An unflinching kiss-off song...It shouldn't work, but it does"; **NME** - "Filled with melodramatic piano chords and overdone vocals, it's a histrionic ballad that you can imagine accompanied with bombastic visuals and a ton of pyro".

The Way I Loved You ****
(Taylor Swift - John Rich)
Produced - Nathan Chapman & Taylor Swift
Released - November 22 2008
Chart peak positions
  Hot 100 #72
RIAA Certification - Gold

Taylor describes the story behind the song: "I got this idea for a song about being in a relationship with a nice guy who is punctual and opens up the door for you and brings you flowers...but you feel nothing. The whole time you're with him, you're thinking about the guy who was complicated and messy and frustrating."

Co-writer John Rich was a former member of the band Lone Star before joining up with fellow country singer Big Kenny to form the duo Big and Rich, who went on to top the country charts with 'Lost in This Moment' in 2007. The lyric hint is "We Can't Go Back".

Vulture - "Swift often plays guessing games about which parts of her songs are autobiographical, but this one is explicitly a fantasy"; **NME** - "Lacks the radio-ready hooks and megawatt moments of Swift's other tunes".

Forever & Always ***
(Taylor Swift)
Produced - Nathan Chapman & Taylor Swift
Released - November 11 2008

Chart peak positions
  Hot 100 #34; Country Digital Songs #44; Canada #32
RIAA Certification - Platinum

The song inspired by the brief relationship with Joe Jonas, which ended with the now-famous "27-second" phone call just a month before *Fearless* was released. As a result, it became a last-minute addition to the album. Although never revealing his name in the song, Taylor recalled: "'Forever & Always' is about when I was in a relationship with someone and I was just watching him slowly slip away. I don't know why, because I wasn't doing anything different. I didn't do anything wrong. He was just fading. It's about the confusion and frustration of wondering why? What changed? When did it change? What did I do wrong? In this case, the guy I wrote it about ended up breaking up with me for another girl. Guess I know why he was fading…"

Jonas later told *Cosmopolitan* that they were still "cool" and still on friendly terms. Asked about him being the inspiration behind the song, he said: "It's part of being a musician, I guess. You write songs about each other."

Taylor reflected on her emotive style of writing: "That emotion of rejection, for me, usually starts with this pretty melody that's easy to sing along with, then in the end I'm basically screaming it because I'm so mad. I'm really proud of that." The lyric hint is "If We Play These Games, We're Both Going to Lose".

Add a star for the beautiful piano version on the platinum edition.

Vulture - "This blistering breakup song was the one that solidified Swift's image as the pop star you dump at your own peril"; **NME** - "Swift manages to evoke the crushing feeling of a crumbling relationship in under four minutes"; **Rolling Stone** - "A blast of high-energy JoBro-baiting aggro".

The Best Day ****
(Taylor Swift)
Produced - Nathan Chapman & Taylor Swift
Released - November 22 2008
Chart peak positions
  Hot 100 Bubbling Under #3; Hot Country Songs #45
RIAA Certification - Gold

A gift for her mother Andrea, and appreciation for all the support and sacrifice she has given her while growing up and embarking on her music career. Apparently written and recorded during the summer of 2007 while on tour with Brad Paisley, Taylor managed to keep it a secret until Christmas, when she played it to her mother, along with a specially-made music video of home movies which she synched to the song. Taylor recalled in an interview for AOL Music: "She didn't know that it was me singing until halfway through the song, at which point she burst out crying…My mom and I have been best friends since I was born."

In an interview with the tv show *Dateline*, Andrea recalled: "I'm looking on the tv and this video comes up with this voice that sounds exactly like Taylor's. And I looked over at her and she said, 'I wrote it for you, Mom.' And that's when I lost it. And I've lost it pretty much every time I've heard that song since."

Speaking to CMT News, Taylor gave an insight into their close relationship: "Out in the big world, I've learned to appreciate my mom. I realise how smart she is. I know my mom knows more than I do. Our arguments become discussions. We are together on the bus or at home all the time, and it works for us." The lyric hint is "God Bless Andrea Swift".

Vulture - "Mom gets the verses while Dad is relegated to the middle eight - even in song, the Mother's Day - Father's Day disparity holds up"; **Rolling Stone** - "A weapons-grade tearjerker and not to be trifled with in a public place"; **NME** - "It's a sweet, if somewhat cloying look at the early years of the planet's biggest pop star".

Change ***
(Taylor Swift)
Promo single
Produced - Nathan Chapman & Taylor Swift
Released - August 8 2008
Chart peak positions
  Hot 100 #10; Pop 100 #21; Hot Country Singles #57
RIAA Certification - Gold

Taylor writes about being an underdog and never getting due recognition or winning awards, and looks no further than her own record label, Big Machine, as she explained to AOL Music: "When you're at a record label that had 12 employees, you have to work harder to get on major tours. You have to work harder to get presenter slots on award shows. There was this moment where I sat there and was like, 'When are we going to get a fighting chance? We're the smallest record label in Nashville, but we want this really bad'."

After starting the song, she left it for a while, waiting for the right time to finish it and hoping that the big break would eventually come. That came the night she won the CMT Horizon Award in November 2007: "I looked over and saw the president of my tiny, little record label crying ... That's when I finished it, because I knew I couldn't finish it until something like that happened. It was absolutely the most amazing night of my life, getting to see the emotion of all the people who worked so hard for me." The lyric hint is "You Made Things Change for Me".

The completed song was recorded in December 2007 in one take. As an emotional call-to-arms, it would later be chosen as one of the patriotic songs to be included on the *AT & T Team USA Soundtrack* for the 2008 Olympic Games in Beijing and featured as the backing track for the televised highlights.

Two versions of a music video were directed by Shawn Robbins. The first was filmed at the ballroom in the Scottish Rite Cathedral in Indianapolis with Taylor wearing a white cocktail dress and black cowboy boots, performing with her band in the empty ballroom. An alternate video features footage of the US Olympic Team at the 2008 Summer Games. Both versions were premiered on NBC in August 2008.

Vulture - "A bit of paint-by-numbers inspiration"; **NME** - "It's easy to be cynical about it all, but it gave Swift her first US top 10, so maybe the message got through after all".

Jump Then Fall **
(Taylor Swift)
Fearless platinum edition
Produced - Nathan Chapman & Taylor Swift
Released - October 26 2009

Chart peak positions
Hot 100 #10; Hot Country Songs #59; Alternative Streaming Songs #32;
Canada #14; Australia #98
RIAA Certification - Gold

According to Taylor, a song "about jumping then falling into the most magical summer love imaginable", and wanting the other person in the relationship to take a chance on you. Another song rumoured to be about Joe Jonas. The song would later be included on the soundtrack to Taylor's movie debut, *Valentine's Day*, in February 2010.

Vulture - "An effervescent banjo-driven love song"; **Rolling Stone** - "Ironclad rule of pop music: Songs about jumping are never a bad idea"; **NME** - "The bouncing banjo-led number is sickly sweet, but lacks much depth".

Untouchable ****
(Taylor Swift - Cary Barlowe - Nathan Barlowe - Tommy Lee James)
Fearless platinum edition
Produced - Nathan Chapman & Taylor Swift
Released - October 26 2009
Chart peak positions
Hot 100 #19; Alternative Streaming Songs #9; Hot Country
Songs #57; Canada #23

A song originally performed by the rock band Luna Halo, formed in 1999 by Nathan Barlowe and Jonny MacIntosh, with Nathan Chapman's brother Cary later replacing McIntosh. As Scott Borchetta was a fan of the band, Taylor decided to record one of their songs, giving the original upbeat track a much slower and more soothing feel, and thereby adding her name to the writing credits. Co-author Tommy Lee James, a full-time Nashville songwriter, was credited for writing a number of chart-toppers for some of the leading country artists.

Vulture - "It's nearly impossible to think this was ever not a Taylor Swift song"; **NME** - "Sweet, but largely unexciting"; **Rolling Stone** - "A rare case where she retools somebody else's song on one of her proper albums".

Come in With the Rain ***
(Taylor Swift - Liz Rose)
Fearless platinum edition
Produced - Nathan Chapman & Taylor Swift
Released - October 26 2009
Chart peak positions
Hot 100 #30; Canada #40

Perhaps written about one of Taylor's first boyfriends, she uses this old expression that means when bad times come, people come to their senses and realise that what they wanted was there all the time. In relationship terms, it was like growing tired of trying to get a guy who likes you to realise it, and instead just waiting until that person realises it for himself.

Vulture - "Follows the Swift template a tad too slavishly"; **NME** - "It's a nostalgic snapshot at Taylor's life before world domination became the main priority".

Superstar ***
(Taylor Swift - Liz Rose)
Fearless platinum edition

81

Released - October 26 2009
Produced - Nathan Chapman & Taylor Swift
Chart peak positions
  Hot 100 #26; Alternative Streaming Songs #14

Banjo-driven ballad written about having an infatuation for a male celebrity and, although realising that he'll probably never notice her, still dreaming that he feels the same way about her. Although never revealing a name, it has been speculated that it could be referring to Arkansas-born country artist Joe Nichols, and even singer Jack Owen, who Taylor had opened for in 2006.

The song had originally been released to radio stations as a promotional cd on the tiny independent label Majorly Indie, just prior to her signing with Big Machine.

Vulture - "A relic of an unfamiliar time when Swift could conceivably be the less-famous person in a relationship"; **NME** - "A syrupy song about Swift fancying a celebrity, the puppy love of 'Superstar' is innocuous but bland".

The Other Side of the Door ***
(Taylor Swift)
Fearless platinum edition
Produced - Nathan Chapman & Taylor Swift
Released - October 26 2009
Chart peak position
  Hot 100 #23; Alternative Streaming Songs #11

Yet another breakup song in which Taylor inadvertently ends a relationship with a guy and then wishes she could take him back, although not having the courage to do so. In an iTunes interview, she explains how she would relish all the drama: "It talks about when you're in a fight with someone you're in a relationship with and you're like, 'Leave me alone, don't ever talk to me - I hate you!' But what you really mean is, 'Please go buy me flowers and beg that I forgive you and stand at the door and don't leave for three days'."

Vulture - "Saved from mediocrity by a gutsy outro"; **Rolling Stone** - "This would be the ultimate Swift song - except there are over a hundred better ones"; **NME** - "Features a deliciously dramatic guitar solo and even more melodrama".

"One of pop's finest songwriters"

Fearless was more than just Taylor's mainstream breakthrough album, it would go on to break more chart records than any of her albums. Debuting on top of the Billboard Hot 200 chart on November 29th, it would remain there for a total of 11 non-consecutive weeks. In the first week alone, it sold 592,000 copies, the largest sum for a country album since the Eagles' *Long Road Out of Eden* in 2007, which sold 711,000. Not only that, it became the longest chart-topper since Santana's *Supernatural* 12-week run back in 1999 and 2000; the longest reign on the charts for the decade; the longest chart-topper by a female country artist; the longest run in the Top Ten by a country artist (58 weeks); and, at the age of 20, she became the youngest artist to have the year's best-selling album and the only female country artist to do so. It also became the second biggest-selling album of the last five years, behind Adele's *21*.

On the Billboard Country chart, it also debuted at the top spot, spending a total of 35 non-consecutive weeks there. It would eventually receive diamond certification in the US for sales in excess of 7.5 million, and quadruple platinum in Canada. It would also become her first worldwide hit, with chart placings in the UK, Australia, New Zealand and the Far East, with total worldwide sales in excess of 12 million, making it the most successful of her career (so far).

The following year, the album won Taylor her first Grammy for Album of the Year, making her the youngest ever artist to receive it, beating 21-year-old Alanis Morrisette's *Jagged Little Pill* in 1996. *Fearless* also became the first album in history to win all four major awards for Album of the Year, when it also received the AMA, ACM and CMA honours, thus making it the most awarded album in the history of country music.

Pitchfork - "Swift captures and bottles a girlish sense of romantic excitement and suburban anguish that is all too fleeting, before real adulthood and the depths of the world's cruelty actually hit her"; **Rolling Stone** - "It's hard not to be won over by the guilelessness of Swift's high-school-romance narratives"; **The Guardian** - "A record that does something bland and uninventive but does it incredibly well"; **Slant** - "However poor her singing voice may be, she does possess a clear, if still immature, voice as an artist. It's troubling that the album does not show significant refinements of the promise she demonstrated on her debut, but Swift's age still gives her ample time to hone her craft into something more substantial and more sophisticated. Does Swift have the potential to make a great album? Perhaps. But *Fearless* certainly isn't it"; **Washington Post** - "She's an equally talented songwriter, but her consistency can often slip into uniformity. Here's how almost all of the songs on *Fearless* work: inviting verses, soaring choruses, a driving bridge, a final stripped-down verse and one last uber-chorus for the road. Rinse and repeat"; **New York Times** - "Teenage subject matter notwithstanding, there's nothing naïve about this young singer's music; her second album is every bit as elegantly designed as her 2006 debut. Ms Swift is one of pop's finest songwriters, the country's foremost pragmatist and more in touch with her inner life than most adults"; **USA Today** - "You just can't fake this kind of innocence and wonder that ring through the glowing title track and the moonstruck single 'Love Story', or the guileless urgency and unmannered precociousness marking more bittersweet songs such as 'Fifteen' and 'White Horse'".

To be classed as "one of pop's finest songwriters" was high praise indeed for 20-year-old Taylor, and clear indication that the crossover from country to mainstream was well and truly on course. And it was not by accident, as she explained to *Rolling Stone*: "I'm inspired by all kinds of different sounds and I don't think I'd ever be someone who would say, 'I will never make a song that sounds a certain way, I will never branch outside of genres', because I think that genres are sort of unnecessary walls."

Taylor struggled to accept some of the criticism. She described *Fearless* as the same as *Taylor Swift* - "just two years older." Rather than seeing it having crossover appeal, she preferred to call it "spillover" as she still considered herself a country artist who wrote country songs, but having the luck to have them played on pop radio.

Speaking to *Billboard*, Taylor recalled how she was blown away by the album's success: "It's really hard for me to wrap my mind around that one. In a business

83

where longevity is what you aim for and hope for and strive for, having my album on the charts that long just absolutely floors me. That is such a long time…"

That success soon had the television producers clambering over each other to get her on their chat shows, but first came the Grammy Nominations Concert in Los Angeles on December 3rd. Nominated for Album of the Year, she joined other nominees that included the Foo Fighters, David Grohl, Celine Dion, Mariah Carey, John Mayer, B B King, and Christian Aguilera, and then took the stage to sing a wonderful cover of Brenda Lee's 'I'm Sorry', followed by another emotional rendition of 'White Horse'.

Two days later, she guested on *The Tonight Show with Jay Leno* to sing 'White Horse' and 'Our Song', before flying back to Nashville the next day to appear on *CMT's Giants: Alan Jackson,* a tribute to the 50-year-old country legend, and sing his 2002 hit 'Drive (For Daddy Gene)'. According to *People* magazine, Taylor called Jackson "one of my songwriting heroes" and cited 'Drive' as the song that "really bonded my dad and I."

On Christmas Day, Taylor was in Las Vegas for *The Today Show*, performing an emotional 'Christmases When You Were Mine', and the more traditional 'Silent Night', and what had been an incredible year finally came to an end with a second stint on *Dick Clark's New Year's Rocking Eve*, with an electrifying four-song setlist of 'Picture to Burn', 'Love Story', 'Forever & Always' and 'Change'.

Perhaps an even bigger indication of her success was the appearance in stores of a tiny Taylor Swift doll aimed at younger Swifties, complete with a miniature sparkling guitar.

Success was coming in all shapes and sizes.

This Ain't a Fairytale

"No matter how many break-up songs you write, no matter how many times you get hurt, you will always fall in love again"

Planning the tour

On January 10th 2009, Taylor became the youngest country artist to guest on the iconic *Saturday Night Live*, performing 'Love Story' and 'Forever & Always', but the highlight of the month was on the 29th, with the announcement via her website of a forthcoming *Fearless* Tour, due to start in April. Taylor had not rushed into this, deciding instead to wait a while and gauge the response to her latest album. She was aware of how some artists had organised tours too soon, and with ticket sales not going as well as expected, this had resulted in half-empty arenas with unsold seats being curtained off. Taylor recalled: "I never wanted to go into an arena and have to downsize it so there were only 5,000 people there. So, we waited a long time to make sure the headlining tour was everything we wanted a headlining tour to be."

In the initial press release for the *Fearless* Tour, it was announced that it would cover both the US and Canada, with a total of 54 cities, and the supporting artists would be Taylor's friend Kellie Pickler and the recently-formed country band Gloriana, who were just about to release their debut single, 'Wild at Heart'. Speaking to *MTV News*, Taylor said: "For the past three years I've been writing down ideas for ... a headlining tour, and I get to do one now. It is unbelievable to me that this is actually happening. But I'm planning the stage, and the wheels are turning."

Taylor need not have worried over ticket sales. When the first batch were released on February 6th, the shows sold out almost immediately, the one at the Staple Center in Los Angeles in just two minutes. The following week, New York's 40,000-seat Madison Square Garden sold out in record-beating 60 seconds, with similar stories emerging at venues across the country as tickets became available.

Taylor's creative mind was in overdrive, and, having toured with many established artists, she had closely observed their performances and stage settings and come up with ideas of her own. The most important thing now was that whatever had to be done, she would be calling the shots, whether it be the music, the settings, the costumes, or the choreography. For many observers, it looked like this was something she was born to do.

In her blog, she wrote: "I'm in heaven right now. Constantly having meetings with the video crew and the lighting guys and the carpenters and the band and running through things over and over and over again." These were not going to be just ordinary concerts; these were going to be sonic and visual extravaganzas.

On February 8th, Taylor was in Los Angeles for the Grammy Awards, and despite, surprisingly, not receiving any nominations, she performed 'Fifteen' with her friend, 16-year-old Miley Cyrus, the star of Disney's billion-dollar franchise *Hannah Montana,* who had already a trio of million-selling soundtrack albums, as well as her own debut, *Breakout,* in 2008. While Taylor provided quiet accompaniment on acoustic guitar, the two starlets sang with a maturity well beyond their combined years. Taylor enjoyed her friendship with the "Teen Queen", saying: "Our personalities are opposite, so it works."

At the beginning of the following month, Taylor headlined the Florida Strawberry Festival in Plant City with a 14-song setlist, including a cover of Jesse McCartney's 'Leavin''. At the time, Taylor was scheduled to appear on the cover of the latest issue of *Rolling Stone*. A writer on the magazine's website revealed: "She really is like a tomboy. I asked her if she likes to get manicures, and she was like, 'No, I don't do that.' She doesn't go get massages; she eats crappy food. What's not to love about that?"

To promote the forthcoming British release of *Fearless* on March 9th, Taylor crossed the Atlantic to appear on the ITV chat show *Loose Women* on February 18th, performing 'Love Story' with her band.

Returning to the States, she was surprised to find that she was indeed gracing the cover of *Rolling Stone* with the heading 'Secrets of a Good Girl'. However, few secrets were actually revealed. In the interview recorded earlier, she made it clear she had never smoked or drunk alcohol, and any questions about her love life were smartly avoided by keeping it focused on her music: "I feel like whatever you say about whether you do or you don't, it makes people picture you naked. And as much as possible I'm going to avoid that."

Meanwhile, Taylor had recorded a duet with 32-year-old singer John Mayer on his single 'Half of My Heart' from his album *Battle Studies*. That March, Mayer had tweeted about wanting to record the song with Taylor: "Waking up to this song idea that won't leave my head. 3 straight days now. That means it's good enough to finish. It's called 'Half of My Heart' and I want to sing it with Taylor Swift. She would make a killer Stevie Nicks in contrast to my Tom Petty of a song." In an interview for the Fuse channel, he was asked why he chose Taylor, since she was only 19 years old, and he replied he was not doing it just to sell more copies for diehard Swift fans that would buy the album for that one song.

Released on June 21st, the song reached #25 on the Hot 100 and #2 on the Adult Top 40 chart, eventually achieving platinum status.

But we hadn't heard the last of John Mayer.

TV and the movies

It was soon announced that Taylor was to appear in an episode of the popular CBS series *CSI: Crime Scene Investigation.* It had always been a dream of Taylor's to appear in what was her favourite show. She told CBS News: "I've always joked around with my record label and my mom and everybody. All my friends knew that my dream is to die on *CSI*. I've always wanted to be one of the characters on there that they're trying to figure out what happened to."

However, it wasn't long before she got her wish. *CSI* producer Carol Mendelsohn heard about her dream and invited her to a meeting where they explained the character they had in mind. Haley Jones was a troubled teenager with anger-management problems and a boyfriend who was a drug addict. It was poles apart from Taylor's own personality, but she rose to the challenge and was given the part in the upcoming episode of season nine.

Entitled 'Turn, Turn, Turn', it was aired on March 5th, and, true to wishes, her character ends up being accidentally stabbed with scissors by her mother. Also featured in the show was a snippet of her song 'You're Not Sorry'. Taylor's acting debut proved a big success, and could have led to a parallel career if music hadn't remained such a massive part of her future life.

The same night *CSI* was aired, Taylor was in Melbourne on the second night of a short Australian tour which culminated on March 14th with the Sydney Sound Relief Concert, organised to raise funds for those affected by the devastating fires and floods that had hit the country in February. At the Sydney Cricket Ground, Taylor and her band joined a list of artists that included Coldplay, Barry Gibb and Marcia Hines, and, although suffering from a cold and feeling tired, she performed a rocking set of four songs - 'You Belong with Me', 'Our Song', 'Love Story', and 'Change'. In her first visit down under, she had no trouble making a wonderful first impression.

Just a month later, Taylor was in Las Vegas for the ACM Awards. Nominated in four categories, which included Entertainer of the Year, Top Female Vocalist, and Video of the Year (for 'Love Story'), she walked away with the prestigious Album of the Year for *Fearless*, making her the youngest artist to do so.

During the star-studded show, hosted by country legend Reba McIntire, Taylor gave two excellent performances. 'Picture to Burn' was introduced by veteran country duo Kix Brooks and Ronnie Dunn after singing their famous line, "She blew through the door like TNT". A superb rendition of 'You're Not Sorry' was then performed at the piano following a piece of introductory wizardry by illusionist David Copperfield.

Meanwhile, Taylor's fans were about to see her make her movie debut, with the release on April 10th of the teen comedy *Hanna Montana: The Movie*, an adaption of Miley Cyrus's hugely popular Disney Channel TV series. Filming had begun a year before in Los Angeles and Tennessee, and Taylor was approached about using her music in the film. Taylor recalled: "When I got an e-mail from Disney saying they wanted a song that was perfect to fall in love to and sort of a country waltz, I sent them 'Crazier' and they loved it." She wrote the song with producer Robert Ellis Orrall, who had worked with her on *Taylor Swift* and *Beautiful Eyes,* and it was produced by Nathan Chapman. Taylor also co-wrote 'You'll Always Find Your Way Back Home' with Martin Johnson of the band Boys Like Girls, which was featured as the movie's closing number.

Taylor told the film officials that she would also be happy to perform a song in the movie, and they obliged by giving her a cameo role singing 'Crazier' at a fundraising open-mic concert to save a local park from developers. The scene was shot in a single day, leading director Peter Chelsom to note: "She only did one day, but I've made a very big mental note to work with her again. If she walked in the room right now, I would say, 'Can we meet and talk about films you might want to do?' I don't have anything concrete, but I would be very keen to do something with her."

Crazier ***
(Taylor Swift - Robert Ellis Orrall)
Label - Walt Disney
Promo Single
Produced - Nathan Chapman
Released - March 20 2009
Chart peak positions
 Hot 100 #17; Pop 100 #28; UK #100; Canada #63; Canada Digital #30; Australia #57
RIAA Certification - Platinum

Although not quite fitting in with the general plot, 'Crazier' went on to receive rave reviews, even overshadowing Miley's own performance in the lead role.

AllMusic - "The comparison [with Swift] is not flattering to the movie's star"; **Entertainment Weekly** - "A pretty, yearning ballad"; **TV Guide** - "When genuine teen star Taylor Swift shows up to perform...she demonstrates all the spontaneity and authenticity that Miley Cyrus lacks"; **Vulture** - "It's kind of a snooze on its own, but compared to the other songs on the soundtrack, even Swift's leftovers shine"; **NME** - "Bad luck, Miley".

Taylor invited actor Lucas Till, who had played Miley's love interest in the movie, to appear in her music video for 'You Belong with Me', which would have its premiere on May 2nd. Taylor recalled that he was the embodiment of a "dreamy guy", and just perfect for the role in what would become an award-winning video.

Fearless on tour

On April 23rd, the *Fearless* Tour kicked off at the Roberts Municipal Stadium in Evansville, Indiana, with the city council president dubbing it "Taylor Swift Day" and presenting her with the key to the city. Taylor had chosen this modest venue after performing at the Wild Horse in Nashville when she was 16 and meeting a group of girls who had driven all the way down from Evansville to see her perform.

Taylor had the support of her regular band The Agency, so-called because she felt they all looked like secret agents in the video for 'Picture to Burn'. Originally brought together with the help of Al Wilson, her original drummer, it now consisted of Paul Sidoti on guitar; Grant Mickelson on lead guitar; Amos Heller on bass; Mike Meadows on guitar, banjo, cello, and synthesisers; Caitlin Evanson (Emily Poe's replacement) on guitar, fiddle and backing vocals; and Liz Huett, also on backing vocals. Taylor recalled: "I couldn't live without them. They are my favourite people in the world...[my] wonderful loving family". Also accompanying Taylor on the road was her mother Andrea, dubbed by the crew "Momma Swift", who was there to look after her daughter's needs. Scott Swift, too, made regular appearances, usually distributing pictures of Taylor to her fans.

The 90-minute shows were set in three "acts", complete with visuals, graphics and theatrics, with various costume changes and set designs, including an illuminated fairytale castle. Taylor excelled herself in connecting with her audience, even those in the "cheap seats", and especially younger fans who she often handed out bracelets to. She was probably one of the first artists to embrace the "hand heart", a method of holding up her hands in a heart shape to show them her love.

After just six concerts in the States, Taylor crossed the Atlantic for the second time to perform two sold-out shows at London's Shepherd's Bush Empire beginning on May 6th. *The Guardian* wrote: "Her regulation blonde bounciness and bubbly ditties about high school Romeos make her deceptively similar to the likes of Miley Cyrus - there is also a matter of her gushing about our 'adorable accents'- it seems Swift really cares what she is doing."

While in London she also performed 'Love Story' on the music show *Later with Jools Holland*, and 'Teardrops on My Guitar' on the teatime *Paul O'Grady Show*. Taylor-mania had well and truly arrived on foreign shores.

At the end of the month, Taylor was back in New York for *The Today Show*, with outdoor performances of 'Love Story', 'You Belong with Me' and 'Teardrops on My Guitar'. Co-host Matt Lauer then made a special request for her to do one more, and she obliged by performing a rocking version of 'Our Song'. *Seventeen* magazine reported: "Taylor was super nice, thanking everyone profusely for standing out in the foul weather, and then signing autographs and taking pictures with all her fans before and after the show. Tay Tay was totally blinged out in an amazing sparky blue dress - with a sparkly guitar to match!"

The tour continued into the summer, taking in the Benjamin Music & Arts Festival (Bama Jam) in Alabama, and the Country USA and Chippewa Valley Country Festivals in Wisconsin. In June, Taylor took time out from her own tour to open for country singer Keith Urban for nine selected dates as part of his *Escape Together* World Tour, starting in Cincinnati and ending in Kansas City in early July.

In June, Taylor, accompanied by brother Austin, attended the CMT Music Video Awards in Nashville. The organisers had asked her to appear as part of the intro, and in an interview with *Rolling Stone* she recalled: "One of the first things that came to mind was that I really, really want to be able to rap and go to the mall and go to those kiosk things and go buy bling and experience rapping in front of a car with spinners for the first time." In a pre-recorded video with rapper T-Pain, who was flown in specially for the shoot in blazing hot weather, they performed a spoof of 'Love Story' called 'Thug Story', with Taylor as T-Swizzle, adorned with bling and a mouth full of diamonds, having T-Pain poking fun at her good-girl image and her apparent penchant for knitting and making cookies while still being a thug.

Once the surprise subsided and the laughter died down, the serious stuff began, and Taylor went on to perform 'You Belong with Me' and then join Def Leppard on their 'Pour Some Sugar on Me', performed in pure rock-chick style. Their lead singer Joe Elliott said: "Taylor's such a bundle of energy!"

After showcasing her incredible versatility, she went on to win awards for Video of the Year and Female Video of the Year, both for 'Love Story'. In her acceptance speech, she once again singled out her fans: "Reading your letters and reading your MySpace comments, anytime I have a bad day, you make those days good."

August found Taylor in the UK ahead of her first outdoor concerts there for V-Fest, held in Chelmsford, north of London, and at Weston Park in Staffordshire. While there, she also appeared on the morning show *GMTV*, performing 'You Belong with Me', while also taking part in a number of radio interviews. Asked if she was still able to keep her feet on the ground, she told the hosts: "It still feels very surreal to me...you know, when it all hits me, because I just try to keep my life as normal as possible. I still go to the grocery store. I still do all the things that I used to do, it just takes a little longer and I'm talking to a lot more people and signing autographs now."

Around this time, Taylor purchased her first home - a 3,240 square-foot, year-old condo, right in the heart of Nashville's Music Row. The property featured floor to ceiling windows that showcased the Nashville skyline.

She also managed to take some time out from her touring schedule to appear in another movie. This time it was the romantic comedy *Valentine's Day,* and it had all started with a phone call from director Garry Marshall, asking her if she wanted to be in the movie. Because of her tour commitments, Taylor couldn't commit to a big role, so Marshall wrote a smaller part for her. With a star-studded cast that included Julia Roberts, Bradley Cooper and Kathy Bates, Taylor plays the sweet and innocent teenager Felicia Miller, whose boyfriend is played by 17-year-old Taylor Lautner, better known for appearing as a werewolf in the *Twilight* series. In a later interview for *Rolling Stone*, Lautner revealed how much he enjoyed working with Taylor, two years his senior: "We got along great. We instantly clicked. And she's an amazing girl. Aside from being beautiful, she's extremely funny, charismatic and fun to be around, and so we definitely get along. We're close."

When asked about a possible romance, Taylor told CMT Radio: "I don't know, he's an amazing guy and we're really close..." The movie would be released the following February.

Taylor also offered the film's producers a song she had written back in the summer of 2008 called 'Today Was a Fairytale', about a girl reflecting on a magical date. It was readily accepted, and, along with the *Fearless* track 'Jump Then Fall', would be included in the movie soundtrack when released in January 2010.

Stepping on the kitten

Another big night for Taylor came on September 13th with the MTV Video Music Awards at Radio City Music Hall in New York. Nominated for Best Female Video for 'You Belong with Me', she was up against Beyoncé, Lady Gaga, Kelly Clarkson, Katy Perry and Pink. After the show got underway with a moving tribute to Michael Jackson, who had died that June, Taylor was presented with the award for 'You Belong with Me'. Grasping the trophy, she began her acceptance speech: "Thank you so much! I always wondered what it would be like to maybe win one of these someday, but never actually thought it would happen. I sing country music, so thank you so much for giving me a chance to win a VMA Award..."

That's as far as she got. As 27 million viewers looked on, hip-hop star Kanye West suddenly appeared from stage right, snatched the microphone from her hand, and said: "Yo, Tay, I'm really happy for you and I'm gonna let you finish, but Beyoncé had one of the best videos of all time! One of the best videos of all time!" (referring to her 'Single Ladies (Put a Ring on It)').

Taylor stood there looking visibly stunned, and as the cameras panned away, viewers caught a glimpse of Beyoncé looking horrified at what was happening. Taylor was seen glancing down at the floor and mouthing "What?" before being escorted away. Realising that this wasn't a gimmick, the audience began booing the rapper as he was ushered off the stage, giving the audience the finger as he left.

After a dressing down by management, he was asked to leave. Sadly, Taylor had actually thought the crowd had been booing her.

To make matters worse for the young singer, as soon as West had handed the microphone back to her, it meant her time was up, and the producer cut to a video of Tracy Morgan and Eminem. Minutes after the incident, MTV chairman and CEO Judy McGrath was seen frantically typing into her phone when rapper Diddy came up to her, and simply said: "It's rock & roll." According to *Rolling Stone*, McGrath answered: "And the applause for [Taylor] will be louder."

Rapper Wale, who was serving as MC for the house band, told the crowd, "You can't fault a man for speaking his mind", a comment that was immediately met by boos from the audience. According to sources for *Rolling Stone,* when West was promptly tossed out of the building he headed to the Spotted Pig, a West Village haunt. Meanwhile, backstage, Fall Out Boy's Patrick Stump told a reporter for the magazine: "I'm assuming based on the amount of Hennessey I saw [West] drink that he was not all there."

Although still flustered and confused with what had just happened, Taylor managed to compose herself, change into a red dress, and then leave the venue for the planned performance of 'You Belong with Me'. After the pre-recorded section filmed at nearby 42nd Street subway station, it cut to the spectacular live performance with Taylor on top of a yellow cab right outside the venue. It was a credit to her professionalism, but sources at the event reported that once back in the dressing room, Taylor let down her shield and burst into tears, with none other than Beyoncé's father trying to comfort her.

Meanwhile, Taylor's outraged mother had tried to confront West before he left, but all she got from him was a repeat of his statement about the video. To her credit, Beyoncé showed both her class and compassion when it was her turn to accept her award in the Video of the Year category (something that seems to have slipped West's mind), and she invited Taylor back on stage to finish her disrupted speech. In matching crimson dresses, the pair of them embraced with a sisterly hug and received a standing ovation.

Interviewed immediately after the show, Taylor said: "I was standing on stage and was really excited because I had just won the award, and then I was really excited because Kanye West was on the stage, and then I wasn't so excited anymore." Asked if she had any hard feelings toward him, she replied: "I don't know him. I've never met him…I don't want to start anything."

But the damage had been done. This young star had been publicly humiliated. Reaction to what had happened soon followed, and many fellow artists rallied around with their support - apart, of course, from certain fellow rappers. One of the most outspoken critics of West's actions was Pink, who allegedly was escorted from the venue for fear of attacking West. Never one to hold back her words, she tweeted: "Kanye West is the biggest piece of shit on Earth. Quote me. My heart goes out to Taylor Swift. She is a sweet and talented girl and deserves her moment. She should know we all love her. Beyoncé is a classy lady. I feel for her too. It's not her fault at all, and her and Taylor did their thing. And douche bag got kicked out."

Even the oft-outspoken Liam Gallagher of Oasis launched his usual tirade of abuse: "If I ever win any more f**king awards, I'd personally invite him to get up and f**king take my award off me! That was rude what he did to that girl. So yeah, give me that award and see where it goes. It will roll out of his f**king arse!" Kelly Clarkson mockingly wondered if West had "got hugged enough" as a child, while Katy Perry gave him short shrift with a simple: "F**k you, Kanye. It's like stepping on a kitten."

In the blink of an eye, it had all gone viral on social media. Even President Obama was quick to comment, and when asked by CBNC if the incident had upset his daughters, made the off-the-cuff remark: "The young lady seems like a perfectly nice person...he's a jackass." Ex-President Jimmy Carter also chimed in to condemn West's actions as "completely uncalled for."

Kanye West, of course, had a chequered history of being arrogant, outspoken, and a regular gatecrasher when it came to award ceremonies, so this should not have been too much of a surprise, and it was rumoured that he had been drinking heavily on the night. But when things cooled down it was time to reflect. He quickly placed a public apology on his blog: "I'm sooooo sorry to Taylor Swift and her fans and her mom...I'm in the wrong for going on stage and taking away from her moment! ... Beyoncé's video was the best of this decade!! I'm sorry to my fans if I let you guys down!! I'm sorry to my friends at MTV. I will apologise to Taylor 2mrw. Welcome to the real world! Everybody wanna booo me but I'm a fan of real pop culture!...I'm not crazy, y'all, I'm just real...I really feel bad for Taylor and I'm sincerely sorry!! Much respect!!"

Appearing on the *Tonight Show with Jay Leno* the day after the show, West put his bad behaviour down to the loss of his mother two years ago, and, while shedding some tears, confessed: "It's been extremely difficult, just dealing with the fact that I hurt someone or took anything away...but I need to, after this, take some time off and just analyse how I'm going to make it through the rest of my life, how I'm going to improve...It was rude, period....And you know, I'd like to apologise to her in person. And I wanted to..."

The following day Taylor went on the daytime chat show *The View* to perform 'You Belong with Me' and she gave her take on events that night to host Barbara Walters: "Well, I think my overall thought process was something like, 'Wow, I can't believe I won, this is awesome, don't trip and fall, I'm gonna get to thank the fans, this is so cool. Oh, Kanye West is here. Cool haircut. What are you doing there?' And then, 'Ouch.' And then, 'I guess I'm not gonna get to thank the fans.'" She then described how she had to get over the shock and continue with the show: "You know, I'm not gonna say that I wasn't rattled by it, but I had to perform live five minutes later, so I had to get myself back to the place where I could perform..." She then praised all the support she had received: "Well, there were a lot of people around that were just saying wonderful things and just having my back. I never imagined that there were so many people out there looking out for me. It was really wonderful to see people defending me, so I didn't have to."

MTV's publicist for the award show then told the press that West had phoned Taylor and personally regretted what he had done, and that she had accepted the apology. Taylor, desperate to put it all behind her, told ABC News Radio: "He was very sincere in his apology and I accepted that apology." Some reports even had the two of them at the same costume ball in New York where, perhaps to diffuse an awkward situation, they just gave each other a high-five.

The following year, West would claim on New York's Hot 97 Radio that his attack on Taylor was not wrong, but just badly mis-timed: "My timing was definitely extremely off and the bigger plans, the bigger fight - how do you go about it? How do you go about getting it done?"

One thing was for sure. Taylor's career was not damaged by the incident; it was only enhanced. Unbeknown to West, kittens have sharp claws. KanyeGate wasn't over. It had only just begun.

The sad ending for Tay-Tay

On October 8th, it was announced that the second leg of the *Fearless* Tour would commence in February in Australia and then return to the States for a further 37 shows in 29 cities, including Canada.

Meanwhile, Taylor took a short break following the concert at Minneapolis on October 11th. Two weeks later she was in Los Angeles, guesting on *Dancing with the Stars* and performing 'Jump Then Fall', 'White Horse' and 'Love Story'. Around this time rumours were circulating about a real-life romance with her *Valentine's Day* on-screen boyfriend, Taylor Lautner. The couple had been spotted together at a basketball match and a hockey game, and also having a romantic dinner at a steak house in Beverly Hills. He was also seen watching one of Taylor's concerts in Chicago. The tabloids were now on the case and watching every move she made. Eventually, Lautner dropped a hint: "The very funny thing is that all of you have seen every single move I make, so I guess I can leave that up to you to decide."

On November 7th, Taylor was invited to New York to guest-host the hugely popular *Saturday Night Live,* becoming only one of a dozen people to do so in the show's 35-year history. Opening with the self-mocking 'Monologue Song', she made reference to Joe Jonas, Taylor Lautner - "the werewolf from *Twilight*" - and, not surprisingly, Kanye West. Critics raved about her performance on the show, with *Entertainment Weekly* calling her "the season's best host so far". After all the mocking, Taylor went on to perform a spirited 'You Belong with Me' and an acoustic 'Untouchable'.

The CMA Awards in Nashville came four days later, and it proved to be one of the highlights of Taylor's year. During the show she performed 'Forever & Always' and an acoustic 'Fifteen', and took away all four awards for which she had been nominated, beating some of the biggest names in country for Entertainer of the Year, Album of the Year, Female Vocalist of the Year and Music Video of the Year (for 'Love Story'). She was also presented with the prestigious International Artist Achievement Award. In one of her emotionally charged acceptance speeches, she paid special tribute to her band members, who then joined her on stage.

A week later she headed off to the UK to resume the *Fearless* Tour with new dates announced for London's Wembley Stadium and Manchester's Evening News Arena. As her regular support acts Gloriana and Kellie Pickler were unable to join her, Justin Bieber was brought in to support her. Before the two shows, Taylor returned as a guest on the *Paul O'Grady Show* and performed 'Fifteen'.

The night before the Wembley concert, Taylor appeared via video link at the AMAs in Los Angeles, where she won five of the six awards she had been nominated for - Artist of the Year, Favourite Pop/Rock Female Artist, Favourite Country Female Artist, Favourite Country Album, and Favourite Adult Contemporary Artist. She only lost out with the award for Favourite Pop/Rock Album, which went to the late Michael Jackson's *Number Ones*.

During the sold-out Wembley concert, Bieber broke his foot while performing the opening lines to 'One Time', but still managed to finish the song and perform at Manchester the following day. Taylor was overwhelmed by the audience reaction that night and told them: "Every time I hear the word Manchester, I won't be able to stop smiling - I love you!"

Apparently, three shows that were supposed to be held in Germany never materialised, so Manchester became the final concert for the first leg of the tour. Reuters News identified the success of the tour: "The key selling point on display was Swift's relatability. She's not just another oversexed, underdressed prefab-pop Barbie, but rather the girl next door who's had her heart broken and takes refuge in music she actually sings, plays and writes…She has a likeable stage presence that's not overly polished and even was slightly awkward at times."

The year ended on a sad note, especially for Taylor Lautner. After just three months it had become apparent that he was more into her than she was into him. By her 20th birthday on December 13th, it was all over. There were also rumours that his previous girlfriend, Disney star Selena Gomez, wanted him back. A close source explained the split to *Us Weekly*: "There was no chemistry and it felt contrived…They plan to stay friends." The beautiful ballad 'Back to December', on Taylor's next album, is reputedly her sweet way of apologising to him.

Speaking Now

"There is a tendency to block out negative things, because they really hurt... I can't stop feeling those things, so I feel everything. And that keeps me who I am"

"People throw rocks at things that shine"

On January 22nd, Taylor was in Los Angeles to take part in *Hope for Haiti Now*, a charity telethon aimed at raising funds for victims of the earthquake that had struck the small country a week before and claimed some 200,000 lives. Broadcast from LA, New York and London, artists included Bruce Springsteen, Coldplay, Alicia Keys, Stevie Wonder and Madonna. Taylor chose to perform 'Breathless', a song written by Kevin Griffin and originally recorded by New Orleans alt-rock band Better Than Ezra for their 2005 album *Before the Robots*. According to MTV News, the "breathtaking" performance seemed "far beyond her young age."

Made available for download, Taylor's 'Breathless' peaked at #72 on the Hot 100; #116 in the UK, and #49 in Canada.

On the same day as the concert, the single of 'Today Was a Fairytale' was released, ahead of the premiere of *Valentine's Day* the following month.

Today Was a Fairytale ***
(Taylor Swift)
Single
Label - Big Machine
Produced - Nathan Chapman & Taylor Swift
Released - January 19 2010
Chart peak positions
  Hot 100 #2; Hot Country Songs #41; AC #21; Adult Top 40 #21; Hot Country
  Songs #41; Mainstream Top 40 #20; UK #57; Canada #1; Australia #3; NZ
  #29; Japan #63
RIAA Certification - Platinum

Despite being blocked from topping the Hot 100 chart by Kesha's 'Tik Tok', it still received 325,000 downloads, breaking the record held by Britney Spears' 'Womaniser' for the most first-week download sales by a female artist.

Slate - "The song is a funny mix: some of her tightest songwriting to date, but some of her laziest lyrics"; **Billboard** - "Her vocals display a growing maturity that could entice her few remaining doubters"; **NME** - "A classically Swiftian country ballad stuffed full of romantic lyrics. It's lovely"; **Rolling Stone** - "A plainspoken and genuinely touching play-by-play recap of a worthwhile date".

If this wasn't enough success to begin the new year, news came that Taylor had been nominated for eight Grammy Awards. During rehearsals she said: "Being at the Grammys is a beautiful thing. To be nominated eight times is unfathomable to me, like, I'm floating this week, as I have been since the nominations came out, and just the chance to perform again this year is wonderful."

At the star-studded ceremony in Los Angeles, on the last day of January, Taylor won four of the eight nominations - Album of the Year and Best Country Album for *Fearless*, and Best Country Song and Best Female Country Vocal Performance for 'White Horse'. She became the youngest ever artist to receive the prestigious Album of the Year award. In her emotional acceptance speech, she said: "I hope you know how much this means to me and all my producers that we can take this back to Nashville. This is the story that when we're eighty years old and we're telling the same story again and again, this is the story we're going be telling..."

It may not have been apparent at the time, but *Fearless* had just become the most awarded album in the history of country music.

Unfortunately, there was one part of the awards show that Taylor wouldn't be keen to retell. After a lacklustre performance of 'Today was a Fairytale', she surprised everyone by singing a duet with the legendary Stevie Nicks, on both the classic Fleetwood Mac hit, 'Rhiannon', and also 'You Belong with Me'. The reviews next day were both stinging and heartbreakingly bad. Some critics wrote that Taylor was noticeably "badly off-key", that the duet with Nicks was "alarmingly under-rehearsed", and that the Fleetwood Mac singer was looking "annoyed" at Taylor's "warbling". *The Washington Post* even called it an "incredibly wretched vocal performance" with "off-key caterwauling". Worst of all, even some of Taylor's fans were critical and told her so on social media.

It was a bitter pill for Taylor to swallow. Scott Borchetta saw it for himself: "It's that classic thing that critics do of building something up and then wanting to tear it down." If there was a problem with her voice, her label boss came to her defence, blaming an "inner-ear volume problem" as the cause of her failure to hit the right notes. He pointed out that her voice wasn't perfect, but she was conveying the emotion of the song and sometimes that can lead to imperfections in her vocals. Sometimes the best emotional singer can eclipse the best technical one, and that's what many listeners prefer to hear.

Taylor was of the same mind, and in an interview for the *Los Angeles Times* explained: "It's really more about portraying the song in a way that gets the feeling across, rather than every phrase being exactly perfect. I think it's the writer in me that's a little more obsessed with the meaning of the song than the vocal technique. All that stuff is like math to me. Overthinking vocals and stuff - I never want to get to that point."

Taylor would never forget the episode and would single out one critic in particular, Bob Lefsetz, when he became the subject of the satirical song 'Mean', destined for the next album.

Almost immediately after the Grammys, Taylor flew out to Australia for the next leg of the *Fearless* Tour, which commenced in Brisbane on February 5th. While there she flew over to Japan for the first time to appear on two of their chat shows with a performance of 'You Belong with Me', a song which she also performed in Sydney for the show *So You Think You Can Dance Australia*. On February 24th, by way of thanking country radio for their support, Taylor performed a special concert at their 2010 Seminar in Nashville.

The trouble with John Mayer

Resuming the tour at Tampa at the beginning of March, rumour had it that Taylor was now romantically involved with singer-songwriter John Mayer, who at the time was having treatment for a vocal problem. Twelve years Taylor's senior, he was reported to be a serial womaniser with a string of high-profile relationships. Taylor was a longtime fan of his music and they began complimenting each other on blogs. She had already contributed vocals on the song 'Half of My Heart' in 2009, apparently sitting on his lap during the recording and behaving like teenagers.

According to the *National Enquirer*, Andrea had tried to tell Mayer to stay away from Taylor, and that she would never let him get close enough to break her daughter's heart. She needn't have worried, as the relationship ended shortly after. In true fashion, a disgruntled Taylor would pen the song 'Dear John' about him on her next album.

The lack of boyfriends raised the inevitable media questions about her virginity, and she felt like she was being constantly hounded to tell the truth about her sex life. Even when she did admit to her chastity, no one believed her anyway.

Fortunately, this constant scrutinising of her personal life didn't deflect her from what was more important in her life.

On April 18th, it was time for the ACM Awards in Las Vegas. Taylor was nominated for three awards - Entertainer of the Year (losing to Carrie Underwood), Top Female Vocalist (losing to Miranda Lambert), Song of the Year ('You Belong with Me' with Liz Rose - losing to Lady Antebellum's 'Need You Now') and Video of the Year ('You Belong with Me' - losing to Miranda Lambert's 'White Liar'). During the show, Taylor performed 'Change' in a suspended cage and wearing a white dress, before suddenly tearing it away to reveal a black outfit underneath to complete the song on stage. It seemed a far cry from the Grammys debacle with the singer now in spellbinding form.

Toward the end of the month, Taylor flew down to Alabama for a surprise visit to Auburn University, and, in particular, two college boys, Ryan Leander and Michael Wekall, who had performed three elaborate challenges in order to get the chance to meet and get a hug from the singer.

The *Fearless* Tour finally came to an end on July 10th at the Cavendish Beach Music Festival in Canada. The 105 shows grossed $65.5 million and had been watched by an estimated 1.2 million fans across four continents.

Farewell to fairytales

Over the last few months, while on the road and in between winning awards, Taylor had been writing songs for the new album, and recording was already underway at a number of studios in Nashville, Hollywood and Kentucky.

Taylor revealed her mindset at the time to *USA Today*: "There is a tendency to want to get thick-skinned. There is a tendency to block out negative things, because they really hurt. But if I stop feeling pain, then I'm afraid I'll stop feeling immense excitement and epic celebration and happiness. I can't stop feeling those things, so I feel everything. And that keeps me who I am."

The original title of the album was going to be *Enchanted,* but that was about to change, as Scott Borchetta recalled for Reuters: "We were at lunch, and she had played me a bunch of the new songs. I looked at her and I'm like, 'Taylor, this record isn't about fairy tales and high school anymore. That's not where you're at. I don't think the record should be called Enchanted.' After the discussion, Swift then excused herself from the table. By the time she came back, she had the *Speak Now* title, which comes close to representing the evolution that the album represents in her career and in her still-young understanding of the world."

The album's new name was also seen to be a metaphor for Taylor now taking back firm control of her life, ridding herself of her feelings of fairytale enchantment, and speaking out more to change teenage infatuations into more real-life adult relationships.

Unlike *Fearless*, *Speak Now* would see a clear departure from Taylor's country style, moving more toward a bona fide pop album. It would also be her first solo effort, as she explained on a live webcast: "I actually wrote all the songs myself [but] it didn't really happen on purpose, it just sort of happened. Like, I'd get my best ideas at 3am in Arkansas, and I didn't have a co-writer around." Nathan Chapman would also be the sole producer, and he revealed: "We deliberately went back to our initial way of working together. We had an unlimited budget and could have gone and recorded the whole album in the Bahamas, used any studio we liked and whatever musicians we wanted. But we decided to bring it back to the basics on purpose, because we wanted to keep it about the music and our chemistry."

Many of the songs were recorded in Chapman's basement in Nashville, and according to Taylor they "got a magical first-take vocal." Comparing it to previous albums, Chapman noticed how Taylor had changed in her outlook on life: "She's left home, she's living on her own now, and she's seeing the world in a different way after growing up a bit." Label boss Borchetta was confident about the success of another album: "Look, if she can produce a superior third album, one that's as big as the last two…well, when's the last time somebody did that?"

Once again it would be the opposite sex that formed the subject matter for the songs, with the usual sprinkle of romance, revenge and regret added to the mix. What her fans could expect she made very clear: "Whatever I go through in life will be reflected directly in my music." In another interview she described the new album as a "collection of confessions - things I wish I had said when I was in the moment."

Here was a girl who had had a rollercoaster of a ride over the last twelve months, and was now ready to open her heart the only way she knew how. She told NPR: "When I first started writing songs, I was always scared that my songs were too personal - like, if I put someone's name in a song, people won't relate to it as much. But what I saw happening was, if I let my fans into my life and my feelings and what I'm going through - my vulnerabilities, my fears, my insecurities - it turns out they have all those things, too, and it kind of connects us."

Meanwhile, there were things to address closer to home. On May 10th a vicious storm hit Nashville and the surrounding area, and the torrential downpour lasted three days, leaving 30 dead and thousands homeless. In an interview for AP, Taylor said: "Being at home during the storm, I honestly could not believe what has happened to the city and the people I love so dearly." In the subsequent telethon organised by the locals, Taylor donated half a million dollars to help those most in need.

Sadness and success

During the spring, it was reported that Taylor was dating 28-year-old Canadian actor Cory Monteith, best known for his portrayal of Finn Hudson in the tv show *Glee*. They had first been spotted having dinner together at a pre-Grammy party in January and later reported to be seen holding hands and gazing into each other's eyes at a Hollywood bowling alley. He had made his feelings about Taylor clear in an interview for *Us Weekly*: "She's lovely. I think talent is attractive." Whatever form their relationship took, by May it had apparently fizzled out. Without naming names, Taylor later told Yahoo Music: "A guy that I just barely knew put his arm around me by the water and I saw the entire relationship flash before my eyes, almost like some weird science-fiction movie." The song 'Mine' on the new album was apparently written about him.

Monteith would go on to date his *Glee*-co-star Lea Michele, but in July 2013 he was found dead in a Vancouver hotel room, allegedly from a drug overdose. On hearing the news, Taylor posted on her Twitter account: "Speechless, and for the worst reason."

At the end of May, Taylor was at the Tiger Stadium in Baton Rouge for the first day of the inaugural Bayou Country Music Superfest. Held over the Memorial Day weekend, her 17-song setlist included the song 'I'm Only Me When I'm with You', for which she was joined by her tour support, Kellie Pickler and Gloriana. The festival season continued on July 10th with a similar performance at the Cavendish Beach Music Festival in Canada.

On August 4th, the song 'Mine' was released as the first single taken from *Speak Now*, two months ahead of the album, and shortly followed by a music video. At the time, Taylor was on a promotional visit to Japan and found out by texts and tweets that it had just debuted at number three on the Hot 100. The signs were looking good.

A month later, Taylor was invited to sing at the Louisiana Superdome for the NFL kick-off game between the New Orleans Saints and the Minnesota Vikings. Taking the stage to sing 'Mine' and 'You Belong with Me', she wore a shimmering dress, sparkling necklace, and black boots, but the performance was dogged by an apparently turned-down microphone that made her vocals seem drowned out by the instrumentation.

September also saw a return to the MTV Video Music Awards, this time held in Los Angeles. News came that Kanye West would be appearing and had written a song called 'Runaway' that he wanted to perform with Taylor. Some of its inspiration came from last year's incident with Taylor during her acceptance speech, with West exiling himself in Hawaii and recording an album almost in reclusion. Of course, Taylor turned down the offer to sing with him, and instead performed one of her new songs, 'Innocent', the lyrics of which hinted at a little forgiveness for his actions. In contrast, West's song was laced with profanities and hints of having a dig at Taylor. The evening saw Taylor nominated for Best Female Video for 'Fifteen', but the award went to Lady Gaga's 'Bad Romance'.

The following month found Taylor once more in Europe, singing 'Mine' on the Italian version of *The X Factor* in Milan, and then repeating the performance on the French chat show *Le Grand Journal* in Cannes two weeks later. She returned to the States just in time for the official release of *Speak Now* on the 25th.

On the eve of the album's release, Taylor gave an interview for the *Chicago Tribune*: "The whole process of songwriting starts out in a very lonely place for me... I sit down to write a song because I'm feeling a very intense emotion, usually an intense form of pain. And I sit there and I'm writing it, and I'm thinking that I'm the only person who has felt this kind of sadness... And then, the next part, something magical happens. I put that song on an album and it goes out into the world. Then I get to stand on a stage and sing that song to people who are singing the words back. At that point, I don't feel like I'm alone anymore. We're all there in this arena, singing these same words because obviously we've all felt that same kind of sadness."

In the album's "letter of introduction", Taylor gave an insight into the background of each track and gave some sound advice to her fans: "Words can break someone into a million pieces, but they can also put them back together. I hope you use yours for good, because the only words you'll regret more than the ones left unsaid are the ones you use to intentionally hurt someone... I don't think you should wait. I think you should speak now. Love Taylor."

As on her debut album, she left a taunting postscript: "To all the boys who inspired this album, you should've known."

SPEAK NOW
Label - Big Machine Records
Produced - Nathan Chapman & Taylor Swift
Released - October 25 2010
Singles - 6
Chart peak positions
  Hot 200 #1; Country Albums #1; UK #6; Canada #1; Australia #1; NZ #1
RIAA Certification - 6 x Platinum
Selected awards and nominations
2011 ACM Awards - Album of the Year (nominated)
2011 CMA Awards - Album of the Year (nominated)
2011 ACA Awards - Album of the Year (nominated)
2011 AMA Awards - Favourite Country Album (won)
2011 Billboard Music Awards - Top Country Album (won)
2011 Billboard Music Awards - Top Billboard 200 Album (nominated)
2011 Canadian Country Music Association - Top Selling Album (won)
2012 Grammy Awards - Best Country Album (nominated)

Mine ****
(Taylor Swift)
1st Single
Produced - Nathan Chapman & Taylor Swift
Released - August 4 2010
Chart peak positions
  Hot 100 #3; AC #1; Hot Country Songs #2; Hot Digital Songs #1; UK #30;
  Canada #7; Australia #9; Japan #6
RIAA Certification - 3 x Platinum
Selected awards and nominations
2011 Billboard Music Awards - Top Country Song (nominated)

2011 BMI Country Awards - Publisher of the Year (won)
2011 BMI Country Awards - Award-Winning Song (won)
2011 CMT Music Awards - Video of the Year (won)
2011 CMT Music Awards - Female Video of the Year (nominated)
2011 CMT Music Awards - Web Video of the Year (nominated)
2012 BMI Pop Awards - Award-Winning Songs (won)

A song about Taylor's tendency to run from love for fear of something going wrong and getting hurt, but remaining hopeful of one day finding a love that will last. Rumours abound that it's about ex-boyfriend, *Glee* star Cory Monteith. Taylor wrote on her website: "Lately I've had this bad habit of running away from love. Kind of getting to the place where it's about to commit, and then you just, like, run in the opposite direction. 'Mine' is about the idea that I could find someone who would be the exception to that, someone who would be so sturdy and so much of a sure thing that I wouldn't run from it." The hidden message for the song is "Toby", a reference to the song's music video star Toby Hemingway. Although not romantically linked, she had noticed him wearing her lucky number 13 on a t-shirt in his movie, *The Covenant*.

The song was chosen as the album's first single after she and producer Nathan Chapman made a demo in his basement, and then looked at each other, realising "This is it. This is the one." The track was leaked online days before its official release, forcing the label to ship copies off to country radio stations.

The music video was directed by Roman White with Taylor (making her directional debut). She chose her friend Jaclyn Jarrett, daughter of wrestler Jeff Jarrett, to play the younger version of herself. Shot at locations in Maine, it features British actor Toby Hemingway as the love interest she eventually marries. Taylor had been impressed with him after watching him in the film *Feast of Love* in 2007.

The video had its premiere on CMT on August 27th 2010.

Chicago Tribune - "Simple but honest expressions of emotion"; **Vulture** - "Swift packs in so many captivating turns of phrase here, and she does it so naturally"; **NME** - "Pure Swift…a country pop epic, with more of a narrative in each verse than an entire Nicholas Sparks novel".

Sparks Fly ****
(Taylor Swift)
5th Single
Produced - Nathan Chapman & Taylor Swift
Released - July 18 2011
Chart peak positions
  Hot 100 #17; Hot Country Songs #1; Canada #28
RIAA Certification - Platinum
Selected awards and nominations
2012 BMI Awards - Top 50 Songs (won)
2012 BMI Awards - Publisher of the Year (won)
2012 Teen Choice Awards - Choice Country Song (won)

Written when Taylor was 16 about a "crush" on 24-year-old country singer Jake Owen, who she had recently opened for at one of his shows and sang with in a bar in Portland, Oregon. Apparently considered for *Fearless*, it failed to make the cut and was destined for obscurity, but with it having gained popularity with fans when performed live, she reworked the lyrics for the new album, with fewer hints about Owen. Taylor revealed on her website that the song "is about falling for someone that you maybe shouldn't fall for, but you can't stop yourself because there's such a connection, there's such chemistry…".

The lyric hint is "Portland Oregon".

The music video was directed by Christian Lamb and features clips of Taylor in various performances from the *Speak Now* tour, including the rain-sodden night at Foxborough. It was premiered on Taylor's official website on August 10th 2011.

Country Universe - "'Sparks Fly' proves how evocative those turns-of-phrase can be in the right context. To that end, 'Sparks Fly' plays as a template as much as it does as a standalone single, and it's a testament to everything Taylor Swift gets right"; **Pitchfork** - "It appears here with all its fireworks and rain-soaked drama, a call to arms for people who'd been following since the beginning"; **Rolling Stone** - "It shows off her uncanny power to make a moment sound gauchely private and messily public at the same time".

Back to December *****
(Taylor Swift)
2nd Single
Recorded - Capitol Studios
Produced - Nathan Chapman & Taylor Swift
Released - November 15 2010
Chart peak positions
  Hot 100 #6; AC #14; Hot Country Songs #3; Adult Top 40 #11; Mainstream Top 40
  #11; Canada #7; Australia #26; NZ #24
RIAA Certification - 2 x Platinum
Selected awards and nominations
2011 ACA Awards - Female Video of the Year (nominated)
2011 BMI Awards - Publisher of the Year (won)
2011 BMI Awards - Publisher of the Year (won)

Taylor's apology for ending the relationship with her *Valentine's Day* co-star Taylor Lautner, and reputedly written on a napkin in an airplane bathroom. In an interview for Comcast, she said that it was a song "that addresses a first for me, in that I've never apologised to someone in a song before. This is about a person who was incredible to me - just perfect in a relationship, and I was really careless with him. So, this is a song full of words that I would say to him that he deserves to hear." The hidden lyrics in the booklet spell out the word TAY.

It was also her first song to feature orchestral arrangements. Lautner later confirmed in a Facebook Live interview that the song was about him.

The wonderful music video was directed by Yoann Lemoine and shot just before Christmas 2010. Lemoine told MTV that he was inspired by the film *E.T.* and had a certain aesthetic he was looking for to capture the chilly clip that has Taylor finding herself and her home covered in snow while contemplating the best way to apologise to her former boyfriend for breaking his heart. The scenes featuring Taylor were shot in Nashville, while upstate New York was used for her ex, played by male model Guntars Asmanis. Lemoine said that Asmanis was the perfect choice: "I wanted a boy that was fragile and beautiful. I didn't want to go for a hunk or a perfect cheesy boy that would have killed the sincerity of the video."

The video was premiered on CMT and GAC on January 13th 2011.

Rolling Stone - "Swift's voice is unaffected enough to mask how masterful she has become as a singer"; **New York Post** - "It's a very surprising, and somewhat brilliant, apology track where Taylor sings about wishing to fix a relationship she wished she wouldn't have ruined in the first place"; **Engine 145** - "That unbridgeable rift between earnest desire and harsh reality makes this song a true heartbreaker"; **Vulture** - "The key to a good apology has always been sincerity, and whatever faults Swift may have, a lack of sincerity has never been one of them"; **NME** - "Unflinching and honest, with Swift taking responsibility and asking for forgiveness after a breakup".

Speak Now ****
(Taylor Swift)
Produced - Nathan Chapman & Taylor Swift
Released - October 5 2010
Chart peak positions
  Hot 100 #8; Hot Country Songs #58; Canada #8; Australia #20; NZ #34
RIAA Certification - Gold

A song inspired by one of her friends discovering their high school sweetheart was getting married to someone who was treating him horribly, and Taylor imagining the same thing happening to her. It has also been suggested to have been inspired by singer Hayley Williams of the rock band Paramore, who had to attend the marriage of ex-boyfriend and former band mate Josh Farro in 2010.

In the song Taylor dreams of gatecrashing her ex-boyfriend's wedding so he won't marry someone who doesn't treat him right. In an interview with Yahoo! Taylor explained: "One of my friends, the guy she had been in love with since childhood, was marrying this other girl. And my first inclination was to say, 'Well, are you gonna speak now?' And then I started thinking about what I would do if I was still in love with someone who was marrying someone who they shouldn't be marrying. And so, I wrote this song about exactly what my game plan would be."

The single became Taylor's sixth Hot 100 top ten debut, setting a record for the most top ten debuts in the history of the chart (beating Mariah Carey's five entries in the 1990s).

The lyric hint is "You Always Regret What You Don't Say".

About.com - "The song is sweet, funny, bratty, and edgy all at the same time. Taylor Swift remains one of the most gifted young lyricists"; **Entertainment Weekly** - "Her expressive delivery of the lyrics makes up for any shortcomings as a technical vocalist"; **Vulture** - "It's hard not to smile at the unabashed silliness"; **NME** - "Some of Swift's most vibrant storytelling...it's a brilliantly intricate story"; **Rolling Stone** - "Tay in stalker mode...crouching behind the curtains in the back of the church, waiting to pounce".

Dear John *****
(Taylor Swift)
Produced - Nathan Chapman & Taylor Swift
Released - October 25 2010
Chart peak positions
  Hot 100 #54; Country Digital #4; Canada #68

Written about the short relationship with singer-songwriter John Mayer, and how she disregarded all the warnings from family and friends. On her website, Taylor revealed that the song "is sort of like the last email you would ever send to someone that you used to be in a relationship with. Usually, people write this venting last email to someone and they say everything that they want to say to that person, and then they usually don't send it. I guess by putting this song on the album I am pushing send." Taylor also drops subtle hints in the music, adding guitar slurring in the background, a technique common in Mayer's songs.

After hearing the song, Mayer felt "really humiliated", and he later hit back in an interview for *Rolling Stone*: "It made me feel terrible because I didn't deserve it. I'm pretty good at taking accountability now, and I never did anything to deserve that. It was a really lousy thing for her to do... I will say as a songwriter that I think it's kind of cheap songwriting. I know she's the biggest thing in the world ...but I think it's abusing your talent to rub your hands together and go, 'Wait till he gets a load of this!' That's bullshit."

Taylor called Mayer's claim of being humiliated "presumptuous" in *Glamour* magazine, and preferred not to get drawn into a war of words: "I let all the gossip live somewhere else. If you go too far down the rabbit hole of what people think about you, it can change everything about who you are."

In 2013 Mayer hit back and released his single 'Paper Doll' from his album *Paradise Valley*, which many took as being about Taylor. Two years later he confirmed it, although annoyed by the column inches it had received: "It never got listened to as a song. It became a news story because of the lyrics."

At a little over six minutes, it remains the longest album track of Taylor's career. The lyric hint is "Loved You from the Very First Day".

Insider - "A masterclass in emotional breakup ballads"; **Hollywood Reporter** - "A brilliant song, and not necessarily an easy one to listen to...at least until the chills-inducing climax"; **Slant** - "It's a slight departure for Swift. She's a lot of things, but subtle isn't one of them, and it's impossible to think of this song as directed toward anyone but Mayer"; **Rolling Stone** - "A slow-burning, methodical, precise, savage dissection of a failed, quasi-relationship, with no happy ending, no moral, no solution, not even a lesson learned - just a bad memory filed away".

Mean ****
(Taylor Swift)
3rd Single
Produced - Nathan Chapman & Taylor Swift
Released - March 13 2011
Chart peak positions
  Hot 100 #11; Hot Country Songs #2; Canada #10; Australia #45
RIAA - 3 x Platinum
Selected awards and nominations
2011 ACA Awards - Female Singer of the Year (nominated)
2011 CMA Awards – Song of the Year (nominated)
2011 CMA Awards - Music Video of the Year (nominated)
2011 MTV Music Video Awards - Best Video with a Message (nominated)
2011 Teen Choice Awards - Choice Country Song (won)
2012 ACM Awards - Video of the Year (nominated)
2012 BMI Awards - Top 50 songs (won)
2012 BMI Awards - Publisher of the Year (won)
2012 Grammys - Best Country Solo Performance (won)
2012 Grammys - Best Country Song (won)

A banjo-laden song apparently written about music critic Bob Lefsetz, who had always given Taylor good reviews until her performance with Stevie Nicks at the

Grammys in 2010, claiming not only that she couldn't sing, but that it would shorten her career overnight. Taylor revealed on her website: "I get it that not everyone is going to like everything that you do, and I get that no matter what, you're going to be criticized for something. But I also get that there are different kinds of ways to criticize someone. There is constructive criticism. There's professional criticism. And then, there's just being mean. There's a line that you cross when you just start to attack everything about a person, and there's one guy who just crossed the line over and over again."

Speaking to *Parade*, she elaborated about the criticism: "Some days I'm fine and I can just brush it off and go about my day, but some days it absolutely levels me. All I can do is to continue to try to work hard every single day and feel everything. I think it's important for me to feel things because then I write a song about them…" Ironically, the song went on to win two Grammys and a string of other awards.

The lyric hint is "I Thought You Got Me".

The music video was directed by Declan Whitebloom and shot over two days in Los Angeles, with the Orpheum Theatre serving as a backdrop. He was full of praise about Taylor's involvement in the production, as it was very personal to her. The film, which also features actor Joey King, consists of different scenes of bullying from different time periods, and according to the director was inspired by Taylor's performance at the Grammys in 2004. It was premiered on CMT on May 6th 2011.

Vulture - "One of Swift's most naturally appealing melodies and the joyful catharsis that comes with giving a bully what's coming to them"; **Rolling Stone** - "a banjo-core Tay-visceration of people who are mean, liars, pathetic, and /or alone in life, including the ones who live in the big cities"; **NME** - "A celebration of self-empowerment sees Swift slamming bullies over joyous banjo strums".

The Story of Us ****
(Taylor Swift)
4th Single
Produced - Nathan Chapman & Taylor Swift
Released - April 19 2011
Chart peak positions
  Hot 100 #41; AC #23; Adult Top 40 #31; Mainstream Top 40 #21; Canada #70
RIAA Certification - Platinum

One of the last songs written for the album, relating to an awkward moment when Taylor found herself sitting just a few seats away from her ex-boyfriend John Mayer at the 2010 CMT Music Awards, and how they both tried to ignore each other's presence. Apparently, she came up with the idea for the song after returning home and telling Andrea how it had felt "standing alone in a crowded room." Talking to *USA Today,* she said: "I just wanted to say to him, 'Is this killing you? Because it's killing me.' But I didn't. But I couldn't. Because we both had these silent shields up." She also recalled for MTV News: "Afterward, I just felt so empty, like we were both fighting this silent war of pretending we didn't care that the other was there."

Taylor said of the song: "Anytime I'm on stage or watching the music video, the first thing that comes into my mind is the person I wrote the song about. It's like the first thing that you think of in the moment that inspired the song, which is that excruciating, awful moment when you run into your ex for the first time."

The lyric hint is "CMT Awards".

Noble Jones directed the music video, which featured actor Caleb Campbell as her love interest. It was shot at Vanderbilt University, where Taylor and her ex-boyfriend, both students, meet up again after their relationship has ended. We see flashbacks of how his cheating caused their breakup. Taylor said: "The biggest difference between the new video and all the other ones is that I love to make a happy ending happen, and with this video, it doesn't happen." It premiered on MTV on May 24th 2011.

NME - "A break-neck tune, it's a catchy nugget of country-pop".

Never Grow Up *****
(Taylor Swift)
Produced - Nathan Chapman & Taylor Swift
Released - October 25 2010
Chart peak positions
 Hot 100 #84; Country Digital #1
RIAA Certification - Gold

Reputedly the last track added to the album, this heartfelt ode to childhood is about growing up and all the fears that it may bring. Written when Taylor was about 18 or 19, Taylor's friend, model Jamie King, had recently had a baby boy, Leo, and she had been asked to be a godmother: "I was holding this little baby the other night, and I was just thinking differently. When you're holding onto something that's so innocent and so perfect and has no idea what's coming for it with the world. The world is going to throw so many things at you as we grow up."

Taylor later elaborated on her website: "Growing up happens without you knowing it. Growing up is such a crazy concept because a lot of times when you were younger you wish you were older. I look out into a crowd every night and I see a lot of girls that are my age and going through exactly the same things as I'm going through. Every once in a while, I look down and I see a little girl who is seven or eight, and I wish I could tell her all of this. There she is becoming who she is going to be and forming her thoughts and dreams and opinions. I wrote this song for those little girls."

The song was later used in 2012's "Lily's Wal-Mart Christmas Commercial". The lyric hint is "Moved Out in July".

Pitchfork - "A quiet acoustic ballad that draws the clearest line to her old material"; **Rolling Stone** - "A folksy fingerpicking change of pace…pining for childhood innocence - though it feels more like a leftover from the debut"; **Vulture** - "This one is so well-observed and wistful about the idea of children aging that you'd swear she was secretly a 39-year-old mom"; **NME** - "This ballad moment peers out into a dimly lit crowd, and sees Swift dealing out her best live advice for younger fans in particular".

Enchanted ****
(Taylor Swift)
Produced - Nathan Chapman & Taylor Swift
Released - October 25 2010
Chart peak positions

Hot 100 #75; Country Digital #11; Canada #95
RIAA Certification - Gold

Originally the title for the album. Another song about infatuation, this time for singer Adam Young, the man behind the electronic music project called Owl City, who had released a debut album *Ocean Eyes* in 2009, which included the six-times platinum single 'Fireflies'. Taylor had first met him at one of his concerts in September 2009, as she later revealed: "I had talked to him on email or something before, but I had never met him. And meeting him, it was this overwhelming feeling of: 'I really hope that you're not in love with somebody.' It was just wonderful, that feeling. Like, 'Oh my gosh. Who's he with? Does he like me? Does he like somebody else? What does it mean?'" She emailed him afterward from her hotel room: "Sorry I was so quiet. I was just wonderstruck meeting you".

Young later responded in song form, admitting he had feelings for her too: "I'll be the first to admit I'm a rather shy boy, and since music is the most eloquent form of communication I can muster, I decided to record something for you, a sort of a 'reply' to the breathtaking song on your current record. You are a true princess from a dreamy fairy tale, and above all, I just want you to know...I was enchanted to meet you, too."

The lyric hint is "Adam".

Vulture - "It's a glittery ode to a meet-cute that probably didn't need to be six minutes long, but at least the extended length gives us extra time to soak up the heavenly coda"; **NME** - "One of Taylor's most underrated songs. A fairytale epic that acts as an elder sibling to 'Love Story', it captures the dizzy infatuation of a new romance".

Better Than Revenge **
(Taylor Swift)
Produced - Nathan Chapman & Taylor Swift
Released - October 25 2010
Chart peak positions
Hot 100 #56; Country Digital #6; Canada #73
RIAA Certification - Gold

Reputedly about actress Camilla Belle, the girl who "stole" the heart of Joe Jonas while he was still dating Taylor. Writing in *The Guardian*, Taylor said: "I was 18 when I wrote [the song]. That's the age you are when you think someone can actually take your boyfriend. Then you grow up and realise no one can take someone from you if they don't want to leave." She also commented: "I think she probably thought I forgot about it, but I didn't."

Camilla's response came in 2016 in a tweet during Taylor's high-profile feud with Kanye and Kim, leading fans to see it as a shot at Taylor: "No need for revenge. Just sit back and wait. Those who hurt you will eventually screw up themselves & if you're lucky, God will let you watch." Although only rumoured to be about Camilla, the line at the end of the song, "so much better", could also be referring to the name of a song by the Jonas Brothers.

The lyric hint is "You Thought I Would Forget".

Vulture - "A nasty little song that has not aged well. Whether a straightforward imitation of Avril Lavigne's style or an early attempt at 'Blank Space'- style self-satirization, the barbs never go beyond bratty"; **NME** - "Across Taylor Swift's entire back catalogue…[it's] perhaps best suited to soundtracking an angsty high school drama".

Innocent ****
(Taylor Swift)
Produced - Nathan Chapman & Taylor Swift
Released - September 12 2010
Chart peak positions
 Hot 100 #27; Country Digital #2; Canada #53

It's hard to imagine this song not being about Kanye West's interruption of Taylor's speech at the 2009 VMAs and not too surprising if it is. But it makes a point of learning from your mistakes and becoming a better person, something the rapper could not bring himself to do. She also performed it at the 2010 ceremony, with West in attendance. In a later Yahoo! Live interview, Taylor said: "When it comes to making an album, if you make everything general and kind of gloss over your actual, raw feelings, that doesn't benefit anyone. As far as what I feel and what level to feel it, I can't really control any of that. It's just how things hit you, and what you let in is definitely something you've got to find a balance for."

The lyric hint is "Life Is Full of Little Interruptions".

Taylor opened up in an interview with *New York* magazine: "I think a lot of people expected me to write a song about [West]. But for me, it was important to write a song *to* him…It doesn't really add anything good if I start victimising myself and complaining about things…I feel everything. I've never had this thick skin that can't be…It's not like I am bulletproof in any sense of the word."

'Innocent' would certainly prove the point with portraying Taylor in a more mature, sensitive light.

Washington Post - "A small masterpiece of passive aggressiveness, a vivisection dressed up as a peace offering"; **Vulture** - "Swift turns in a tender vocal performance, though the lyrics could stand to be less patronizing".

Haunted ****
(Taylor Swift)
Produced - Nathan Chapman & Taylor Swift
Released - October 25 2010
Chart peak position
 Hot 100 #63

Notable for its dramatic intro, this song is about a past relationship, the memory of which will never go away. Although never confirmed, Joe Jonas was put in the frame as being the inspiration. Taylor revealed on her website that the song "is about the moment that you realise the person you're in love with is drifting and fading fast. And you don't know what to do, but in that period of time, in that phase of love, where it's fading out, time moves slowly. Everything hinges on what the last text message said, and you're realising that he's kind of falling out of love. That's a really heartbreaking and tragic thing to go through, because the whole time you're trying to tell yourself it's not happening. I went through this, and I ended up waking up in the middle of the night writing a song about it."

To reflect the song's emotional intensity and the chaotic confusion Taylor was looking for, strings were recorded at Capitol Studios with maestro arranger Paul Buckmaster.

This should have been a bigger hit had it not been overshadowed by so many great tracks. The lyric hint is "Still to This Day".

Celeb Mix - "'Haunted' will forever remain as an epic orchestral power ballad for nostalgic Swifties like ourselves to return to. We can live with that"; **Rolling Stone** - "Enchanted to meet you, Goth Taylor. We'll meet again"; **Vulture** - "She almost pulls it off, but at this point in Swift's career her voice wasn't quite strong enough to give the unrestrained performance the song calls for"; **NME** - "Lacks the nuance that some of her enchanting, happy ending filled romances boast".

Last Kiss ****
(Taylor Swift)
Produced - Nathan Chapman & Taylor Swift
Released - October 25 2010
Chart peak positions
 Hot 100 #71; Country Digital #9; Canada #99

An epic emotional ballad about Taylor's feelings for Joe Jonas and how for a time she thought their relationship would never end. Taylor wrote on her website: "'Last Kiss' is sort of like a letter to somebody. You say all of these desperate, hopeless feelings that you have after a break-up... You feel anger, and you feel confusion, and frustration. Then there is absolute sadness. The sadness of losing this person, losing all the memories, and the hopes you had for the future." The hidden message in the song is "forever & always", the name of the song she wrote about him soon after their break-up, and, less noticeably, the song has a 27-second intro, the time that famous phone call had taken for Joe to tell her it was over.

The lyric hint is "Forever and Always".

Rolling Stone - "When you're already wrung out from sad songs and begging for mercy, this six-minute quasi-doo-wop ballad creeps up on you to inflict more punishment. One of those flawless Nathan Chapman productions - so sparse, so delicate, flattering every tremor of her voice"; **Vulture** - "A good-bye waltz with an understated arrangement that suits the starkness of the lyrics"; **NME** - "A plodding waltz".

Long Live (We will be remembered) ****
(Taylor Swift)
Recorded - Blackbird Studios, Nashville TN
Produced - Nathan Chapman & Taylor Swift
Released - March 1 2012
Chart peak positions
 Hot 100 #85; Country Digital Songs #13

Taylor's tribute to all the people who had helped her in the last couple of years, especially her producer, her band and her legion of Swifties. Possibly written after the show at the Gillette Stadium in Foxborough on June 5th, Taylor recalled how the song "talks about the triumphant moments that we've had in the last two years...about how I feel reflecting on it. The song for me is like looking at a photo album of all the award shows, and all the stadium shows, and all the hands in the air in the crowd. It's sort of the first love song that I've written to my team."

In 2012 Taylor released a new version of the song as a single, taken from the Brazilian edition of Taylor's live album, *Speak Now World Tour - Live.* It featured new verses written and performed by Brazilian singer Paula Fernandes, who shared writing credits, and reached the top five in her country's charts.

The music video featuring Fernandes was directed by Eduardo Levy and had the two singers performing while connected by satellite.

The lyric hint is "For You".

Rolling Stone - "An arena-slaying rock anthem to cap off *Speak Now*, for an ordinary girl who suddenly gets to feel like she rules the world for a minute or two"; **Vulture** - "Ostensibly written about Swift's experiences touring with her band, but universal enough that it's been taken as a graduation song by pretty much everyone else".

Ours *****
(Taylor Swift)
Speak Now North America Deluxe Edition Disc 2
6th Single
Recorded - Blackbird Studios, Nashville TN
Produced - Nathan Chapman & Taylor Swift
Released - November 2 2011
Chart Peak Positions
  Hot 100 #13; Hot Country Songs #1; UK #181; Canada #68; Australia #91
RIAA Certification - Platinum
Selected awards and nominations
2012 ACA Awards - Female Singer of the Year (nominated)
2012 ACA Awards - Female Video of the Year (nominated)
2012 CMT Awards - Female Video of the Year (nominated)
2013 BMI Country Awards - Country Awards Top 50 Songs (won)

Superb song about a relationship she had that nobody approved of, and believed by some to be another one about John Mayer. Taylor told VH1: "I wrote it about this guy nobody thought I should be with. So, I wrote this song specifically just to play it for him, just to show him, I don't care what anyone says." The song became Taylor's sixth chart topper on Billboard's Country Songs, also making her the first female in the chart's history to begin her chart history with 15 consecutive top ten entries.

The music video was devised by Taylor and directed by Declan Whitebloom. Taylor said: "I had a very definite idea of what I wanted this video to be." The resultant film shows Taylor working in an office, where everything and everybody is seemingly conspiring to make her day worse. Only when she turns on her computer and sees clips of her and her boyfriend (played by Zach Gilford) does she feel happier. The video ends with her going to meet him at the airport after he's been working overseas, and she runs to embrace him.

The video had its premiere on E! News on December 2nd 2011.

Vulture - "Even if this song never rises above cuteness, it is *incredibly* cute".

If This Was a Movie **
(Martin Johnston - Taylor Swift)
Speak Now North America Deluxe Edition Disc 2
Promo Single
Produced - Martin Johnston & Taylor Swift
Released - November 8 2011
Chart peak positions
  Hot 100 #85; Country Digital #13

A song about breaking up with someone, then dreaming that the love lost would return as it often does in the movies. It was co-written with Martin Johnston, lead singer of the rock band Boys Like Girls, and possible inspiration for her song 'Love Story'. Many commentators believe this track is another one about ex-boyfriend John Mayer.

Vulture - "The mirror image of 'White Horse', which makes it feel oddly superfluous"; **NME** - "Frustratingly repetitive. With its droning guitar licks and dreary chorus, it stutters toward the finish line".

Superman *
(Taylor Swift)
Speak Now North America Deluxe Edition Disc 2
Promo single
Produced - Nathan Chapman & Taylor Swift
Released - November 8 2011 (Amazon and I-Tunes)
Chart peak position
 Hot 100 #26

About a boy who breaks up their relationship, but hopes he will eventually return to her when the time is right. Taylor explained before one of her performances: "This was a guy I was enamoured with. The song got its title by something that I said randomly in conversation. When he walked out of the room, I turned to one of my friends and said, 'It's like watching Superman fly away'."

It could be another about John Mayer, as Superman was apparently his favourite superhero. If it was true, he would become the possible inspiration for four songs on the album, a sort of record in itself.

Rolling Stone - "Lois Lane fantasy, left off Speak Now for good reason".

"A songwriter beyond her years"

In a later interview for MTV, Taylor reflected on the theme of the album, and the tendency of not wanting to say the wrong thing: "In your personal life, that can lead to being guarded and not making what you feel clear in the moments that you're feeling it. For me, it's never really fearing saying what's on your mind in my music, but sometimes having a problem with it in life. Sometimes you lose the moment... I just keep going back to Speak Now, because I think it's a metaphor for so many things we go through in life, the moment where it's almost too late, and you've gotta either say what it is you're feeling or deal with the consequences forever."

Taylor had nothing to fear over her third album receiving positive reviews:

Los Angeles Times - "She makes memorable music by homing in on the tiny stuff: the half-notes in a hummed phrase, the lyrical images that communicate precisely what it's like to feel uncomfortable, or disappointed, or happy"; **New York Times** - "A bravura work of nontransparent transparency...the most savage of her career, and also the most musically diverse. And it's excellent too, possibly her best"; **AllMusic** - "She writes from the perspective of the moment yet has the skill of a songwriter beyond her years... She may be not a girl, and not yet a woman, but on Speak Now she captures that transition with a personal grace and skill that few singer songwriters have"; **Washington Post** - "ridiculously entertaining... lengthy, captivating exercise in woo-pitching, flame tending and score-settling... [although occasionally] stretched thin"; **Rolling Stone** - "These 14 tunes chronicle the hopes and dreams of boy-crazy small-town Everygirls, and Swift wrote them all by herself"; **The Guardian** - "A conscious attempt to move beyond those childish things while retaining her balance of maturity and relatability"; **Chicago Tribune** - "There's no question that she's put herself in the place of being a role model for these young women. I think there's a whole lot in her music - the whole diary aspect, using her own emotions to talk about her challenges - that encourages young people to do the same thing. I think she's made it more comfortable for young people to express what's going on with themselves, which is so key to their survival of those horribly awkward and sometimes dangerous years"; **Slant** - "*Speak Now* is no masterpiece, though it's sure to be hailed as such in some circles. But it's an album that finds Swift getting an awful lot of difficult stuff right, and it makes it clear what she still needs to develop in order to refine her craft even further".

Speak Now became another record breaker. All 14 tracks on the standard album and three bonus tracks charted on the Hot 100, with 11 of them charting concurrently, becoming the only album in history to have 17 Hot 100 hits, four of which were top ten. Taylor also became just the third artist in history and the first female artist to have over ten concurrent Hot 100 hits.

At the time of writing, it remains the fastest selling digital album by a female artist in the US, with a total of 278,000 copies, and the fast-selling album in the US by a female country artist, with first-week sales of 1.04 million. Taylor also became the first artist to have singles enter the Hot 100 top ten in successive weeks, with 'Speak Now' on October 23rd and 'Back to December' seven days later.

To top it all, it still remains the best-selling self-written album of all-time.

Meanwhile, on October 22nd, the three-part television mini-documentary *Journey to Fearless* had its television premiere on the recently formed Hub Network. Directed by Don Mischer and Ryan Polito, it was a behind-the-scenes look at the recent tour. Shown over three days, the first 43-minute episode was entitled *Dreaming Fearless,* in which Taylor discussed her rise to stardom, the move to Nashville, and the album's release. The second episode, *Becoming Fearless*, showed the preparation involved in the tour, while in the last part, *Living Fearless,* she shared her video diaries with the spotlight on the final concert in Boston. Altogether, there were clips of 14 live performances.

The documentary was released on dvd and Blu-ray through Shout! Factory a year later.

On October 26th, the day after *Speak Now* was released, Taylor appeared with her band on *The Today Show* at New York's Rockefeller Center. Once again with sparkly dress, matching guitar, and knee-high boots, she sang 'Mine', 'Speak Now' and 'Love Story'. Talking to host Ann Curry, she said that she couldn't believe all the praise the new album was receiving: "Oh my gosh! It's unbelievable when you put two years of your life into something, having it be received like that is incredible. I'm so happy because this album means a lot to me...I've never written an entire album on my own before, so songwriting is my favourite thing. It's all what makes life more sense to me." The singer also remarked that as far as relationships went, she was keen to keep her fans guessing: "One of my goals has been to stay the same person, [a] songwriter. I'm always going to write about my life."

That same day, she guested on *The Late Show with David Letterman* and sang 'Speak Now', apparently unrattled by Letterman's "you smell like expensive wood" comment, and next day completed the trio of guest spots in the Big Apple with a stint on the morning show *Live with Regis and Kelly* with another performance of 'Mine'.

It would prove to be a frantic time for the singer. At the beginning of November, she was in Los Angeles to appear on *The Ellen De Generes Show,* with performances of 'You Belong with Me', 'Back to December', and an acoustic 'Mine'. During the chat with Ellen, she was grilled about her love life, past and present, and tried her best to dodge questions by focusing on the album. She revealed how writing the music had been an emotional process: "I'd have nightmares in the middle of the night that *Rolling Stone* hated it. I was really nervous about it, because taking this on, you're taking a lot of ownership of whether people like it or don't." On the subjects for her songs, Taylor insisted that her plan was "to continue to never tell."

Dating Jake

Although nothing had yet been made official, Ellen had asked Taylor about her love life and whether she was optimistic: "Well, why wouldn't anyone be?" The comedienne then quipped: "Especially if your boyfriend is Jake Gyllenhaal, because he's very handsome. Y'all are just hanging out though, right?" A picture of the two of them was being shown on the screen at the time, and Taylor didn't deny or confirm they were an item. It transpired that actress Gwyneth Paltrow had been their matchmaker and had hosted a dinner in London for the couple.

Almost coinciding with the album's release, she had first been seen backstage at a recording of *Saturday Night Live* in New York with the star of the movies *Donnie Darko* and *Brokeback Mountain*, and was there apparently to support Taylor's actor friend Emma Stone, who was guesting on the show. The couple were also seen together walking around Brooklyn and having brunch together. 29-year-old Gyllenhaal had been split from girlfriend, actor Reece Witherspoon, for almost ten months after a two-year-long relationship.

Taylor cancelled plans to be at home for Thanksgiving to spend it with Gyllenhaal in New York, where she met his family, including actor sister Maggie and her husband Peter Sarsgaard. She then returned the compliment and invited him to spend some time in Nashville. While busy promoting his latest movie *Love & Other Drugs*, it was reported that he had spent £100,000 to have Taylor flown out to London on a private jet to spend some time with him at the Dorchester Hotel. According to a report in *Us Weekly*, Taylor "was totally smitten. She loves how nice and affectionate he is", while Jake "likes that Taylor is sweet, low-key and very easy to be around."

The day after the *Ellen* show, Taylor was a guest on the 200th episode of *Dancing with the Stars* in Los Angeles. With a glittering guitar and wearing a champagne-coloured dress, she performed 'Mine' while professional dancers twirled on the ballroom floor in front of her, and then sang 'White Horse' in front of a screen

113

showing past moments from the show. Talking to the singer afterward, host Tom Bergeron pretended to faint, leaving Taylor to take over hosting duties, which she did just fine.

A week later, the awards season commenced with the CMAs in Nashville. Nominated for Female Vocalist of the Year, she lost out to Miranda Lambert, but made up for it with the best performance of the night, a spellbinding rendition of 'Back to December' at the piano. Wearing a beautiful long, white, empire-waist gown, iconic red lipstick, and her curly hair swept into an updo, she looked every inch a grown-up lady and no more the teenage starlet, and the turn-of-the-century, mist-covered setting, and cello and violin accompaniment, gave the most ethereal quality to the performance.

Four days after the award show, Taylor was in London for the BBC Radio 1 Teen Awards at London's Hammersmith Apollo. Despite performing 'Love Story', 'Speak Now' and 'Mine', she failed to impress her British fans enough to pick up any awards. Back home that same day, NBC aired a Thanksgiving special called *Taylor Swift - Speak Now,* with performances filmed in New York and Los Angeles.

A few days later, Taylor made a whistle-stop visit to Japan, where she and the band performed 'Mine' and 'You Belong with Me' on the show *Music Station*, with enthusiastic accompaniment from several Japanese male singers. In the meantime, fans were kept in suspense no longer, when, on November 23rd, various media outlets, including *Billboard* and MTV News, announced that the anticipated *Speak Now* World Tour would commence in February 2011.

Two days after the announcement, Taylor attended the AMAs in Los Angeles and came away with the award for Favourite Country Female Artist, beating her closest rivals Miranda Lambert and Carrie Underwood. During the show, she once again performed a mellow 'Back to December', this time on a grand piano on an elevated platform slowly lowered to a stage adorned with sparkling trees and moonlit night sky. Wearing a black trouser suit, and sporting another new hairstyle, this time poker-straight and tied back, she finished the performance by standing and singing a short rendition of One Republic's ballad 'Apologise', a song about being too late to say sorry. It would be taken by many to be seen as her reaching out and apologising for the way she had treated ex-boyfriend Terry Lautner. It must have had the Swifties tweeting comments until their fingers bled.

Although not actually admitting Lautner was the inspiration, Taylor did tell MTV News: "Well, I've always sort of written songs about situations in my life, things that needed to be said. I write songs about people who deserve to have songs written about them, and whatever they need to hear, whatever is the right thing to say to that person, ends up being said. I've never felt the need to apologise in a song before. But in the last two years I've experienced a lot, [including] a lot of different kinds of learning lessons, and sometimes you learn a lesson too late and at that point you need to apologise because you were careless."

For her 21st birthday, on December 13th, Taylor was thrilled when Gyllenhaal bought her a $11,000 guitar signed by the legendary country star Chet Atkins, and, according to *In Touch* magazine, she also received a white gold, diamond-encrusted bracelet costing $100,000. However, on her actual birthday, Taylor threw a party for friends and her management team, but Gyllenhaal was noticeably absent, having gone to Los Angeles for Christmas. Instead, Taylor took a short vacation with Andrea and Austin to the Turks and Caicos Islands.

According to *Us Weekly*, this signalled the end of their brief relationship and claimed: "He said he wasn't feeling it anymore and was uncomfortable with all the attention they got. He also said he could feel the age difference. Taylor is really upset. We told her not to move so fast with this but she didn't listen." Some reports indicated it had ended with a simple phone call.

Gyllenhaal was indeed an intensely private man, and their dual fame and the media attention it attracted was all the more difficult for him. Although in public their happiness was undeniable, the publicity had undermined what was most important to him, his privacy. Taken by some to have just been a publicity stunt, there was no denying Taylor was heartbroken. Some unreliable sources revealed she had stopped eating and was shielding her pain by working herself to death at the gym.

A year later she would reveal her heartbreak to *Vogue*: "I really have this great life right now, and I'm not sad and I'm not crying this Christmas, so I am really stoked about that. I am not gonna go into it! It's a sad story!... I can deal with someone who's obsessed with privacy. People kind of care if there are two famous people dating. But no one cares that much. If you care about privacy to the point where we need to dig a tunnel under this restaurant so that we can leave, I can't do that." True to form, Taylor would soon write several songs about her experience.

2010 came to an end with *Speak Now* still holding the top spot on the charts and with Taylor's earnings for the year estimated to be an incredible $45 million. She also became the latest face of *CoverGirl* magazine, a dream she had held since a little girl, which was now a reality. It went a long way to lifting her spirits and made her look toward the new year, and a new world tour, with more confidence.

Taylor was riled up and ready for the next chapter in her career, and what many critics saw as the start of her supernova phase.

Tour Time

*"I loved being able to thank my fans for this life they've given me. Being on tour,
I get a nightly reminder of how lucky I am to get to stand on giant stages
and sing for sold-out crowds"*

Hitting the road again

For Taylor, the new year would be all about the music, with no relationships to
speak of, and, surprisingly, only one television chat show appearance. The focus
now was on promoting the new album, but first there was another award ceremony
to attend. The People's Choice Awards were held in Los Angeles and broadcast on
CBS. Although not performing on the night, she was nominated in the category of
Favourite Female Artist, but lost out to Carrie Underwood. However, she did win
Favourite Country Artist, and had it presented to her by none other than the great
Elton John.

At the end of January, Taylor was in Cozumel, Mexico, performing a short set
for 250 prize-winning passengers of the Royal Caribbean's *Azure of the Seas*, the
world's newest and largest cruise ship, at their outdoor AquaTheater. According to
MTV Buzzworthy, the singer rehearsed for her set in one of the ship's loft suites
before being ushered to the stage via a private elevator, and used Tom Petty's
'American Girl' as her introduction song before treating the audience to a mix of
fan favourites and one or two covers.

With that out of the way, work began on finalising details for the forthcoming
Speak Now World Tour which was set to begin on February 9th in Singapore,
commencing Stateside in Omaha on May 27th, and ending in Dallas in October.
There would be a total of 87 shows in 19 countries, with plans to add additional
dates in Australia and New Zealand. Tickets would be going on sale for $25.

Taylor knew very well what this would mean to her fans: "I'm so excited to go
back out on tour again in 2011. The *Fearless* Tour was so much fun and even more
unforgettable than I ever imagined, and I can't wait to get back out and play my
new music from *Speak Now*! The fans have been so amazing and I'm thrilled to
play in new cities around the world and meet even more of my fans in 2011."

Joining the band for the tour was rhythm guitarist Jody Harris.

Compared to the previous tour, this would be on a different scale, with the
majority of the venues being huge stadia or arenas with 50,000 seats or more.
Because of tour commitments, Taylor would be unable to attend the Grammys in
Los Angeles on February 13th, and, besides, she had not received any nominations
because *Speak Now* had been released a few weeks after the deadlines set. That
would now have to wait until next year.

When the tour finally kicked off in Singapore, the fans were treated to something
very special and very different to what had been seen before. With her love for
stage productions, Taylor and her team had unleashed a theatrical and logistical
extravaganza, which over the next eight months would involve 130 personnel,
travelling from city to city in 13 buses, and 21 trucks loaded with 62 tonnes of

equipment, including 116 speakers and 350 lights, and a wardrobe for the nine costume changes in each show.

The lavish sets included a sweeping staircase, illuminated trees, and a Juliet-style balcony that could be raised above the audience. Taylor revealed: "One of my favourite things about this tour - although it's a very theatrical show, is that it really reminds me a lot of my favourite musical theatre productions in its scenery, costumes, and production - there are lots of moments in the show that are very spontaneous."

Then there was having to choose the 15 or so songs to be performed: "We spent months going over the set list and thinking where things would go, which ones would segue well into other songs and how we could tell individual stories. I didn't want to tell one big story. I wanted each song to have its own story."

The remainder of February saw the tour visiting South Korea, Japan, the Philippines and Hong Kong. Taylor felt honoured performing for her non-English speaking fans: "I look down and I see all the fans singing the words to my songs, having written the lyrics, knowing that they connect in countries where English really isn't spoken by everyone. It means the world to me."

The European leg of the tour commenced in Brussels on March 6th, and throughout the rest of the month took in the Netherlands, Norway, Germany, Italy, France, Spain and Ireland, and included three dates in England at venues in London, Birmingham and Manchester. For this leg, the supporting act included Scottish group Martin and James. Following the UK dates, there was a two-month break before commencing the North America leg.

In the first week of April, Taylor attended the ACM Awards in Las Vegas. With banjo in hand, she performed 'Mean' on a country-porch setting, and then went on to win the award for Entertainer of the Year. Accepting the award, she said: "This is the first time that I've ever won this and I'm just losing my mind. The fact that this is from the fans makes it so beautiful."

Two days later she flew to London with the band to appear on BBC Radio 1's *Live Lounge* series, performing an acoustic set of 'Story of Us' and a cover of London-based band Mumford & Sons' 'White Blank Space', a track from their 2009 album *Sigh No More*. The performance was also televised.

On a sadder note, it had been reported that, sometime in 2011, Taylor's parents had separated, without telling anyone about it. Having been too worried that the news would offset Taylor's career, Andrea and Scott had remained silent about their marriage issues and refused to get the press involved throughout the legal process. According to *Entertainment News*, the fact that Andrea accompanied her daughter on tour whilst Scott tended to stay behind may have posed a significant challenge to their marriage of over 20 years.

In the meantime, Taylor had taken her father's advice to invest her money wisely. *Us Weekly* reported that she had bought herself a new $3.6 million mini-mansion in the celebrity hotspot of Beverly Hills. The one-and-a-half acre Cape Cod-style house boasted four bedrooms, four bathrooms, and a sports court within the private grounds (the home was reportedly sold on in 2018 in an off-market deal for $4 million). Around the same time, Taylor had also bought her parents a $1.4 million home in Nashville. According to a source close to the singer, the recently-renovated property was an "incredible house." It was also said that Taylor had purchased her own private 12-seater jet for a reported $40 million, with her lucky number 13 painted on the nose.

On May 6th, the bullying-themed music video for the song 'Mean' was released on CMT, and would prove to be one of the most empowering of Taylor's career. Although reviews were mixed about its actual intent, Taylor had seemingly reached out to touch many groups of people. Citing her parents for giving her this lesson in life, Taylor wrote: "Why make life miserable for someone when you could be using your energy for good? We don't need to share the same opinions as others, but we need to be respectful. When you hear people making hateful comments, stand up to them. Point out what a waste it is to hate, and you could open their eyes."

The New York Times saw Taylor as being "part of a new wave of young (and mostly straight) women who are providing the soundtrack for a generation of gay fans coming to terms with their identity in a time of turbulent and confusing cultural messages."

Taylor was in Los Angeles in May, making her only tv chat show of the year with her fourth appearance on *The Ellen de Generes Show*. During the interview, Taylor talked about opening up her tour rehearsals to fans in order to raise funds for the victims of tornadoes in the south, and also spoke about how she would never complain about living her personal life in the public eye: "I think it's just obnoxious if I complain about anything. You know, I hear people talk about like, 'Oh, the intrusion on my privacy.' It's like there are a million other jobs you could have had. And for me, I've just come to an acceptance of the fact that this is my life, and if somebody wants to hide a relationship or had privacy issues, then we don't have the same viewpoint. Cause for me, it's just like, live your life. If people happen to take pictures, you laugh about it in the car afterward."

Following the interview, Taylor wore a sassy schoolgirl-inspired outfit to perform 'The Story of Us', and after the show took the time to surprise one of her fans in the audience with a basket of memorabilia and VIP passes to her show. Just over a week later, she was in Las Vegas for the Billboard Music Awards. Nominated in six categories, she won for Top Billboard 200 Artist and Top Country Artist.

By the end of the month, it was time to hit the road again, with the US tour once again commencing in Omaha, Nebraska, and continuing across the country throughout the summer, including several dates in Canada. The supporting artist for these concerts was the Christian rock band NeedtoBreathe from South Carolina.

Taylor began to surprise her fans at certain concerts with appearances by special homegrown guests to perform duets of one of their hits with the singer. They included Justin Bieber ('Baby'), Tim McGraw ('Just to See You Smile'), Shawn Colvin ('Sunny Came Home') and the legendary James Taylor ('Fire and Rain'), who was chosen for the final show of the leg at New York's Madison Square Garden on November 22nd.

James Taylor recalled: "We just hit it off. I loved her songs, and her presence on stage was so great…When she called and asked if I would join her at the end of the last concert to celebrate the end of a successful tour on her part, I jumped in."

118

Wonderstruck

During the summer, Taylor had also been offered the voice part of tree-loving Audrey in the 3D animated movie *The Lorax*, based on the popular children's book by Dr Seuss. Audrey was the love interest of idealistic 12-year-old Ted Wiggins, played by the young actor Zac Efron. In an interview for MTV, Taylor talked about the voiceover part: "It's a completely different space that you go to in your head. It's very different from when you're singing songs that you wrote...With this, you're sitting there in a booth by yourself having conversations with no one."

Released the following March, it would lead to some speculation that Taylor and Zac had become an item off screen as well. It was also reported that she had purchased another house for her parents by shelling out $2.5 million on a prime piece of real estate nestled in the elite Forest Hills suburb of Nashville. Set in six lush, landscaped acres, the four-bed Greek Revival-style mansion, which boasted a guesthouse and pool house, had been built in 1934 for the US ambassador to Denmark, and was later owned by Luke Lewis, chairman of Universal Music Group.

Now her parents, who may or not have been living apart by now, would have the likes of Nicole Kidman and Keith Urban as celebrity neighbours. Taylor was certainly showing her deep appreciation for Andrea and Scott Swift and the sacrifices they had made in the past to give her every chance of fulfilling her dreams. But with Forbes having already announced the singer's earnings for the year, it was hardly making a dent in her bank balance.

And it wasn't just in her family where Taylor's generosity was displayed. In August, she found a window in the tour schedule and treated all the girls who performed on stage with her to a three-day mini-vacation in Charleston, South Carolina. Also that month, Fox aired the Teen Choice Awards live from Los Angeles, with Taylor coming away with six awards, including Ultimate Choice, Best Female Artist and Best Country Song (for 'Mean').

That summer it was announced on Taylor's website that she had gone into partnership with Elizabeth Arden to launch a fragrance called Wonderstruck, a name referring to a line in the song 'Enchanted'. It went on sale in stores for around $60 in October, no doubt helped by an expensive tv promotion campaign, which showed Taylor dressed "in a romantic, frilly gown with a ruffly train and her signature blonde tendrils and bright red lips." On its release, Taylor explained: "I wrote the lyric, 'I'm wonderstruck, blushing all the way home' ...about the first time you meet someone. A fragrance can help shape someone's first impression and memory of you. It's exciting to think that Wonderstruck will play a role in creating some of those memories." In the debut ad, Taylor teased that it was "the beginning of something magical."

In November, Taylor was back in Nashville for the CMA Awards, and following a performance of 'Ours', her latest single, she was presented with her second award for Entertainer of the Year by country legend Reba McIntire. She also had nominations in three other categories - Female Vocalist, Album of the Year (for *Speak Now*), Song of the Year and Music Video of the Year (both for 'Mean') - but failed to pick up an award.

In her acceptance speech, Taylor gave special thanks to all the fans that attended her recent concerts, and also to those artists who answered her call and duetted with her on the tour. She also hinted that she had been writing songs for her next album and making demos in Nathan Chapman's basement.

Although losing out at the CMA Awards, better news came eleven days later at the AMAs in Los Angeles. Although it proved to a big night for Adele, it was Taylor who came away with the award for Artist of the Year, as well as Favourite Country Female Artist and Favourite Country Album.

That same month, *Speak Now World Tour - Live* was released on cd and dvd. It featured all 17 performances from various shows on the North American leg, including her covers of 'Bette Davis Eyes' and Train's two smash-hits, 'Drops of Jupiter' and 'Hey, Soul Sister'. Directed by Baz Halpin, it peaked at #11 on the Hot 200 chart, and #2 on Top Country Albums. Two tracks from the album also charted, with the live version of 'Drops of Jupiter' reaching #7 on the Hot 100 Bubbling Under chart and #22 on Country Digital; and 'Back to December/Apologise/You're Not Sorry' making #45 on Country Digital. A special Target edition dvd also contained home videos and rehearsal footage.

The Hunger Games

In the meantime, Taylor was making yet another venture into movies. During the summer of 2011 top producer T-Bone Burnett had been tasked with recording a soundtrack album for the forthcoming dystopian sci-fi movie, *The Hunger Games,* directed by Gary Ross and starring Jennifer Lawrence. For the project, Burnett got together a range of artists including Maroon 5 and Arcade Fire. Taylor was asked to contribute two songs, one a solo effort and the other a collaboration with The Civil Wars, the alternative country duo consisting of Joy Williams and John Paul White, whose debut album *Barton Hollow* would go on to win a Grammy the following year. Sometime in the fall, Burnett got them together at his Los Angeles home, and between them they came up with the haunting folk-ballad 'Safe & Sound' in just two hours.

Taylor recalled: "The Civil Wars had a show that night in LA, so they raced right over to T-Bone's house. There are so many things he could've done production-wise to make that song bigger sonically than it is, but I think that would have possibly been a mistake. For him to have left the song as a lullaby is brilliant."

On December 22nd, Taylor tweeted some of the song's lyrics, saying: "Something I've been very excited about for a very long time is going to be happening very soon, and I'm not referring to Christmas…And this is it, the big surprise…Go get it! #TheHungerGames."

The haunting music video was directed by Philip Andelman and has Taylor walking barefoot through a forest in Watertown, Tennessee, wearing a long white gown, while The Civil Wars are seen singing along whilst inside a cottage in front of a fire. Some of the shots show Taylor in a cemetery sitting atop the graves of a couple who died in 1853, and there are also many references to the movie, including Taylor finding a mockingjay pin. The video had its premiere on MTV on February 13th 2012.

120

Safe & Sound (featuring The Civil Wars) ****
(Taylor Swift - Joy Williams - John Paul White - T Bone Burnett)
Label - Big Machine
Single
Produced - T-Bone Burnett
Released - Dec 26 2011
Chart peak positions
  Hot 100 #30; Hot Digital #19; UK #67; Canada #31; Australia #38; NZ #11
RIAA Certification - 2 x Platinum
Selected awards & nominations
2012 CMT Awards - Video of the Year (nominated)
2012 CMT Awards - Collaborative Video of the Year (nominated)
2013 Golden Globes - Best Original Song (nominated)
2013 Grammys - Best Song Written for Visual Media (won)
2013 Grammys - Best Country Duo/Group Performance (nominated)

Within minutes of its release, it became the top trending topic on Twitter in the US and the second hottest topic worldwide. Both the song and the music video received mixed reviews: **Rolling Stone** - "[Swift's] prettiest ballad"; **The Wall Street Journal** - "The new song has a rural feel, but doesn't sound like a commercial country song. The music is acoustic and contemplative, and the lyrics, while outwardly soothing, have an undercurrent of hurt and dread"; **Idolator** - "With sparse, eerie production...is one of Swift's most beguiling singles. Her breathy vocals have never been better utilised & the menacing lyrics are a testament to her songwriting versatility. It should've been bigger"; **Vulture** - "Her best soundtrack by a country mile. Freed from the constraints of her usual mode, her vocals paint in corners you didn't think she could reach"; **NME** - "This pretty, stripped-back track is enthralling".

The other song Taylor recorded for the soundtrack was her self-penned 'Eyes Open', although it would not be included in the movie itself.

Eyes Open ***
(Taylor Swift)
Label - Big Machine / Republic
Single
Produced - Nathan Chapman &Taylor Swift
Released - March 27 2012
Chart peak positions
  Hot 100 #19; AC #21; Hot Country Songs #50; Adult Top 40 #11; Mainstream
  Top 40 #20; UK #70; Canada #34; Australia #37; NZ #6
RIAA Certification - Platinum
Selected awards & nominations
2012 Teen Choice Awards - Choice Single by a Female Artist (won)

Taylor had already debuted the song a week or so earlier during the final concert of the *Speak Now* tour in Auckland, and she told the audience: "I'm really excited about it...but, I mean, you don't think I'd get in trouble if I played it now? Probably not, right?"

Vulture - "With guitars seemingly ripped straight out of 1998 alt-rock radio, this one's most interesting now as a preview of Swift's *Red* sound"; **Rolling Stone** - "Finally, her long-overdue metal move"; **NME** - "Sees Swift go stadium rock. Too bad hair-whipping number's repetitive chorus begins to grate".

121

The soundtrack album, *The Hunger Games: Songs from District 12 and Beyond,* was released on March 16th 2012 and debuted at #1 on the Hot 200. The following week it sold 100,000 digital copies, making it the highest one-week total for a theatrically released soundtrack in digital history. 'Safe & Sound' would become the most successful of the album's 16 tracks, and both of Taylor's songs would be nominated for awards.

Taylor's final honour of 2011 came when *Billboard* named her their Woman of the Year, having "already made a major impact on music and has been an incredible role model for aspiring singer/songwriters and young women everywhere."

It had certainly been an incredible twelve months for the 22-year-old singer, and in her Christmas message for her fans she wrote: "I hope they feel appreciated by me. My life would look nothing like this without them."

Lady in Red

"I look back on this as my true breakup album, every other album has flickers of different things. But this was an album that I wrote specifically about pure, absolute to the core, heartbreak"

Losing out with Les Mis

2012 would be the year that Taylor's bright star would go nebula. The world tour, soon to be coming to an end, had exceeded all expectations, and, together with the sale of her first three albums, had made her a very rich woman, named by *Forbes* as the highest-earning artist under 30, overtaking Rihanna and Justin Bieber, and also heading *Billboard*'s list of the Top 40 money makers in music.

Magazines were falling over each other to get her face on their cover, starting in February with *Vogue's* "Cool new look for America's Sweetheart". Designers were clamouring to dress her for the upcoming awards ceremonies, and companies from around the world were offering her fortunes to promote their products. Even film companies were now sending her scripts.

Taylor took the term "fashion icon" with a pinch of salt, and explained to *Vogue*: "I don't ever want to be that person whose self-image overtakes who they are." Whether she liked it or not, Taylor was now well and truly pop royalty.

In January, Taylor went to see The Civil Wars perform in a sold-out concert at the Ryman Auditorium in Nashville, and was invited by the duo to join them on stage for an impromptu performance of 'Safe & Sound'.

That same day, it was revealed by CBS News that she had been approached by film director Tom Hooper for a role in his new movie *Les Misérables,* which starred Hugh Jackman and would be out at the end of the year. In an interview for *Variety*, five years later, Taylor recalled: "[Hooper] called me in for Cossette [eventually played by Amanda Seyfried]. And I said, 'I'm not a soprano, but I loved Éponine's song ['On My Own'], so can I audition for Éponine?' I went through the whole process of flying to London. I did a screen test with Eddie Redmayne and pretended to die in his arms, which was fabulous, but I didn't get the role and [Samantha Barks], who played it on the West End, got the role and was absolutely phenomenal. But I had a great time with it. I just thought, if I ever got a chance to work with him, I know that would be a great experience."

The chance to work with Tom Hooper in a musical would be coming her way again in a few years, but with results no one could have really predicted.

Hitting back

The Grammy Awards took place in Los Angeles on February 12th, the day after the tragic death of Whitney Houston in that very town. Although the night belonged to Adele, winning all six of her nominations, Taylor netted the awards for Best Country Song and Best Country Solo Performance (both for 'Mean'), but lost out on Best Country Album to Lady Antebellum's *Own the Night*.

Accepting her award for 'Mean', Taylor said: "There is no feeling quite like writing a song about someone who is mean to you and makes your life miserable and winning a Grammy for it." While performing the song, it was noticeable that on her banjo were scrawled the lyrics: "Someday...I'll be big enough so you can't hit me." As well as a standing ovation, she received an apologetic review from *Time* magazine: "Tonight, Swift delivered her comeback on-key and with a vengeance...OK, Taylor. This is a great song, and you're younger, cuter, and more talented than any professional critic who has ever cut you down. You win."

Meanwhile, at least where social media was concerned, the focus on Taylor seemed to be back on her love life, with the inevitable rumours of a relationship with Zac Efron, her voiceover co-star on *The Lorax*. At the premiere of the movie on March 2nd, the two of them had performed a "dance-dare" on the orange carpet to the song 'Sexy and I Know It'. However, all rumours were dispelled when they both appeared as guests on *The Ellen de Generes Show* on February 21st, where the mischievous host called them "a cute couple."

During the show they were handed guitars as they sat on the couch and sang Foster the People's 'Pumped Up Kicks', with Taylor revealing she had taught Zac a few chords on the guitar. With Ellen still referring to them as a couple, she quickly pointed out: "We are not a couple. He's awesome, we are not a couple though. You hear people get together when they're shooting movies, co-stars. But not, like, animated co-stars - You know what I'm saying? Oh my God, as we were recording our voiceovers on separate coasts, we really connected" (although they changed the lyrics especially for the show).

Also on the social media radar was Taylor's relationship with film and television actor Dianna Agron, best known for a role as the snotty high school cheerleader in *Glee*. The pair of them had been friends for a while, seen together at Dianna's circus-themed 26th birthday party in Los Angeles and at a lavish party for Hollywood star Shirley MacLaine at the Beverly Hills Hilton and then dining at their famous Polo Lounge.

After being seen together wearing matching floral dresses at a West Hollywood restaurant, Dianna was asked by chat show host Jimmy Kimmel if they were actually dating, and she replied: "That would be great. Wouldn't that be juicy?" and then, turning to the camera, she blew a kiss and purred "Hi, Taylor."

Woman of the Year

On March 2nd, the final leg of the *Speak Now* tour resumed in Perth, Australia, and ended in Auckland, New Zealand, on the 18th. The support artist for these last concerts was the Nashville band Hot Chelle Rae. The *New Zealand Herald* spoke for many Kiwis when it claimed: "We're unlikely to witness a show like that again in a long, long time. Maybe ever." The tour had a total of 110 two-hour shows and a setlist of some 17 songs, had sold an estimated 1.6 million tickets and grossed $123.7 million.

Returning to the States, Taylor received the Nickelodeon Kids' Choice Big Help Award for her charity work and had it presented to her by First Lady Michelle Obama. Unbeknown to many, Taylor had made a number of donations, including $75,000 to her old Hendersonville High School for refurbishing their auditorium, and an incredible $4 million pledged to fund a new education centre at Nashville's Country Music Hall of Fame and Museum. Other sizeable donations went to charities such as Elton John's AIDS Foundation, Oxfam and Unicef.

Taylor would always be paying it forward for her success.

As well as having the honour of meeting the First Lady at the awards ceremony, Taylor had also met 18-year-old Harry Styles, the charismatic member of British band One Direction, who, after shooting to overnight superstardom on *The X Factor,* had signed a £2 million record deal with Simon Cowell. They would soon be recording their second album, and would go on to claim the record of having their first two albums debut at #1 on the Hot 200 chart.

During the show, Taylor was seen dancing with her friend Selena Gomez along to the band's performance of 'What Makes You Beautiful', and apparently told Selena's boyfriend and fellow-nominee Justin Bieber how much she liked the British heartthrob. Rumour has it that she then went backstage to meet the band and jokingly fanned herself when being introduced. Following their meeting, Styles told *Seventeen* magazine that the attraction was reciprocal: "She honestly couldn't be a sweeter person. She's genuinely nice and extremely talented, and she deserves everything she has."

It may be possible that the two of them started a discreet relationship while he was still in the country. If true, it would turn out to be short lived, as the band soon flew off to begin their Australian tour, with one source telling Radar Online that Styles had promised Taylor he wouldn't see anyone else while he was away. Understandably, she was heartbroken when later shown pictures of him kissing model Emma Ostilly, who had appeared in one of the band's earlier videos. The source also revealed: "Taylor was crushed over Harry the first time they dated, and like she always does, she penned a song about him to deal with her broken heart." Her feelings that, somehow, she could give him another chance and still make the relationship work inspired the song 'I Knew You Would Be Trouble', which would appear on her new album.

By early November, Taylor and Styles would once again be in the media spotlight, but in the meantime, any disappointment she may have harboured was soothed by the fact that she would soon be involved in a summer romance that involved a member of one of America's most famous dynasties, the Kennedys.

At the beginning of April, the night after meeting both Michelle and Styles, Taylor attended the ACM Awards in Nashville, and, with her parents in attendance, was presented with the prestigious award for Entertainer of the Year for the second year running.

That same month, it was reported in *Variety* that Taylor was being tipped for the role of singer Joni Mitchell in a proposed movie, *Girls Like Us*, based on the best-selling book by Shelia Weller about the lives of Joni, Carole King and Carly Simon. Although Alison Pill had already auditioned for the role of Carole, Taylor revealed that nothing was set in stone and clearly many scripts had made their way into her hands: "I've been reading scripts for five years, and you just don't know what ones are going to get greenlit and which ones aren't, so I can't talk about it unless it's the real thing." Sad to say, she heard nothing more of the project.

In May, Taylor made a personal phone call and sent flowers to the family of Sgt Wade Wilson who had recently been killed in Afghanistan. Wilson was a huge fan of the singer, and, according to a comrade who messaged Taylor, "even slept with a poster of you in between our beds." Although unable to attend his funeral, Taylor asked if she could wear his dog tags in her next video to show her support for his military service.

At the Billboard Music Awards in Las Vegas that same month, Taylor received the award for Woman of the Year, introduced by the legendary Kris Kristofferson, who said: "At an age when most of us are thinking just about what to do with our lives, Taylor's become one of the most successful recording artists in the history of music, and she's done it the old fashioned away, by always speaking her truth, beautifully."

But success didn't always go Taylor's way. At the CMT Awards in Nashville in June, she lost out in the nominations for the music videos of 'Safe & Sound' and 'Ours'.

Taylor and the Kennedys

According to Yahoo.com, it all started with Taylor being a long-time admirer of the Kennedy dynasty, and she had even written a song on her new album inspired by Bobby and Ethel Kennedy's courtship in the "summer of 45". Hearing that Taylor was a fan, Ethel's daughter, Rory, got in touch with her people in the summer of 2011 and asked for concert tickets for herself and her daughters. When they met the singer backstage, Taylor asked if it would be possible to meet Ethel in person, and she did so a short time later.

In January 2012, Rory had invited Taylor to the premiere of the documentary about her mother, and whilst there, she was invited by Ethel to spend a fourth of July weekend at the Kennedys' home at Hyannis on Cape Cod. According to the biography *The Kennedy Heirs*, Taylor at first was seen to spent a lot of time with aspiring actor Patrick Schwarzenegger, the son of Arnie and Maria Shriver, although a romance was never confirmed. Once Patrick had departed, Taylor's attention turned to his cousin, Conor Kennedy, grandson of Robert F Kennedy, whose mother had committed suicide a few months before. Taylor was seen as "a real shoulder to cry on" and really smitten with Conor.

By mid-August it seemed the romance was in full swing. A source revealed to the *New York Times*: "I was a little surprised. It's been two weeks and he's in love, he thinks of her as his girlfriend - not just friends or dating. He calls her his girlfriend." The couple were often pictured hand-in-hand and kissing around beautiful Cape Cod and Nantucket, putting Swifties into a frenzy on Twitter. A *New York Post* insider commented: "Taylor has a really generous and positive spirit, and the whole Kennedy family loves her. It has been a very difficult time for Conor, losing his mother, and Taylor has great positive energy. She is definitely helping him through this."

When work commitments took her away from the Cape, it was not unusual for Taylor to send her private jet to pick Conor up so he could be with her.

The couple had also reportedly gatecrashed the Boston wedding of Bobby's granddaughter, Kyle Kennedy, to Liam Kerry, after being told by Kyle's mother Victoria that Taylor's presence would no doubt draw attention away from the bride. They arrived anyway and sure enough all attention was on Taylor. According to her stepmother, who confirmed the story on *Today*, Victoria asked Taylor to leave, but said the singer "seemed to look right past me" and she felt as if she was "talking to a ghost." To diffuse an awkward situation, the couple left. Apparently, there was an argument later with Taylor, who still thought they had been invited. Taylor's spokesperson denied Victoria's story and said that there was an invitation and that the bride had welcomed Taylor to the party. Taylor got in touch with Ethel and cleared the air, saying it was all just a misunderstanding.

Within a matter of weeks, Taylor had bought a $4.9 million seven-bed oceanfront mansion near the Kennedy compound, but the move had made Conor nervous, and according to one of his friends, he was feeling she was getting "a little too attached", spending all that money to be near him. According to one anonymous source, it was claimed that Taylor had been seen scribbling "Taylor Swift Kennedy" in her notebook, "just to see how it looked."

By early October, Taylor's fairytale romance had come to an abrupt end. While one of Conor's friends claimed: "She was more obsessed with the idea of dating a Kennedy, than the actual Kennedy she was dating", another source offered in *Us Weekly*: "They quietly parted ways a while ago. It was just a distance thing. No hard feelings. They're fine."

Taylor sold her Hyannis home seven months later, banking a million-dollar profit.

"A thirst for learning"

With broken relationships very much in the back of Taylor's mind, it was time to focus all her energies on completing the new album. Although she was happy to be working again with producer Nathan Chapman, she felt that by following the same songwriting formula that was evident on *Speak Now,* it would "diminish her creativity." In an interview for yahoo.com she explained: "When I was approaching the idea of making this album...it took two years. In the first year, I wrote a lot of things on my own and kind of produced them with Nathan the way that we always do things. And my label came to me and they said, 'You're done. This record is finished. Congratulations.' And I looked at my label head, Scott Borchetta, and I said, 'I just don't think we are. Because I think it's good, but I don't think it's different enough. And I don't think we're covering enough new ground here'."

Taylor elaborated that when making the fourth album you have two choices, either doing things the way they had been done before, or switching and going "outside your comfort zone." Taylor had always been eager to see and understand how different producers worked in the studio: "I didn't want the albums to have a definitive sound that was all reminiscent of each other. But the emotions I felt in the last two years were all very singular. Each one of them felt so different from every other feeling. It was very scattered all over the place. So, I wanted the album to reflect how those feelings felt. And the way that the album ended up working, it ended up being a cohesive thing. It ended up working in that they are all woven with the same kind of lyrical stories."

With this in mind, Taylor saw the new album as a statement of her "thirst for learning" the craft of studio production and embarked on reworking the songs, experimenting with different styles, and engaging with musicians she admired so she could learn all their techniques. But as a songwriter, she also had to prioritise the lyrics over production and find the best way to translate her emotions into a song. That process would always precede the method of production. Unlike *Speak Now,* she would also invite co-writers, something that had worked so well on *Fearless,* where she would outline her emotions to other writers and then gain ideas on how to convey her stories.

Taylor explained the reason for the album's title, *Red*, and how it epitomised all the different emotions she had been experiencing in the "semi-toxic" relationships in the last two years: "All those emotions - spanning from intense love, intense frustration, jealousy, confusion - in my mind, all those emotions are red. There's nothing in between; there is nothing beige about any of those feelings."

It was beyond doubt that with this album, Taylor's lyrics would be scrutinised more than ever before, due to the number of past relationships. She revealed: "I think what I've learned recently is that it's not…heartbreak that inspires my songs. It's individual people that come into my life. I've had relationships with people that were really substantial and meant a lot to me, but I couldn't write a song about that person for some reason. Then again, you'll meet someone that comes into your life for two weeks and you write an entire record about them."

The first song Taylor wrote for *Red* was as far back as late 2010, when 'All Too Well' was penned during a rehearsal for the world tour. Since that time, it had been a test of her creativity to get the desired sounds for the songs she had written. She asked Borchetta to bring in top Swedish producer and songwriter Max Martin, the man behind hits such as Britney Spears' 'Baby One More Time' and the Backstreet Boys' 'I Want It That Way'. Taylor had always been impressed by the way his songs "can just land a chorus", and added: "He comes at you and hits you and it's a chorus - all caps, with exclamation points."

Joining Martin was his frequent collaborator and fellow-Swede, Shellback (aka Karl Shuster), who had just co-produced Maroon 5's multi-platinum 'Moves Like Jagger'. Martin and Shellback would bring their trademark electronic production to the several songs they would be working on. Taylor and Borchetta also brought in experienced producers Dann Huff, Dan Wilson, Jeff Bhasker, Butch Walker, and Jacknife Lee for some of the tracks.

Taylor would end up writing more than 30 songs for *Red*, with 16 making the final cut, 10 of which she was sole writer. She was also thinking ahead about how the songs would be performed in concert. The visuals were becoming an integral part of her songwriting process.

With the release of *Red* pencilled in for October, it was time to begin promoting some of the new songs. But before that came the Teen Choice Awards in Los Angeles on July 22nd, in which she won in all the categories she had been nominated in - Female Artist, Country Music Artist - Female, Country Song (for 'Sparks Fly') and Best Single-Female (for 'Eyes Open').

September saw the promotional schedule get into full swing. On the 6th Taylor attended the MTV Awards in Los Angeles, and for the show's finale performed a television debut of her sensational new song, 'We Are Never Ever Getting Back Together', which had been released the previous month, along with the music video, which was now being replicated on stage. Dressed in the theme of her upcoming album, she danced around the stage wearing a red-and-white striped sweater, classic black shorts, and bright-red sneakers, and throwing on a pair of black sunglasses to give her that extra attitude.

Ronan

The following day, the mood changed dramatically when Taylor took part in the charitable telethon *Stand Up to Cancer*, broadcast on all four major networks. Taylor had written a song called 'Ronan', based on a blog called "Rockstar Ronan" by Maya Thompson, whose son had died of neuroblastoma in May 2011, a few days short of his fourth birthday. Maya had continued the blog after his death by writing heartbreaking letters to her late son and raising both money and awareness for childhood cancer. Taylor heard about her blog and contacted her by voicemail: "Hey Maya, this is Taylor Swift. There's something coming up that I really wanted to talk to you about and just kinda get your ideas on…"

With Maya's permission, Taylor wrote the song, using Maya's quotes from her blog and giving her credit as co-writer. The pair met in October 2011 when Taylor invited Maya to come to one of her concerts in Arizona, and it was there that she first told her about how her blogs had inspired her to write and produce the song. Maya described her reaction later: "The tears started pouring down my cheeks as soon as I heard her say those words. But her words didn't stop there. Not only did she write a song for you, but she wanted to know if it would be alright to perform it on the nationally televised show."

In one of the most moving songs of her career, Taylor's emotional performance received universal acclaim. Tim McGraw closed the show with his own poignant song, 'Live Like You Were Dying', a tribute to his father who had also died of cancer.

Ronan *****
(Taylor Swift - Maya Thompson)
Single
Label - Big Machine
Produced - Taylor Swift
Released - September 8 2012
Chart peak positions
 Hot 100 #16; Hot Digital Songs #2; Hot Country Songs #34
RIAA Certification - Gold

Released on iTunes immediately after the broadcast, 'Ronan' was downloaded a quarter of a million times in its first week alone, and debuted at #2 on the Hot Digital Songs chart, being blocked from the top spot by Taylor's own 'We Are Never Ever Getting Back Together'. All proceeds were given to Taylor's Charitable Fund.

Rolling Stone - "[It] movingly channels a mother's heartbreak and loss"; **Arizona Republic** - "Displaying an empathy, a depth and a level of emotional maturity that place this poignant ballad clear at the opposite end of the artistic spectrum from her latest hit… 'Ronan' may well be her finest hour as an artist"; **Vulture** - "One of the most empathetic songs in Swift's catalogue, as well as her most reliable tearjerker".

Taylor would remain an advocate for children with cancer and maintain a close relationship with Maya and her family.

A week after the telethon, Taylor made her first appearance in South America when she flew to Rio de Janeiro for a televised free concert called *Taylor Swift: Showcase Brazil*. During the show, she performed a selection of her hits as well as a spectacular duet of 'Long Live' with Brazilian country singer Paula Fernandes. A promo single of them performing the song had been released in March 2012, along with a music video showing them seemingly performing together, but actually connected by satellite from their respective countries. Fernandes was also given co-writing credits for adding verses in Portuguese. The single peaked at #5 on Brazil's Hot 100 Airplay chart.

Three years later, a spokesperson for Taylor would contact BuzzFeed News to refute viral rumours on social media, saying that "there is absolutely no truth" to reports that Taylor had declined invitations to play concerts in Brazil because her mother wouldn't let her perform "in third world countries". Nevertheless, it would be July 2020 before she returned to perform in South America.

Later in the month, Taylor made her debut at the popular iHeartRadio Music Festival in Las Vegas. Following a high-octane performance from Pink, Taylor stepped out in a sequinned top, which was later swapped to an equally glittery dress, to play some of her best-known songs. In October, she was in London to promote the imminent release of *Red*, and also appeared once again at BBC Radio 1's Teen Awards at Wembley Arena, with performances of 'You Belong with Me', 'Love Story', 'Red', and 'We Are Never Ever Getting Back Together'. A week later she performed the last song as a guest on UK's *The X Factor*.

Returning home the next day, the singer delivered an intimate acoustic set for students of Harvey Mudd College at the Bridges Auditorium in Claremont. The performance was recorded for the televised series *VH1 Storytellers* to be aired the following month. During the show, Taylor shared personal stories and candidly answered questions from students. The concert was the grand prize in an online voting competition "Taylor Swift on Campus" won by Harvey Mudd.

Sad, Beautiful, Tragic

On October 22nd, after two years of writing and recording, the long-anticipated album *Red* was released.

In the liner notes, Taylor writes: "There's something to be proud of about moving on and realising that real love shines golden like starlight, and doesn't fade or spontaneously combust. Maybe I'll write a whole album about that kind of love if I ever find it, but this album is about the other kinds of love that I've recently fallen in and out of. Love that was treacherous, sad, beautiful, and tragic. But most of all, this record is about love that was **red**".

Boy, were her fans ready for this one…

RED
Label - Big Machine Records
Produced - Taylor Swift, Nathan Chapman, Jeff Bhasker, Dann Huff, Jacknife Lee,

Max Martin, Shellback, Butch Walker & Dan Wilson
Released - October 22 2012
Singles - 7
Chart peak positions
  Hot 200 #1; Country Albums #1; UK #1; Canada #1; Australia #1; NZ #1
RIAA - 7 x Platinum
Selected awards and nominations
2013 CMA Awards - Album of the Year (nominated)
2013 ACM Wards - Album of the Year (nominated)
2013 AMA Awards - Favourite Country Album (won)
2013 Billboard Music Awards - Top Album (won)
2013 Billboard Music Awards -Top Country Album (won)
2013 Canadian Country Music Associations Awards - Top Selling Album (won)
2014 Grammys - Album of the Year (nominated)
2014 Grammys - Best country album (nominated)
2014 CMA Awards (Australia) - Top Selling International Album of the Year (won)

State of Grace ***
(Taylor Swift)
Promo single
Recorded - Blackbird Studios, Nashville TN
Produced - Nathan Chapman & Taylor Swift
Released - October 16 2012
Chart peak positions
  Hot 100 #13; Country Digital Songs #36; UK #36; Canada #9; Australia #44;
  NZ #20
RIAA Certification - Gold

For all its paradoxes and contradictions, this perfect introduction to the album can also be looked on as its conclusion, with a warning that love can be both wonderfully good and devastatingly bad, dependent on all its inherent complexities. True love, after all, is worth fighting for. Appearing on *Good Morning America,* Taylor explained: "I wrote this song about when you first fall in love with someone - the possibilities, kind of thinking about the different ways that it could go. It's a really big sound. To me, this sounds like the feeling of falling in love in an epic way." Some commentators interpret clues found in the song as being about ex-boyfriend Jake Gyllenhaal.

With its full-blown stadium-rock intro and lyrics full of romance and sentiment, seldom before had one of her songs been so rich and heavy, and it was praised by most reviewers as being a marked departure from Taylor's usual country pop, with its much broader sound being evidence of her taking inspiration from alternative rock bands. The song was released as the fourth and final single off the album, and the only promo that didn't have an official release.

Add two stars for the acoustic version included as a bonus track on the deluxe edition, which brings a whole new dimension to the song.

The lyric hint is "I Love You Doesn't Count After Goodbye".

Los Angeles Times - "It has a strong U2 streak to it, with feedback- and echo-drenched guitars and some of her most for-the-rafters vocals yet... It's the least obviously 're-inventing' single from the album so far"; **MTV** - "Its sparkling production and powerhouse vocals definitely has the record in the realm of pop, but Taylor's country twang isn't too far behind either"; **Entertainment Weekly** - "While Swift's songs are usually quite lyrically driven (and this is a good thing), 'State of Grace' is more about the build - that dawning sense of triumphant wonder that accompanies love - and the extended instrumental breaks provide a more forceful, mature impact than Swift's standard sass"; **Billboard** - "Eloquently and effortlessly extends Swift's genre reach"; **Vulture** - "Big, expansive rock track, which sent dozens of *Joshua Tree* fans searching for their nearest pair of headphones. Another surprise: that she never tried to sound like this again. Having proven she could nail it on her first try, Swift set out to find other giants to slay"; **NME** - "One of her grandest love songs in arena-rock drag".

Red ***
(Taylor Swift)
5th Single
Recorded - Blackbird Studios, Nashville TN
Produced - Taylor Swift, Dann Huff & Nathan Chapman
Released - June 21 2013
Chart peak positions
  Hot 100 #6# Country Songs #2; Country Airplay #7; Hot Digital #2;
  UK #26; Canada #5# Canada Country #17
RIAA Certification - 2 x Platinum
Selected awards & nominations
2014 CMT Music Awards - Female Video of the Year (nominated)
2014 CMT Music Awards - Video of the Year (nominated)
2014 BMI Awards - Publisher of the Year (won)

According to Taylor's journal, the album's title song was written on a red-eye flight to Nashville on September 7th 2011 and recorded the following day. As Taylor explained, the song compares different emotions to colours: "This relationship that I had that was, like, the worst thing ever and the best thing ever at the same time. I was writing this song and I was thinking about correlating the colours to the different feelings I went through. You have the great part of red, like the red emotions that are daring and bold and passion and love and affection. And then you have on the other side of the spectrum, jealousy and anger and frustration..."

The lyric hint here is "SAG", which could be interpreted as Swift and Gyllenhaal, or maybe even Sagittarius, their mutual star sign. Others have speculated that it's about John Mayer, who has a neurological condition that makes one see colours based on the intensity of different sounds. Award-winning Nashville producer Dan Huff was drafted in to work on this and two other tracks, with Taylor having admired his work with Rascal Flatts and Keith Urban. Like the previous track, the acoustic version found on the Deluxe Edition is sublime and worth an extra star.

The music video was directed by Kenny Jackson and features footage from the *Red* Tour. It was released on July 3rd 2013.

Taste of Country - "Songs like 'Red' add depth to the young star's catalog. As always, the magic isn't necessarily in the voice, it's in the inspired interpretation of brilliant lyrics"; **Billboard** - "The song hinges on the electronic 'R-r-red' that punctuates the chorus; for some, it's a deal breaker, but others may find it a bold detail"; **NME** - "The hair-whipping, chorus-screaming title track...is an adrenaline-charged ride".

132

Treacherous ****
(Taylor Swift - Dan Wilson)
Recorded - Ballroom West, LA; Marlay Studios, North Hollywood
Produced - Dan Wilson
Released - Oct 22 2012
Chart peak positions
  Hot 100 Bubbling Under #2; Hot Country Songs #26; Alternative
  Streaming Songs #40; Canada #65

The perfect bridge between the opening track and the one that follows. Taylor writes about how she would fight to protect a relationship that she knows is dangerous. It was co-written and produced by Dan Wilson, front man of the band Semisonic, who had also recently shared the writing credits for Adele's massive breakthrough hit, 'Someone Like You'. Taylor already had a melody in mind, but together they turned it into something quite special, and just when it was deemed completed, they gave the song an added dimension with a much rockier chorus, contrasting superbly with the almost-whispered verses that *Billboard* described as "hushed, confessional beauty".

Talking to *Taste of Country,* Taylor explained: "We came up with a way to say, you know, 'This is dangerous and I realise that I might get hurt if I go through with this, if I move forward with you. But…but I want to.' You know? It's like that kind of conflicted feeling of it being a risk every time you fall in love - especially with certain types of people." Wilson recalled the pleasure of working with Taylor: "An interesting quality, objectively speaking, was how on fire she was, the clarity she had. She was so open and excited about the things I would add. She works at a very high level of positivity, and that is rare."

In an interview for *USA Today,* Taylor described the song as detailing a relationship that could only "end in fiery, burning wreckage", but, despite that, had a "magnetic draw that doesn't really let up - you walk toward it anyway". Rumours abound about who she is referring to, with John Mayer and Jake Gyllenhaal again likely candidates. Some, however, link it to Harry Styles.

The lyric hint is "Won't Stop till It's Over".

Billboard - "The guitar strum and percussion sit at a steady simmer before flaring up at the finale - an emotional moment to be sure, but one that unfortunately steers away from the hushed, confessional beauty of the verses"; **Rolling Stone** - "Taylor braves the ski slopes of love, with a seething acoustic guitar that finally detonates halfway through"; **Hollywood Reporter** - "Her nearly whispered vocals neatly put across the tentativeness of her sensuality in falling for a bad boy"; **NME** - "[It] eventually grows to a subtle roar, and details a pairing that's gradually unravelling like a ball of twine"; **Vulture** - "Swift has rarely been so tactile as on this intimate ballad, seemingly constructed entirely out of sighs".

I Knew You Were Trouble *****
(Taylor Swift - Max Martin - Shellback)
3rd Single
Recorded - MXM Studios, Stockholm; Conway Studios LA
Produced - Max Martin & Shellback
Released - December 10 2012
Chart peak positions
  Hot 100 #2; AC #5; Adult Top 40 #1; Country Airplay #55; Dance/Mix Show
  Airplay #18; Mainstream Top 40 #1; Rhythmic #21; UK #2; Canada #2;

Australia #3; Japan #51
RIAA Certification - 7 x Platinum
Selected awards and nominations
2013 MTV Video Music Awards - Best Female Video (won)
2013 MTV Video Music Awards - Video of the Year (nominated)
2013 Teen Choice Awards - Choice Single by a Female Artist (nominated)
2013 Radio Disney Music Awards - Song of the Year (won)
2014 BMI Awards - Award-Winning Song (won)
2014 BMI Awards - Publisher of the Year (won)

Taylor expresses her guilt and blames herself for a toxic relationship destined to fail. She explained the song's inspiration to MTV News: "It's about, like, knowing the second you see someone, like, Oh, this is going to be dangerous, but look at me going in there anyway. I think that for me, it was the first time I ever noticed that in myself, like when you are curious about something you know might be bad for you, but you know you are going to go for it anyway, because, if you don't, you'll have greater regrets about not seeing where that would go."

The song's hidden message, "When You Saw My Dancing", is strongly rumoured to be about Harry Styles and their first meeting at the Nickelodeon Kids' Choice Awards in March, when she was seen dancing along to One Direction's performance. Speculation about it referring to Styles was strengthened at the Brit Awards, where he was due to attend, and talking about performing the song there, she said: "Well, it's not hard to access that emotion when the person the song is directed at is standing by the side of the stage watching."

However, Taylor later said that she wrote this song and 'Treacherous' about the same person, fuelling speculation that it could be about either John Meyer or Jake Gyllenhaal.

While on *Good Morning America,* Taylor said: "It's a song about, kind of, being frustrated with yourself because here you are heartbroken and you knew when you first saw that person, you saw all these red flags and you just went for it, anyway. So, shame on me."

In a dramatic move from country to pop, the multi-award-winning song was cited as the "most radical sonic innovation on the album", with its collision of r&b, electric pop, punk-rock, dubstep and dance hall, mixed together into a "country-fused feast" of a record, and, arguably, Taylor's best example of her ability to jump genres with ease.

Taylor had first written the melody on the piano and had taken it to producers Martin and Shellback, who then worked with her to "infuse a little bit of dubstep." Taylor had been an admirer of dubstep since listening to some of Ed Sheeran's music. As a result, the song "sounds just as chaotic as the feeling was when I wrote it."

Explaining to *Time* magazine, she said: "I didn't even know that that's really what we were doing with the track - I just knew I wanted it to sound a certain way; and that's what people have been calling it." She also revealed to *Billboard*: "[The] song was a big signal flare. When I did something like that, that I thought people were going to be freaked out over, and it ended up spending seven weeks at No.1 on the pop charts, I felt like I had tried on something new that fit really well."

The song became the third single from the album, and the cd was sold by itself or as part of a package that included a t-shirt, a *Red* drawstring backpack, and a spiral notebook.

New York Times - "[The production is] a wrecking ball, changing the course not just of the song, but also of Ms Swift's career"; **Hollywood Reporter** - "In essence, it's a great rock & roll song - and an emotional one, though the ear candy elements disguise that at first"; **Billboard** - "While it's not as smoothly executed as 'State of Grace', watching Swift try her hand at electro-country is darn entertaining"; **Vulture** - "The adventurous vocals and vivid lyrics keep the track from going off the rails"; **NME** - "Swift's most brilliantly bombastic release".

All Too Well *****
(Taylor Swift - Liz Rose)
Recorded - Pain in the Art Studios, Nashville TN
Produced - Taylor Swift & Nathan Chapman
Released - October 22 2012
Chart peak positions
  Hot 100 #80; Hot Country Songs #17; Country Airplay #58; Canada #59
RIAA Certification - Gold

The first song written for the album is still widely regarded as one of Taylor's best compositions and certainly her best collaboration with songwriter friend Liz Rose. This heart-wrenching, confessional melodrama came about after a six-month-long case of writing block following the painful breakup of a relationship. She told *USA Today*: "There's a kind of bad that gets so overpowering you can't even write about it."

As the album's emotional centrepiece, it portrays through vivid imagery the lingering memories, best and worst, of a lost relationship. In an interview for Pop Dust, Taylor revealed she had started writing the song during a soundcheck on the *Speak Now* tour: "I was just playing these chords over and over on stage and my band joined in and I went on a rant...I was going through a really hard time then, and my band joined in playing."

Taylor has always remarked that this song was the hardest to write on the album, saying: "It took me a really long time to filter through everything I wanted to put in the song without it being a 10-minute song, which you can't put on an album. I wanted a story that could work in the form of a song."

Taylor called on her old friend Liz Rose for help, saying, "Come on over, we've gotta filter this down." Liz later told *Rolling Stone* how she was preparing to move from Nashville to Dallas when she got the unexpected call from Taylor, who said to her: "I've got this thing and I really need you to help me with it. Can you write today? What are you doing today?" Liz then drove over to Taylor's house: "She had a story and she wanted to say something specific. She had a lot of information. I just let her go. She already had a melody and she started singing some words, and I started writing things down, saying 'Ok, let's use this, let's use that...It was the most emotional, in-depth song we've ever written'."

The song was originally 10-15 minutes long, but Liz helped her cut it down to "the important pieces" and a more album-friendly length. Even then, it would become the longest track on the album at 5.28 minutes.

Taylor's richly-detailed lyrics are mesmerisingly beautiful: memories of a symbolic old scarf; road trips and getting lost; autumn leaves dancing on a breeze, and dancing to the light of a refrigerator. This is Taylor at the very zenith of her songwriting craft.

According to some blogs, the hidden message in the lyrics, "Maple Lattes", refers to the coffees she and Jake Gyllenhaal had shared. Also, the scarf referenced in the song is likely to be about the one she was seen wearing in photographs taken of the couple together.

While introducing the song during her *Reputation* Tour, she told her fans how their relationship toward the song had meant as much to her as the song meant: "You turned this song into a collage of memories of watching you scream the words to this song, or seeing pictures that you post to me of you having written the words to this song in your diary, or you showing me your wrist and you have a tattoo of the lyrics to this song underneath your skin. And that is how you've changed the song 'All Too Well' for me."

The song did not, however, come without a little controversy. Folk singer Matt Nathanson claimed on Twitter that some of Taylor's lyrics had been taken from 'I Saw', a song he had written in 2003. Taylor was in fact a fan of his music, and she may have unintentionally "borrowed" his lyrics by having them in the back of her mind. Where he writes the following line, "…and I'll forget about you long enough to forget why I need you", Taylor's line is "…and I forget about you long enough to forget why I needed you".

Nathanson accused Taylor of being caught *Red*-handed, and in the tweet that was later deleted, he said: "She's definitely a fan…and now she's a thief." This resulted in a flood of angry tweets directed at him by Swifties, and he replied: "Come on, @taylorswift13 fans. Why ya gotta be so mean." Maybe the similarity is purely coincidental, so let's just leave it there.

Sadly, there was no music video made for this iconic song, but we still have several incredible live performances to treasure.

Rolling Stone - "So casually cruel in the name of being awesome…on the best day of your life you will never inspire a song as great as 'All Too Well', or write one"; **Bustle** - "'All Too Well' is one of those songs that's cathartic to listen to, whether you're singing along with Swift live at a concert or screaming the lyrics by yourself in the car"; **NME** - "Swift takes you on the entire journey of a relationship, and it's masterful - just as we've come to expect from her"; **Beyond the Stage** - "It's a beautiful masterpiece lyrically and vocally while it equally breaks your heart because you probably relate to it more than you want to"; **Billboard** - "Just like that, Swift snaps back to her core demographic"; **Vulture** - "This is Swift at her most literary, with a string of impeccably observed details that could have come out of a *New Yorker* short story".

22 ****
(Taylor Swift - Max Martin - Shellback)
4th Single
Recorded - MXM Studios, Stockholm; Conway Studios LA
Produced - Max Martin & Shellback
Released - March 12 2013
Chart peak positions

Hot 100 #20; AC #19; Adult Top 40 #9; Mainstream Top 40 #12; UK #9;
Canada #20; Australia #21; NZ #23
Selected awards & nominations
2015 BMI Awards - Award-Winning Song (won)
2015 BMI Awards - Publisher of the Year (won)

A joyful and romping synth-driven song about being young and confident, without any fears of getting older and having some "reckless" fun along the way. Apparently, the inspiration for writing the song came on a plane journey around the time of her 22nd birthday, and, in the album's booklet, the lyric hint namechecks four of her closest friends at the time - stylist Ashley Avignone, actor Dianna Agron, jewellery designer Claire Kislinger, and singer Selena Gomez, all of whom appear in the music video for the song, letting loose, and celebrating all the good things in their lives, and poking a little fun at some of the sadder times.

Taylor wrote: "For me, being 22 has been my favourite year of my life. I like all the possibilities of how you're still learning, but you know enough. You still know nothing, but you know that you know nothing. You're old enough to start planning your life, but you're young enough to know there are so many unanswered questions."

In an interview for radio host Ryan Seacrest, she revealed: "I wrote this about my friends, like finally I've got this amazing group of girlfriends and we tell each other everything, we're together all the time."

In 2012's *VH1Storytellers*, she said: "It's kind of like a message in a bottle, you write a song and you can send it out into the world and the person you wrote it about might hear it, and they might end up knowing what you think about them or how you feel about them."

The music video was directed by Anthony Mandler and was shot in Malibu in February 2013. It features Taylor having fun on trampolines and the beach and holding a house party for her celebrity friends. It had its debut on March 13th 2013.

Billboard - "Arguably Swift's most blatantly "pop" song of her career...Even when she's having fun, Swift is succinctly communicating conflicting emotions"; **Digital Spy** - "[Swift]continues to cross over into the pop charts with yet another snagging ditty...She may have already achieved more during her youth than most do in their lifetime, but with one more pop smash to add to their repertoire, it seems she's only just getting started"; **NME** - "A gargantuan cut of bubble-gum pop, and somehow Swift turned it into a milestone".

I Almost Do ***
(Taylor Swift)
Recorded - Pain in the Art Studios & Blackbird Studios, Nashville TN
Produced - Taylor Swift & Nathan Chapman
Released - October 22 2012
Chart peak positions
Hot 100 #65; Hot Country Songs #13; Canada #50

A ballad about the conflicting feelings of wanting to take someone back who keeps calling you for another chance, but knowing full well such a move would be ill-judged due to all the hurt it may bring. The song is often compared to the other album tracks 'We Are Never Ever Getting Back Together' and 'Sad Beautiful Tragic'. Taylor described her feelings in writing the track on her Paint the World Red website's secret clues: "So you're sitting there and wondering where they are

137

and hope that they think about you and that you're almost picking up the phone to call, but you just can't. I think I needed to write this song in order to not call that person actually. I think that writing the song was what I did instead of picking up the phone."

The song's "never, ever" refrain makes its second appearance on the album, having been heard on 'State of Grace', and would now make way for its grand appearance on the following track.

The lyric hint is "Wrote This Instead of Calling".

Rolling Stone - "For almost any other artist, 'I Almost Do' would have been a career peak. A *Red* slow jam that could have worked even better sped up into a punked-out rocker - though it's plenty affecting as is"; **Vulture** - "The kind of plaintive breakup song Swift could write in her sleep at this point of her career, with standout guitar work and impressive vulnerability in both lyrics and performance"; **Billboard** - "A slow grower, with shards of ace songwriting presenting themselves over time"; **NME** - "Exploring the internal battle between moving forward and looking back, the poignant ballad fuses country-pop with soft-rock, and the result is a brutally honest and quietly powerful song".

We Are Never Ever Getting Back Together ***
(Taylor Swift - Max Martin - Shellback)
1st Single
Recorded - MXM Studios, Stockholm; Conway Studios LA
Produced -Max Martin & Shellback
Released - August 13 2012
Chart peak positions
 Hot 100 #1; AC #10; Adult Top 40 #7; Country Airplay #13; Dance/Mix Show
 Airplay #21; Hot Country Songs #1; Mainstream Top 40 #2; UK #4; Canada #1;
 Australia #3; NZ #1; Japan #2
RIAA Certification - 6 x Platinum
Selected awards & nominations
2013 ACM Awards - Best Music Video (nominated)
2013 Billboard Music Awards - Top Streaming Song (Video) (nominated)
2013 Billboard Music Awards - Top Country Song (won)
2013 BMI Awards - Award-Winning Song (won)
2013 CMT Music Awards - Video of the Year (nominated)
2013 Grammys - Record of the Year (nominated)
2013 Teen Choice Awards - Choice Country Song (won)
2014 BMI Pop Awards - Award-Winning Song (won)

With the title speaking for itself, this crazy and catchy bubblegum-pop song is gleefully described by Taylor as "a really romantic song...touching and sensitive...to my lovely ex-boyfriend." She conceived the idea for the song along with collaborators Max Martin and Shellback after a friend of one of her ex-boyfriends apparently came to the studio and told her of the rumours circulating that the estranged couple were back together again. After he left, Taylor was asked by the producers what all this meant, and she described it as "break up, get back together, break up, get back together, just, ugh, the worst." When Taylor picked up her guitar and began singing "We are never ever..." the song took little time for them to develop it into the girl-power anthem it was destined to become.

Taylor recalled having a hilarious time recording the song, and that the two producers delivered just what she was looking for. Speaking to *USA Today*, she recalled: "It's a definitive portrait of how I felt when I finally stopped caring what my ex thought of me. He made me feel like I wasn't as good or as relevant as these hipster bands he listened to...So I made a song that I knew would absolutely drive him crazy when he heard it on the radio."

The song became the first in Taylor's career to top the Hot 100 and her eleventh top ten hit, tying with Kenny Rogers' record for the most top ten hits by a country artist in chart history. She also became the first female country artist to top the Hot 100 since Carrie Underwood's 'Inside Your Heaven' in 2005. On the Hot Country Songs chart, it became the first song to remain at #1 for three weeks since Rogers's 'Lady', which held that position for six weeks in 1980.

The lyric hint is "I Stopped Caring What You Thought".

One of Taylor's most popular videos, it was directed by Declan Whitebloom, who had previously worked on 'Mean' and 'Ours'. Filmed in one continuous shot, it features Taylor in a number of outfits, beginning with pyjamas, recounting her relationship with her ex-boyfriend (played by Noah Mills). Taylor recalled how she wanted it to be as "quirky as the song sounds...There's just knitting everywhere; there's just random woodland creatures popping up." It was premiered on several channels on August 30th 2012, and was the first of her videos shot in 4K resolution.

Rolling Stone - "A perfect three-minute teen tantrum"; **Billboard** - "Swift has tossed out a lead single that's at once bold and familiar"; **Country Universe** - "If she'd downplayed the sarcastic delivery and grating vocal runs, this would be a decent record. As it is, it's only listenable for its sheer audacity, a novelty that wears off quickly after a handful of listens"; **Entertainment Weekly** - "Sounds like a brighter, more-polished Avril Lavigne tune, with an undeniable, instantly catchy hook...Sure, it isn't very country...but somehow I doubt her loyal fanbase will mind - they'll be too busy singing along"; **Vulture** - "Like all hyper-efficient products it feels like a visitor from some cold algorithmic future: The sense of joy here is so perfectly engineered that you get the sense it did not come entirely from human hands".

Stay Stay Stay ***
(Taylor Swift)
Recorded - Blackbird Studios, Nashville TN
Produced - Taylor Swift & Nathan Chapman
Released – October 22 2012
Chart peak positions
  Hot 100 #91; Hot Country Songs #24; Canada #70

Taylor again longing to find true love and imagining what a perfect relationship would be like, and how they would make up following a fight. She based the daydreaming song on what she had seen of real relationships not being perfect: "There are moments where you're sick of that person, you get into a stupid fight, [but] it's still worth it to stay in it. There's something about it that you can't live without. In the bridge it says, 'I'd like to hang out with you for my whole life', and I think that's what's probably the key to finding the one, you just want to hang out with them forever."

The song serves as a perfect counterpoint to the previous track, as it describes "how amazing it is to meet someone new."

The lyric hint is "Daydreaming About Real Love".

Vulture - "Swift broke out her southern accent one last time for this attempt to homespun folk, which is marred by production that's so clean it's practically antiseptic"; **NME** - "Atop chronically catchy ukulele, she details a more generous kind of love that's still worth fighting for".

The Last Time (featuring Gary Lightbody) **
(Taylor Swift - Gary Lightbody - Jacknife Lee)
7th Single
Recorded - The Garage, Topanga Cyn, CA
Produced - Jacknife Lee
Released - November 4 2013
Chart peak positions
  Alternative Streaming Songs #49; UK #25; Canada #73

Looked at from the perspective of both sides of a long-standing but failing relationship, Taylor trades verses with Snow Patrol's Gary Lightbody in a song that relates the "vicious cycles of both heartbreak and forgiveness." The hidden message "LA on Your Break" is maybe a hint that the breakup occurred with her while he was taking time out in Los Angeles, and thereby bringing Jake Gyllenhaal forward as a suspect, as it looks like he was doing just that, promoting a movie, rather than being with Taylor for her birthday.

Speaking to NPR, Taylor said: "The idea was based on this experience I had with someone who was kind of this unreliable guy. You never know when he's going to leave, you never know when he's going to come back, but he always does come back...He's saying, 'This is the last time I'm going to do this to you', and she's saying, 'This is the last time I'm asking you this: Don't do this again'."

Produced by Jacknife Lee, noted for his work with Snow Patrol and U2, the emotional tension between the two characters is intensified by the atmospheric use of solemn strings and bass, which "feels like a worn-out beat that drags on to represent that sinking feeling."

The music video, directed by Terry Richardson, uses footage of the *Red* Tour concert in Sacramento on August 27th 2013. It had its premiere on Vevo and YouTube on November 15th 2013.

PopCrush - "They go the darkly romantic route on this song. It's the most mature and adult contemporary track on the record, and if worked correctly by her label, it could introduce Swift to a whole other world of fans and radio programmers, not to mention injecting her with a dose of credibility. It's also sort of epic"; **Taste of Country** - "[The album's] only pure skip-ahead moment"; **Vulture** - "Feels about ten minutes long"; **Rolling Stone** - "Unfortunately, their voices don't mesh at all".

Holy Ground****
(Taylor Swift)
Recorded - Enormous Studios, LA
Produced - Jeff Bhasker
Released - October 22 2012
Chart peak positions
  Hot 100 Bubbling Under #12#; Hot Country Songs #32; Alternative Streaming
  Songs #64; Canada #89

Taylor reminisces about a lost relationship and the "holy ground" on which they shared memories - memories that are still safe and sacred, not deemed as just being wasted time, and mistakes made are just lessons to be learned. When she started writing the song, Taylor invited Jeff Bhasker to produce this track and 'The Lucky One', having been captivated by his work with indie band Fun and their 2011 hit 'We Are Young', especially with its drum instrumentation.

Taylor explained the meaning of the song: "I wrote about the feeling I got after years had gone by and I finally appreciated a past relationship for what it was, rather than being bitter about what it didn't end up being." On working with Bhasker, she recalled: "He's just so talented, and so I called him and I said, 'I wrote this song. I really want you to work on it with me.' And I played it for him and he was like, 'Let's go! This is great!' and he did such an amazing job on it." Bhasker's production makes the song sound different from all of Taylor's previous work.

The song's hidden message, "When you came to the show in SD", assumes it's about her relationship with Joe Jonas, who had been spotted watching Taylor's San Diego concert during the *Speak Now* tour.

Idolator - "The most startling song on the album…A storming drum beat brings a sense of urgency that Swift's sprawling soft-rock productions have rarely had. But the lyrics are classic Swift, with a couplet that's brilliantly tight and so obvious it seems like it should have been the hook in a thousand pop songs already": **Vulture** - "This chugging rocker nails the feeling of reconnecting with an ex and romanticizing the times you shared, and it livens up the back half of *Red* a bit"; **NME** - "This galloping soft-rock moment celebrates whirlwind romances, and comes with a chorus perfect for shouting along to on road trips"; **Rolling Stone** - "Nobody does zero-to-60 emotional peel out like our girl, and 'Holy Ground' is her equivalent of Evel Knievel jumping the Snake River Canyon"; **Slant** - "Tracks that work best are those on which the production is creative and contemporary in ways that are in service to Swift's songwriting".

'Holy Ground' certainly fits that bill. Add a star for the beautiful BBC *Live Lounge* version.

Sad, Beautiful, Tragic ****
(Taylor Swift)
Recorded - Pain in the Art Studios, Nashville TN
Produced - Taylor Swift & Nathan Chapman
Released - October 22 2012
Chart peak positions
  Hot 100 Bubbling Under #18; Hot Country Songs #37; Alternative Streaming
  Songs #69; Canada #92

With some regret, Taylor looks back on another doomed relationship. Similar in sentiment to 'Back to December', it was written on a ukulele during the *Speak Now* tour. Taylor explained in an interview with *Billboard* how the story was close to her heart: "I remember it was after a show and I was on a bus thinking about this relationship that ended months and months before. The feeling wasn't sadness and anger or those things anymore. It was wistful loss. And so, I just got my guitar and I hit on the fact that I was thinking in terms of rhyming; I rhymed magic with tragic, changed a few things and ended it with what a sad beautiful tragic love affair. I wanted to tell the story in terms of a cloudy recollection of what went wrong. It's kind of the murky gray, looking back on something you can't change or get back."

Taylor recorded the song the same day at Chapman's studio and made the decision to kept the authentic first-take vocals for the final polished version.

The song has been linked to several of Taylor's past relationships. According to CelebBuzz, it may have been Jake Gyllenhaal, as the relationship being on "New York time" points in his direction, while Fandom.com suggests the probability of it being about old flame Terry Lautner.

The lyric hint is "While You Were on a Train".

Billboard - "[The song] finds her working her best Hope Sandoval impression on a slow dance number about a dead love affair"; **Vulture** - "Another glacially paced song from the back half of *Red* that somehow pulls off rhyming "magic" with "tragic"; **NME** - "This gloomy tune sees Swift reflect on a relationship"; **Rolling Stone** - "Such an underrated *Red* gem, one she's almost never sung live, but it was one of her templates for the sound of *folklore*".

The Lucky One ****
(Taylor Swift)
Recorded - Enormous Studios, LA
Produced - Jeff Bhasker
Released - October 22 2012
Chart peak positions
Hot 100 Bubbling Order #13; Hot Country Songs #33, Alternative Streaming Songs #63; Canada #88

Taylor's cautionary tale about the perils of celebrity, fearing what fame could do to her in the future. Reportedly written during her Australian tour, she tells of a star who had it all, but after her closely guarded secrets were being leaked by the tabloids and exposed on social media, gave it all up and went away to live a life of solitude. Narrated in the third person, it is rumoured to be about Joni Mitchell, Britney Spears, and British singer Kim Wilde, who apparently gave up her career as a singer to become a landscape gardener, or, as Taylor puts it, "chose the rose garden over Madison Square."

The main melody of the song is also similar to that of Wilde's 'Four Letter Word'. Taylor made a point not to reveal any names, and the hidden message here is "Wouldn't you like to know".

Producer Jeff Bhasker revealed this track was one of his favourites: "I was really impressed when she brought that. That track falls into a little bit more of a Springsteen, Joni Mitchell vein, which I think shows a lot of maturity and what a good songwriter she is. The lyrics are kind of about her, it has a story, and I think she's talking about Joni Mitchell rejecting fame, even though she never mentions her...To be able to express your feelings through music, that's what it's all about."

There is no doubt that Taylor is also singing about herself, as she revealed: "Your life is constantly being analysed. There's a lot of trade-offs. There's the microscope that's always on you. The camera flashes, the fear that something you say will be taken the wrong way and you'll let your fans down. There's the fear that you'll be walking down the street and your skirt will blow up and you'll be in the news for three months...You're scared of lots of things for a lot of the time, but the trade-off of being able to get on a big stage and sing your songs - is worth it."

In this most intriguing of songs, Taylor sees herself as the lucky one.

Vulture - "A plight-of-fame ballad from the back half of *Red*, with details that never rise above cliché and a melody that borrows from the one Swift cooked up for 'Untouchable'"; **NME** - "Possibly, it could also be a reflection of Swift's future fears".

Everything Has Changed (featuring **Ed Sheeran**) ****
(Taylor Swift - Ed Sheeran)
6th Single
Produced - Butch Walker
Released - July 16 2013
Chart peak positions
 Hot 100 #32; AC #11; Adult Top 40 #8; Mainstream Top 40 #14; UK #7; Canada
 #28; Australia #28; NZ #22
RIAA - 2 x Platinum
Selected awards & nominations
2014 BMI London Awards - Award-Winning Songs (won)
2015 BMI Awards - Award-Winning Songs (won)
2015 BMI Awards - Publisher of the Year (won)

In perhaps Taylor's most famous collaboration, the song explains how your life can be turned upside down after falling in love and "you're thinking of two instead of one." With its hidden message of "Hyannis Port", it obviously points to her fairytale fling with Conor Kennedy and was written while, or just before, she dated him.

Taylor had been a fan of British singer Ed Sheeran since being blown away by seeing his 'Lego House' music video while touring in Australia. Asked about working with Sheeran, she told *The Sun*: "He comes from such a sincere place as a writer, and his songs move you in every direction emotionally. That's something I was so inspired by."

When Taylor returned home, a friend told her that he wanted to work with her. Speaking to *The Sun*, she said: "We both reached out to each other's camps at the same time. I showed up at his hotel in Arizona and we just wrote songs all day. Then he came and hung out at my house in LA and we spent all night sitting on the kitchen floor laughing, writing songs and harmonising." In an interview with MTV, she also revealed that the song was written while sitting and bouncing on a trampoline in her backyard in May 2012.

According to Sheeran it was Taylor who wrote most of the song, although they had a friendly battle over one chord. Apparently, she just pointed out to him all of her awards she had on the wall. Although never originally intended as a duet, they had so much fun writing the song, it just felt right.

The music video was directed by Philip Andelman and shot in Oak Park, California, and at the Medea Creek Middle School in San Antonio. It features two young children portraying what seems to be young versions of the singers, meeting each other on a school bus, and then having "youthful play" together. It's only when the bus comes to pick them up that Taylor and Sheeran appear as the parents of their child counterparts.

The video was released on Taylor's Vevo channel on June 6th 2013.

Vulture - "It's a sweet duet and Sheeran's got a roughness that goes well with Swift's cleaner vocals, but the harmonies are a bit bland"; **Billboard** - "Thematically, this is Swift at her most familiar and clichéd, but Sheeran's tender harmonies lend the song some much-needed depth"; **NME** - "Warm, fuzzy, and firmly hanging onto its rose-tinted glasses".

Starlight ***
(Taylor Swift)
Recorded - Blackbird Studios, Nashville TN
Produced - Taylor Swift, Nathan Chapman & Dann Huff
Released - October 22 2012
Chart peak positions
  Hot 100 Bubbling Under #5; Hot Country Songs #28; Alternative
  Streaming Songs #56; Canada #80

Where the previous track was supposedly about a Kennedy, this is most definitely inspired by the family, and the teenage romance between Conor's grandparents, Robert and Ethel. Taylor spoke about it at the Ripple of Hope Gala in December 2012: "It's inspired by a photograph that I saw, and it's a black and white photo. I saw it about two years ago, and this was before I knew anything extensive about, you know, Robert Kennedy and Ethel. I just saw this picture of these two young kids dancing...and below, it said, 'Ethel and Robert Kennedy, 1945, at age seventeen'. And I wrote this song, just based on what I saw in the picture."

With its hidden message "For Ethel", Taylor thought about what that night must have been like and the fun these two teenagers were no doubt having. When she got the chance to meet Ethel and play her the song, "she just loved it."

Taylor again asked Dann Huff to co-produce with Chapman: "I didn't choose them because I wanted to force my style on them; I chose them because I wanted to learn from them."

Billboard - "Every Swift album as of late has one danceable, fists-in-the-air love anthem...and 'Starlight' fills that role for *Red*".

Begin Again *****
(Taylor Swift)
2nd Single
Produced - Dann Huff, Nathan Chapman, Taylor Swift
Released - October 1 2012
Chart peak positions
  Hot 100 #7; Hot Country Songs 10; UK #30; Canada #4; NZ #11
RIAA - Platinum
Selected awards & nominations
2013 ACA - Female Singer of the Year (nominated)
2013 ACA - Country Awards - Female Video of the Year (nominated)
2013 ACA - Video of the Year (nominated)
2013 BMI Awards - Publisher of the Year (won)
2013 BMI Awards - Country Top 50 Songs (won)
2013 CMT Music Awards - Female Video of the Year (nominated)
2014 Grammy Awards - Best Country Song (nominated)

For the album's final track, Taylor wrote this gentle and optimistic country song about the vulnerability of starting a new relationship after experiencing a horrible breakup. With the album studded with songs that explore other genres, it shows that Taylor has not severed her country roots.

Taylor described the song as getting through a painful breakup, still being sad and a little insecure about herself, and then having the courage to start again: "It's about, kind of, the vulnerability involved with that, and the idea that you realise

144

that, wow, this could be great." With such a tumultuous album about the pain of breakups and bad relationships, it's heartwarming to see Taylor end it on an optimistic and confident note that it's never too late to begin again.

The lyric namechecks singer James Taylor, the guy she was named after, while the hidden message is "I Wear Heels Now".

The music video was directed by Philip Adelman and shot on location in Paris, with Taylor, in various costumes, walking, cycling, and shopping in the city, interspersed with scenes featuring a potential love interest, played by Vladimir Perrin. It was released on October 17th 2012.

Vulture - "Swift's sequencing genius strikes again: After the emotional roller coaster of *Red*, this gentle ballad plays like a cleansing shower... Of all Swift's date songs, this one feels the most true to life; anyone who's ever been on a good first date can recall the precise moment their nervousness melted into relief"; **NME** - "Marking one of *Red's* more pointed returns to her country roots"; **Rolling Stone** - "Sweet Baby Tay drops a deceptively simple ballad that sneaks up and steamrolls all over you, as an unmelodramatic coffee date leads to an unmelodramatic emotional connection".

The Moment I Knew ***
(Taylor Swift)
Red Deluxe Edition
Promo single
Recorded - Pain in the Art Studios, Nashville TN
Produced - Taylor Swift & Nathan Chapman
Released - January 8 2013
Chart peak positions
  Hot 100 #64; Alternative Streaming Songs #32

A song about Taylor's 21st birthday when her boyfriend Jake Gyllenhaal failed to show up, thereby signalling the end of their relationship. She called it "the worst experience ever." The track is notable for producer Nathan Chapman playing almost every instrument during the recording at his Nashville studio.

Vulture - "If you're the type of person who stays up at night remembering every inconsiderate thing you've ever done, the level of excruciating detail here is like a needle to the heart"; **Rolling Stone** - "A sombre piano ballad about getting stood up on your 21st birthday".

Come Back...Be Here ****
(Taylor Swift - Dan Wilson)
Red Deluxe Edition
Promo single
Recorded - Ballroom West LA; Marlay Studio, Hollywood & Instrument Landing,
  Minneapolis
Produced - Dan Wilson
Released - January 8 2013
Chart peak position
  Alternative Streaming Songs #39

Wonderful ballad in which Taylor writes about a failed long-distance relationship, and during the launch party for the album she explained: "It's a song I wrote about this guy that I met. You know, you meet someone and then they just kinda happen to go away, and it's, like, long distance all of a sudden. And you're like, b-b-but, come back, be here! So, it's a song that I wrote about having distance separate you, which is something I face constantly."

Although never confirmed, it's hard to imagine it not being about Harry Styles, when their brief relationship ended with him going on tour to Australia with One Direction.

It is one of two songs on the album produced and co-written by Dan Wilson, the other being 'Treacherous'.

Vulture - "A vulnerable track about long-distance love, with simple sentiments overwhelmed by extravagant production"; **NME** - "A weepy ballad where Swift reminisces over a lost love"; **Rolling Stone** - "A yearning prayer for a rock & roll boy on tour, weak in the knees as she pleads for him to jet back on any terms he chooses".

Girl at Home**
(Taylor Swift)
Red Deluxe Edition
Promo single
Recorded - Pain the Art Studios, Nashville TN
Produced - Nathan Chapman & Taylor Swift
Released - January 8 2013
Chart peak position
  Alternative Streaming Songs #51

In an interview with Yahoo, Taylor said the song "is about a guy who had a girlfriend, and I just felt like it was disgusting that he was flirting with other girls." This, of course, had happened to her in the past, and it has been suggested that Zac Efron had been trying to date Taylor while still seeing another girl.

It was another song recorded at Chapman's Nashville studio, with him playing most of the instruments.

NME - "[The song] fuses the driving country of *Red* with bleeping 8-bit sounds, and is a sweet but bland tune"; **Vulture** - "A singsongsy melody accompanies a largely forgettable lyric"; **Rolling Stone** - "A perfunctory cheating-is-bad homily with barely any chorus".

A fine fantasy

In an interview for *Billboard* eight years later, Taylor revealed: "I look back on this as my true breakup album, every other album has flickers of different things. But this was an album that I wrote specifically about pure, absolute to the core, heartbreak." The album perfectly illustrates the uneasy reality of how even the best and most enduring relationships can end in heartache and pain. It's a clear sign of Taylor's maturity that love with all its complexities just ain't no fairytale. The innocence and optimism displayed on previous albums has been replaced by trepidation and insecurity, with all emotions laid bare; her ex-lovers being almost demonised by her lyrics. The music world had just seen Taylor come of age.

The album's cover of Taylor, with downcast eyes and face partially in the shadow of her wide-brimmed hat, has been favourably compared to that of Joni Mitchell on her album *Blue*.

Red had debuted on the Hot 200 at #1 with first-week sales of 1.21 million, becoming her third consecutive chart topper. It also claimed the largest single-week sales of 2012, surpassing Garth Brooks' 1998 album *Double Life* as the fastest-selling country album. As a result, Taylor became the first solo female with two million-selling weeks on the Hot 200. *Red* went on to spend a total of seven non-consecutive weeks in the chart, making her the first female artist to achieve the record of The Beatles in having three consecutive studio albums each spend six or more weeks at #1, with *Fearless* having spent eleven weeks and *Speak Now* six. It was also the third time that an album by Taylor had peaked at #1 in the last week before Christmas.

Pitchfork - "An album of disappearances, of things that have gone or are just about to go missing - lost relationships, old sounds, previous Taylor Swifts, each photographed just as they're receding out of frame...a once potential and hazy inspiration now coming into view"; **Rolling Stone** - "A 16-song geyser of wilful eclecticism that's only tangentially related to Nashville...One of the best stories in pop. When she's really on, her songs are like tattoos"; **The Guardian** - "How she's had time to open her door to such a parade of lovers good and bad, God only knows...Add to this the many vulnerable poses struck by this Brunhilde of a rock star, this asbestos and iron-clad Amazonian of a woman, and it's clear that *Red* is another chapter in one of the finest fantasies pop music has ever constructed"; **NPR** - "Given her recent high-profile feuds and controversies, *Red* showcases a version of Swift we may never hear from again".

Within a month of its release, *Red* had sold 2.8 copies worldwide, and became the second-highest-selling album of 2012. It also topped the charts in six English-speaking countries, including being her first UK chart-topper, and went top five in other countries, including Austria, Germany, Italy, Mexico, Norway, South Africa, Spain and Japan.

On the day after the album's release, Taylor began the promotional campaign in earnest with three televised appearances with the band, beginning at Times Square with a live performance of 'We Are Never Ever Getting Back Together', 'Red' and 'Love Story' for *Good Morning America;* a performance of 'WANEGBT' on *The View,* and finally 'Red' on *Late Night with David Letterman.*

Toward the end of October, Taylor guested on the primetime special *All Access with Katie Couric - A Special Edition of 20/20* to announce the launch of a North American tour in early 2013 in support of her new album, and, speaking on WRVW Radio, said it would be "nothing like any other tour before." She also performed 'WANEGBT' on *Dancing with the Stars* in Los Angeles.

In the meantime, Taylor made her debut on the cover of *Rolling Stone* for their October issue, complete with the tagline "The Heartbreak Kid".

The following month saw no let-up in the schedule. First came the CMAs in Nashville. Too late for the album to receive nominations, Taylor lost out to Blake Shelton for Entertainer of the Year, and to Miranda Lambert for Female Vocalist of the Year. During the show, Taylor performed 'Begin Again' in a beautiful red dress, with a Parisienne-inspired setting emulating the music video.

Ten days later, she was in Frankfurt, Germany, for the MTV Europe Music Awards, coming away with nods for Best Female, Best Live Act (for the *Speak Now* tour) and even Best Look, maybe not the most prestigious of awards, although one of the highlights of the night was her circus-themed performance of 'WANEGBT', complete with ringmaster outfit and riding crop.

Back with Harry

Returning home from Europe, this was followed by a trip to Los Angeles on November 15th for her debut live television performance of 'State of Grace' on *The X Factor,* for which she wore a black fedora, white button-down, black flood pants, and glittery shoes. During the show, Taylor was seen holding hands with Harry Styles, who was also there to perform. During the rehearsals, Styles sat with Andrea in the audience to watch her do a soundcheck, and then ran on stage, threw a surprised Taylor over his shoulder, and rushed off with her. Radio host Mario Lopez later revealed to his listeners that he had seen them walking "hand in hand" and declared: "You heard it here first. [They're] officially hanging out."

Almost overnight, they had suddenly regained their place as the coolest celebrity couple in Christendom and been dubbed "Haylor". *Look* magazine claimed via a source that Taylor had instructed an estate agent to find her a home close to Styles in London. Although never confirmed, it did not detract from the fact that Taylor was well and truly back with the British singer. In an interview for *Parade*, she admitted: "I think every girl's dream is to find a bad boy at the right time, when he wants to not be bad anymore."

With *Red* selling 1.2 million copies in its first week alone, Taylor decided to purchase another property in Los Angeles. The $1.8 million retro-home was a change in architectural style for the singer. According to the *Los Angeles Times*, the single-storey, four-bedroom house was reportedly used to host guests while she lived in her Beverly Hills residence. It would be sold in 2018 for $2.7 million, making her a tidy profit.

Taylor was still in Los Angeles on November 18th to attend the AMA Awards. After singing 'I Knew You Were Trouble' she picked up the award for Favourite Female Country Artist. *Billboard* reported on the performance: "The stage details...which featured dance manoeuvres as elegant as the masquerade ball knickknacks surrounding them, couldn't mask the stark maturity the 22-year-old conjured with every movement. From the careful high-heel steps toward the audience in the first chorus to the vivacious dress swap mid-song, Swift oozed confidence...and let the goody-two-shoes image start to fly away."

Later in the month, she turned the tables on Styles and went out alone to Tokyo to promote the album on the *Sukkiri Morning Show* and perform 'WANEGBT' for her legion of Japanese Swifties. Before returning home, she flew to Sydney for *The Today Show* and to attend the ARIA Music Awards. Although having no nominations, she performed 'WANEGBT' and 'I Knew You Were Trouble'. Overwhelmed by the fans' reaction, she tweeted: "The fans at the Arias came out in full force! This is insane!"

On the first day of December, Taylor performed at the *KIIS FM Jingle Ball* in Los Angeles, along with Ellie Goulding, One Republic and the Jonas Brothers, and she closed the show with five of her hits, using her signature red microphone. Returning to New York, she was spotted next day with Styles walking around Central Park Zoo and carrying a friend's baby.

Another big night for Taylor came two days later when she was a guest at the Ripple of Hope Gala at New York's Marriot Marquis and honoured with an award by the Kennedy family for her charitable and philanthropic efforts, joining the list of recipients that included President Clinton and Archbishop Desmond Tutu. Presenting the award, Kerry Kennedy said: "This world demands the qualities of youth: not a time of life but state of mind, a temper of the will, a quality of imagination, a predominance of courage over timidity, of the appetite for adventure over the life of ease. Here's a young woman - 22 years old - who has put herself out in the world, and in an incredibly powerful and strong way."

During the gala, Taylor performed an emotional 'Starlight' for Ethel Kennedy, while perhaps wondering why Conor Kennedy was nowhere to be seen.

Immediately after the show, Taylor rushed over to Madison Square Garden where Styles and One Direction had been playing to a sell-out crowd, and spent the rest of the night at an after-show party along with the band's families and invited friends that included Ed Sheeran. After spending the night at the hotel, Taylor returned to Nashville where, on December 5th, she co-hosted the televised *Grammy Nominations Concert Live!* along with rapper LL Cool J. To her surprise, she was up for three awards - Record of the Year (for 'WANEGBT'), Best Country Duo/Group Performance, and Best Song Written for Visual Media (both for 'Safe & Sound').

Not wanting to be away from Styles for too long, she flew back to New York where they were spotted having a romantic dinner, followed by a get-together with friends at the Crosby Street Hotel, including Dianna Agron and Emma Stone.

In an interview with *Cosmopolitan*, Taylor was asked about relationships and replied: "How to make them last. I've never had a really long relationship, so I have no idea what that's like...Wish me luck for the future." When it became Styles' turn to comment, while the band made their final appearance at the *Z100 Jingle Ball*, he simply replied: "I just bumped into her at the zoo and then I don't know..."

After the show, Taylor offered Styles a flight home in her private jet, although there was also room for the rest of the band. While in England, Taylor was seen backstage with him at the *X Factor Finale* in Manchester on December 9th. By this time, the rest of the band were becoming less impressed with the amount of time he was spending with Taylor. For her 23rd birthday, Styles took her for a meal in his favourite pub in Cheshire, and was reported to have bought her gifts worth over £1,000. Over the Christmas period, he showed Taylor around the Lake District, while accompanied by his mother.

With more promotional duties ahead, Taylor flew out to Germany to appear on a live television show. Meanwhile, BBC Radio 1's Nick Grimshaw, a friend of Styles, revealed to the *Daily Mirror*: "Harry really likes Taylor; he's fallen for her in a big way...it seems to be that she's the one for him - for now, anyway."

The couple returned to the States, where Styles met Taylor's family, and then spent a few days in Utah skiing with her and her brother, and hanging out with friends Justin Bieber and Selena Gomez.

The magic doesn't last

There were rumours that Styles was going to accompany Taylor to Australia over Christmas, where she was due to do some promotional work. According to the *New York Daily News*, Styles declined the offer, saying he wanted to spend Christmas at home. However, after buying each other expensive presents, they reunited in New York just in time to see Taylor perform at *Dick Clark's New Year's Rockin' Eve* in Times Square.

MTV News reported: "In the moments before the clock struck 2013, she was right in the thick of the action, standing among the crowd with Styles...The two shared a New Year's kiss and hug to the tunes of 'Auld Lang Syne' and the Frank Sinatra classic 'New York, New York'."

After seeing in the New Year together, Taylor tweeted how thrilled she was and looking forward to 2013. It was around this time that Taylor's protective father Scott reportedly told Styles to slow things down in a man-to-man conversation. He knew only too well how her heart had been broken in the past. *The Sun on Sunday* revealed that they had already talked about getting married, and that Scott didn't want to see them split up. On New Year's Day, the couple jetted off for a relaxing and romantic getaway in the British Virgin Islands.

In a candid interview for *The Guardian*, Taylor revealed: "I think the one thing I'm really afraid of is...that the magic doesn't last. The butterflies and daydreams of love, all these things I hold so dear, are going to leave some day..."

Indications that all was not well in the "Haylor" world came when Taylor cryptically tweeted lyrics from the song 'I Knew You Were Trouble', which was supposedly written after their first breakup, and Swifties around the world got their feathers ruffled when pictures emerged of the couple holidaying in the British Virgin Islands. They showed Styles partying with friends in a hot tub on billionaire Richard Branson's privately-owned Necker Island, while a sorrowful-looking Taylor was sitting all alone on a boat on the neighbouring island of Virgin Gorda. It was then reported that she flew home alone three days earlier than planned. A short while later Styles was again pictured in a hot tub, this time with British blonde Hermione Way, one of the stars of the reality show *Start-Ups: Silicon Valley,* who would tweet in response to media allegations: "What happens on Necker, stays on Necker."

It was soon revealed that the couple had indeed split up, apparently after an "almighty row" and words said that they probably both regretted. Stories from a number of sources emerged in the press over why they split, with rumours that Taylor was becoming "too demanding", that she was prioritising her own career commitments over Styles', and that she criticised him about his intentions toward other women and had told him that he was "lucky" to be with her. Radar Online also brought attention to Styles beginning to get cold feet about becoming tied down.

Disregarding the emotional implications for Taylor, both critics and fans alike became cynical about it all, suggesting it could all have been a PR exercise to promote both her album and One Direction's upcoming tour. *The National Enquirer* suggested that Taylor may not have even been aware that Styles' people had gone to great lengths to put them together as she was "such a huge star." *The*

Guardian, however, dismissed the allegations and just looked on it for what it probably was, just "true love in our time."

It was a glorious time to be a Swiftie. After a whirlwind relationship that had lasted a mere 65 days, Twitter exploded with their predictions of the song titles Taylor might use to write about Styles, and in a matter of hours after the split was announced, the hashtag #HaylortBreakUpSongTitles would become Twitter's number one trending topic around the world.

For now, Taylor would be focused solely on her career, and Swifties and the media would have to wait over two long years before she would strike up another celebrity relationship. It was time to clear her head of bad thoughts and be focused. There was an incredibly busy year ahead, with more promotional work and a world tour already being planned. Putting her past relationships behind her, she revealed with characteristic maturity:

"That's the thing with love: it's going to be wrong until it's right. So, you experience these different shades of wrong, and you miss the good things about those people and you regret not seeing the red flags for the bad things about those people, but it's all a learning process."

Heroes and Villains

"I woke up [one morning] at 4am, and I [decided the album is] called 1989. I've been making 80s synth pop, I'm just gonna do that. I'm calling it a pop record. I'm not listening to anyone at my label. I'm starting tomorrow"

Roasting time

2013 began like previous years with award ceremonies. On January 9th, Taylor was in Los Angeles for the People's Choice Awards, honouring the best in popular culture. With the *Red* album not being eligible due to its release date, Taylor received nominations for Favourite Song ('WANEGBT') and Favourite Female Artist, but came away with their award for Favourite Country Artist. Wearing an immaculate plunging white gown, she took to the stage to accept the award from one of the hosts, actress Olivia Munn, who remarked, "This is a little awkward." In the hilarious scene that followed, Taylor embraced a stony-faced Munn, and as the award was handed over, she snatched it out of her hands. Taylor played along, saying, "This always happens to me...God!" Munn replied: "And it will always happen Taylor, this is your lot in life."

Taylor had been well and truly Kanye-d, but once she had her claws firmly gripped on the award, she addressed her fans with another passionate speech: "You guys have blown my mind with what you've done for this album *Red* and I just want to thank you for caring about my music and for caring about me. Thank you so much, you guys. I love you."

But the joke didn't end there, as she then had to exit the stage to One Direction's 'Live While We're Young'.

There were also reports that Taylor was on the rebound and had asked her friend, actress Jennifer Lawrence, to introduce her to 38-year-old actor Bradley Cooper. According to Radar Online, he politely declined as she was "far too young for him."

At the Golden Globes in Beverly Hills four days later, Taylor and her co-writers were nominated for 'Safe & Sound' in the category for Best Original Song, but lost out to Adele's Bond anthem, 'Skyfall'. Taylor once again looked stunning in a Donna Karen gown, but, by the end of the show, she would be feeling hurt by a joke that backfired. Hosts Tina Fey and Amy Poehler opened the show, with Fey making a wisecrack: "You know, Taylor Swift, stay away from Michael J Fox's son." Handsome 23-year-old Sam Fox was appearing as the evening's "Mr Golden Globe" with the task of escorting award winners onto the stage. As Poehler apparently urged Taylor to "go for it", Fey interjected: "No. She need some 'me' time to learn about herself."

Apart from upsetting the singer, it also unsettled Sam's father, who later responded in *Vulture* magazine: "I don't keep up with it all. Taylor Swift writes songs about everybody she goes out with, right? What a way to build a career." His disapproval of the way the singer wrote about her ex-boyfriends led to Fox receiving a backlash of hateful tweets from Swifties, but Taylor responded by saying that she had received an apology from Fox and all was now good. Even Sam chipped in to tweet, "Hope you gave her my #".

According to sources for *USA Star*, Taylor's feelings had taken a real beating: "She can't snap out of it. Taylor is putting on a brave face to the public but she is a complete mess. Taylor thought Tina's taunt was a low blow and she bawled herself to sleep that night. That's when it hit her that she has such a horrible reputation, and it can affect her professionally."

In an interview for *Vanity Fair*, Taylor referenced one of her favourite quotes: "There's a special place in hell for women who don't help other women." According to *Hollywood Reporter*, Fey hit back: "It was just a joke, and I think it was actually a very benign joke. Well, I feel bad if she was upset...I am a feminist and she is a young and talented girl. That being said, I do agree I am going to hell. But for other reasons. Mostly boring tax stuff."

Those in the business knew only too well that this kind of celebrity roasting at awards was par for the course. Taylor now had to realise that. Despite all her riches and fame, she had to grow thicker skin to be able to deal with it, or stand the risk of becoming an even bigger target.

Although she would still see herself as the girl who wrote songs in her bedroom, she was so much more than that, and whatever curveballs were thrown at her - and they would surely come - she had to keep control of her emotions and put her feelings into her songs, not display them for an unsympathetic media to ridicule.

Oh, to be in England

Two weeks later, Taylor and her band were in Madrid for Los Premios 40 Principales 2012, a ceremony honouring the best in Spanish and international music. In a daring white mini-dress, Taylor performed an acoustic version of 'Love Story' and 'WANEGBT', and won their award for Best International Act. She also appeared on the Spanish chat show *El Hormiguero*.

This was followed toward the end of January with the NRJ Music Awards, presented by the popular French radio station in Cannes. Wearing a lacy black dress and knee-high leather boots, she repeated her earlier performance but came away with no prize. One Direction were also at the show to accept the award for Best International Group, but Taylor and Harry Styles managed to avoid each other.

During the show, Taylor had said that she wanted to do more than just work, and, moving on to Paris, she took a day out to explore the city. After doing a filmed radio interview, she performed a televised live show called *Off Live - Taylor Swift Live on the Seine*. Taking place aboard the exclusive Yachts de Paris barge in the City of Light, the intimate acoustic set included hits from the *Red* album and was well appreciated by the small audience. One reviewer wrote: "If you question just how great she is as an artist, watch this performance. Your mind will quickly be changed. It's raw, beautiful and unforgettable, just like Swift herself." Also that evening she appeared for a second time on the popular nightly chat show *Le Grand Journal*.

Taylor was nominated for three awards at the Grammys, held in Los Angeles the second week of February. Prior to performing, she was a little nervous and told Seacrest: "Oh my God, it's Grammy week, it's so hectic. I have a lot to plan for with the opening performance, and I'm just really hoping all the pieces come together this week. Because this is when it gets really crazy, but it's all very exciting too."

She need not have worried. During a spectacular performance of 'WANEGBT', she took at dig at Styles by breaking into a deep British accent and changing part of the lyric to "I'm sorry, I'm busy opening up the Grammys - and we're never ever getting back together." Huffpost were there to report on her performance: "She rocked a bedazzled white top hat and tails. Her over-the-top performance included men on stilts, ballerinas, and dancers dressed as rabbits." On the night, she and her writing collaborators won the award for 'Safe & Sound' in the category of Best Song Written for Visual Media, but lost out for Best Country Duo-Performance. 'WANEGBT' also failed to win Record of the Year.

Mocking her ex didn't stop there. While in Malibu, filming the music video for her next single, '22', she wore a similar knitted beanie hat to the one he often sported while they were together.

Harry Styles was out of her life, for sure, but far from out of her thoughts. At the Brit Awards in London later in the month, the two of them were kept well apart to avoid any confrontation. When asked about Taylor in *Grazia* magazine, Styles said: "I'm not worried about seeing her at all. She's a sweet girl, you know, I don't have a bad word to say about her."

During the show, Taylor was presented with her first-ever Brit Award for Best International Female Solo Artist and treated her British fans with a fine performance of 'I Knew You Were Trouble', wearing a white geometric gown. MTV News described what happened next: "As the performance continued with all its dancer-filled madness and Swift sauntering around the stage, her gown was pulled off to reveal a sexy, body-hugging black leotard, and her hair was released from its prim bun. From there, the hair tossing kicked into high gear, and the song broke down into a massive dance break, with Swift shaking her hips as the song's dubstep and EDM influences reached heightening levels."

While in London, Taylor also appeared as a guest on the popular *Graham Norton Show* and again sang 'I Knew You Were Trouble'. Returning home, she guested on Country Radio Seminar's *New Faces of Country Music Show* in Nashville, joining country duo, Florida Georgia Line, for an impromptu version of their chart-topping song 'Cruise'. *Taste of Country* reported: "With no loud and proud intro, no fanfare and no warning, Swift showed up for the second verse. Wearing a simple and tight black dress and knee-high boots, Swift looked sexy and she certainly enjoyed herself, performing with the band, sashaying across the stage and rocking out."

A few days later, Taylor was back in London to perform '22' for the BBC charity show *Let's Dance for Comic Relief.*

Painting the world *Red*

Tickets for the forthcoming *Red* Tour had gone on sale on November 16th, with reports that the album had already sold 1.55 million copies, and she assured her fans that they would have everything to do with what she played. Meanwhile, there would be some new faces added to The Agency. Gone was longtime backing singer

Elizabeth Huett, who left to pursue other projects, and in her place came Starlight - a quartet of backing singers who would also have a choreography for each song. They were Kamilah Marshall, Melanie Nyema, Eliotte Nicole Woodford and Clare Turton Derrico. There would also be a group of 15 dancers joining her on stage for certain numbers. Longtime drummer Al Wilson would also be leaving during the tour to pursue other opportunities and was replaced by Matt Billingslea.

The sheer scale of the shows was impressive, with massive visuals and multi-level stages, all carefully designed to give each performance an added visual experience for the fans, and, as expected, there would be more costume changes than ever before.

Taylor spoke to *Taste of Country* about it being a more sophisticated set: "The way I kinda look at this tour, from an aesthetic point of view, from the way the visuals are, I really think that my last two tours, if I were to pick a place where they would exist, it would be a fantasy world where there are princesses and fairies and castles. If this tour existed in a place, it would exist in a city. It's a glammed-up vision of what I would wear every day. Or a rocked-out version of what I would wear out at night."

As before, Taylor would make each show different, switching some songs and doing covers with other artists. Her mother would also accompany her on the road, supplying moral support and helping hands as before. Among the artists supporting this time were country artists Florida Georgia Line, Brett Eldredge and Joel Crouse. But best of all, Taylor would have her close friend and soulmate Ed Sheeran along for all the dates on the seven-month-long North American leg.

In a later interview, Sheeran said: "I'm loving it. I've been very fortunate with the tour that I've been invited on…I go there, hang out with Taylor, I play a show, do my duet with her, then I hang out a bit more and then I go. So, really, it's a nice tour."

In the recent past, Taylor had walked on stage to Tom Petty's 'American Girl', but as a sign of her growing maturity, it would now be Lenny Kravitz's 'American Woman'.

As with previous tours, the concerts kicked off in Omaha on March 13th. The *World-Herald* wrote the next day: "For the first four songs of Swift's kick-off concert of the *Red* Tour, screams, whistles and cheers melded with her powerful backup band to create a relentless cacophony. One suspects, though, that few in the packed CenturyLink Center crowd of 13,800 needed to make out Swift's vocals above the din. They could listen inside their brains as they revelled in the dancers, the pyrotechnics, the sexy band members and backup singers and, of course, Swift herself."

However, fans were a little disappointed to find out there would be no encore.

Following the show in Newark, New Jersey, later in the month, *Rolling Stone* was full of praise: "Seeing Taylor Swift live in 2013 is seeing a maestro at the top of her or anyone's game. No other pop auteur can touch her right now for emotional excess or musical reach - her punk is so punk; her disco is so disco. The red sequins on her guitar match the ones on her microphone, her shoes and 80 percent of the crowd … She's a master of every rock-star move, except the one about dialling it down a notch. But who would ever want that?"

Over the months, there were the inevitable breaks from the tour to make special appearances, attend various award shows, and even buy some property. In April, Taylor attended the ACMs in Los Angeles. Although failing to win any of her four nominations, she had the chance to sing for the first time with her hero Tim McGraw, and, along with Keith Urban, performed the smash hit 'Highway Don't Care', while wearing a stunning black Elizabeth & James dress. The performance would also be featured on *Tim McGraw's Superstar Summer Night* show in Las Vegas the following month.

Also that month it was reported that Taylor had paid cash for a seven-bed, nine-bathroom vacation home called Holiday House, situated on a breathtaking five-acre plot atop the highest point in Watch Hill, Rhode Island, overlooking Block Island Sound and Montauk Point. The property had once belonged to socialite Rebekah Harkness, who would later be the inspiration for the song 'The Great American Dynasty'. At a cost of $17.8 million, it was rumoured that Taylor had bought the mansion after breaking up with Conor Kennedy, whose family home was just a few miles away in Hyannis.

In May, Taylor attended the Billboard Awards in Las Vegas and won an incredible eight out of her ten nominations, including Artist of the Year, Top Country Artist, Top Country Album, and Top Country Song. Accepting the top award from Celine Dion, she once again paid tribute to the 3.7 million fans who had bought *Red*: "Thank you for making my music the soundtrack to your crazy emotions. You are the longest and best relationship I have ever had."

During the show, Taylor sang '22' with a posse of Cirque du Soleil performers and the hip-hop dance crew Jabbawockeez, with a routine that took her from backstage dressing room, through the audience, and onto the stage for an incredible showstopper.

Days after the show, she spoke to *Billboard*: "I loved being able to thank my fans for this life they've given me. Being on tour, I get a nightly reminder of how lucky I am to get to stand on giant stages and sing for sold-out crowds. Now I have so many girls my age coming up to me and saying, 'I've listened to you for seven years.' It's crazy to me that that we've been in each other's lives that long and it still feels new. But, hey, I guess that's what real love feels like."

A most harrowing time

One of the most harrowing times of Taylor's career came on June 2nd. During a meet and greet event held before the concert at the Pepsi Center in Denver, David Mueller, a radio host for the local station KYGO, was alleged to have groped Taylor while he posed for a photo with her and his then-girlfriend Shannon Melcher, who also worked for the radio station. According to the singer, Mueller had reached under her skirt and grabbed her rear.

Immediately after the photo was taken, Taylor told her mother Andrea what had allegedly happened, and then they met with her management team backstage, including her "senior manager" Frank Bell, her radio promotions director. Before the concert got under way, Taylor's team approached Mueller and accused him of inappropriately touching the singer, before removing him from the venue and issuing him a life-time ban against ever attending another one of her concerts.

The following day Bell called Robert Call, vice-president of KYGO, to tell him what had happened. Call then suspended Mueller without pay, citing the morality clause in his contract, while an investigation got under way. Being shown the photo by Bell, Call acknowledged the "inappropriate placement of Mueller's hand" but claimed it did not show that he had lifted Taylor's skirt and touched her.

Executives of KYGO, including attorney Eddie Haskell, Mueller's boss, held a meeting with Call, and then met up with Mueller, who denied touching Taylor. According to court documents they determined he had lied about the incident and changed his story. On June 4th, Call fired Mueller.

That would not be the last word, but, in the meantime, the shows had to go on.

The day after the meet and greet incident, Taylor joined rock legends The Rolling Stones onstage in Chicago for part of their *50 and Counting* Tour and duetted with Mick Jagger on 'Tears Go By', a song he admitted they hadn't done live in a long time. Taylor sauntered onto the stage wearing a short black dress and handled the second verse by herself, then joined Jagger for what appeared to be a kind of formal dance as if at a glittering ball. Unfortunately, it was one of those rare times when two different voices just didn't gel, and Taylor's high vocal was sadly off-kilter.

Nevertheless, it was a special night for Taylor to be in the company of music royalty, and she tweeted her 28 million fans: "Filing this under "never in my wildest dreams". Thank you @rollingstones for inviting me to Chicago to sing with you".

Two days later came the CMTs in Nashville, and a performance of 'Red'. MTV News was there to see it: "Taylor did a complete 180 from soft and sweet to strong and sultry with this red and black performance outfit." However, she failed to win her brace of nominations.

Shortly afterwards, she flew to the UK with Ed Sheeran and the band to perform on the finale of *Britain's Got Talent* on June 8th, with what would be a world exclusive of 'Everything Has Changed'. *Hollywood Life* noted how the two of them "looked so romantic" as they sang, with Taylor looking "adorable" in black shirt, skirt and brogues. Even her fans were quick to tweet how they looked to be more than just friends. Of course, both would deny all the rumours.

Back in March, Sheeran had been seen leaving Taylor's hotel room at 4am, but he quickly denied they were dating. He told TVNZ: "I did go to her hotel; I did stay there til four, and I did leave in the same clothes. But I was playing her my new record. It was strictly that kind of thing. Literally, I went in there and we passed the guitar back and forth and played songs to each other." When asked if they had kissed, he replied: "I'm a professional."

Taylor took part in Macy's July 4th Fireworks Spectacular in New York, along with fellow artists Mariah Carey, Cher and Tim McGraw, and performed 'WANEGBT' and 'Everything Has Changed' with Sheeran. At Foxborough, Massachusetts, later in the month, she treated the 110,000 fans by inviting legendary singer Carly Simon to perform her iconic 'You're So Vain' with her.

In August, Taylor received four nominations at the Teen Choice Awards and won Female Country Artist and Country Song (for 'WANEGBT'). Just one night after a dramatic performance of 'Red' at the CMTs in Nashville, she headlined the first night of the CMA Music Festival there. As well as her own set, she was joined by country giants Tim McGraw and Keith Urban for another performance of 'Highway Don't Care', which had been pre-recorded in June. Speaking to *USA*

Today, Taylor described how the brief set had just been a teaser for her fans: "It's starting...When the anxiety starts, the writing happens right after, usually. Whatever I write in the first year is going to get thrown away. I'm going to like it, but it's going to sound like the last record. The second year usually sounds like the next project."

The month ended for Taylor with the MTV Video Awards in New York where she received the nod in the category for Best Female Video for 'I Knew You Were Trouble'.

The North American leg of the *Red* Tour finally came to an end with the second of two nights at Nashville's Bridgestone Arena on September 21st, and Taylor took a well-earned break from touring before the Oceania leg commenced at the end of November.

Magical movie moments

It had been announced in September that Taylor had been cast in a supporting role for the dystopian movie *The Giver,* a film adaptation of the award-winning novel by Lois Lowry. Directed by Phil Noyce, Taylor plays the character of Rosemary, the daughter of the titular Giver, and, in an appearance of just a few minutes, is shown in flashback playing at a piano, alongside movie legend Jeff Bridges.

Taylor had been a fan of Lowry's novel since elementary school, and credits reading it with changing her outlook on life. She told Bustle.com: "The fact that it celebrated all the things that I hold really dear and are most important to me, like our history and our music and our art and our intellect and our memories, I think that really had a great deal to do with why I wanted to be a part of this." Once offered the part, it was an easy decision for her to accept: "I just immediately thought, I'm gonna say yes to this. If it's anything like the effect the book had on me, then I'm gonna do this."

Production got under way in Cape Town on October 7th and had Taylor wearing a brown wig to erase her pop star image. Noyce recalled: "Being vulnerable comes very naturally to her, because she's a conduit of emotions in her work. So, she just has to go to the place, as I kept reminding her, that she goes to when she writes."

Taylor revealed that Harvey Weinstein, the movie's producer, had attended her launch party for *1989* and had offered her a supporting role in the film, but confirmed they were never alone together: "He'd call my management and be like, 'Does she have a song for this film?' And I'd be like, 'Here it is'." At the Golden Globes, she never hung out with him, sensing there was a vibe: "I would never vouch for him. I believe women who come forward, I believe victims who come forward. I believe men who come forward." While insisting he never propositioned her, she said: "If you listen to the stories, he picked people who were vulnerable, in his opinion. It seemed like it was a power thing. So, to me, that doesn't say anything - that I wasn't in that situation."

The movie would finally be released on August 15th 2014.

Taylor's film work didn't stop there. At the end of 2012, Simon Cowell had completed production of a movie called *One Chance*, a biopic of carphone salesman turned opera singer Paul Potts, the first winner of *Britain's Got Talent* in 2007, and starring James Corden. He approached Taylor to write a song for the soundtrack, and she came up with 'Sweeter Than Fiction', co-written with Jack Antonoff of the indie band Fun. In an interview she explained why she wanted to do the song: "Getting to see the struggles and triumphs of someone who never stopped chasing what he was after really inspired me. It's a beautiful movie and I just wanted to share it with everybody."

Taylor was desperate to record the song and put pressure on her label to let her put her break on hold to release it. Talking to BBC's *Newsbeat*, she said: "I had to fight to do this because I try to take a break in between albums and try to give people a minute to not hear me on the radio. I had to go around and ask people, Can I please, please put something out, even though we're supposed to be going quiet."

Despite her label's reluctance to put any music out before the next album, Taylor insisted on being a part of *One Chance* and got her way.

Sweeter Than Fiction ***
(Taylor Swift - Jack Antonoff)
Single
Label - Big Machine
Produced - Jack Antonoff & Taylor Swift
Released - October 21 2013
Chart peak positions
  Hot 100 #34; Hot Digital Songs #6; UK #45; Canada #17; Australia #44; NZ #26
Selected awards and nominations
2014 Golden Globes - Best Original Song (nominated)

This was Taylor's first collaboration with Jack Antonoff. The single was released along with the movie soundtrack on October 21st. The album included Taylor's song and tracks featuring Paul Potts. The movie was released four days later.

Taylor's fifth movie song garnered varying reviews:

Entertainment Weekly - "Uplifting without being hokey and sweet with being cloying"; **Vulture** - "So sugary that a well-placed key change in the chorus is the only thing that staves off a toothache"; **NME** - "This John Hughes-channelling tune is a new-wave belter that forecast the shimmering synth-pop of ...*1989*"

On becoming Taylor's 43rd Top 40 entry on the Hot 100, it equalled Aretha Franklin for the second-most top 40 entries for a female in the chart's history. With 114,000 downloads it also peaked at #6 on the Hot Digital chart, tying with Rihanna for the most top ten digital hits. The song would also go on to receive a Golden Globe nomination.

Pure pop, not country

For Taylor, the main focus this summer would be on writing and recording material for a proposed new album. In Taylor's words, it had been a snap decision: "I woke up [one morning] at 4am, and I [decided the album is] called *1989*. I've been making 80s synth pop, I'm just gonna do that. I'm calling it a pop record. I'm not listening to anyone at my label. I'm starting tomorrow."

Just eight months after the release of *Red*, Taylor was already thinking about how she was going to give the new release a fresh feel: "I think you need to change up your influences. I think you need to be inspired by different things than you were inspired by before."

Taylor was indeed looking to depart from her country/pop experimenting and make it "blatant pop". As she told *Rolling Stone*: "At a certain point, if you chase two rabbits you lose them both." To emphasise the point, she revealed she would not be attending any country award shows or going on country radio to promote it. Apparently when she turned in the finished songs to label boss Scott Borchetta, he said: "This is extraordinary - it's the best album you've ever done. Can you just give me three country songs?" Taylor responded: "Love you, mean it, but this is how it's going to be." Borchetta finally conceded and agreed that they would not be promoting the album on country radio.

In response to the songwriting process, she told *Rolling Stone*: "The floodgates just opened the last couple weeks. I'm getting to that point where I'm irritating to be around because I'll be with you for half the conversation and then the second half of the conversation, I'm clearly editing the second verse of whatever I'm writing in my head."

Taylor also revealed that there would be no dissing of ex-boyfriends on the album, a first for the singer, and although relationships would be covered, there would be no score-settling but mostly romantic nostalgia: "Different phases of your life have different levels of deep, traumatising heartbreak. And in this period of my life my heart was not irreparably broken. So, it's not a boy-centric album, because my life hasn't been boy-centric."

The title for the new album, *1989*, is of course the year she was born, but in the songs, there are influences of some of her favourite 80s artists, such as Annie Lennox, Phil Collins, and Peter Gabriel, who she had enjoyed watching on VH1.

Swift explained how it was a very experimental time in pop music, with people realising songs didn't have to be done with the standard formula of guitars, drums and bass, but could use all manner of electronic instruments and vocal techniques. She also saw that what was happening in music was also happening in culture, with people seizing opportunities to be different and live how they wanted to live. There were no rules, and this is how she saw the album. She could make an album with whatever producer or musicians she liked, and write songs to convey her thoughts, whatever they might be.

Taylor was becoming the most clean-cut, sweet-as-apple-pie rebel in the music business.

To make the transition from country to pop, she looked no further than Max Martin and Shellback as her "dream collaborators", as they had done sterling work on *Red*. In an interview for AP, Taylor said: "I'll bring in ideas and they'll take such a different turn than where I thought they were going to go, and that level of unexpected spontaneity is something that really thrills me in the process of making music...I love people who have endless strange and exciting ideas about where music can go."

As Taylor knew only too well, taking risks can bring huge rewards.

Taylor invited Jack Antonoff, who had worked with her on 'Sweeter than Fiction', to collaborate on two of the songs, and also Ryan Tedder, lead vocalist of the band One Republic, whose work Taylor had long admired. He would also produce two songs. Tedder spoke about Taylor's work ethic and perfectionism in

160

an interview for *Time*: "Ninety-five times out of 100, if I get a track to where we're happy with it, the artist will say, 'That's amazing.' It's very rare to hear, 'Nope, that's not right.' But the artists I've worked with who are the most successful are the ones who'll tell you to my face, 'No, you're wrong,' two or three times in a row. And she did."

Another part of the creative team was English producer Imogen Heap, who was enlisted to help Taylor finish one of the songs. Her longtime collaborator and close friend Nathan Chapman would also be on hand.

Recording of the album continued over the next few months, with a release date set for October 2014.

Rocking with royalty

On November 3rd, Taylor was back in London for *The X Factor*, duetting with Gary Lightbody for 'The Last Time'. The *London Metro* wrote: "The pair took to the stage wearing all black outfits…and it seems Taylor's chic get-up wasn't to the taste of many *X Factor* viewers."

The remainder of the month consisted of almost back-to-back award shows. One of the most emotional evenings of Taylor's career came at the CMAs in Nashville, when the night truly belonged to the singer. With her parents and Austin looking on, she delighted the star-studded audience with a wonderful stripped-down version of 'Red', together with her own "unplugged" band consisting of country luminaries Alison Krauss, Edgar Meyer, Eric Darken, Sam Bush and Vince Gill. Later in the evening, she was presented with the International Artist Achievement award, a great prize in itself, but that would be eclipsed by being bestowed with CMAs' prestigious Pinnacle Award, the highest honour of the evening, "recognising her groundbreaking place in music history." Seldom had such an award been given to one so young.

To present the award, some of the biggest names in country music, ones that Taylor herself had supported in the past, gathered on stage - Tim McGraw, Faith Hill, Brad Paisley, Keith Urban, George Strait and Rascal Flatts. Before the presentation, a video was aired showing other A-list celebrities paying tribute. Carly Simon: "She knows how to include her audience in the way she delivers the song"; Ethel Kennedy: "Taylor, knowing at an early age that she had the opportunity to use her celebrity as a force for good, and with that head start, she's already making a difference in the lives of children"; Mick Jagger: "Taylor had such an amazing stage presence. She really connects with her fans"; and Justin Timberlake: "From a country boy at heart, I'm so proud of you and can't wait to see what new pinnacles you decide to reach."

Other tributes came from Julia Roberts, Reese Witherspoon and Ellen De Generes. Wearing a long red gown, Taylor ended her emotional acceptance speech: "You've made me feel so special right now."

Another successful night came at the AMAs in Los Angeles on November 24th, when Taylor did an almost clean sweep, with five wins from six nominations - Favourite Female Country Artist, Artist of the Year, Favourite Pop/Rock Female Artist, Favourite Country Female Artist and Favourite Country Album for *Red*. Receiving the Artist of the Year award for the second time, she praised her fans:

"I'm 23 and I have no idea what's gonna happen to me in my life, but I figure if you've decided on something as wonderful as this, then we're pretty much in it together."

Three days later, Taylor rubbed shoulders with real royalty when she attended the Winter Whites Gala at London's Kensington Palace, an event in aid of the youth homelessness charity Centrepoint. Looking resplendent in an angelic white, off-the-shoulder gown, with her hair in old-school Hollywood curls, she sang a couple of hits and then was invited by fellow-guest Jon Bon Jovi to join him on stage, along with Prince William, to help sing the classic 'Living on a Prayer'.

In an interview for *The Guardian*, Taylor reflected on the song 'Love Story' and how it "has references to palaces, princes and princesses and it is very strange that I end up playing it in a palace…I don't think I've ever played at a palace before, so it is really wonderful." Full of praise for Prince William for helping put the event together, she was also wrong-footed by some questions about the prince from a royal correspondent for *The Times*, telling him: "I love your accent, I just don't know what you're saying."

It was indeed a surreal experience for Taylor. Here she was, meeting a real-life prince and future king in a real-life palace, and looking every inch a princess herself.

Sometimes, even for a starry-eyed farm girl from Pennsylvania, fairytale dreams do eventually come true.

Red down under

The day after her royal engagement, Taylor flew out to New Zealand to commence the Oceania leg of the *Red* Tour, beginning in Auckland on November 29th. This was followed by dates in Sydney, Brisbane, Perth and Melbourne. Supporting her were the American band Neon Trees and Australian singer Guy Sebastian.

On the first day of December, she attended the ARIA Awards in Sydney and was presented with the award for Best International Artist. *The Guardian* reviewed the Sydney show on December 4th: "The night had all the hallmarks of a glitzy extravaganza: fireworks, hydraulics, dancers. stilt-walkers, tickertape and of course, plenty of costume changes. Swift variously donned a red dress, t-shirt and shorts, a cream ballgown (ripped off to reveal a racy black number) and finished the show in a jewel-encrusted ringmaster jacket."

The *Sydney Morning Herald* was not impressed: "For a female to write about her feelings, and then be portrayed as some clingy, insane, desperate girlfriend in need of making you marry her and have kids with her, I think that's taking something that potentially should be celebrated - a woman writing about her feelings in a confessional way - and turning it and twisting it into something that is frankly a little sexist."

Ten days later, the Melbourne show brought a break in the tour until resuming the following February.

Taylor had become the first solo female artist in 20 years to headline a national stadium tour in Australia (the last being Madonna in 1993), and the crowd of over 40,900 at Sydney's Allianz Stadium set a record for her being the first female artist in history to sell out the stadium since its opening in 1988.

Between the Brisbane and Perth shows, Taylor had flown to New York on December 10th for her first Victoria's Secret Fashion Show and two headline-catching performances. The first was part of the British Invasion segment, joining the band Fall Out Boy, for their 'My Songs Know What You Did in the Dark / Light Em Up' set, with Taylor suitably decked with a Britannia theme, a reworking of Geri Halliwell's Union flag dress. The second was for the Snow Angels segment and a superb rendition of 'I Knew You Were Trouble', almost outdoing all the models with her shimmery minidress, even two of her best friends Martha Hunt and Karlie Kloss, members of the so-called "Swift squad".

The Squad

The Swift squad was the name given to Taylor's elite posse of A-list pals who hung out with her over the years. The girlie gang has included models, actresses, singers, entrepreneurs, and even loyal school friends, and Taylor pulls out all the stops to have fun with them, whether it be Fourth of July parties, red carpet events, or even appearances in her music videos. One of the original members was Disney star and singer Selena Gomez, close friends since meeting Taylor at a Jonas Brothers concert in 2008, when both of them were dating band members Joe and Nick. Karlie Kloss, one of the world's leading models, became friends with Taylor in January 2012 with the singer tweeting that she wanted to bake cookies with her, and Karlie replying "Your kitchen or mine?" Models Lily Aldridge, Cara Delevingne, and Martha Hunt all became friends after meeting Taylor at the VS Show. There was also Brittany LaManna and Abigail Anderson, both childhood friends. Later additions to the squad included model Gigi Hadid and indie-band guitarist Alana Haim.

Sadly, some friendships were destined not to last.

By the end of the year, rumours spread that Taylor's friendship with singer Katy Perry had come to an end. In an interview for one of his country's newspapers, the *Daily Examiner*, Aussie dancer Lockhart Brownlee reported that he and two of Katy Perry's other former dancers had left Taylor's *Red* tour in 2012 to join Perry for her forthcoming *Prismatic* world tour: "Obviously we were with Katy for two and a half years, she's like family to us. So, we were like, 'Absolutely.' We weren't really dancing in Taylor's tour anyway, so I had got a little bored, and I really wanted to do a promo tour... Taylor is very untouchable. When we did see her, we had so much fun with her, but she's a lot more protected than Katy."

Although the seeds for bad blood between them had been sown, they would remain buried until coming to the surface in September 2015.

Guess We're Not in Nashville Anymore

"Music is art, and art is important and rare. Important, rare things are valuable. Valuable things should be paid for. It's my opinion that music should not be free"

"A true arena-rock goddess"

What a mind-blowing year it had been for Taylor, just barely 24 years old. With a record-breaking tour well on the way to being completed, sales of her album *Red* had taken her total record sales beyond 26 million, and her music had been downloaded by fans an incredible 75 million times across five continents, making her the top digital singles artist of all time. She had performed in some of the world's great arenas and also some of its more intimate settings, and had even performed in a real-life royal palace and had high-fived the future King of Great Britain. It was also reported that Taylor now topped the industry chart for the highest earners in 2013, with around $39 million during the year.

What's more, Taylor also became the first artist since The Beatles (and the only female artist in history) to log six or more weeks at #1 with three consecutive studio albums.

With the glossy mags having little gossip about the singer, after a year almost devoid of relationship rumours, the music press was now taking Taylor more seriously. The well-respected *Rolling Stone* had celebrated her tour as "seeing a maestro at the top of her game, or anyone's game... A true arena-rock goddess at an amazing peak." The *New York Times* was of a similar mind: "A king-size spectacle... Taylor Swift off-script is very much like Taylor Swift on-script: not just the brains of the operation, but the brawn, too, the unflappable force that ensures stuck landings." The *New Yorker* magazine had no qualms stating she was "the biggest pop star in the world."

One of Taylor's biggest assets was her continuing ability to communicate with the fans who were sharing her incredible journey, even factoring them in when making professional or personal decisions. Since day one, she had vowed to "let them in on everything." Instead of relying on a posse of corporate employees, she was still able to look after her own affairs, albeit with a little input from well-meaning Swifties.

As a songwriter, Taylor's life experiences had gone a long way to enriching her craft, and the vivid imagery of her writing was now being compared favourably to lyric luminaries like Joni Mitchell, Neil Young and Bruce Springsteen. Her love for music was paramount, as she explained to the *Philadelphia Inquirer*: "I think anyone, when they come across something that fascinates them more than anything they've ever seen - and that's what music does for me - I think when each person finds that in their life, that's when they become driven. That's when they grow up. I was just kind of a fluke in that I found mine age 10. I was like: I found this. There's no way I can let it go."

With all that was happening to her right now, Taylor was still finding it a little difficult to believe it was all for real.

As for her love life, Taylor hadn't dated anyone since Harry Styles, a year ago. In an interview for *Rolling Stone*, she explained: "I feel like watching my dating life has become a bit of a national pastime, and I'm not just comfortable providing that kind of entertainment anymore. I don't like seeing slideshows of guys I've apparently dated. I don't like giving comedians the opportunity to make jokes about me at awards shows. I don't like it when headlines read, 'Careful, bro, she'll write a song about you', because it trivialises my work. And most of all, I don't like how all these factors build the pressure so high in a new relationship that it gets snuffed out before it even has a chance to start. And so, I just don't date."

Taylor would be true to her word for many months to come.

From Nashville to New York

In January, Taylor won the People's Choice Favourite Country Artist for the second year running, and at the Golden Globes in Los Angeles the song 'Sweeter than Fiction' picked up a nomination for Best Original Song.

The following month came the Grammys, for which Taylor had already won seven awards. Now she had the chance to showcase the beautiful song 'All Too Well'. In the most gorgeous of gowns, she sat at the piano and gave the audience a stunning performance of what is arguably her finest composition. But the night would be tinged with some disappointment, losing out on all four nominations for Album of the Year, Best Country Album, Best Country Song ('Begin Again') and Best Country Duo/Group Performance ('Highway Don't Care').

In an interview for *Vanity Fair*, Taylor also described her feelings the moment Daft Punk beat *Red* for Album of the Year: "When they announced the album of the year winner, it was like, 'And the album of the year goes to Raaaaaaandom Access Memories, Daft Punk.' They really dragged out 'Raaaa', and I was like, for a second there, kinda thought we had it. And we didn't."

Taylor gave it some thought in an interview: "Maybe I did not make the record of my career. Maybe I need to fix the problem." She made it clear that shiny trophies were not that important, but were a good motivator: "We don't make music so that we can win a lot of awards, but you have to take the cues from somewhere if you're going to evolve."

During the month, it was reported that Taylor had once more dipped into the property market and purchased two adjacent penthouses in the Tribeca area of New York for nearly $20 million. The two properties had been previously bought by film director Peter Jackson in 2008, who tried unsuccessfully to list them together five years later. Taylor now renovated them into one large condo that boasted ten bedrooms and ten bathrooms. Taylor was soon spotted "taking a leisurely stroll by herself" and visiting the Metropolitan Museum of Modern Art, where she was seen standing transfixed before an oil painting of Vigo the Carpathian for hours on end.

On February 1st, the last leg of the *Red* Tour kicked off in Europe, with five sell-out concerts at London's 15,000-seat O2 Arena, supported by British band The Vamps. The *London Evening Standard* wrote: "Unquestionably the most popular pop star on the planet, Taylor Swift brought her all-conquering, all-singing and dancing, almighty *Red* tour to the O2 over the weekend. Those who wondered why the 24-year-old, Nashville-based, Pennsylvania-born stockbroker's daughter has eclipsed Beyoncé, Rihanna, Lady Gaga and the rest, need wonder no more... More tellingly still, the breadth of ideas, the invention, and the sharp songwriting confirmed Taylor Swift as Madonna's less sexualised, less needy heiress." *The Times* opined: "A perfect balance between professionalism and intimacy. The biggest thing in music."

Surprisingly, throughout April and May, Taylor would fail to win any of the nominations at the ACM, Billboard or CMT Awards.

Following the final show in London on February 11th, it was announced that, in response to strong demand, the tour would be extended in the spring to the Far East for seven dates. In May, Taylor and her team arrived in Shanghai aboard a specially-charted AirAsia flight painted in *Red* livery and adorned with images of the singer. The concert became the fastest sell-out in Chinese history with all 18,000 tickets sold in 60 seconds. Further dates followed in Japan, Indonesia, and the Philippines, with a planned concert in Bangkok cancelled due to political unrest.

The final show of the *Red* Tour took place in Singapore on June12th. The figures were impressive. Since tickets went on sale on November 16th 2012, over 1.7 million had been sold, generating a revenue of over $150 million. It became the highest-grossing tour by a country artist in history, surpassing the record held by Tim McGraw and Faith Hill's headlining *Soul2Soul* Tour, which had brought in $141 million.

Following the Asian tour, work on the new album was nearing completion. Meanwhile, in August, Taylor picked up the award for Top Female Country Artist at the Teen Choice Awards in Los Angeles, and later that month performed her new song 'Shake it Off' at the MTV Video Music Awards in Inglewood. *Billboard* described her performance: "Wearing a two-piece outfit decorated with shimmering fringe, Taylor and a team of tuxedo-clad dancers took the stage with a classy, 20s-themed performance of the upbeat pop banger..."

With the new album completed, Taylor recalled how her relocation to New York had been one of its inspirations: "I was so intimidated by this city for so long...I thought I would never be able to make it here, because I wasn't something enough - bold enough, brave enough to take on this huge city in all its blaring honesty. And then at a certain point I just thought, 'I'm ready'."

Running out of stream

In July 2014 Taylor wrote an article in the *Wall Street Journal*:
"In recent years, you've probably read the articles about major recording artists who have decided to practically give their music away, for this promotion or that exclusive deal. My hope for the future, not just in the music industry, but in every young girl I meet...is that they all realize their worth and ask for it. Music is art, and art is important and rare. Important, rare things are valuable. Valuable things should be paid for. It's my opinion that music should not be free, and my prediction is that individual artists and their labels will someday decide what an album's price point is. I hope they don't underestimate themselves or undervalue their art."

On November 3rd, Taylor pulled her entire catalogue from the Swedish streaming service Spotify as an act of protest against its ad-funded "free" tier - specifically, the fact that, at the time, artists couldn't choose to only release their music on their paid-for premium offering.

Spotify soon responded: "We hope she'll change her mind and join us building a new music economy that works for everyone." Launching a social media campaign to persuade her to return, they claimed that 16 million of their 40 million users had played Taylor's music in the last 30 days and it was appearing on 19 million playlists.

Taylor had previously delayed her album *Red* going on Spotify when it was first released, declaring on Yahoo Music: "[All] I can say is that music is changing so quickly, and the landscape of the music industry is changing so quickly, that everything new, like Spotify, all feels to me a bit like a grand experiment. And I'm not willing to contribute my life's work on an experiment that I don't feel fairly compensates the writers, producers, artists, and creators of this music. And I just don't agree with perpetuating the perception that music has no value and should be free…"

Spotify's co-founder and CEO, Daniel Ek, reacted later: "Taylor Swift is absolutely right; music is art, art has real value, and artists deserve to be paid for it…", then stated that an artist like Taylor was on track to earn $6 million a year. Label boss Scott Borchetta disputed these figures and claimed the singer had received "less than $500,000" in the last year of domestic streaming, with Spotify then counter-claiming that Taylor's total payout for streaming was a global figure of $2 million, and that Borchetta's figure only covered Taylor's payment for streams in the US, which was not its largest market.

According to Borchetta, Taylor's earnings from streaming her videos on Vevo was more than the payout from Spotify, and in an interview for *Time*, said: "The facts show that the music industry was much better off before Spotify hit these shores." He said that Taylor's was "arguably the most important current catalog there is", stating that the streaming service "is about each individual artist, and the real mission here is to bring…attention to it."

In a radio interview with Nikki Sixx on November 7th, Borchetta explained the reason for pulling out of Spotify: "Big Machine is rewarding fans that pay for music," he said, and that letting people listen to Taylor's music for free would be "completely disrespectful" to fans that paid for her music. As a result, the label drew a line between services that offered free, ad-supported listening and the ones that offered only paid subscriptions. "Now if you are a premium subscriber to Beats Music or Rdio or any other services that don't offer just a free-only, then you'll find her catalog."

No sooner had Taylor departed from Spotify than other artists like Jason Aldean, the Black Keys, Radiohead and Coldplay followed suit, choosing to delay their album's streaming release in order to encourage listeners to buy or download the album before it became available to stream. Borchetta said: "I've had calls from so many other managers and artists. There's a big fist in the air about this."

In the meantime, Taylor and her label kept *1989* only on paid subscription-required streaming platforms such as Beats and Rhapsody.

In June the following year, Apple Music became her next target. In an open letter, she told them she was withholding the album due to her concerns over the unfairness of their three-month free trial offered to subscribers. Arguing that Apple had the money to cover the cost, she said: "I find it to be shocking, disappointing, and completely unlike this historically progressive and generous company… Three months is a long time to go unpaid, and it is unfair to ask anyone to work for nothing. We don't ask you for free iPhones. Please don't ask us to provide you with our music for no compensation."

The very next day, Apple reversed its payment policy, with CEO Eddie Cue tweeting: "We hear you @taylorswift13 and indie artists. Love, Apple". Speaking to AP, he praised Taylor's stance: "When I woke up this morning and I saw Taylor's note that she had written, it really solidified that we needed to make a change." Responding to the news, Taylor tweeted: "I am elated and relieved. Thank you for your words of support today. They listened to us."

Apple Music was launched on June 30th with each individual subscriber paying $9.99 per month in the US and £6.30 in the UK.

Meanwhile, the dispute with Spotify continued for months. In November 2016 the company's head of content programming spoke to *Music Week*: "I've every good reason to be very optimistic Taylor Swift will be coming back to Spotify. I'm not saying it's done, but the indications are good", and, sure enough, on June 9th 2017, Taylor's management announced: "In celebration of *1989* selling over 10 million albums worldwide and the RIAA's 100 million song certification, Taylor wants to thank her fans by making the entire back catalog available to all streaming services." This led to some cynics pointed out that the timing had coincided with the launch of a new album by rival Katy Perry.

Nevertheless, Taylor was perhaps one of just a handful of artists with a big enough fan base to be able to boycott Spotify without doing harm to their record sales.

In an interview for CBS *This Morning,* Spotify's Daniel Ek spoke about how he convinced Taylor to come back: "I should've done a much better job communicating this, so I take full ownership of that. I went to Nashville many, many times to talk to [Taylor's] team, spent more time explaining the model, why streaming mattered. And the great news is I think she saw how streaming was growing. I think she saw the fans were asking for it. So eventually when the new album came out, she came to Stockholm and spent some time there, figuring out a way that made sense to her."

Spotify declared that it had been a main contributor to reversing the downward financial trajectory of the music industry, and that streaming would continue to play a major part in the industry's success.

That, of course, was still very much in the future.

War begins with Katy

Right now, Taylor was promoting *1989* through product endorsements with Diet Coke, Keds and Subway, and on August 18th she held a live stream on Yahoo! sponsored by ABC News, in which she announced the details of *1989* and the release of the song 'Shake It Off' and its accompanying music video. As a further way of connecting with her fans, she hand-picked a number of fans, based on their engagement on social media, to various "*1989* Secret Sessions" which were held at her various homes across the country and in London throughout September.

Arrangements were made for the fans to meet at a certain location and they were then bussed to one of her properties. A short video was released showing behind-the-scenes footage of the various events, with Taylor baking cookies for the fans as they got ready to see her perform, but no hints to what was played.

On September 8th, ahead of the release of *1989*, Taylor gave an interview for *Rolling Stone* and was asked about the inspiration for the song 'Bad Blood'. Although no names were mentioned, she revealed: "For years, I was never sure if we [her and Perry] were friends or not. She would come up to me at awards shows and say something and walk away, and I would think, 'Are we friends, or did she just give me the harshest insult of my life?' She did something so horrible. I was like, 'Oh, we're just straight-up enemies.' And it wasn't even about a guy! It had to do with business. She basically tried to sabotage an entire arena tour. She tried to hire a bunch of people out from under me. And I'm surprisingly non-confrontational - you would not believe how much I hate conflict. So now I have to avoid her. It's awkward, and I don't like it."

The following day, Perry hit back at the allegation and tweeted: "Watch out for the Regina George in sheep's clothing..." in reference to the villainous *Mean Girls* movie character played by Rachel McAdams. It didn't take too much taxing of the brain to realise that Taylor had been speaking about Perry in the interview. The war was on...

During the month, Taylor flew out to Germany to perform the new single at the German Radio Awards in Marl. PopCrush was there to record her performance of 'Shake It Off': "Showing off her midriff in a two-piece black ensemble outfit with matching high heels, Swift's live performance was noticeably more subdued compared to her performance...at the MTV Video Music Awards - with little dancing and no costume changes. Still, though, she keeps the spirit of the song alive as she works the stage with the same fierce attitude and carefree confidence, inspired by the track's lyrics."

On September 19th, Taylor performed a five-song set at the iHeartRadio Music Festival at the MGM Grand Garden Arena in Las Vegas. According to *Billboard*, the performance was "pure bubblegum", as she took to the stage in a jewel-encrusted light pink two-piece. During the performance of 'Shake It Off', Taylor went across to her trombonist and playfully "smacked his ass" as if he was one of her well-publicised haters, and later revealed: "I was so happy tonight, it made it impossible to remember the times in the past that I haven't been."

The following month saw a return to Paris to promote the new song, beginning with appearances on the nightly talk show *Le Grand Journal*, and the chat show *C à Vous* the following day. During an interview for the radio station NRJ, she was asked by a fan why she was ditching guitars for automated drums and layered vocals on her new album, and explained: "I just felt myself gravitating towards making pop music." Another fan told her how he was being made fun of and perceived as being gay for listening to the singer's "girl" music. She responded: "Listening to my music is just as manly as growing out a full beard. It's just like chopping up trees in the backyard and building a log cabin. Everyone knows that. You tell them that."

Taylor then moved on to London for several appearances. For BBC Radio 1's *Live Lounge* series, she performed 'Shake it Off', 'Love Story' and 'Riptide', a cover of the Vance Joy song, and the following day was a guest on *The X Factor*, performing 'Shake it Off'. The *Daily Mirror* was there to report: "Taylor gave an energetic performance with a troop of backing dancers, leaving the crowd screaming as they applauded the singer with a standing ovation. Her mic was a little low at the start of the track, but the tech team swiftly sorted it out so Taylor could go on to finish her performance in style."

Remaining in London, Taylor then took part in *Stand Up to Cancer*, performing a parody of her new song called 'Bake it Off' with celebrity chef Jamie Oliver, and two days later appeared at the Radio 1 Teen Awards to sing 'Love Story'. Immediately after the London shows, she flew out to Australia to appear on their version of *The X Factor* in Sydney, once again debuting her latest single.

After the whirlwind promotional tour, Taylor was back home to guest on *Jimmy Kimmel Live*. During the show, Taylor exacted revenge on the show's booker, who in the past had refused to let a certain 14-year-old starlet sing on the show. Kimmel named and shamed him, and then had him "thrown" out of the studio. Hollywood Boulevard was then shut down as Taylor rocked the town with 'Shake It Off' and 'Out of the Woods'.

The following day, Taylor took part in *We Can Survive*, CBS Radio's annual breast cancer research benefit at the Hollywood Bowl. Among the mainly-female artists were Alicia Keys, Lady Antebellum, Jennifer Lopez and Ariana Grande, but, as *Rolling Stone* reported, it was Taylor who stole the show with her four-song set: "Swift…was the most commanding personality on the stage and the one most frequently name-checked by other artists, many of whom seemed aware they were playing in her shadow…Swift worked the crowd into a sing-along froth, danced like a happy antelope and used the word 'frenemies' when introducing 'Shake It Off'."

Back in the UK at the end of the month, Taylor's London appearance on the chat show *Alan Carr Chatty Man* was aired (but probably pre-recorded during her earlier visit).

On October 27th, the day of the new album's release, Taylor was in New York for one of her Secret Sessions with iHeartRadio, held for specially invited fans. With a five-song setlist and dressed in sequinned all-white, she performed on a Manhattan rooftop with the Empire State Building providing her with a once-in-a-lifetime light show. Her appearance on *The Ellen De Generes Show* was also aired that same day, with performances of 'Shake it Off' and 'Out of the Woods'.

Songs from the Big Apple

Taylor's self-styled first "official pop album" was digitally released in both standard and deluxe editions on October 27th, with the deluxe edition, and its three bonus tracks, being made available exclusively through Target. A physical cd of the deluxe edition was released the same day.

Unlike previous albums, the songs' hidden messages in the liner notes form a clever story in 13 sentences: "We begin our story in New York. There once was a girl known by everyone and no one. Her heart belonged to someone who couldn't stay. They loved each other recklessly. They paid the price. She danced to forget him. He drove past her street each night. She made friends and enemies. He only saw her in his dreams. Then one day he came back. Timing is a funny thing. And everyone was watching. She lost him but she found herself and somehow that was everything".

1989
Label - Big Machine Records
Recorded – Conway Recording, LA; Jungle City NY; Lamby's House, Brooklyn; MXM
  Stockholm; Pain in the Art, Nashville; Elevator Nobody, Goteborg; The Hideaway Studio.
Produced - Max Martin; Taylor Swift, Jack Antonoff, Nathan Chapman, Imogen Heap,
  Mattham & Robin, Ali Payami, Shellback, Ryan Tedder & Noel Zancanella
Released - October 27 2014
Singles - 7
Chart peak positions
  Hot 200 #1; Country Albums #1; UK #1; Canada #1; Australia #1; NZ #1
RIAA Certification - 9 x Platinum
Selected awards and nominations
2015 AMA Awards - Favourite Pop/Rock Album (won)
2016 iHeart Radio Music Awards - Album of the Year (won)
2016 Grammys - Album of the Year (won)
2016 Grammys - Best Pop Vocal Album (won)

Welcome to New York ***
(Taylor Swift - Ryan Tedder)
Recorded - Conway Recording, LA
Produced - Ryan Tedder, Noel Zancanella & Taylor Swift
Released - October 20 2014
Chart peak positions
  Hot 100 #48; Alternative Streaming Songs #3; UK #39; Canada #19; Australia
  #23; NZ #6
RIAA Certification - Platinum

The full-blown pop sound of the opening track signals Taylor's firm-footed departure from her country roots, introducing to the fans both a new sound and a new lifestyle. Speaking to E!Online, she revealed: "I dreamt and obsessed over moving to New York, and then I did it. The inspiration that I found in that city is hard to describe and to compare to any other force of inspiration I've ever experienced in my life. I approached moving there with such wide-eyed optimism and sort of saw it as a place of endless potential and possibilities. You can kind of hear that reflected in this music and this song especially."

In an interview for *Rolling Stone* in September 2014, Taylor revealed: "I really like my life right now...I love the album I made. I love that I moved to New York. So, in terms of being happy, I've never been closer to that."

Some $50,000 from sales of the single went to New York's public school system, and, in return, the city made her a tourism ambassador.

Some commentators look at the song as the last in a trilogy, with 'A Place in This World', describing where she needs to be, and 'Mean', in which she promises that "someday I'll be living in a big ol' city". The song is later featured in the animated movie *The Secret Life of Pets*.

In the liner notes, Taylor describes her feelings about the move to the Big Apple. "I think you have to know who you are and what you want in order to take on New York and all its blaring truth."

The lyric hint is "We Begin Our Story in New York".

Entertainment Weekly - "It's the *Sex in the City* tour version of New York, so much so that one almost expects it to make a stop at Magnolia Bakery. It honours the city…but only skims the surface"; **Time** - "A new kind of equality anthem"; **USA Today** - "Swift could not care less that the story has been told ten thousand times because it's her story, and she's going to sing about it in a way that every other person in the country is going to want to sing along. This is going to be the next New York anthem. Don't fight it. It's already over"; **The Observer** - "The album's scene-changing opener, proffering 80s pop as its signature sound. Swift may have been born on 13 December 1989, but here she is claiming the 80s - gated drums, synth-pop - as a formative influence"; **Vulture** - "When it's not taken as a mission statement, 'Welcome to New York' is totally tolerable, a glimmering confetti throwaway with lovely synths"; **Rolling Stone** - "The most authentic New York thing about it is how it sends people into spasms of mouth-foaming rage"; **NME** - "With its bouncing bassline and hand-clapped beats, it's a bombastic tribute to the Big Apple".

Blank Space *****
(Taylor Swift - Max Martin - Shellback)
2nd Single
Recorded - MXM Studios, Stockholm, Conway Recording LA
Produced - Max Martin & Shellback
Released - November 10 2014
Chart peak positions
 Hot 100 #1; AC #1; Adult Top 40 #1; Dance Club Songs #23; Latin Airplay #48;
 Mainstream Top 40 #1; Rhythmic #14; UK #4; Canada #1; Australia #1;
 NZ #2; Japan #45
RIAA Certification - 8 x Platinum
Selected awards and nominations
2015 AMA Awards - Song of the Year (won)
2016 BMI Awards - Award-Winning Songs (won)
2016 Grammys - Record of the Year (nominated)
2016 Grammys - Song of the Year (nominated)
2016 Grammys - Best Pop Solo Performance (nominated)

Taylor uses her "serial dater" image to her advantage, with a satirical nod to her flirtatious reputation and string of former boyfriends, and how it spoils her once-wholesome image.

For *GQ* magazine, she explained: "You take your creative license and create things that are larger than life …That is not my approach to relationships. But is it cool to write the narrative of a girl who's crazy but seductive but glamorous but nuts but manipulative? That was the character I felt the media had written for me, and for a long time I felt hurt by it. I took it personally. But as time went by, I realized it was kind of hilarious."

In the song, Taylor even includes the noise of a pen clicking toward the end of the chorus, suggesting the character is writing her new lover's name in her "blank space".

Taylor realised that the whole idea of doing a song poking fun at herself was risky, but she need not have worried: "The fact that it ended up being a sort of shining spot on the album is really exciting for me." By releasing this, Taylor was sending out a note to the tabloids - she is one step ahead of them by mocking her own headlines. The mark of an incredibly wise woman completely in command. In an interview for *NME*, Taylor said: "It's so opposite my actual life. Half the people get the joke, half the people really think that I was like really owning the fact that I'm a psychopath… I have no complaints to how things turn out."

The lyric hint is "There Once Was a Girl Known by Everyone and No One".

When released, 'Blank Space' set a record by replacing Taylor's own 'Shake It Off' at #1 on the Hot 100, the first time a female had de-throned herself in the history of the chart. By doing so, she became the first lead artist to simultaneously occupy the top two positions since 2012, when her songs 'Ronan' and 'We Are Never Ever Getting Back Together' occupied the top two positions. It also remained on top of the charts for seven consecutive weeks, making it Taylor's longest reign at #1.

The music video was directed by Joseph Kahn and based on Taylor's idea to be portrayed as a "crazy villain" who has broken up with so many guys that maybe the problem is not them, but her. The three-day shoot took place in September 2014 at Oheka Castle in West Hills, New York, and on the Woolworth Estate in Glen Cove. The love interests are played by Sean O'Pry and Andrea Denver, and the video's symmetrical framing style was inspired by the Kubrick movie *A Clockwork Orange*.

Taylor had planned to release the video on *Good Morning America* on November 11th, but it was accidentally leaked by Yahoo! the day before, forcing her to post it on her Vevo account shortly after.

BuzzFeed - "Swift's brilliance is in how she always manages to make her glamorous love life sound so ordinary, and essentially the same as any other girl her age who hasn't settled down just yet"; **Cosmopolitan** - "She also asserts her right to short flings and one-night stands…which is a far cry from the teenager who was marrying her high-school sweetheart back in 'Love Story'. Pop Taylor is awesome"; **NME** - "Instead of moping about the portrait being painted of her, Taylor's vengeance came in the form of this unspeakably infectious pop parody, mocking her detractors over bubblegum hooks"; **The Observer** - "An out and out pop song with an intriguingly skeletal undercarriage. There is a rewarding pen click when Swift prepares to write down this man's name"; **Vulture** - "Swift's long history of code-switching works wonders for her here, as she gives each line just the right spin - enough irony for us to get the jokes, enough sincerity that we'll all sing along anyway": **Rolling Stone** - "A double-venti celebration of serial monogamy for Starbucks lovers everywhere".

Style ****
(Taylor Swift - Max Martin - Shellback - Ali Payami)
3rd Single
Recorded - Conway Recording, LA
Produced - Max Martin, Shellback & Ali Payami
Released - February 9 2015
Chart peak positions
  Hot 100 #6; AC #1; Dance/Mix Show Airplay #6; Dance Club Songs #44;
  Mainstream Top 40 #1; UK #39; Canada #19; Australia #23; NZ #6
RIAA Certification – 3 x Platinum
Selected Awards & nominations
2016 BMI Pop Awards - Award Winning Song (won)
2016 BMI Pop Awards - Publisher of the Year (won)

Perhaps inspired a little by her time with Harry Styles, Taylor writes about a tumultuous relationship where the two people keep coming back together, using the metaphor "never going out of style" to symbolise the cycle they have found themselves in.

In an interview with Ryan Seacrest, she explained: "I love comparing these timeless visuals with a feeling that never goes out of style…The two people are trying to forget each other. So, it's like, 'All right, I heard you went off with her', and well, I've done that, too…What happens when you grow up is you realise the rules of relationships are very blurred and that it gets very complicated very quickly, and there's not a case of who is right or who is wrong."

The instrumental for the song was originally written by producer Ali Payami and guitarist Niklas Ljungfelt for themselves. Ljungfelt played it to Max Martin at the latter's studio, and when Taylor got to hear it, she decided to record it for herself with added drums and synthesisers, and also using ostinato, the same musical phrase over and over.

The lyric hint is "Her Heart Belonged to Someone Who Couldn't Stay".

Kyle Newman directed the music video on location in Los Angeles over four days. To play her love interest Taylor contacted British actor Dominic Sherwood, a mutual friend, about a month before, who at the time was working on the movie *Billionaire Ransom*. Despite no clear narrative, the video features flashbacks of the two of them together in various settings.

Taylor planned to premiere the video on *Good Morning America* on February 13th 2015, but the Canadian music channel Much released it the night before, with Taylor uploading it to her Vevo account the same day.

Pitchfork - "Seems like a distilled look at a future version of Taylor Swift. Though it is structured like so many of her previous tracks, it's not her meticulous songwriting that throws you into a headrush. Instead, it's her vocals, tense and restrained, misting emotion in cascading sighs and implied ellipses"; **The Independent** - "The shallow - possibly skewed? - vision of Swift's own self can almost be ignored by the time the bridge rolls around"; **Vulture** - "Despite the dress-up games in the chorus, this is one of the rare Swift love songs to feel truly adult: Both she and the guy have been down this road too many times to bullshit anymore"; **Rolling Stone -** "Full of hushed-breath melodrama, where even the guy taking off his coat can feel like a plot twist"; **NME** - "It's Swift at her best".

Out of the Woods *****
(*Taylor Swift - Jack Antonoff)*
6th Single
Recorded - Jungle City Studios, NY; Conway Recording LA
Produced - Jack Antonoff & Taylor Swift
Released - January 19 2016
Chart peak positions
  Hot 100 #18; AC #20; Adult Top 40 #11; Mainstream Top 40 #12; UK #136;
  Canada #8; NZ #6
RIAA Certification - Platinum

A song about trying to hang on to a fragile relationship destined to end, and then pondering over past mistakes that both parties have made, while also capturing some of the excitement and anxieties of their time together. Taylor explained: "It kind of conjured up all these feelings of anxiety I had in a relationship where everybody was watching, everybody was commenting on it. You're constantly just feeling like, Are we out of the woods, yet? What's the next thing gonna be? What's the next hurdle we're gonna have to jump over? Are we gonna make it to the next week?"

In an interview for NPR, Taylor explained the lyrics: "That line is in there because it's not only the actual, literal narration of what happened in a particular relationship I was in, it's also a metaphor. 'Hit the brakes too soon' could mean the literal sense of, we got in an accident and we had to deal with the aftermath. But also, the relationship ended sooner than it should've because there was a lot of fear involved."

With its hidden message, "They Loved Each Other Recklessly", speculation over who the song is about had fans in a frenzy. The bridge section references a snowmobile accident that Taylor had with Styles, and there's even specific mention of a paper airplane necklace, which the two of them wore when together. Taylor revealed: "That song touches on a huge sense of anxiety that was, kind of, coursing through that particular relationship, because we really felt the heat of every single person in the media thinking they could draw up the narrative of what we were going through and debate and speculate. I don't think it's ever going to be easy for me to find love and block out all those screaming voices."

Taylor cited the song as one of her favourites, as it "best represents *1989*". It became her 61st record to enter the Hot 100. For a female artist, only Aretha Franklin had scored more chart entries with an incredible 73.

The cinematic music video was directed by Joseph Kahn and was filmed on location in the mountains of Queenstown and on the Bethells Beach in New Zealand. A severe storm caused a week-long delay. In the video Taylor is shown battling through what appears to be an enchanted forest forming around her as she runs from a pack of wolves. She then appears in different settings, including snowy mountains, barren landscapes, and burning forests, before finally reaching a shore, with a caption that reads: "She lost him, but she found herself, and somehow that was everything". The video was premiered on *Dick Clark's New Year's Rocking Eve* show on December 31st.

New York Magazine - "Seems to herald an exciting, unexpected, and mature new direction in Swift's sound"; **The Guardian** - "A beautiful, churning incantation, set delicately on that tipping point between casual fling and heartfelt romance"; **Time** - "It's the furious chant of that anthemic chorus, all breathless urgency, and the left-of-centre production that help Swift perform the niftiest sleight of hand"; **Rolling Stone** - "Antonoff was just learning how to record her voice, and wow, he wasn't even halfway there yet - it's the production equivalent of a snowmobile wreck", **NME** - "It's a breathless, honest depiction of a lost relationship, and one of Swift's greatest triumphs".

All You Had to Do Was Stay ***
(Taylor Swift - Max Martin)
Recorded - Conway Recording, LA
Produced - Max Martin, Shellback & Mattman & Robin
Released - October 27 2014
Chart peak positions

Hot 100 Bubbling Under #14; Canada #92; Australia #99
RIAA Certification - Gold

A song about a crumbling relationship that falls apart due to her lover's indecision, and another example of Taylor's tendency to always make the fifth track on the album an emotional ballad. In an interview with Ryan Adams, she explained: "I had a dream that my ex showed up at my door, knocked on the door, and I opened it up and I was about ready to launch into, like, the perfect thing to say, and instead, all that would come out of my mouth was that high-pitched chorus of people singing 'stay!'"

The lyric hint is "They Paid the Price".

Cosmopolitan - "Men: If you break up with your girlfriend this winter and want to know what she'll listen to while she curses your memory over red wine and dance parties, this song is the answer"; **Vulture** - "Came to its writer in a dream. Inspiration works in mysterious ways"; **Rolling Stone** - "A *1989* banger that could have made an excellent single".

Shake It Off ****
(Taylor Swift - Max Martin - Shellback)
1st Single
Recorded - MXM Studios Stockholm, Conway Recording LA
Produced - Max Martin & Shellback
Released - August 18 2014
Chart peak positions
  Hot 100 #1; AC #1; Adult Top 40 #1; Country Airplay #58; Dance Club Songs
  #17; Latin Airplay #48; Mainstream Top 40 #1; Rhythmic #17; UK #2; Canada
  #9; Australia #3; NZ #3; Japan #34
RIAA - Diamond
Selected awards and nominations
2015 BMI Pop Awards - Award-Winning Songs (won)
2015 BMI Pop Wards - Publisher of the Year (won)
2015 Grammys - Record of the Year (nominated)
2015 Grammys - Song of the Year (nominated)
2015 Grammys - Best Pop Solo Performance (nominated)
2015 Billboard Music Awards - Top Streaming Song (video) (won)
2015 Billboard Music Awards - Top Hot 100 Song (nominated)
2015 Billboard Music Awards - Top Digital *Song* (nominated)
2015 iHeartRadio Music Awards - Song of the Year (won)

In what is arguably Taylor's most famous song, she shakes off all of her critics and haters, and has more fun than them by just being herself and doing whatever makes her happy. She explained to *Billboard*: "That song is essentially written about an important lesson I learned that really changed how I live my life and how I look at my life. I really wanted it to be a song that made people want to get up and dance at a wedding reception from the first drum beat. But I also wanted it to be a song that could help someone get through something really terrible."

In another interview for ABC News, she said: "People will find anything about you and twist it to where it's weird or wrong or annoying or strange or bad. You have to not only live your life in spite of people who don't understand you, you have to have more fun than they do", while on her own YouTube channel she claimed: "I've learned a pretty tough lesson that people can say whatever they want about us at any time, and we cannot control that. The only thing we can control is our reaction to that."

For *Rolling Stone*, she put it more bluntly: "I've had every part of my life dissected...When you live your life under that kind of scrutiny, you can either let it break you, or you can get really good at dodging punches. And when one lands, you know how to deal with it. And I guess the way I deal with it is to shake if off."

According to Taylor's journals, the song was written over two days in February 2014, and the chorus first came to her after hearing producers Martin and Shellback play a beat.

The lyric hint is "She Danced to Forget Him".

As the first single taken from the album, 'Shake It Off' spent a total of four weeks at #1 on the Hot 100 and remained on the chart for 50 weeks. It became the most successful single of her career, with sales of well over 5.4 million in the US alone, giving it diamond status.

The music video was directed by Mark Romanek with choreography by Tyco Dioro, with filming taking place over three days in Los Angeles in June 2014. Taylor recalled how she visualised a humorous depiction of her trying to find her true identity: "It takes a long time to figure out who you are and where you fit in the world." In the video she is portrayed as clumsy when it comes to dance moves: "I'm putting myself in all these awkward situations where the dancers are incredible, and I'm having fun with it, but not fitting in...I'm being embarrassingly bad at it. It shows you to keep doing you, keep being you, keep trying to figure out where you fit in in the world, and eventually you will." The final scenes have Taylor dancing with fans who had been handpicked by her via social media. The video was released on August 18th, the same day as the single.

Billboard - "The song suggests the world's biggest country star now belongs to a different genre entirely. The completed transition is jarring, but the impeccable pop stylings make it easy to swallow"; **The Guardian** - "The incongruent blend of modern dance, ballet, and breakdancing is fun, but the conceit falls flat. Taylor is a little too skilled a dancer for the comedy to really work"; **The Daily Beast** - "We are in a new phase of Taylor Swift's career. It is, apparently, one in which she feels comfortable using the term 'sick beat'. Taylor Swift is now a pop star. Ugh"; **Vulture** - "The spoken-word bridge and cheerleader breakdown...might be the worst 24 seconds of the entire album"; **Rolling Stone** - "A clever transitional single - great verses, grating chorus, pithy lyrics with a shout out to her obvious inspiration, Robyn's 'Dancing on My Own'"; **NME** - "There's no two ways about it: 'Shake it Off' is a stone-cold smash".

I Wish You Would ***

(Taylor Swift - Jack Antonoff)
Recorded - Lamby's House Studios, Brooklyn; Conway Recording, LA
Produced - Taylor Swift, Jack Antonoff, Max Martin & Greg Kurstin
Released - October 27 2014
Chart peak position
  Canada Digital #58

A song about wanting a guy to come back to her and start over, because she misses him and feels sorry for breaking up with him in the first place, with the twist that neither one knows how the other feels. According to a fan who attended one of Taylor's Secret Sessions, it was revealed that it was written a couple of months after Taylor and Harry Styles broke up and then decided to become friends again and that the song was about a time when Styles pulled up at her house and was deciding whether or not to see her, while she was in the bedroom wishing he would make the first move and come back to her. The truth behind that story has never been confirmed.

The lyric hint is "He Drove Past Her Street Each Night".

The song would not have been out of place on *Red*. Taylor described working with Antonoff in her voice memo for the song: "We were hanging out and he pulled out his phone and goes, 'I made this amazing track the other day. It's so cool. I love these guitar sounds.' And he played it for me and immediately I could hear this finished song in my head, and I just said, 'Please, please let me have that. Let me play with this, send it to me'."

Taylor was on tour at the time, and she played the track on her laptop while recording herself singing the vocal on her phone. Antonoff loved the result.

Vulture - "You get the sense it might work better as a bleachers song".

Bad Blood (featuring Kendrick Lamar) *
(Taylor Swift - Kendrick Lamar)
4th Single
Recorded - MXM Studios, Stockholm, Conway Recording, LA
Produced - Max Martin, Shellback & Ilya
Released - May 17 2015
Chart peak positions
  Hot 100 #1; AC #9#; Adult Top 40 #4; Dance/Mix Show Airplay #5; Dance
  Club Songs #37; Mainstream Top 40 #1; Rhythmic #6; UK #4; Canada #1;
  Australia #1; NZ #1
RIAA Certification - 6 x Platinum
Selected awards and nominations
2015 MTV Video Music Awards - Video of the Year (won)
2015 MTV Video Music Awards - Best Collaboration (won)
2015 MTV Video Music Awards - Best Female Video (won)
2015 MTV Video Music Awards - Best Pop Video (won)
2015 MTV Video Music Awards - Best Direction (nominated)
2015 MTV Europe Music Awards - Best Video (won)
2015 MTV Europe Music Awards - Best Song (won)
2015 UK Music Video Awards - Best Pop Video International (won)
2015 UK Music Video Award - Best Styling (won)
2015 AMA Awards - Collaboration of the Year (nominated)
2015 BMI Awards - Award-Winning Song (won)
2015 BMI Awards - Publisher of the Year (won)
2016 Grammys - Best Pop Duo/Group Performance (nominated)
2016 Grammys - Best Music Video (won)

The album's fifth single was inspired by the feud between Taylor and her nemesis Katy Perry, and the allegation that the singer had tried to "sabotage" the *Red* tour by trying to hire three of her dancers. The hidden message is "She Made Friends and Enemies" and the song also features American rapper Kendrick Lamar.

The remixed version of 'Bad Blood' debuted on the Hot 100 at #53 and jumped to #1 a week later, making it the largest jump to the top in the chart's history. Taylor also became the first artist since Adele in 2011 to yield three chart toppers from the same album.

The Grammy-award winning music video was directed by Joseph Kahn and produced by Taylor. It was shot in Los Angeles in April 2015 and features an ensemble cast of singers and fashion models dubbed Taylor's "squad" with their appearances during the subsequent tour. With the story set in London, Taylor's character is betrayed by her secret agent partner and prepares to exact revenge with the help of her friends. Each member chose their character's name, and they included Catastrophe (Taylor); Arsyn (Selena Gomez); Lucky Fiori (Lena Dunham); Welvin da Great (Lamar); The Trinity (Hailee Steinfeld); Dilemma (Serayah); Slay-Z (Gigi Hadid); Destructa X (Ellie Goulding); Homeslice (Martha Hunt); Mother Chucker (Cara Delevingne); The Crimson Curse (Hayley Williams), Frostbyte (Lily Aldridge); Knockout (Karlie Kloss); Domino (Jessica Alba); Justice (Mariska Hargitay); Luna (Ellen Pompeo), and Headmistress (Cindy Crawford). It was not too hard to see that the villain of the video closely resembled a look which Perry once had.

The video was premiered during the Billboard Music Awards on May 17th 2015, and then broke Vevo's record by receiving 20.1 million views in its first day of release,

Rolling Stone - "Melodically parched, lyrically unfinished, rhythmically clunky"; **Spin** - "Disappointingly bland"; **New York Magazine** - "Brainless, evil pop": **Vulture** - "The lyric here indulges the worst habits of late-period Swift - an eagerness to play the victim, a slight lack of resemblance to anything approaching real life - attached to a schoolyard-chant melody that will never leave your head, even when you may want it to"; **NME** - "Would have been right at home on …villainous *Reputation*... Instead, though, it felt like an outlier on *1989*".

Wildest Dreams ****

(Taylor Swift - Max Martin - Shellback)
5th Single
Recorded - MXM Studios, Stockholm; Conway Recording, LA
Produced - Max Martin & Shellback
Released - August 31 2015
Chart peak positions
 Hot 100 #5; AC #2; Adult Top 40 #1; Dance/Mix Show Airplay #1; Mainstream
 Top 40 #1; Rhythmic # 5; UK #40; Canada #4; Australia #3; NZ #8
RIAA Certification - 4 x Platinum

A plea for her lover to remember their best moments after what appears to be an inevitable breakup. Taylor told *Rolling Stone*: "I think the way I used to approach relationships was very idealistic. I used to go into them thinking, 'Maybe this is the one - we'll get married and have a family, this could be forever.' Whereas now I go in thinking, 'How long do we have on the clock - before something comes along and puts a wrench on it, or your publicist calls and says this isn't a good idea?'"

There were numerous lyric changes between the original and studio versions, and, according to the liner notes, the beats heard at the start of the song resemble Taylor's heartbeats. The lyric hint is "He Only Saw Her in His Dreams".

Reaching #5 on the Hot 100, the song became Taylor's fifth consecutive top ten hit from the album. Singing with luscious "breathy" vocals, Taylor knows her lover is not suitable for her and warns him that after the breakup he will have haunting memories of their time together. Its sultry, dramatic atmosphere led some reviewers to compare the song to the music of Lana Del Ray, particularly her 2012 album *Born to Die*.

Add a star for the Grammy Museum acoustic version in 2015.

179

The cinematic music video was helmed by Joseph Kahn and tells the story of an old-school Hollywood romance between actors on a movie set in Africa in the 1950s. Taylor's premise was that with no social media at the time, it would be impossible for actors not to fall in love if they were isolated together for so long. Inspiration also came from classic movies such as *The African Queen*, *Out of Africa*, and *The English Patient,* all of which were set in Africa in the 1950s. Taylor plays the leading lady, Marjorie Finn (a reference to her grandmother Marjorie Finlay), while Scott Eastwood (son of actor Clint) portrays leading man Robert Kingsley (combining the name of Taylor's grandfather and her own father's middle name). The two of them fall in love, but it comes to an end after a fight on set. Then, after watching the premiere back home, she sees him with his wife and leaves in a hurry, with Kingsley then running outside to watch her limousine drive away.

The video had its premiere at the pre-show for the MTV Video Music Awards on August 31st 2015.

Billboard - "Swift flat-out mimics her [Del Ray] ... it's hard to tell if the song is homage or a parody"; **The Guardian** - "If 'Wildest Dreams' bears a hint of Lana Del Ray, there's something hugely cheering about the way Swift turns the persona of the pathetic female appendage snivelling over her bad-boy boyfriend on its head"; **Rolling Stone** - "The song sounds stronger and stronger over the years"; **Vulture** - "Swift is in full control of her instrument here, with so much yearning in her voice that you'd swear every breath was about to be her last. For a singer often slammed as being sexless, those sighs in the chorus tell us everything we need to know"; **NME** - "A synth-pop beauty".

How You Get the Girl ***
(Taylor Swift - Max Martin - Shellback)
Recorded - MXM Studios, Stockholm; Conway Recording LA
Produced - Max Martin & Shellback
Released - October 27 2014
Chart peak positions
 Hot 100 Bubbling Under #4; Canada #81
RIAA Certification - Gold

Taylor gives advice to a guy who wants to get his girlfriend back, suggesting they use better ways than she herself had used in the past, such as the time-honoured: Profess that you love her - "for worse or for better...forever and ever".

She explained to Radio.com: "I wrote about how you get the girl back if you ruined the relationship somehow and she won't talk to you anymore. All the steps you have to do to edge your way back into her life, because she's probably pretty mad at you. So, it's kind of a tutorial. If you follow the directions in the song, chances are things will work out. Or you may get a restraining order." It has been rumoured that the song was inspired by the on/off relationship between Selena Gomez and Justin Bieber.

The lyric hint is "Then One Day He Came Back".

Cosmopolitan - "I dare you to listen to this song one time and not have it stuck in your head forever. It's not possible. So how do you get the girl, Taylor? Short answer: Be honest. Long answer: 'How Do You Get the Girl' on repeat for the next five hours": **Vulture** - "The breeziest and least complicated of Swift's guy-standing-on-a-doorstep songs": **Rolling Stone** - "A seminar on girls' hearts and the

180

wooing thereof, with Coach Taylor offering a pep talk to girl-curious boys everywhere"; **NME** - "Taylor's full with useful tips for winning an ex back after an unwise dumping. She's even got a script ready".

This Love ****
(Taylor Swift)
Recorded - Pain in the Art Studios, Nashville TN
Produced - Taylor Swift & Nathan Chapman
Released - October 27 2014
Chart peak positions
  Hot 100 Bubbling Under #19; Canada #84
RIAA Certification - Platinum

The one true ballad on the album, and Taylor's only self-penned song, it's about trying to live without the person you love after a breakup, with the knowledge that if you let someone free, love will come back to you.

As documented by Tumblr, Taylor described how the song originated as a poem: "I was writing in my journal about something that had happened in my life - it was about a year ago - and I just wrote this really, really short poem…All of a sudden in my head I just started hearing this melody happen, and then I realised it was going to be a song."

The lyric hint is "Timing Is a Funny Thing".

Another one of her favourite tracks on the album, Taylor described it as "kind of like hypnotic in a way, and it's kind of somewhat romantic and wistful and relaxing." The wash of synths manages to evoke the sound of waves on the shore, and used as a metaphor, it describes the hope that love can come back to you like an ocean tide.

Slate - "The slowest, haziest song on the album"; **Vulture** - "Like an imperfect poached egg, it's shapeless but still quite appetising": **Rolling Stone** - "A meditative *1989* nocturne - half acoustic introspection, half electro reverie - as she genuflects in the midnight hour"; **NME** - "Feels remarkably maudlin when nestled in between the bevvy of synth-pop bops that [the] album holds".

I Know Places ****
(Taylor Swift - Ryan Tedder)
Recorded - Conway Recording, LA
Produced - Taylor Swift, Ryan Tedder & Noel Zancanella
Released - October 27 2014
Chart Peak Position
  Canada Digital #51
RIAA Certification - Gold

A song about the problems of a high-celebrity couple having to hide from the media circus to get some privacy.

Speaking to *Billboard*, Taylor revealed: "I had this idea of like, you know, when you're in love - along the lines of 'Out of the Woods' - it's very precious, it's fragile. As soon as the world gets a hold of it, whether it's your friends or people around town hear about it … it's kind of like the first thing people want to do when they hear that people are in love is just kind of try to ruin it, if they're not the greatest human beings…I kind of was in a place where I was like, 'No one is gonna sign up for this. There are just too many cameras pointed at me. There are too many

181

ridiculous elaborations on my life. It's just not ever gonna work.' But I decided to write a love song, just kind of like, 'What would I say if I met someone really awesome and they were like, hey, I'm worried about all this attention you get?' So I wrote this song called 'I Know Places' about, like, 'Hey, I know places we can hide. We could outrun them.'"

Taylor uses the metaphor of a fox hunt, where its only chance of escape is in its cunning ability to find a hiding place. Some reviewers see the song reflecting Taylor's early relationship with Harry Styles.

Co-writer Noel Zancanella had worked with co-producer Tedder before, and had co-authored One Republic's hit 'Good Life'.

The lyric hint is "And Everyone Was Watching".

Cosmopolitan - "It brilliantly mixes angry, sexy Taylor on the verses with anthemic, arena-filling Taylor on the chorus. One million teenage girls just made 'They are the hunters; we are the foxes' their Twitter bio"; **Vulture** - "As a slice of gothic pop-star paranoia, it gives a much-needed bit of edge to *1989*; **NME** - "A song that explores falling in love amid high pressure fame, and finding places to outrun the cameras".

Clean ****
(Taylor Swift - Imogen Heap)
Recorded - The Hideaway Studio
Produced - Taylor Swift & Imogen Heap
Released - October 27 2014
Chart peak position
 Canada Digital #45

In the final track on the standard album, Taylor finds herself emotionally and mentally drowning after a breakup and unable to move on until she is "clean". One of the last two songs written for *1989*, it came about as Taylor was shopping in London and suddenly realised she was in the same city as someone she used to date and hadn't even thought about it for weeks.

Speaking to *Elle*, she said: "A heartbroken person is unlike any other person. Their time moves at a completely different pace than ours. It's this mental, physical, emotional ache and feeling so conflicted. Nothing distracts you from it. Then time passes, and the more you live your life and create new habits…You hope [this person's] fine. The first thought that came to my mind was - I'm finally clean."

Some of Taylor's fans take the meaning of being "clean" in more basic terms, with those struggling with addiction, abuse, and mental illness, seeing it as being "literally clean". The singer immediately accepted the fans' meaning once she heard it. It was not just about losing someone you love; it was also about losing yourself, about moving on and looking after yourself mentally.

The song was co-written by the highly regarded English Grammy award-winning musician Imogen Heap, who also provides the haunting background vocals. The lyric hint is "She Lost Him but She Found Herself and Somehow That Was Everything". Add a star for the acoustic version.

Vulture - "This is *1989*'s big end-of-album-catharsis song, and the water imagery of the lyrics goes well with the drip-drip-drip production": **Rolling Stone** - "An intense finale for the all-killer homestretch of *1989*"; **NME** - "With chiming

182

soft-rock instrumentals, and gorgeous layered vocals, it's an unfussy song that's filled with Swift's impressive turn of phrase".

Wonderland ***
(Taylor Swift - Max Martin - Shellback)
1989 Deluxe Edition
Recorded - Conway Recording, LA
Produced - Max Martin & Shellback
Released - October 27 2014
Chart peak position
  Hot 100 #51

The first of three bonus tracks, this uses the story of *Alice in Wonderland* as inspiration. Taylor describes a toxic relationship in which the two lovers tumble "down the rabbit hole" and find a place "where life was never worse or never better" and enjoy a state of wanderlust. With it having a major theme of insanity, Taylor posted a lyric teaser on her Instagram: "You searched the world for something else to make you feel like what we had. And in the end, in Wonderland, we both went mad."

Suggestions that the song could be about Harry Styles were given credence when she sang it at the 2013 Grammys, dressed as the Mad Hatter with backing dancers resembling Wonderland characters, and using an English accent as part of the performance. And the lyric reference to having green eyes also could link the song to her former beau.

PopMatters - "The epic 'Wonderland' features Swift's best vocal work on the record and finds a melodramatic sweep that would obliterate the charts if someone hadn't wrongly convinced her to hold it from the proper record"; **Vulture** - "A deranged bonus track that sees Swift doing the absolute most"; **Rolling Stone** - "Taylor...fits right in on the other side of the looking glass, with white rabbits and Cheshire cats. Feed your head!"

You Are in Love ***
(Taylor Swift - Jack Antonoff)
1989 Deluxe Edition
Recorded - Jungle City Studios, NY; Conway Recording, LA
Produced - Taylor Swift, Jack Antonoff & Max Martin
Released - October 27 2014
Chart peak position
  Hot 100 #83

A soulful song inspired by the relationship of producer Jack Antonoff and Taylor's friend Lena Dunham. Speaking on Jimmy Kimmel's chat show, she explained: "Jack sent me this song. It was just an instrumental track he was working on and immediately I knew the song it needed to be. And I wrote it as a kind of commentary on what their relationship has been like."

In another interview, she revealed: "It was the most beautiful, poignant, simple track I've ever received and I wrote it really quickly. I remember writing it really fast, because I just remember thinking it sounded so much like the sound of like, actual love. True love. Live through thick and thin, sickness and health love."

Vulture - "The best of Swift's songs idealizing someone else's love story"; **NME** - "It's inoffensive, but you can see why it was only bunged on the end of the deluxe edition of the album".

New Romantics ****
(Taylor Swift - Max Martin - Shellback)
1989 Deluxe Edition
7th Single
Recorded - MXM Studios, Stockholm; Conway Recording, LA
Produced - Max Martin & Shellback
Released - February 23 2016
Chart peak positions
  Hot 100 #46; AC #18; UK #132; Canada #58; Australia #35; Japan #90
RIAA Certification - Gold
Selected awards & nominations
2016 Teen Awards - Choice Song - Female Artist (nominated)

The seventh and final single off *1989*. With a more mature mindset, Taylor takes a satirical view on love and the way young adults approach it. With the knowledge now that love isn't a fairytale, and chances of a happily ever after less likely, she sees it's better to live your life freely and not take relationships too seriously. Speaking to *Cosmopolitan*, she said: "People will say, let me set you up with someone, and I'm just sitting there saying, 'That's not what I'm doing. I'm not lonely; I'm not looking.' They just don't get it. I've learned that just because someone is cute and wants to date you, that's not a reason to sacrifice your independence and allow everyone to say whatever they want about you. I'm not doing that anymore."

The music video was released on April 6th 2015 exclusively on Apple Music. Directed by Jonas Akerlund, it features clips of Taylor performing the song during the *1989* Tour.

Pitchfork - "A surging, euphoric song…Swift's voice is processed and couched in thrilling yelps and sighs, crunchy synth, and galloping drums"; **Washington Post** (on the song's hook) - "Somewhere between mouldy emo and the back pages of a high school literary magazine"; **New York Magazine** - "[A failed attempt at] writing a big generational anthem"; **Vulture** - "Like '22', an attempt at writing a big generational anthem. That it was left off the album proper suggests Swift didn't think it quite got there"; **Rolling Stone** - "Having written a work of genius, exceeding even the wildest hopes any fan could have dreamed, she left it off the damn album, a very New Romantic thing to do"; **NME** - "It should have been a single! The sparkling success is pure euphoria".

"The most impressive sleight of hand"

It was a time when the music industry was seeing a sharp decline in record sales brought about by the growing number of streaming platforms. But not when it came to Taylor Swift, whose albums had been selling like it was 1979. With her two previous albums each selling over a million copies within their first week, she was established as one of the best-selling digital artists in the world. Adding this to her potentially risky decision to completely break away from her country roots, it was feared that predicted first-week sales of *1989* would be in the region of 600,000 to 750,000.

They need not have worried. *1989* shot straight to #1 on the Hot 200, making her the first artist to have three albums each selling a million copies in its first week;

to have the first album of 2014 to exceed a million sales; and the second female artist to have two albums each having five Hot 100 top ten hits.

1989 remained on top of the charts for 11 non-consecutive weeks, and spent a full year in the top ten. It eventually went on to achieve worldwide sales of over 10 million, making it Taylor's second most successful album behind *Fearless*. All but one of its seven singles ('New Romantics') went on to achieve platinum or multi-platinum status, with 'Shake It Off' becoming the most successful single of her career.

This album, and the two to follow, *Reputation* and *Lover*, would solidify her place as a true pop superstar.

The Guardian - "[Her co-producers] make umpteen highly polished pop records every year, but they're seldom as clever or as sharp or as perfectly attuned as this, which suggests those qualities were brought to the project by the woman whose name is on the cover"; **Time** - "The most impressive sleight of hand yet, shifting the focus away from her past and on to her music which is as smart and as confident as it's ever been"; **New York Times** - "By making pop with almost no contemporary references, Ms Swift is aiming somewhere even higher, an emotive timelessness few pop stars even bother aspiring to"; **Billboard** - "[Taylor's] rare ability to write to multiple audiences and ages even more universal ...[and] expertly sets up the next chapter of what is now even more likely to be a long career"; **Vogue** - "A joyful reminder of just how fun it is to love every second on a pop record, no strings attached. Perhaps the critical community has been expecting too much from pop these days"; **Rolling Stone** - "This is still an artist who likes to let it rip, deeply weird, feverishly emotional, wildly enthusiastic. *1989* sounds like Taylor Swift even when it sounds like nothing she's ever tried before".

Her music, now taken much more seriously by her would-be critics, even led to some of the biggest names in the industry singing her praises. Even the venerable Neil Young referred to her as "a great writer."

The backlash

While the music of *1989* was still being lauded, there had been growing media criticism over music videos made for two of the album's hit singles. Where 'Shake it Off' had received accusations of "racist and cultural appropriation", the video for 'Wildest Dreams' had received an immediate backlash on its release. *The Huffington Post* claimed it "channels white colonialism", and that "instead of the cultural appropriation that has become almost status quo in today's pop music, Swift has opted for the bolder option of actually just embodying the political exploitation of a region and its people." The *Daily Mail* accused it of having "a major race problem" adding: "The video wants to have its old-school Hollywood romance but ends up eating some old-school Hollywood racism, too... Just because you represent the past or pay respect to it doesn't mean you need to recreate its worst aspects." *The Atlantic* opined: "The past is beautiful until you're reminded it's ugly."

NPR claimed: "Swift's music is entertaining for many. She should absolutely be able to use any location as a backdrop. But she packages our continent as the backdrop for her romantic songs devoid of any African person or storyline, and she sets the video in a time when the people depicted by Swift and her co-stars killed, dehumanised and traumatised millions of Africans. That is beyond problematic…We don't totally blame Taylor Swift, but the people behind the video should have done a little more research. They should have wondered how Africans would react. This nostalgia that privileged white people have for colonial Africa is awkwardly confusing to say the least and offensive to say the most."

New York Magazine defended the video, saying that the accusations were "overblown", suggesting that we should all "take a deep breath, exhale, and direct our rage toward something that matters."

Amid all the accusations of racist connotations, Kahn defended both Taylor and his work. In a public statement, he said: "We collectively decided it would have been historically inaccurate to load the crew with more black actors as the video would have been accused of rewriting history. This video is set in the past by a crew set in the present…The reality is not only were there people of colour in the video, but the key creatives who worked on this video are people of colour. I am Asian American, the producer Jill Hardin is an African-American woman, and the editor Chancler Haynes is an African-American man."

Speaking to *Vulture*, Kahn said he realised that a video with two whites having a romance in Africa during an era of segregation would be a minefield in the culture wars and that he tried to come up with ways to incorporate Africans into the film to make it work. At first, he wanted to cast an African as the director of the movie being portrayed in the video, but said he would then be accused of "whitewashing history and pretending apartheid didn't exist." He also rejected the idea of featuring an African movie crew in the video, suggesting it would appear "like you're running a plantation."

Although Taylor herself made no comments, she donated proceeds from advertisements linked to her video to the charity African Parks Foundation of America, and they issued a statement: "We are honoured that Taylor Swift is donating all proceeds from her newest video 'Wildest Dreams' to African Parks. We thank her for shining the spotlight on Africa's wildlife, and for helping us conserve and protect many of the world's threatened species."

"The most enthusiastic, obnoxious person"

Three days after the release of *1989*, Taylor continued with its promotion. On October 28th she guested on *The Late Show with David Letterman* and performed 'Welcome to New York' with her band. During the interview, Taylor discussed her new role of Global Ambassador for New York City and her love affair with the Big Apple. Imagining how the powers-that-be had chosen her for the role, she said: "She's the most enthusiastic, obnoxious person to ever love New York. She loves it with, like, 18 exclamation points after it, underlined."

Two days later she was on *Good Morning America*, singing three songs live from Times Square, including 'Out of the Woods'.

Meanwhile, Taylor had just launched what would be her fourth fragrance, entitled "Incredible Things", which had a gold cap embossed with the number 13. The press release from Elizabeth Arden stated: "Taylor lives her life with an open heart, and by sharing her personal stories through music, art and fragrance, she helps inspire her fans to follow their heart, to be their own artist - to do incredible things. Channeling Taylor's inherent ability to see beauty in the world, she encourages her fans to do the same."

On November 3rd, following weeks of speculation by fans and the media alike, Taylor announced on Twitter: "So yeah, #The1989WorldTour is happening!! ...I CANNOT WAIT". According to her official site, it would kick off in Bossier City, Louisiana, on May 20th, and finish in Australia in December. Vance Joy would be the main support for the North American gigs. The Australian singer had had his smash hit 'Riptide' covered by Taylor during BBC's *Live Lounge* segment in London in October. Canadian artist Shawn Mendes would also appear at selected concerts. Tickets would go on sale on November 14th.

That same month, Taylor jetted off to Japan to promote the tour and perform on several of their television shows. Back in Nashville, she lost out with her nomination for Best Female Artist at the CMA Awards. However, returning home for the AMAs in Los Angeles on the 23rd, she performed 'Blank Space' as a live recreation of its music video, and was then presented with the Dick Clark Award for Excellence by Diana Ross, in recognition of her being the first artist to have three albums debut with more than a million copies sold in their first week.

During her acceptance speech, Taylor took a subtle shot at Spotify: "What you did by going out and investing in music and albums is saying you believe in the same thing I believe in. That music is valuable and should be consumed in albums, and albums should be consumed as art and appreciated."

Two days later, Taylor was in New York to perform 'Blank Space' on *The Voice*, acting out the lyrics with lots of hair flips, silly faces and hand gestures. One reviewer noted: "It feels like Taylor's comfortable with and in on the jokes about her love life and more than willing to poke a little fun at herself, even on live television."

As the festive season got under way, there were the customary appearances on the iHeartRadio Jingle Ball Tour and a number of dates in London, including Capital FM Radio's Jingle Bell Ball and another appearance at the Victoria's Secret Fashion Show, where she sang 'Blank Space' and 'Style', while once more sharing the stage with Snow Angel supermodels that included Karlie Kloss and Lily Aldridge.

According to Capital FM Radio, "she arrived onto the stage in a sexy black and gold cropped top and hot pants...showing off those loooong legs and flashing a smile at the crowd!" Like the Angels, Taylor had several costume changes, which *Us Weekly* described as "a cleavage-bearing slip with a cream-coloured floor-length robe over a satin negligee... [and], while singing the Harry Styles-inspired tune 'Style', she bared even more in sheer black lace lingerie."

Brand Swift

The tremendous year finally came to a close with another guest spot on *Dick Clark's New Year's Rockin Eve* in New York's Times Square and performances of 'Welcome to New York' and 'Shake It Off'.

Just ten years ago Taylor was no more than a blip on music's radar, just beginning to get noticed for her amazing songwriting talent and charismatic personality. In the decade that followed, the transition from teen idol to global icon had not only seen her become one of music's highest earners, but also an undeniably powerful presence in the industry and a force now to be reckoned with.

In a candid interview for *Time* magazine, Taylor was asked about what writing a song does for her: "Being a celebrity means you lock your doors and close your windows and don't let people in. Being a songwriter means you're very attuned to your own intuition and your own feelings even if they hurt. So, I approach it much more from a songwriter's perspective. But I do know how to pull myself out now, from that constant, never-ending, bottomless rabbit hole of self-doubt and fear. I've been able to write songs and feel better. They clarify and simplify the emotions that you're feeling. Nothing you do is going to make the pain stop. It just helps to have it clarified and simplified."

Although Taylor had her music to thank for most of her income, another key factor in terms of commercial success was Swift as a brand. At 24, her untarnished image as "America's Sweetheart" still remained intact, and, as a much-sought-after advertising partner, would see her endorsing products for massive companies like Elizabeth Arden, Cover Girl, Sony, Keds Footwear, and Target. Even then, she didn't escape some moments of controversy. In 2011 Taylor had her first run-in with the photoshop police when Cover Girl's parent company Procter & Gamble were forced to pull a printed ad for not being able to prove that a mascara range showing an airbrushed image of the singer actually "enhanced lashes" as claimed.

Nevertheless, more recently, Diet Coke had her walking her long legs all the way to the bank with an estimated figure of $26 million to appear in several of their tv ads. Where there is power, there is always money, and in the twelve months between June 2014 and June 2015, Taylor will have had career earnings of an estimated $80 million.

Apart from the continuing success, what had changed in recent years was public scrutiny toward her. Whether it be her spats with Kanye West and Katy Perry, political opinions, such as her support for feminism, or even her frequent public appearances with her so-called "squad" of celebrity friends, it looked to some that she was doing it to keep her name in the news headlines, and, as a result, was now eroding the sense of authenticity she had so far maintained.

Like a number of artists, Taylor had her fair share of haters, no doubt exaggerated by social media, but due to her incredible stoicism, she would, in her own words, continue to shake them off.

With all the complexities of stardom, maybe it was time for her to take a break. But not just yet. There was another world tour to prepare for.

The Most Spectacular Tour

"I was very adamant that every decision I've made creatively in the past had to be almost flipped.
You're not going to see me playing a banjo"

New year and a new guy

2015 began with a trio of honours at the People's Choice Awards in Los Angeles, winning Favourite Song (for 'Shake It Off'), Favourite Female Artist, and Favourite Pop Artist. Less success came the following month at the Grammys, where she failed to pick up awards after nominations for Record of the Year, Song of the Year, and Best Pop Solo Performance (all for 'Shake It Off').

Meanwhile, Katy Perry was interviewed by *Billboard*, and, when asked about the past magazine profiles and subtweets regarding her relationship with Taylor, she simply remarked: "If somebody is trying to defame my character, you're going to hear about it."

In February, Taylor was invited to *Saturday Night Live's* 40th Anniversary Special after-show party in New York, where she rubbed guitars with the legendary Paul McCartney, performing 'I Saw Her Standing There' and 'Shake It Off', along with Jimmy Fallon and Dan Aykroyd.

One particularly notable date in Taylor's journal came that month with the Elle Style Awards in London. Backstage at the show, British singer Ellie Goulding introduced Taylor to her friend, Calvin Harris (real name Adam Wiles), the 31-year-old Scottish singer-songwriter, DJ, and producer. Harris had previously dated British singer Rita Orr, and had only recently split with his former girlfriend, model Aarika Wolf. Wearing a sultry, emerald-green Julien Macdonald dress, Taylor must have made an eye-catching first impression.

The following evening, they were apparently both spotted at the Brit Awards in London, where she performed 'Blank Space' and won International Solo Female Artist. As well as being seen chatting backstage with Mick Jagger, they were holding hands and looking cosy with one other at the after-show party. *The Guardian* commented on her performance: "'Blank Space' is her bunny-boiler anthem where she doesn't entirely convince us she's driven insane by lust into courting a series of players - and its minimalist verses make for a rather tempered, non-bombastic opener. She does a perfectly pleasant vocal performance held aloft by big backing vox and strummed guitars..."

Through a source, *Heatworld* magazine alleged that Harris later sent a private jet to pick Taylor up and fly her out to Las Vegas to watch him play one of his regular DJ concerts at the MGM Grand nightclub. Reports also claimed Ellie Goulding, Selena Gomez and the Haim sisters were also in tow, and the girls were all seen "having fun" standing with Harris behind his booth.

The couple-to-be would announce many months later that they had begun dating on March 6th. That month, the two of them were snapped exiting a food store in Nashville and wearing matching shaded outfits, and in no time at all the picture went viral on social media. *Cosmopolitan* saw it as possible bad timing for Taylor, as it had just been announced that Taylor's best friend and soulmate Ed Sheeran was now single.

While in Nashville, Taylor and Harris were seen kissing at hometown singer Kevin Chesney's *Big Revival* Tour on the 26th, where Taylor joined him on stage during the second verse of his hit single 'Big Star' and swapped lead vocals. Three days later she was in Los Angeles for the iHeartRadio Music Awards, winning the categories of Artist of the Year, Song of the Year ('Shake It Off'), and Best Lyrics ('Blank Space'). During the show, Taylor was a little starstruck herself when she was invited to play guitar on Madonna's performance of 'Ghosttown'. Even without singing herself, Taylor, towering over the diminutive legend, still managed to steal some of her thunder.

While still not officially a couple, Taylor and Harris added fuel to the media fire in April, when they appeared at the Troubadour in West Hollywood to see Taylor's friends Haim perform at a benefit concert, and were once again sporting matching outfits. The celebrity coupling was seen as being taken to the next level with each public sighting.

Family crisis

On April 19th came an emotional evening at the ACM Awards, held in Dallas, where Taylor was presented with their 50th Anniversary Milestone Award by none other than her mother Andrea, who addressed the audience in surely one of the most heartfelt introductions ever given to an artist: "I've watched this milestone artist from the time she was a tangled hair little girl growing up on our farm; full of imagination and creativity, until right now as she prepares for her next world tour. And ever since then, her favourite thing in the world to do has been to write a song, tell a story, play a guitar or a piano. And I've seen those things carry her through every emotion, every experience in her life, good or bad... For many years I was her constant companion, and I witnessed a young girl with very few friends become a young woman with many, learning to stand up for herself and the things she believes in, being brave enough to explore her musical curiosity, having a voice for those against those who hate, and giving of herself to those in need, and like many of you out there tonight with children of your own, I am a very proud mom."

In turn, Taylor thanked the country music community for accepting with good grace her decision to explore other genres and make a pop album, and also how thankful she was to have learned to write songs in Nashville.

That emotional evening had come just a matter of days after ABC News reported that Taylor had put this message on Tumblr about her 57-year-old mother: "I'm writing to you with an update I wish I wasn't giving you, but it's important and I'm used to sharing important events in my life with you...This is something my family and I thought you should know about now. For Christmas this year, I asked my mum that one of her gifts to me to be going to the doctor to get screened for any health issues, just to ease some worries of mine. She agreed, and went in to get checked. There were no red flags and she felt perfectly fine, but she did it just to get me and my brother off her case about it."

190

Then came the bombshell: "The results came in, and I'm saddened to tell you that my mum has been diagnosed with cancer... She wanted you to know because your parents may be too busy juggling everything they've got going on to go to the doctor, and maybe you reminding them to go get checked for cancer could possibly lead to an early diagnosis and an easier battle...I hope and pray that you never get news like this."

Although not going into any more detail, Taylor felt it was right for her fans to know, even though she was struggling to come to terms with the news herself.

With Andrea undergoing treatment, it must have been truly hard for Taylor to focus on the upcoming tour, but rehearsals had to go ahead, and she informed her fans that her mother would probably not be able to attend some of the concerts in her role of tour "ambassador". Only time would tell.

Getting ready for the road

Seven months in the planning, Taylor was involved in every single aspect. This time she was looking to make it feel to *all* the fans like a more intimate setting, which had been challenging in the large arenas of the *Red* tour. Speaking to *Time* magazine, she expressed that her goal was "for those people in the very top row [to] feel like they got an intimate, personal experience." Her choice of special guests would include not just fellow singers, but actors, models, and even some sports stars.

Taylor would still enjoy the wonderful support of her musician family, although there had been a couple of changes in the Agency. Although backing singers the Starlights would continue to be an integral part of the performances, lead guitarist and fan favourite Grant Mickelson had parted ways to pursuit other projects, as had violinist and backing singer Caitlin Evanson, soon to become a big star in her own right. Musical director David Cook was also on board to provide additional keyboards.

With *1989* being an album of essentially full-blown pop music, it would be like having to start all over from scratch. Taylor told *Rolling Stone*: "I was very adamant that every decision I've made creatively in the past had to be almost flipped. You're not going to see me playing a banjo. It's not a country show, it's not a multi-genre show, and it's not a mixed-influence show."

Three months were spent in rehearsals, "replicating the sonic quality of the album", with producer Max Martin sitting down with the musicians and taking each song one at a time to explain what had to be achieved to create the "glistening bounce" he and Taylor were looking for. The dozen or so male dancers also went through four weeks of choreography with the singer to perfect their routines.

Unlike some of her previous tours, which had included a more balanced mix of old and new songs, the main focus for *1989* would be songs taken from the album, and due to fans making it a multi-platinum success, Taylor felt assured it was the right thing to do: "If this album hadn't been so impactful to the fans, if they hadn't gone out and broken so many records and made sure that I knew that this album was the most important one to them and the one they liked the most, I probably would have had to pull more old hits into the set." Even the few old popular hits that remained were done differently, adding or removing certain instruments. There would also be less drama, with none of the theatrical costumes of the previous tours. Instead, this was a chance to make it all about fashion statements, with no expense spared. Before all the shows, flashing bracelets would be handed out to the audience, which could be programmed to change colour during the performances, another cool way of connecting with the fans.

Taylor's celebrity squad also had a big part to play, with huge visuals of them basically narrating the show by giving their perspective of how they saw the singer and the songs at this stage of her career. In Taylor's words, "it almost feels as if you are in a different world."

The logistics for staging the tour were as impressive as the performances. It would involve 26 semi-trailer trucks and 11 buses carrying 146 people to each venue, and, in each city, some 125-150 extra people were hired for the offloading and stage setup, which could take anything from a few hours to a couple of days, depending on the type of venue.

1989 - The great tour begins

What was destined to become the highest-grossing tour of the year kicked off with three warm-up concerts. The first two were in front of 55,000-strong audiences at the Tokyo Dome on May 5th and 6th, followed by one in Las Vegas on May 15th as part of Rock in Rio USA, a spin-off to the Brazilian festival.

During the Vegas show, Taylor's friend Lena Dunham made the best video quote of the evening, saying: "I'm surprised when she walks down the street stray cats don't follow her like the patron saint." Highlights of Taylor's performance included a beautiful acoustic 'Wonderland', a fiery rendition of 'Bad Blood', and a chance to duet on Ed Sheeran's 'Tenerife Sea'; his own set had preceded her two-hour stint. However, the show, which got under way at 11.30pm, was not without its mishaps. Not only did Taylor's vocals keep cutting out, but there were also problems with the mixing, leading to some of the audience leaving early.

The *Las Vegas Weekly* wrote: "Those who stayed enjoyed a one-of-a-kind performance - fireworks and all - and the chance to see the pop princess in all her glittering glory", while *Billboard* saw it as being evident that "the pop princess had earned her stripes and was well on her way to becoming a queen".

Other reviewers were not so impressed. Vice.com wrote: "Nobody would begrudge Taylor the ability to embrace a growing confidence in her mid-20s, a fantasy to dress fabulous and be The Star. She is! Taylor wants to draw a line under the Swift of yore who dared to try it all (country, pop and dubstep wobbles) and instead establish a homogeneous Pop Star mould with a clear vision and a perma-pout. The problem is, she's no longer making it look easy and her vision doesn't seem that clear."

The first leg of the official tour got under way in Bossier City, Louisiana, on May 20th, and took in another eight cities around the country right through till mid-June, finishing with two nights in Philadelphia, again in front of a sell-out crowd of 50,000.

On June 19th, the short European leg began in Cologne, followed by Amsterdam, and then moved to the UK for sell-out dates in Glasgow, Manchester and London.

During the outdoor spectacular in London's Hyde Park, Taylor told the 65,000 audience: "This is one of those nights where I'm aware I'm going to be taking mental snapshots so I can remember this night for the rest of my life."

In a show themed around female empowerment, Taylor brought on stage to perform 'Style' some members of her celebrity squad - Gigi Hadid, Kendall Jenner, Martha Hunt, Karlie Kloss and Cara Delevingne, along with tennis star Serena Williams. She also duetted with her friend Ellie Goulding on her smash hit 'Love Me Like You Do'. Reviewing the show, *Glamour* magazine wrote: "She's the artist the world can't get enough of right now, and last night cemented that. A show of lights, glitter and kick-ass sisterhood."

The short overseas leg finished with two concerts in Dublin. *The Irish Times* noted: "Swift puts on a reasonably good show of sincerity, much of it well aimed at her demographic. A bit too much oversharing, perhaps, and far too much chat, but as major gigs go, Swift kicked it into touch."

With the shortest of breaks, the four-month-long main part of the tour commenced in Ottawa on July 6th, and was applauded by the *Ottawa Citizen*: "The talented 25-year-old, who's now one of the wealthiest and most influential pop stars on the planet, still seemed like your best friend as she dispensed relationship advice, offered self-love affirmations, and generally spoke from the heart. There were no whips and chains from this gal; even as a dance-floor diva, she's still the wholesome one."

For the majority of the US dates, Taylor would surprise her fans with specially invited guests, as she told *Seventeen*: "They [the fans] know the set list, they know the costumes, they've looked them up. That presented me with an interesting issue. I love the element of surprise…so going on this tour, having people pop on stage that you didn't expect to see."

The list of celebrity appearances would include the likes of Julia Roberts and Joan Baez dancing with her to 'Style' in Santa Clara; John Legend pulled out of the audience in LA to duet on 'All of Me'; rocking with Avril Lavigne on 'Complicated' in San Diego; sharing the microphone with the iconic Steve Tyler for 'I Don't Want to Miss a Thing' in Nashville ; strutting along to 'Satisfaction' with the one and only Mick Jagger on two separate Nashville nights; and duetting on 'Talking Body' with Swedish rock star and Euro sensation Tove Lo in Atlanta.

Although having these special surprise guests joining her on stage was exciting to see, some commentators were more sceptical. Nick Levine of the BBC said it gave the impression that the singer was only doing this to prove the power of her new image as a bona fide pop star, while Kristy Fairclough, professor in popular culture and film, identified a change in the singer's perceived identity: "Her shifting aesthetic and allegiances appear confusing in an overall narrative that presents Taylor Swift as the centre of the cultural universe."

Despite what some critics were thinking, one of Taylor's personal highlights of the tour came at the Staple Center in Los Angeles, where, on the last of five nights performing to a sell-out audience, she was presented by local basketball legend Kobe Bryant with a banner honouring her achievement for a record-breaking 16 sell-out concerts at the famous venue. An attendance milestone for the tour was also achieved at the Gillette Stadium in Foxborough in the last week of July, when Taylor performed in front of a record crowd of 116,849 for each of the two nights.

The final concert in the US took place in Tampa on the night of Halloween, with Taylor's parents both in attendance. The special guest was Idina Menzel, the voice behind Elsa in the smash animated movie *Frozen*. Dressed in an Olaf costume, Taylor duetted with her on 'Let it Go', while surrounded by her dancers all dressed as reindeer. *The Tampa Bay Times* wrote: "No doubt, after more than 70 shows, Swift could use a break. This was a physical show - Swift glistened in the unseasonable heat from her many marches up and down the catwalk. And yet her face betrayed no pain, no disillusionment, no trace she's anything other than 25 and alive."

There would be a break, but not a long one, as extra dates in Asia had been announced during the summer. In a matter of a week Taylor would be in China.

Harris in Wonderland

With the massive tour soon to be completed at the end of the year, it was time to look back on some of the award shows over the past few months. With Andrea's cancer now undergoing treatment, she had been able to attend some of Taylor's concerts and help out as she had always done before.

On May 17th, Taylor had attended the Billboard Music Awards in Las Vegas, and, in a night to remember, won a total of eight awards - Top Artist, Top Female Artist, Top Billboard 200 Artist, Top Billboard 200 album, Top Billboard 100 Artist, Top Digital Songs Artist, Top Streaming Song-Video (for 'Shake It Off') and, last but not least, the Chart Achievement Award. Taylor was accompanied, among others, by Calvin Harris and her brother Austin, whose graduation from Notre Dame she had attended earlier in the day. Taylor's relationship with Harris could not have been made more public during the show. He sat beside her, and they hugged and kissed each time the awards were announced.

Although not performing live at the show, there was the premiere of her music video for 'Bad Blood', which featured a long list of Taylor's squaddies, including Gigi Hadid, Karlie Kloss, and Selena Gomez in a dark wig with bangs that many saw to be a reference to Katy Perry. A few days later, on May 23rd, Taylor tried to suppress the conflict in an interview with the *Daily Telegraph* by saying: "I'm not giving them anything to write about. I'm never going to talk about her in my interviews. It's not going to happen."

The following day Taylor was back in the UK to perform in BBC Radio 1's Big Weekend at Earlham Park in Norwich. According to the *Daily Mirror*, Harris's ex-girlfriend Rita Ora made a sly dig onstage about him, and, to top it all off, the radio played a few of her songs minutes before Taylor took to the stage. As the venue wasn't used to playing host to celebrity A-listers, there were not enough dressing rooms for the stars, and Taylor had to be relocated to the adjacent University of East Anglia building. As a mark of respect for her British fans, she also covered the cost of local cab fares, with each taxi emblazoned with her album cover. Dave Grohl of the Foo Fighters later admitted that Taylor was his guilty pleasure and dedicated the song 'Congregation' to her: "I'm officially obsessed, she might want to get a restraining order."

Even though the tour had kept the two apart for long periods, the relationship between Taylor and Calvin Harris was seen to be blossoming. At the end of May they had been spotted having lunch in New York. A source told E! News: "They are trying to be as private as they can but they are also not afraid or hiding their affection towards each other when they are together in public. They both love New York City and this trip together is really easy and comfortable for them."

On June 9th, Taylor posted her first picture of Harris on Instagram. The blurry black and white photo of her "favourite people", taken in the kitchen, showed Harris along with her girlfriends Gigi Hadid and Karlie Kloss. She tweeted, "They were laughing so hard, the lens couldn't capture it fast enough." The following day Taylor shared a picture showing her and Harris having fun on an inflatable swan, while a source told *Us Weekly*: "They're making time for each other in a way that other guys she's been with haven't before. They're taking it one step at a time." A few days later Taylor was performing in Glasgow in Harris's native country, and she told the enthusiastic audience, "I happen to love Scottish people."

On June 27th, Taylor was at the British Summer Time festival at London's Hyde Park, and during her 19-song set introduced on stage her friends Kendall Jenner, Karlie Kloss and Carla Delevingne. The *Daily Telegraph* called the performance "bedazzling charm."

The next day, Taylor and Harris were spotted looking cosy aboard a boat on the River Thames, double-dating with the then-couple Gigi Hadid and Joe Jonas, and with Karlie also along for the ride. Taylor's friend and would-be matchmaker Ellie Goulding told *The Sun*: "Calvin is a really great mate and he's so fantastic, and Taylor is such a cool person who I love. I thought, 'They're both really awesome and both really tall, they'll be brilliant together'." During the concert in Dublin, Taylor was seen making sweet gestures to Harris while performing 'I Know Places', as he looked on from near the sound desk.

A couple of weeks after spending a Fourth of July holiday together, Harris announced in a radio interview that things were "going absolutely fantastic" between them.

Trouble with Nicki and Katy

When nominations were announced in July for the forthcoming MTV Video Music Awards, Taylor found herself embroiled in more controversy. It began when Trinidadian rap artist Nicki Minaj fired off tweets about her videos for 'Feeling Myself' and 'Anaconda' not receiving top nominations. In one tweet she argued: "When the 'other' girls drop a video that breaks records and impacts culture they get that nomination", while in another she claimed: "If your video celebrates women with very slim bodies, you will be nominated for vid of the year."

Taylor felt that this was aimed at the video for 'Bad Blood' and, in a since-deleted tweet, wrote "I've done nothing but love & support you. It's unlike you to pit women against each other. Maybe one of the men took your slot." This brought a response from the rapper: "Huh? U must not be reading my tweets. Didn't say a word about u. I love you just as much. But you should speak on this." Taylor, to her credit, ended this the only way she could by replying: "If I win, please come up with me!! You're invited to any stage I'm ever on." They would indeed perform together at the ceremony when it took place at end of August.

195

Following the exchange of tweets between Taylor and Minaj, it wasn't long before Katy Perry chimed in with her own response, and on July 22nd tweeted: "Finding it ironic to parade the pit women against other women argument about as one unmeasurably capitalises on the take down of a woman…" Just a few days later at a concert in Foxborough, Taylor was captured on a fan video singing 'Bad Blood' as one of her dancers, dressed in a budget shark costume, slams himself against a window. Taylor then has to pull the microphone away from her face as she laughs. To many, it was an explicit reference to Perry's halftime Super Bowl concert in February, when the now-infamous "left shark" was seen to be struggling with the choreography.

At the finale of one of her five concerts in Los Angeles on August 24th, Taylor finished her last song and was clearly spotted (and caught on camera) saying "I love you" to Calvin Harris, as he watched from the front of the audience.

Ten days later, Taylor attended the MTV Awards in Las Vegas. During the show, she kept her word and joined Minaj on stage to duet on the rapper's smash hit 'The Night Is Still Young', as well as a short snippet of 'Bad Blood'. On the night, Taylor picked up awards for Video of the Year and Best Collaboration (for 'Bad Blood') and Best Female Video and Best Pop Video (for 'Blank Space'). During the show, she even presented the prestigious Michael Jackson Video Vanguard Award to Kanye West, announcing him for having "one of the greatest careers of all time!" As it happened, Minaj picked up the award for Best Hip-Hop Video for 'Anaconda', which had also been nominated for Best Female Video.

Following the incident with Minaj, Taylor's critics began pointing out a narrative of "white victimhood" in her career. In a later interview, she responded, saying she had come to understand "a lot about how my privilege allowed me to not have to learn about white privilege. I didn't know about it as a kid, and that is privilege itself, you know? And that's something that I'm still trying to educate myself on every day. How can I see where people are coming from, and understand the pain that comes with the history of our world?"

Taylor also accepted some responsibility for the tabloid drama that was a result of her overexposure. As an example, she said that if she didn't wish a friend happy birthday on social media, there would be reports about severed friendships. She added: "Because we didn't post about it, it didn't happen - and I realised *I* had done that. I created an expectation that everything in my life that happened, people would see."

Realising that she could never win, she confessed: "I think it happens to women so often that, as we get older and see how the world works, we're able to see through what is gaslighting." ("Gaslighting" is a term that refers to trying to convince someone they're wrong about something even when they're not).

Looking back at the release of *1989* and the subsequent fallout, Taylor said: "Oh my God, they were mad at me for smiling a lot and a quote-unquote acting fake. And then they were mad at me that I was upset and bitter and kicking back." For Taylor, the rules were always being changed.

During August, *Billboard* reported that Taylor would be using Ticketmaster's Verified Fan program to prevent bots and scalpers from purchasing tickets. Named "Taylor Swift Tix", the program allowed fans to purchase tickets in advance of the public on-sale by participating in activities which increased their chances of getting a pre-sale code.

In September, Taylor won a Primetime Emmy Award in Los Angeles in the category of Outstanding Creative Achievement. It was for a free interactive app created by American Express called Upstaged: The Taylor Swift Experience. While filming of the music video for 'Blank Space' was being wrapped in Long Island that month, another film crew were brought in with "groundbreaking 360-degree cameras" to photograph the mansion in the video to create the interactive world of the app, then fleshed out with real details and human characters. It was claimed that "you can choose where you go, who you follow, and what you explore in a stunning [virtual] house filled with characters, objects and scenes." The resulting video game, apparently lasting less than five minutes, was unveiled on *Good Morning America* on November 11th.

Mueller files a lawsuit

On September 10th, former radio host David Mueller filed a lawsuit against Taylor in the US District Court in Denver for defamation and losing his $150,000-a-year job at KYGO Radio. The lawsuit claimed "Mueller lost his job and other prospective business opportunities because of the [sexual harassment] allegations" and was therefore seeking $3 million in damages from the singer. According to *NME*, it also claimed that Mueller had been wrongfully identified, and that his radio colleague, Eddie Haskell, had been the one who had touched her inappropriately.

In the later documentary *Miss Americana*, Taylor said that, at the time, both Mueller's story and the subsequent lawsuit were full of lies, and stated: "There were seven people who saw him do this, and we have a photo of it happening."

On October 28th, Taylor's legal team filed a counterclaim against Mueller for assault and battery, specifically citing "reaching under her skirt and groping her." The lawsuit was for a symbolic one dollar, and it claimed that Mueller had waited too long to deny the allegation after it had been reported. It also detailed that the assault occurred without Taylor's permission and against her will. In documents filed with the US District Court in Colorado, Taylor's attorney wrote: "Mueller's newfound claim that he is the 'wrong guy' and, therefore, his termination from KYGO was unjustified, is specious…Ms Swift knows exactly who committed the assault - it was Mueller." It was also highlighted that Mueller had a troubled employment history, having been "twice terminated from on-air radio positions he held with other radio stations."

The following day, Vox.com reported: "Swift is not backing down in the face of Mueller's 'it wasn't me' defense, asking in the lawsuit for a jury trial; she intends to donate any profits from awarded damages to organizations 'dedicated to protecting women from similar acts of sexual assault and personal disregard.' Regardless of how this legal battle shakes out, Swift's declarative response to Mueller's suit is a power move, one that seeks to make an example of him as a representation of the systemic sexual inequity and harassment faced by female entertainers. It's the most high-profile case in a recent string of sexual harassment claims by women in the entertainment industry. By challenging Mueller's claims, Swift is standing up to the apathy and inertia that fosters that systemic inequality.

For a singer who usually takes the 'shake it off' approach to her critics and accusers, it's a heartening and welcome development."

"The most beautiful chapter in our story"

On the last day of September, while Taylor's team had been preparing to respond to Mueller, Taylor was again in Los Angeles for her very own Attendance Record-Breaking Exhibit in the Clive Davis Theater at the Grammy Museum, in which she performed a short acoustic set that included 'Wildest Dreams', 'Out of the Woods', 'Shake It Off', and 'How You Get the Girl'.

Around this time, it was also reported that Taylor had added to her real estate portfolio with the purchase of the seven-bedroom Beverly Hills mansion previously owned by film producer Sam Goldwyn, for an estimated $25 million. In 2018, she applied for and won landmark status for the estate, ensuring that the home would never be significantly changed or demolished. Being a huge fan of traditional Americana interior design, Taylor decked out the home with a combination of contemporary art pieces and vintage furnishings to restore it to its former glory.

In October, Taylor won the Nashville Songwriters Association award for Songwriter/Artist of the Year for an incredible seventh time, and, at the AMAs in Los Angeles, came away with Favourite Pop/Rock Album and Favourite Adult Contemporary Artist, but lost out to One Direction for Artist of the Year.

Meanwhile, in another interview for *GQ*, Taylor still refused to acknowledge that Kate Perry had been the subject of 'Bad Blood', saying: "I never said anything that would point a finger in the specific direction of one specific person, and I can sleep at night knowing that. I knew the song would be assigned to a person, and the easiest mark was someone who I didn't want to be labelled with this song. It was not a song about heartbreak. It was about the loss of friendship."

On November 7th, the final leg of the *1989* tour began with the first of two concerts in Singapore, before moving on to China for three concerts in Shanghai. Arriving in Australia in early December, Taylor featured in Nova's Red Room: Taylor Swift on Hamilton Island, an intimate concert for just 100 lucky competition winners held at the idyllic location, and with the media turned away for once to allow her some privacy.

Meanwhile, Taylor performed the final shows of the *1989* Tour with a three-night finale in Melbourne, beginning December 10th, and with hometown boy Vance Joy in support. Taylor shared a few photos of the final shows on Instagram: "Melbourne, the first two nights with you have been magical. Tonight, we play this show for the very last time. I'm so honoured I get to share the last night of the *1989* World Tour with all of you. This has been the most incredible adventure. Thank you for all of it."

Alex Dean of *Australia's Daily Review* was not too complimentary about the final show: "To be fair, pop music by nature is seldom genuine or risky, and this tour was a solid representation of how far down that rabbit hole Taylor has gone. Like her album, the show was scripted and polished within an inch of its life. Yes it was fun, yes it was dazzling - but I couldn't help but yearn for a moment of unscripted connection."

Taylor wrote on Twitter: "The *1989* World Tour is officially over, the most beautiful chapter in our story so far...Thank you."

After 85 dates across four continents and in a little over seven months, the *1989* extravaganza had finally come to an end. The statistics were amazing. The first five concerts of the North American leg alone (May 20th-June 6th) had generated a total of $16.8 million from 149,708 ticket sales, with the following three shows in Charlotte, Raleigh and Philadelphia earning $15.2 million from 129,962 ticket sales. By the beginning of August, the tour had grossed $86.2 million from 771,460 tickets at 20 North American concerts, and in October *Billboard* reported the tour had surpassed *Red* as Taylor's highest-grossing tour with sales of $173 million.

The records soon followed. Total earnings for the tour came in at $250 million, making it the world's highest-grossing tour of the year. In the US alone, the figure was $199.4 million, beating the previous all-time record of $192 million set by The Rolling Stones in 2005. The eventual worldwide figures grossed at over $250.7 million from over 2.278 million tickets sold.

On December 13th, the day Taylor celebrated her Christmas-themed birthday party with Harris, she announced a deal had been made with Apple Music to release the movie *The 1989 World Tour - Live,* featuring over two hours of concert footage, mixing in interviews and rehearsals. Filmed at the ANZ Stadium in Sydney on November 28th, there was also additional footage of special guest appearances from other shows on the tour. A week later, the concert was made available for streaming on Apple Music.

Summer of the Apocalypse

"The thing about life is, every time you learn a lesson, another one is waiting
right at the corner.
You never know everything"

Peace with Perry?

Compared to previous years, 2016 would be a rather quiet time for Taylor when it came to live music. There would no festivals, no television appearances to talk about, and only one notable concert. But, as always, there would still be the customary award ceremonies. On January 6th she won both Favourite Female Artist and Favourite Pop Artist at the People's Choice Awards in Los Angeles.

The following month she attended the Grammys there, where she performed 'Out of the Woods'. With a total of five nominations, she won Album of the Year for the second time, Best Pop Vocal Album, and Best Music Video (for 'Bad Blood'), but lost out with 'Blank Space' for Song of the Year, which was picked up by her mate Ed Sheeran for 'Thinking Out Loud' (with co-writer Amy Wadge). He also pipped her for Best Pop Solo Performance.

Huffpost reviewed the performance: "Fresh from her world tour, Taylor Swift absolutely nailed her performance... Swift chose a black, sparkly jumpsuit with long side slits and a daring back for the opener. The 'Style' singer wore her hair short but (of course) had her classic, signature red lip on. The performance set up was simple, with a few backup singers and some trees in the background to go along with the woodsy vibe."

That same month, there were rumours that Taylor and Katy Perry might have reconciled their differences and reached an entente. According to the *New York Times*, Perry revealed that she had thrown a pre-Grammys event with Spotify and had invited "a mixture of new and familiar artists", including both Taylor and Adele. According to the streaming service's director of artist services, Mark Williamson: "We bought into Katy's vision that if we can work together to create these relationships, we're going to benefit long-term, because we're helping to improve their community." Perry remarked: "It's just up to their schedules."

Perhaps due to the fact that both Taylor and Adele had pulled their music from Spotify, it remains unlikely that either of them turned up.

The following month she received special recognition at the BMI Pop Awards in Beverly Hills when she was presented with the first-ever "Taylor Swift Award", in celebration of her "incomparable creative and artistic talent and influence on music lovers around the world." It was only the second time in the 76-year history of Broadcast Music Inc. that they had presented an award in someone's name, the first being Michael Jackson in 1990. Taylor also picked up for the second time their coveted Pop Songwriter of the Year Award for writing four of the year's most-performed songs from *1989* - 'Bad Blood', 'Blank Space', 'Style' and 'Wildest Dreams'.

A few days later, Taylor won Top Touring Artist for *1989* at the Billboard Music Awards in Las Vegas. After that, the rest of the year would be devoted to her personal life, at least as far as the fans and media were concerned.

It had begun oh so well. After spending Christmas with Calvin Harris building a snowman, and then watching him perform at a Las Vegas nightclub party on New Year's Eve, the new year had gotten under way with a source telling E!News that the couple "are definitely talking about their future together and the possibility of one day getting engaged," and, although too busy in the studio to see her win three awards at the Grammys in February, he tweeted: "Congratulations to my beautiful girlfriend."

Hiddleswift

On March 6th, the self-proclaimed anniversary of their first date, Taylor shared a photo on Instagram of a gift that Harris had given her - a gold locket engraved with that particular date. In turn, he posted on Snapchat a video of them celebrating with a cake. A sure sign of the young lovers' feelings toward one another came at the iHeartRadio Music Awards held in Inglewood in April. Taylor trumped Adele by winning both Album of the Year and Female Artist of the Year, as well as the award for Best Tour, and in one of her acceptance speeches, she revealed: "For the first time I had the most amazing person to come home to when the spotlight went out and when the crowds were gone."

During their time together, Taylor wrote a song, sat down at the piano, and did a demo into her iPhone. She then sent it to Calvin, who loved it. After that, they went into the studio and did a full demo together, with Taylor on vocals. The song was called 'This is What You Came For'. Realising that the song would be a hit, and as Taylor had written it for Harris, they both agreed that it would be a bad idea to let it out as a collaboration, as it would more than likely overshadow the song. To retain the publishing rights, Taylor opted to use the pseudonym Nils Sjoberg on the credits.

On April 29th Harris released the song with Rihanna, having presented it to her just two weeks before. It became an instant hit, peaking at #5 on the Hot 100 and #1 on Dance Club Songs. The single also featured Taylor on backing vocals. That same day Harris was interviewed on radio by Ryan Seacrest, and the host asked him: "Will you do a collaboration with your girlfriend?", to which he replied: "You know we haven't even spoke about it. I can't see it happening though."

What happened next would send Swifties into an absolute frenzy of tweeting. On May 1st, Taylor was snapped leaving a dinner held at journalist Anna Wintour's New York home, with British actors Tom Hiddleston and Idris Elba. As reported in *Cosmopolitan*, the following night she was caught on camera dancing with Hiddleston at the Met Gala to Beyoncé's 'Crazy in Love', with "some serious shapes being thrown." Taylor's friend Karlie Kloss was also spotted on the dancefloor. The clip was soon posted on the internet for the entire world to see.

Rumour has it that on the same night, Taylor may have met English actor Joe Alwyn, as was later deduced by Swiftie sleuths with lyrical references to hairstyles in the song 'Dress' being seen as a link to that night.

Two weeks later, MTV UK interviewed Hiddleston about the dance with Taylor, and all he said was: "She was very charming. She is amazing."

The next piece of drama came on May 22nd, when Harris was involved in an accident in Los Angeles. He was a passenger in a Cadillac when a VW Beetle reportedly crashed into him near LA International Airport. Although no one was seriously hurt, he suffered lacerations to his face and was taken to hospital. A post on his Facebook page said doctors had advised him to "rest for a few days", forcing him to cancel a number of concerts, including one in Las Vegas the night of the accident.

The bombshell came on June 1st when, according to *People* magazine, Taylor and Harris had split up. Their source claimed it was mutual and without drama. The following day, E!News shed more light on the revelation with sources of their own. One reported: "Taylor's heart was more in it than he was. He started to lose interest over the past few months, but really tried to not just break up."

Already the media were seeing the writing on the wall, or, in this case, lyrics for her next song. *Cosmopolitan* wrote: "The only good thing we can see coming from this…is another killer album from Taylor. Because we know what this woman does with her feelings and it involves bloody great music."

All was confirmed the next day when Harris made the split official in a tweet: "The only truth is that a relationship came to an end & what remains is a huge amount of love and respect." With Taylor re-tweeting it, it seemed to the world that all was, indeed, amicable. *People* also confirmed that "multiple sources" claimed the couple had gone their separate ways.

Meanwhile, on June 6th, Katy Perry had announced the launch of her new fragrance called "Mad Love", a name many fans recognised from the lyric of Taylor's 'Bad Blood'. According to the Fragrance Shop, it "incorporates the spirit of love at the heart of the fragrance" and is "fruity and irresistible."

A week later, "Hiddleswift" was well and truly on, with *The Sun* printing a world exclusive photo showing Taylor and the 35-year-old star of the popular tv drama *The Night Manager* kissing among a bunch of rocks near Taylor's Rhode Island home. According to reports, Harris unfollowed Taylor and her brother Austin on Twitter and deleted all the couple's pictures from his Instagram account, while Taylor also deleted their pictures taken together. A couple of days later, Harris was confronted by a photographer, who asked: "Did she betray you?" His reaction was surprisingly calm: "It's all good, she's doing her thing…she's doing her thing, dude."

On June 21st it was reported that Hiddleston had met Taylor's parents in Nashville and they had later been spotted dancing together at one of Selena Gomez's gigs, along with fellow-squaddie Abigail Anderson.

The curse of Kanye

Just a year ago, it had seemed like the crazy media dance that was KanyeGate had been put to bed. There had been a hint that West and Taylor would be working on some music together, and Kim Kardashian and her sister Kendall had been to see Taylor at one of her concerts. Even at that year's MTV Video Music Awards, the three of them had appeared to be on friendly terms, with Taylor quoting and mocking West's infamous on-stage interruption when presenting him with the special Video Vanguard Award.

On February 14th 2016 West's latest album, *The Life of Pablo,* was released, containing the track 'Famous', which included the incendiary lyric: "I feel like me and Taylor might still have sex/Why? I made that bitch famous". West also performed the song at the album's premiere at Madison Square Garden. Once heard, it stirred up a hornet's nest of criticism from Taylor's fans, friends and family, especially her brother Austin, who took it that West was taking a shot at her. The track would also be released as a single on April 1st.

Responding to the flood of criticism, West tweeted: "I called Taylor and had an hour-long convo with her about the line and she thought it was funny and gave her blessings", and "I'm not even gone take credit for the idea... It's actually something Taylor came up with..."

The night after the Garden show, TMZ also reported through sources that West had called Taylor prior to the song's release and told her about the lyric being done as a "joke" and that he wanted to make sure "she wouldn't be upset." A short while later, Jon Caraminica of the *New York Times* placed a statement from Taylor's publicist on his Instagram account. According to BuzzFeed, the statement read: "Kanye did not call for approval, but to ask Taylor to release his single 'Famous' on her Twitter account. She declined and cautioned him about releasing a song with such a strong misogynist message. Taylor was never made aware of the actual lyric..."

At the Grammys on February 16th, Taylor unleashed a thinly-veiled dig at West in her acceptance speech for Album of the Year: "I want to say to all the young women out there, there are going to be people along the way who are going to try to undercut your success, or take credit for your accomplishments or fame, but you just focus on the work and you don't let those people sidetrack you. Someday when you get where you're going, you'll look around and you will know that it was you, and the people who love you, who put you there and that will be the greatest feeling in the world."

While making a nightclub appearance a week later, West reiterated his claim that Taylor knew the song's lyrics would reference her, while TMZ showed a video in which he says he called her before the album premiere and told her the line, "I feel like me and Taylor might still have sex" would feature on the record. West claimed that she replied: "Oooh, Kanye, I like that line" before going off on a rant: "Then she won her award and said something completely different. She ain't cool no more. She had two seconds to be cool and she f**ked it up."

Us Weekly meanwhile claimed through a source that Kim was "concerned and frustrated" by her husband's recent behaviour, and, as they were "having big problems that are escalating" was demanding he got therapy.

On April 10th, West performed the song on stage and remarked: "If I get in trouble for saying the truth, what's being said the rest of the time? And I had to fight every day of my life, with the whole world turned against me, for saying out loud what everyone else felt. But that's the job of an artist. A real artist..."

Nearly two months later, on June 16th, *GQ* magazine's cover story featured an interview with Kim, claiming Taylor had lied about not knowing about the lyric and that there was footage of a phone call where she learned about it: "She totally knew that that was coming out. She wanted to all of a sudden act like she didn't. I swear, my husband gets so much shit for things [when] he really was doing proper protocol and even called to get it approved. What rapper would call a girl that he was rapping a line about to get approval? ...[Swift] totally gave the okay. Rick Rubin [producer] was there. So many respected people in the music business heard that [conversation] and knew. I mean, he's called me a bitch in his songs. That's just, like, what they say. I never once think, 'What a derogatory word! How dare he?' Not in a million years. I don't know why she just, you know, flipped all of a sudden..."

She went on to say that when Taylor called West, she told him that at the Grammys she would just say that it was all a joke and that she was "in on it the whole time", instead of dissing her husband "just to play the victim again."

Publicly "cancelled"

Immediately, questions were being raised in the media. It was possible that both parties were telling the truth, at least as both of them saw it. Maybe "sex" had been mentioned, but not the word "bitch". Did West misinterpret Taylor's "noncommittal politeness" as "implicit accord", as suggested in *GQ*? West was well known to have episodes of his life recorded on video for posterity, possibly for future documentaries, so it's equally possible that the phone conversation was filmed.

When asked in the interview with *GQ* whether Taylor and her husband got back in touch, Kim replied: "No. Maybe an attorney's letter she sent saying, 'Don't ever let that footage come out of me saying that. Destroy it...", and then admitted one had been sent. The question was then raised - how did Taylor's people know about the alleged footage if she hadn't realised it had been recorded in the first place? Kim admitted she wasn't sure, but suspected that maybe one of West's team had called someone from Taylor's, which led to a letter being sent from their legal team.

Kim then went on to defend the video: "When you shoot something, you don't stop every two seconds and be like, 'Oh wait, we're shooting this for my documentary.' You just film everything, and whatever makes the edit, then you see, then you send out releases. It's like what we do for our show."

When *GQ* got in touch with West's team, they confirmed both the video footage and the threat of legal action had taken place, but then declined to back it up with further proof. At the same time, Taylor's team, rather than answer questions directly, put out a statement:

"Taylor does not hold anything against Kim Kardashian as she recognises the pressure Kim must be under and that she is only repeating what she has been told by Kanye West. However, that does not change the fact that much of what Kim is saying is incorrect. Kanye West and Taylor only spoke once on the phone while she was on vacation with her family in January of 2016 and they have never spoken since. Taylor has never denied that conversation took place. It was on that phone call that Kanye West also asked her to release the song on her Twitter account, which she declined to do. Kanye West never told Taylor he was going to use the term 'that bitch' in referencing her. A song cannot be approved if it was never heard. Kanye West never played the song for Taylor Swift. Taylor heard it for the first time when everyone else did and was humiliated. Kim's claim that Taylor and her team were aware of being recorded is not true, and Taylor cannot understand why Kanye West, and now Kim Kardashian, will not just leave her alone."

On June 17th, Kim apparently referred to Taylor as a snake on social media: "Wait, its National Snake Day?!?! They have holidays for everybody, I mean everything these days!"

A week later, Taylor had every reason to cry on Hiddleston's shoulder when the music video for 'Famous' was released. Seen as being even more inflammatory than the lyrics, it features a realistic wax model of Taylor naked in a giant bed alongside, among others, similar models of West and his wife, President Trump, George W Bush, Rihanna, and *Vogue* editor Anna Wintour.

The drama continued a few weeks later in a teaser for the July 17th episode of *Keeping Up with the Kardashians,* in which Kim defended "talking shit" about Taylor over the past few months. During the clip, she said: "I feel like I've had it with people blatantly treating my husband a certain way and making him look a certain way. Kanye is always so honest and speaks his mind... At this point, I really don't give a f**k so I'll do whatever to protect my husband."

On July 17th, Kim placed on Snapchat some apparently edited footage of the phone call, with no mention of the "I made that bitch famous" line, and Taylor appearing to perceive it as a "compliment". The following day it drew a response from Taylor on Twitter with a screenshot of a note: "Where is the video of Kanye telling me he was going to call me 'that bitch' in his song? It doesn't exist because it never happened. You don't get to control someone's emotional response to being called 'that bitch' in front of the entire world. Of course, I wanted to like the song. I wanted to believe Kanye when he told me that I would love the song. I wanted us to have a friendly relationship. He promised to play the song for me, but he never did. While I wanted to be supportive of Kanye on the phone call, you cannot 'approve' a song you haven't heard. Being falsely painted as a liar when I was never given the full story or played any part of the song is character assassination. I would very much like to be excluded from this narrative, one that I have never asked to be a part of, since 2009."

Although the heavily edited clip had shown Taylor at least agreeing to the "sex" line on the phone with West, if not the "bitch" part, and pleading the technicality, it would make little difference. When Kim went on Twitter to describe her as a snake, the comparison stuck, as it was taken as proof of her insincerity. Suddenly Taylor found herself very publicly "cancelled".

Moving on, Taylor admitted she stopped trying to explain herself, despite the fact that she could. As she began working on the next album, *Reputation,* she described it as "a think-piece a day that I knew I would never publish: the stuff I would say, and the different facets of the situation that nobody knew."

But why not exonerate herself? In an interview for *The Guardian*, she replied: "Because when people are in a hate frenzy and they find something to mutually hate together, it bonds them. And anything you say is in an echo chamber of mockery...You can either stand there and let the wave crash into you, and you can try as hard as you can to fight something that's more powerful and bigger than you, or you can dive under the water, hold your breath, wait for it to pass and while you're down there, try to learn something."

For now, it seemed like this on-going feud had been put to rest by the trio of megastars, at least, that is, until January 2019....

"The ties were black, the lies were white"

In the meantime, there had been new developments in the Hiddleswift saga. No sooner had the spectre of West been aroused than Taylor had been whisked off to England to meet Tom Hiddleston's mother, before heading off to Rome, where they were snapped in the Vatican wearing saintly whites and holding hands. After that they moved on to Australia's Gold Coast, where he was due to begin the shoot for his new movie *Thor*.

On July 13 TMZ revealed to the world that Taylor was indeed the co-writer with Harris of the Rihanna hit 'This Is What You Came For'. Taking to Twitter, Harris later accused Taylor's team of leaking something she had initially wanted kept secret, even bringing Katy Perry into it: "I know you're off tour and you need something new to try and bury like Katy etc, but I'm not that guy, sorry. I won't allow it." In response, Perry got her tweeting fingers at work and posted a GIF of Hilary Clinton with an infuriated face.

A few days later, Harris was interviewed by *GQ* and apologised for his post-split behaviour:

"It was completely the wrong instinct. I was protecting what I see as my one talent in the world being belittled. It felt like things were piling on top of me and that was when I snapped. It's very difficult when something I consider so personal plays out very publicly. The aftermath of the relationship was way more heavily publicised than the relationship itself. When we were together, we were very careful for it not to be a media circus. She respected my feelings in that sense. I'm not good at being a celebrity. But when it ended, all hell broke loose. Now I see that Twitter thing as a result of me succumbing to pressure. It took me a minute to realise that none of this matters. I'm a positive guy. For both of us it was the wrong situation. It clearly wasn't right, so it ended, but all of that stuff happened afterwards."

While in Australia, Hiddleston was reluctant to talk about the relationship when confronted by the news media, but on July 16th he told *Hollywood Reporter*: "How best to put this? ...The truth is that Taylor Swift and I are together and we're very happy. Thanks for asking. That's the truth. It's not a publicity stunt."

A month later, Taylor released her new single, 'Look What You Made Me Do'. The accompanying music video seemed to include a subtle dig at Harris, with Taylor appearing as a zombie-like character seen digging a grave for "Nils Sjoberg".

On August 14th, Hiddleston again spoke to *Hollywood Reporter*: "I've learned that there are many sides to a story, and that sometimes there are a lot of stories out there which are falsehoods and the hardest thing is to try to not let those falsehoods affect your own life." Ten days later, *Us Weekly* reported the couple had had "a major argument" that had stemmed from Hiddleston's filming schedule in Australia, and that he had tried patching things up by flying to Rhode Island for a "quick, two-day stay."

On September 6th, a *Daily Mail* insider report claimed that Taylor was feeling very "uncomfortable" over Hiddleston's desire to be "so public" with their relationship and his desire for her to accompany him at the upcoming Emmy Awards on the 18th. The report went on to say: "She tried to be ok with it in the beginning, but fears he is in love with the idea of her and not falling in love with her for the right reasons. Taylor is an independent young woman and doesn't feel like she needs a boyfriend to make her complete."

The following day a number of publications claimed it was all over, giving publicity as the reason. Sources for *Us Weekly* stated: "Tom wanted the relationship to be more public than she was comfortable with. Taylor knew the backlash that comes with public displays of affection but Tom didn't listen to her concerns when she brought them up." In the meantime, friends of the British actor insisted it was *him* that dumped *her*.

With fans now anticipating the inevitable response from the singer, they would have to wait for over a year and theorise over the content of her next album. Taylor had indeed been writing songs with an album in mind, still a long way off from being recorded, but its concept may have been influenced to some degree by events of the last few months. In particular, the lyrics "think about the place you first met me" and how "the ties were black, the lies were white" allegedly refer to Hiddleston, and their first meeting, at the Met Gala, back in May.

A soulmate in waiting

On October 12th, just a month after breaking up with Hiddleston, Taylor attended a private Kings of Leon concert, followed by an after-show party at the Bowery Hotel, along with her friends Cara Delevingne, Dakota Johnson, Lorde, Zoe Kravitz, Suki Waterhouse, Lily Donaldson and Martha Hunt. Some unofficial sources say that she may have met English actor, 25-year-old Joe Alwyn there, and a fan website revealed a video showing Alwyn walking in with Hunt and her boyfriend. Alwyn was the star of the new Ang Lee war movie *Billie Lynn's Long Halftime Walk*. Prior to his audition for the much-coveted role, Alwyn had never even stepped in front of a camera. There was also speculation that the meeting may have been instigated by Taylor and Alwyn.

Later that month, Taylor and Katy Perry were spotted at a 30th birthday bash for the Canadian rapper Aubrey "Drake" Graham. Although there was no evidence of any interaction between the two women, it was reported that their mutual ex-boyfriend John Mayer was also a guest.

A year of rare interviews and very few concerts rounded off on October 22nd, when Taylor took part in the pre-race show for the US Grand Prix in Austin, Texas, with an impressive setlist of 17 songs that simultaneously delivered a knock-out blow and treated her fans beyond all expectations. During the show, Taylor debuted a solo piano version of 'This Is What You Came For', the Calvin Harris hit that had become the focal point of a controversy between the former couple when Taylor revealed she had co-written the song after keeping the fact a secret. She told the audience: "I've never played this song live, but if you know it, maybe you could sing along so I know what that feels like with this song?" The audience of 80,000, drawn from around the world, did exactly that. According to *Billboard*, the crowd "cheered particularly loudly when she struck the final note with dramatic intention, raising her finger from the key with ample so-there sass to match her mischievous smirk."

Also that month, Taylor provided a pre-trial disposition for the upcoming trial over the sexual harassment allegations concerned David Mueller: "Right as the moment came for us to pose for the photo, he took his hand and put it up my dress and grabbed onto my ass cheek and no matter how much I scooted over it was still there. It was completely intentional; I've never been so sure of anything in my life." The trial would be set for August 8th.

Taylor was not present at the MTV Video Music Awards at the end of October, having received no nominations, and the following day summed up her state of mind by writing in her journal: "This summer is the apocalypse."

On November 11th, Taylor accompanied her mother and a gaggle of girlfriends to see a screening of Alwyn's latest movie at a theatre in Hollywood. If the couple had been dating at the time, they were certainly off the radar when it came to the media and many online sleuths. This most secret of her relationships would not be made public until the following May.

The single 'I Don't Wanna Live Forever' was released on Republic Records on December 9th. Written by Taylor, along with Jack Antonoff and singer-songwriter Sam Dew, the r&b ballad served as the main theme for the James Foley movie *Fifty Shades Darker*, the sequel to the erotic drama *Fifty Shades of Grey*. Taylor performed the song with English singer Zayn (Malik), who, like Harry Styles, was a former member of the band One Direction. Produced by Jack Antonoff, the vocals were recorded separately - Zayn's at the Rough Customer Studio in Brooklyn, and Taylor's at the Record Plant in Los Angeles.

I Don't Wanna Live Forever - **Zayn/Taylor Swift** ***
(Taylor Swift - Sam Dew - Jack Antonoff)
Label - Republic
Single
Recorded - Rough Customer Studio NY; Record Plant, LA
Produced - Jack Antonoff
Released - December 9 2016
Chart peak positions
  Hot 100 #2; AC #16; Adult Top 40 #2; Dance/Mix Show Airplay #3; Mainstream
  Top 40 #2; Rhythmic #20; Alternative Streaming Songs #2; UK #5; Canada #2;
  Australia #3; NZ #4
RIAA Certification - 4 x Platinum
Selected awards and nominations
2017 MTV Millennial Awards - Best Collaboration of the Year (won)
2017 MTV Video Music Awards - Best Collaboration (won)
2018 Grammys - Best Song Written for Visual Media (nominated)
2018 BMI Awards - Award-Winning Songs (won)
2018 iHeart Radio Awards - Titanium Award (won)

The song became Taylor's 20th Hot 100 top ten hit (and Zayn's second as a solo artist), making her only the sixth female artist to achieve this. It was held off the top spot by Ed Sheeran's 'Shape of You'. On the Hot Digital Songs chart, it became Taylor's 11th chart-topper, tying with Katy Perry as the second-most successful artist in the chart's history, behind Rihanna.

The music video was released on January 27th. Directed by Grant Singer, it features Taylor and Zayn trading vocals on a rainy night in a London hotel. The single also featured on the chart-topping soundtrack album, which was released on February 10th to coincide with the movie's premiere, and the song would go on to receive two Grammy nominations and quadruple platinum status.

Entertainment Weekly - "It's a surprising step from an artist who doesn't exactly make anyone's idea of mood music and who generally prefers to keep her image on the squeakier side of clean"; **Rolling Stone** - "Neither she nor Zayn sound deeply interested in this duelling-falsettos battle".

Although on a personal level it had proved to be tumultuous year for Taylor, it ended on a career high. Forbes reported that the artist had achieved record annual takings of $170 million during the period June 1st 2015 to June 1st 2016, surpassing the $135 million earned by rival Katy Perry in the previous 12 months.

For a short time between 2016 and 2017 it was reported that Taylor rented a townhouse while her Tribeca apartment was being renovated. The three-storey, four-bed, five-bathroom converted carriage house at 23 Cornelia Street had been rented to the singer by former SoHo House executive David Aldea for $39,500 a month. Aldea admitted to vulture.com that he "really didn't know" who Taylor was at the time. "Mind you, I knew her songs because I had them on my running playlist. I just didn't match the name to the song."

Year of the Snake

"I've learned a pretty tough lesson that people can say whatever they want about us at any time, and we cannot control that. The only thing we can control is our reaction to that"

Finding her Prince

On February 4th 2017, Taylor entertained her audience with a 10-song set for DirecTV's *Super Saturday Night* show at the Club Nomadic in Houston. This would be one of only a handful of concerts she would perform this year, as her main focus now would be on writing material for a new album. According to *Rolling Stone*, tickets to the event were given away via promotions, so people in the audience knew they were lucky to be at the show. They didn't realise just how lucky. During the show, Taylor informed the audience that, by attending this one show, they were attending the only planned performance of the entire year.

Taylor then treated them to a spectacular show, packed with some of her biggest hits, a live debut of 'I Don't Wanna Live Forever', and a rare performance of her self-penned 'Better Man', the chart-topping song that had been recorded by the country band Little Big Town. It would go on to win Taylor a Grammy for Best Song the following year. Originally written for the *Red* album, it was presumably inspired by her breakup with Jake Gyllenhaal, and, according to a source from *Us Weekly*, was offered to the band in July 2016 because of their distinct harmonies.

By the spring, reports were emerging that Taylor and Joe Alwyn were indeed dating. A source for *The Sun* revealed they had been an item for a few months: "This isn't a new couple alert or a secret relationship - the only people this has been a secret to is the media because all of us, Taylor and Joe's closest friends and their families, were aware they have known each other for a long time. After her *1989* tour and all the attention Taylor received, she learned she had to be more protective of her personal life and she and Joe decided early on to keep their private life private."

The same source told the paper that Taylor had flown in on a private jet to see Alwyn in London, "and her security has made it a military-like mission to prevent her from being seen...She's been walking around with Joe in London using disguises, like scarves and hats, to keep her identity under wraps."

What Katy did next

Meanwhile, things had remained quiet between Taylor and Katy Perry. That is, until the release of Perry's new album *Witness* in May. Speaking to *Entertainment Weekly*, the singer was asked if any of the songs would be a response to Taylor's 'Bad Blood'. She replied: "One thing to note is: You can't mistake kindness for weakness and don't come for me. Anyone. Anyone. Anyone. Anyone. And that's not to any one person and don't quote me that it is, because it's not. It's not about that. Honestly, when women come together and they decide to unite, this world is going to be a better place. Period. End of story. But let me say this: Everything has a reaction or a consequence so don't forget about that, okay, honey? We got to keep it real, honey. This record is not about anyone else! This record is about me being seen and heard so that I can see and hear everything else! It's not even about me! It's about everything that I see out there that I digest. I think there's a healing in it for me and vulnerability. If people want to connect and be healed and feel vulnerable and feel empowered and strong. God bless and here it is."

The following week Perry released the song 'Swish Swish', which featured rapper Nicki Minaj singing a verse that some commentators could relate to her brush with Taylor at the MTV Video Music Awards in 2017, when Perry made a cheeky reference to Taylor during one of her monologues. Giving viewers a quick recap of what had gone on so far, she said: "Kendrick Lamar: on fire. Ed Sheeran's friends: dead. I for one real skyped with an astronaut, Lorde did Lorde stuff, Pink made a car fly" (In Taylor's new video she appears as a zombie rising from the grave and refers to herself as "dead").

According to *People*, actress Ruby Rose would have none of it, and slammed Perry on Twitter, saying: "I just think with everything that's going on in the world to go from rebranding as a political activist only to ditch it and go low...is...a bummer."

On May 19th, Perry was asked by Jimmy Fallon on *The Tonight Show* if 'Swish Swish' was about Taylor, and she replied: "I think it's a great anthem for people to use whenever someone's trying to hold you down or bully you. It's a liberation from all the negative that doesn't serve you."

Also that month, Perry was a guest on James Corden's *Carpool Karaoke* feature of his late-night show, and, in between the duetting, spoke candidly about the feud with Taylor, saying: "Honestly, it's like she started and it's time for her to finish it." When asked about how it all had started, she recalled: "There's three backing dancers that went on tour with her, right? And they asked me before they went on tour if they could go and I was like 'Yeah, of course. But I will be on record cycle probably in about a year. So be sure to put a thirty-day contingency in your contract so you can get out if you wanna join me when I'm going back on.' So that year came up...and I texted all of them because I'm very close with them and I said, 'Look just FYI, I'm about to start and I want to put the word out there.' And they said 'okay, well we're going to go and talk to management about it.' And they did and then they got fired. And I tried to talk to her about it and she wouldn't speak to me."

Perry added that all attempts to contact Taylor was a "full shutdown", and then added: "She writes a song about me. So, I was like, Cool, cool, cool, so that's how you wanna deal with it? Karma...Now there is the law of cause and effect. You do something and there's going to be a reaction. And trust me daddy, there's going to be a reaction."

In what to some looked like a suspicious move on Taylor's part, she released her entire catalogue to Spotify and other streaming services on June 9th, the same time that Perry released her new album *Witness*. The following day, Perry spoke to *NME*: "No one has asked me about my side of the story, and there are three sides of every story: one, two, and the truth. I mean, I'm no Buddha - things irritate me. I wish that I could turn the other cheek every single time, but I'm also not a pushover, you know? Especially when someone tries to assassinate my character with little girls [Swifties]. That's so messed up!"

In a smart way to promote her new album, Perry allowed her fans to "witness" her online in a massive three-day livestream beginning the same day as Taylor released her music to Spotify. During the stream, she spoke to Ariana Huffington on an episode of her Thrive podcast, which was also featured in *People* magazine. In the somewhat surprising interview, Perry said: "I am ready to let it go. I forgive her and I'm sorry for anything I ever did, and I hope the same for her...I love her, and I want the best for her. And I think she's a fantastic songwriter. Maybe I don't agree with everything she does and she doesn't agree with everything I do, but I just really, truly want to come together in a place of love and forgiveness and understanding and compassion. There's a lot of other things out there in the world that people need to be focused on, and I truly, like, God bless her on her journey. God bless her."

During the livestream event, Perry even changed the lyrics of 'Swish Swish', switching "Don't you come for me, oh, not today" to "God bless you on your journey, oh, baby girl" in the first verse.

Judgement days in Denver

Back in May, US District Court Judge William Martinez had refused to dismiss David Mueller's lawsuit against Taylor and ruled that a jury should decide the case in a Federal court, with a date set for the civil trial to begin in Denver on August 8th. Taylor and Mueller and their legal teams were present at jury selection, and eventually six women and two men were selected, who would decide the outcome of both opposing lawsuits after hearing each party's testimony.

On the opening day of the trial, 55-year-old Mueller was the first to take the stand. He described his encounter with Taylor as "weird and awkward" and went on to testify: "I know my hand was touching her rib or her skirt, and it went behind her, and her hand, or arm, went behind my arm." When he was asked if he had grabbed her bottom, he said, "No, I did not" and he finished his testimony by declaring: "I'm here to prove that I'm innocent. I had a good reputation in radio and I would like to get it back." *NME* reported that he had described the experience "humiliating" and that "It cost me my career, the thing I love to do, my passion."

The following day, it was the turn of Taylor's mother Andrea to testify. According to *NME*, she said: "I went to the dressing room and I saw her face. I could see that there was something horribly wrong. She said: 'Mom, a guy just grabbed my ass.' I wanted to vomit and cry at the same time...she was really shaken. She was humiliated...He sexually assaulted my daughter", and, pointing directly at Mueller, said: "Right there, that guy. I heard it from my daughter's mouth. I know that it happened."

According to BBC News, when asked why she didn't go straight to the police when she was first told by Taylor that she had been assaulted, Andrea replied: "I did not want this event to define her life. I did not want her to have to live through the endless memes and gifs that tabloid media and internet trolls decided to come up with - doctoring the pictures...and making her relive this awful moment over and over again."

That same day, Mueller's radio liaison Frank Bell testified that he had sought "appropriate action" once told by Mueller's employers what had happened.

On August 10th, it was time for Taylor to take the stand and testify. While practising her testimony, she thought she was supposed to be polite to everyone, but by the time she got to court, in her own words, "something snapped." What followed was a brilliant and uncompromising testimony.

According to *NME*, the singer said that it "was a definite grab. A very long grab. It was intentional...He stayed latched onto my bare ass cheek...He stayed latched onto my bare ass cheek as I lurched away from him. [His hand] didn't let go. It was a very shocking thing. I had never dealt with something like this before."

Taylor refused to back down or give ground to Mueller's lawyer Gabe McFarland. According to *Variety*'s Jem Aswad, who praised her performance on the stand, when he claimed there was no sign of her skirt being lifted, she hit back: "Because my ass is located in the back of my body."

Asked if she was critical of her bodyguard, she replied: "I'm critical of your client sticking his hand under my skirt and grabbing my ass." With his claim that no one had actually seen Mueller's hand touch her rear, she responded: "The only person who would have a direct eye line is someone laying underneath my skirt, and we didn't have anyone positioned there." She also rejected the accusation that she had misidentified Mueller: "I'm not going to allow you or your client to say I am to blame. He had a handful of my ass. It happened to me. I know it was him."

At another questioning, *Billboard*'s Gil Kaufmann heard Taylor respond: "It happened to me. I have a 3-D rendition of what happened in my brain. I could have picked him out of a line of 1,000. I know exactly who did this. It is not alleged; it is a fact. You can ask me a million questions about it and I'm never going to say anything different." According to Buzz Feed's Claudia Rosenbaum, Taylor bristled when asked why she hadn't called off the meet-and-greet following the alleged incident. When McFarland said, "You could have taken a break", the singer shot back: "And your client could have taken a normal photo with me."

When asked about the defamation charges that caused Mueller's "humiliation", she replied: "I'm being blamed for the unfortunate events of his life that are a product of his decisions, not mine." Finally, when asked the question of whether she felt Mueller had got what he deserved, she answered: "I don't feel anything about Mr Mueller. I don't know him."

Also testifying that day was the meet-and-greet photographer Stephanie Simbeck, who recalled: "I saw her fall into the female [his then-girlfriend Shannon Melcher], and she had a shocked look, and I saw his hand grab her ass." From where she stood, five feet away, Simbeck couldn't say whether his hand was inside or outside her skirt.

On August 11th, it was the turn of Taylor's former bodyguard Greg Dent. According to *NME*, he said in his testimony: "I saw his hand under her skirt...Her skirt went up...She jumped", and then added that he was positive Mueller had been drinking: "I don't know what level. He was staggering or falling down." When asked why he didn't intervene, Dent replied that he "took his cues" from Taylor, who, apparently, had said she had carried on with the meet-and-greet in order not to disappoint the fans waiting for her.

Also brought to the stand that day was Shannan Melcher, who had also appeared in the photo. Although testifying that she had not seen Mueller acting inappropriately, she added: "I don't have eyes in the back of my head." She admitted the photo was taken quickly, and that Mueller was not close to Taylor when it was about to be taken, but then "we had to dive into the photo." When asked if she had noticed Taylor "lurch" away from Mueller, she said she hadn't.

Judge Martinez threw out Mueller's case against Taylor, who "did not act inappropriately" in contacting KYGO radio to tell them of the incident. Neither did he make a ruling on Taylor's lawsuit against Mueller. That was left for the jury to decide.

In his closing address, McFarland argued why his client would introduce himself by name and then almost immediately afterward reach under the skirt of "one of the planet's, one of the country's, biggest superstars." According to Reuters, as he spoke, Taylor burst into tears.

On the 14th, the jurors took four hours to decide unanimously that Mueller had assaulted Taylor, and they awarded her the requested sum of $1. The singer pledged to donate "an unspecified amount" to organisations aimed at helping victims of sexual assault.

In a statement, Taylor thanked her legal team for "fighting for me and anyone who feels silenced by sexual assault... I acknowledge the privilege that I benefit from in life, in society and in my ability to shoulder the enormous cost of defending myself in a trial like this. My hope is to help those whose voices should also be heard."

To prevent this sexual assault from ever happening again, Taylor had security cameras installed at all her meet-and-greet events, providing video footage from every angle.

Speaking to *The Guardian* two years later, she recalled that time: "Having dealt with a few of them, narcissists basically subscribe to a belief system that they should be able to do and say whatever the hell they want, whenever the hell they want to. And if we - as anyone else in the world, but specifically women - react to that, well, we're not allowed to. We're not allowed to have a reaction to their actions."

Taylor had never wanted the assault to be made public. Despite winning the case, she still felt belittled. This had happened just two months prior to the launch of the #MeToo movement, and she later revealed: "Even this case was literally twisted so hard that people were calling it the 'butt-grab case'. They were saying I sued him because there's this narrative that I want to sue everyone. That was one of the reasons why the summer was the apocalypse."

Fifty shades of success

While this most traumatic of episodes had come to an end, Katy Perry's latest olive-branch gesture had as yet received no response from Taylor, and all had been quiet for weeks. Then, on August 16th, Taylor cleared out her website and all social media accounts and two days later replaced the deleted content with several short videos of a snake.

Five days later, Perry issued a teaser clip ahead of the premiere of the star-studded video for 'Swish Swish', with the intriguing caption, "Countdown to Catastrophe". It immediately caught the attention of Swifties who recalled that Catastrophe was the name of Taylor's character in the video of 'Bad Blood'.

On August 23rd, in what appeared to be a well-timed response, Taylor broke the news on social media that her next album would be called *Reputation*, and that the first single, 'Look What You Made Me Do' would be released the following night, almost coinciding with Perry's video for 'Swish Swish'. The *Space Jam*-inspired 'Swish Swish' video was a not-so-subtle reference to Perry's feud with Taylor and depicted two basketball teams - Perry's Tigers and another called the Sheep (perhaps recalling her tweet referring to Taylor as a "Regina George in sheep's clothing").

Meanwhile, as all this was being played out, Taylor and Zayn had won Best Collaboration for 'I Don't Wanna Live Forever' at the MTV Video Music Awards on August 27th. Katy Perry was host for the evening, and one of the highlights was her performance of 'Swish Swish' with Nicki Minaj, but Taylor seemed to have stolen Perry's thunder. Although not in attendance that evening, the show had the world premiere of the video for 'Look What You Made Me Do'. Its hidden meanings and alleged references to Harris, Perry, West, Kim, et al was taking retaliation to the next level.

The record-breaking and critically-acclaimed video, which had been shot in May, ends with a line-up of "old Taylors" standing in front of a private jet and trading snide comments about the numerous false or exaggerated media portrayals of her that have attacked her reputation. Clever in its conception and spectacular to watch, it displays Taylor at her creative and mischievous best.

Having heard nothing more from Taylor about ending the feud, Perry told SiriusXM: "Listen, I'd love for the beef to end. I'd love to take it off the BBQ. I'm down, but I haven't heard anything of it." That statement brought an end to this chapter in the ongoing bad-blood saga, and all would appear relatively calm for the next nine months. In the meantime, Taylor's new album was taking shape, and while she remained quiet, she would let her song lyrics speak for her.

Meanwhile, in September, Taylor had purchased a three-storey townhouse at 152 Franklin Street, in the Tribeca area of Manhattan, for a reported $18 million. The property consisted of a private cinema, gym, bar, and an enclosed, paparazzi-safe roof garden, and was reported to have been purchased by a lawyer working for Taylor's management team in an off-market deal before it was publicly listed.

Out With the Old

Reputation would become the most widely scrutinised album of her career. Drawing inspiration from what had been a highly-publicised period in both her personal and professional life, its themes were largely based on what were perceived to be the relentless crusades to damage her public image, and on finding new love amid all the turmoil that had been created. During her seclusion from social media, there would be interviews to promote the album, as had previously been done. Working once again with the production team of Jack Antonoff, Max

Martin and Shellback, she had additional help from fellow-Swedes Oscar Holter, Oscar Görres, and Ali Payami.

This time, it would reveal a darker, deeper side to the artist - Old Taylor was dead. This was New Taylor, exposing a vulnerability seldom seen before.

In a later interview with *Entertainment Weekly*, Taylor gave her view on the album's real meaning: "Songwriters need to communicate, and part of communicating correctly is when you put out a message that is understood the way you meant it. *Reputation* was interesting because I'd never before had an album that wasn't fully understood until it was seen live. When it first came out everyone thought it was just going to be angry; upon listening to the whole thing, they realized it's actually about love and friendship, and finding out what your priorities are."

As before, over the course of a year, Taylor had hand-picked 500 fans from around the world for her Secret Sessions and a chance to play them songs from her new album, a month before its worldwide release. On October 18th, Disney/ABC was on hand to film Taylor perform an intimate and extended world premiere of 'New Year's Day' for 100 fans in the candlelit living room of her Rhode Island home. In what would be her first public performance of new music in three years, it was broadcast on November 9th during ABC's drama series *Scandal*, and just a couple of hours before the album was released at midnight. An extended version of Taylor's performance was aired during the movie *The DUFF* the following evening.

In the liner notes to the album, taken by many of her fans as being as important and insightful as the lyrics within, Taylor concluded by saying: "Let me say it again, louder for those in the back...We think we know someone, but the truth is that we only know the version of them that they have chosen to show us. There will be no further explanation. There will be just reputation."

Unlike her previous albums, this time there would be no need for hidden messages.

REPUTATION
Label - Big Machine
Recorded - Conway Recordings, LA; MXM Studios, LA/Stockholm; Rough
  Customer Studio, Brooklyn; Seismic Activities, Portland; Tree Sound, Atlanta
Produced - Taylor Swift, Jack Antonoff, Max Martin & Shellback
Released - November 10 2017
Singles - 6
Chart peak positions
  Hot 200 #1; UK #1; Canada #1; Australia #1; NZ #1; Japan #3
RIAA Certification - 4 x Platinum
Selected awards and nominations
2018 AMA Awards - Favourite Pop/Rock Album (won)
2018 Billboard Music Awards - Top Billboard 200 Album (nominated)
2018 Billboard Music Awards - Top Selling Album (won)
2019 Grammys - Best Pop Vocal Album (nominated)

...Ready for It? *
(Taylor Swift - Max Martin - Shellback - Ali Payami)
2nd Single
Recorded - MXM Studios, LA/Stockholm

Produced - Taylor Swift, Max Martin, Shellback & Ali Payami
Released - October 24 2017
Chart peak positions
 Hot 100 #4; AC #26; Adult Top 40 #10; Dance Club Songs #34; Mainstream
 Top 40 #12; UK #7; Canada #7#; Australia #3; NZ #9
RIAA Certification - 2 x Platinum
Selected awards & nominations
2019 BMI Awards - Award Winning Song (won)
2019 BMI Awards - Publisher of the Year (won)

Based on the caption of one of the polaroids featured in a Target-exclusive magazine, Taylor was writing this song in late December 2016. According to *Entertainment Weekly*, the song focuses on the beginnings of a romantic relationship, and the "reputations and baggage that come before", with lyrics that revolve around a subject she refers to as a "killer", with movie-like imagery of a bank heist, going undercover, ransom and jail.

Speaking to iHeart Radio, she said: "It kind of introduces a metaphor you may hear more of throughout the rest of the album, which is like this kind of crime and punishment metaphor, where it talks about robbers and thieves and heists, and all that. And I found that to be a really interesting metaphor, but twisted in different ways throughout the album. The way that's presented in 'Ready for It?' is, basically, finding your partner in crime, and it's like, 'Oh my god, we're the same, oh my god! Let's rob banks together, this is great!'"

Taylor had first teased a portion of the single, along with 'Look What You Made Me Do' in a commercial aired on ABC's *Saturday Night Football* broadcast between Florida State and Alabama on September 2nd 2017. The same day she announced its release as a promotional single.

With opening sales of 135,000 copies, it became Taylor's 13th chart-topper on Billboard's Digital Songs. On the Hot100 it also became Taylor's 22nd top ten entry, and her 14th top ten debut, setting a record for a female artist, and second most overall behind Drake.

The music video was directed by Joseph Kahn and shot in August 2017. Inspired by movies like *Tron* and *Ghost in the Shell,* the film is a homage to sci-fi and anime and features Taylor playing two roles - that of a cyborg wearing a white bodysuit, and another in which she wears a large black cloak. Once again, it was a video that courted controversy. In the movie *Ghost in the Shell*, Scarlett Johansson had starred as Major Mira Killian (aka Kusanagi), who was an Asian character in the original source material, so this was seen by some as another case "whitewashing" by Taylor. The video had its premiere on October 26th 2017.

Spin - "Part of being a pop star is selling your persona, and at the moment it still feels as if Swift is wearing a costume. And yet, it's hard to imagine any of this mattering. I won't guess at Swift's motivations, but it seems like an indisputable fact that she is being economically incentivised to make songs that sound like a different person. Hopefully, she will simply get better at it...for whatever it's worth [the song], is at least a small step in that direction"; **Newsweek** - "[Ready for It?] is an industrial-coated disaster, a flailing cocktail of grinding synths and faux-rap delivery that's as gratuitous as the ellipses in the title...Swift never summons the swagger to justify those harsh sandpaper synths - she just sounds like she's drowning"; **Billboard** - "Swift has never sang more expressively, not sounded

217

more in tune with the way modern pop production uses the voice as an instrument... [The chorus is one of the] prettiest melodies of her career"; **Vulture** - "The second straight misfire off the *Reputation* rollout"; **Rolling Stone** - "Max Martin really knows how to shape a production around her voice"; **Rolling Stone** - "The chorus has a little air in the mix, giving the room she needs to pull off her intricate breathy effects"; **NME** - "With its dubstep wubs, EDM beats and trappy instrumentals, this messy number feels like a tug of war between this collection of different genres".

End Game (featuring Ed Sheeran and Future) *
(Taylor Swift - Max Martin - Shellback - Ed Sheeran - Nayvadius Wilburn)
3rd Single
Recorded - MXM Studios, LA/Stockholm; Seismic Activities, Portland; Tree
  Sound, Atlanta
Produced - Max Martin & Shellback
Released - November 14 2017
Chart peak positions
  Hot 100 #18; Adult Top 40 #13; Dance/Mix Show Airplay #18; Mainstream
  Top 40 #10; Rhythmic #25; Alternative Streaming Songs #4; UK #49;
  Canada #11; Australia #36; NZ #2
RIAA Certification - Platinum
Selected awards & nominations
2018 Teen Choice Awards - Choice Music Collaboration (nominated)
2019 BMI Awards - Award Winning Song (won)
2019 BMI Awards - Publisher of the Year (won)
2019 BMI London Awards - Pop Award (won)

In this pop-rap song, the only collaboration on the album, Taylor wants to be her lover's soulmate and hopes that the "drama" surrounding her doesn't stop him wanting to be with her because they've already been so close. Although she never mentions a name, Swifties seem certain that its either about Tom Hiddleston or current boyfriend Joe Alwyn. As well as Taylor and Sheeran, the song was also co-written by producer Max Martin, Shellback and the rapper Future (aka Nayvadius Wilburn). Before the song was announced, the words "Eddie" and "Future" were written in graffiti in certain shots of the music video for 'Ready for It?'

According to Sheeran, he was inspired by attending a Fourth of July party at Taylor's Rhode Island residence, where he met an old schoolfriend Cherry Seaborn, a girl he would go on to marry. His verse in the song includes a reference to the movie *Born on the Fourth of July* as a symbol of the beginning of their relationship. He also described how he wrote his verse in a hotel room in New York about 8am, "cause, for some reason I, like, dreamed it in my head what I was gonna do." He typed it out and recorded it the next day and then sent it to Taylor.

In the song, Taylor, Sheeran and Future talk about finding their true love amidst the gossip about their perceived reputations.

'End Game' became Taylor's record-breaking 55th top 40 on the Hot 100.

The music video was again directed by Joseph Khan, and depicts Taylor partying in several locations - with rapper Future on a yacht in Miami, Ed Sheeran in a Tokyo nightclub, and with various friends on a red double-decker bus in London. In one of the London scenes, Taylor is seen playing Snake on a game console, and, in the Tokyo scene, rides a motorbike in a snakeskin-patterned bodysuit - all subtle references to Kim's famous snake tweet. Taylor released the video on her Vevo channel January 12th 2018.

Rolling Stone - "Deeply weird, wildly funny"; **Pitchfork** - "Uninspired"; **The Ringer** - "[Sheeran's] rapping so hard that you can practically smell the sweat he breaks trying to keep up with Future, which blemishes the whole song"; **The Atlantic** - "Maddeningly catchy"; **Vulture** - "A track that sounds unmistakably like a Rihanna reject"; **NME** - "Less spiky than the rest of *Reputation* - instead Swift muses on wanting her relationship to last forever".

I Did Something Bad ***

(Taylor Swift - Max Martin - Shellback)
Recorded - MXM Studios, LA/ Stockholm
Produced - Max Martin & Shellback
Released - November 10 2017
Chart peak positions
  Hot 100 Bubbling Under #14; NZ Heatseeker #5

With lyrics inspired by an episode of the fantasy series *Game of Thrones*, in which Sansa and Arya Stark conspire to kill Littlefinger for his treachery, Taylor writes about her lack of remorse after alleged wrongful behaviours that caused a sensation. Taylor had initially teased fans with the lyric "they're burning all the witches, even if you aren't one" in the music video for 'Ready for It?'

At a Secret Sessions party for *Reputation*, Taylor explained how the idea for the production came to her in a weird dream and she initially developed it on a piano. The sound in her head was "so hook-y and so catchy that I knew it would have to be in a song because it was that annoying." She described the concept to Martin saying she wanted that sound to come post-chorus. As there was no instrument to replicate it, he said he could use her voice by pitching it down to create the desired effect and make her sound "like an enchantress, slash, a dude."

The line "If a man talks shit then I owe him nothing" marked the first time Taylor uses a profanity in a song.

The song should have been the album's lead single, and for a number of reviewers, it was an example of Taylor's new defiant attitude.

Slant - "The album marks a shift from the retro-minded pop-rock of 2014's *1989* toward a harder, more urban aesthetic, and Swift wears the stiff, clattering beats of songs like 'Ready for It?' like body armour. That can make *Reputation* feel impenetrable, leaving the listener to search for the humanity in defiant songs like 'I Did Something Bad'"; **Rolling Stone** - "Despite the Eurodisco bleeps and bloops, this is a total Nineties grunge-rock rager …This is just waiting for her to turn it into a head-banging live guitar monster"; **NME** - "A cavernous slab of EDM, this was basically Swift proving she's a good girl gone bad".

Don't Blame Me ***

(Taylor Swift - Max Martin - Shellback)
Recorded - MXM Studios, LA
Produced - Max Martin & Shellback
Released - November 10 2017

Taylor compares being in love to drug addiction, and writes about being "crazy in love" with someone, despite admitting to herself that she has been a heartbreaker in the past. Possibly taking inspiration from Hozier's 2013 hit 'Take Me to Church' with its sonic and thematic similarities.

The song is rumoured to be about Joe Alwyn, while many believe she could be referring to how the media perceive her.

Spin - "Her voice lilts over the thick, dark production, and she sounds every bit like the fully-realised adult pop star she aimed to be with her earlier singles"; **People** - "Swift continues to spin the public's opinion of her - that she's boy-crazy, that she plays the victim - into sonic gold on the bluesy 'Don't Blame Me'. And this time around, she's unapologetic"; **Vulture** - "A woozy if slightly anonymous love song that comes off as a sexier 'Take Me to Church'; **NME** - "This thundering, foot-stomping, fist-pumping moment...will make you want to set fire to your ex's car..."

Delicate ****
(Taylor Swift - Max Martin - Shellback)
5th Single
Recorded - MXM Studios, LA/ Stockholm
Produced - Max Martin & Shellback
Released - March 12 2018
Chart peak positions
  Hot 100 #12; AC #1; Adult Top 40 #1; Dance/Mix Show Airplay #4; Mainstream
  Top 40 #1; UK #45; Canada #20; Australia #28; NZ #33
RIAA Certification - 2 x Platinum

Where the preceding four tracks reflect Taylor's carefree disinterest in her perceived reputation, this song sees Taylor revealing her inner vulnerability for the first time, and her insecurity about whether her new love interest would be bothered by her blemished reputation.

At the release party, she explained that with this track, "it's like...oh god, what happens when you meet someone who you really want in your life and then you start worrying about what they've heard before they met you? You start to wonder like, could something fake, like your reputation, affect something real, like someone getting to know you. And you start to wonder, um, how much does all that matter?... Kind of questioning the reality and the perception of a reputation what that actually...how much weight it actually has. So, this is called 'Delicate'."

Compared with the album's mainly aggressive electronic sound, critics praised Taylor's songwriting and the more mellow production of the song.

To create the sound that reflects the song's vulnerability, producers Martin and Shellback used a vocoder to manipulate Taylor's voice, as the singer explained: "There's an effect that you may hear on the vocals throughout the rest of the album that is recurring, and it's a vocoder. It's a vocal effect where you sing, and the vocoder splits your voice into chords, and you can play your voice on a keyboard, in chords. So basically, if you're singing the notes of a piano, and you could play your own voice. So that's what you'll hear in the beginning, and throughout the song, and then you'll hear it several times. We tried it in the studio, and I thought it sounded really emotional, and really vulnerable, and really kind of, like, sad but beautiful."

After a slow start on the Hot 100, 'Delicate' eventually broke into the top 40 to extend Taylor's record as the woman with the most Hot 100 top 40 entries (56).

The music video, directed by Joseph Kahn, was shot over two nights at various locations in Los Angeles, including the Millennium Biltmore Hotel and the 7th Street/Metro Center station. It depicts Taylor being interviewed on a red carpet and getting all the usual attention. She is then handed a sparkly note by someone in the crowd, and only when she gets a chance for some privacy does she read it, and then realises she has suddenly become invisible. She then enjoys a brief moment of newfound freedom before once again becoming visible again.

Some commentators saw this as an autobiographical reference, as she had not given press interviews while she had been promoting *Reputation*.

Taylor also directed a "vertical version", shot in just one take in a vertical format, and featuring her singing the song in a park. It was released exclusively on Spotify.

Rolling Stone - "At heart, 'Delicate' is a story about a girl in her room, hearing an electro-beat that lures her to go seek some scandalous adventures in the city lights. In other words, the story of pop music"; **Spin** - "Ethereal lusciousness"; **Billboard** - "The deliberately paced, heavily vocodored 'Delicate' could be the most sensual song Swift's ever written, where she narrates a new relationship that's as thrilling as it is uncertain"; **Vulture** - "With multitracked, breathy vocals, this is Swift at her most tentative…This is the most genuinely sexy song on *Reputation*"; **NME** - "'Delicate' is dazzling".

Look What You Made Me Do **
(Taylor Swift - Jack Antonoff - Richard Fairbrass - Fred Fairbrass - Rob Manzoli)
1st Single
Recorded - Rough Customers Studio, Brooklyn
Produced - Jack Antonoff & Taylor Swift
Released - August 24 2017
Chart peak positions
  Hot 100 #1; AC #19; Adult Top 40 #7; Dance Club Songs #9; Dance/Mix Show
  Airplay #3; Mainstream Top 40 #1; Rhythmic #20; Alternative Streaming Songs
  #1; UK #1; Canada #1; Australia #1; Japan #7
RIAA Certification - 4 x Platinum
Selected awards & nominations
2018 MTV Video Music Awards - Best Art (nominated)
2018 MTV Video Music Awards - Best Editing (nominated)
2018 MTV Video Music Awards - Best visual effects (nominated)
2018 BMI London Awards - Pop Award (won)
2019 BMI Awards - Award Winning Song (won)
2019 BMI Awards - Publisher of the Year (won)

Regarded as Taylor's comeback, the song was released after a year's hiatus from the public spotlight, and the immense media scrutiny that had resulted from the much-publicised disputes with fellow celebrities Kanye, Kim and Katy. The song is considered to be one of pop music's most memorable moments, not for the incredible records broken, but for its controversial content and equally controversial music video, resulting in a frenzied online reception with both lyrics and video being dissected by both press and public in the most clinical and forensic detail, and leading *Rolling Stone* to describe the song's "nightmarish aesthetic" as a continuation of the "antagonistic persona" of 'Bad Blood'.

Taylor revealed that the song started out as a poem she had written about her feelings: "It's basically about realising that you couldn't trust certain people, but realising you appreciate the people you can trust. Realising that you can't just let everyone in, but the ones you can let in, you need to cherish."

Co-writer Jack Antonoff was asked about the song on the red carpet at the VMAs: "[When we wrote the song] she came over to my house. We hung out and wrote the song…We just, were kinda, like, messing around and cooked up all these different ideas together. I love working with people, and I'm blessed to work with people who are always moving forward." In an interview for Stereogum, he said: "The idea there was 'let's make something that doesn't sound like what's going on right now.' Sonically, it was like, 'let's just f**king freak out.' I'm sorta blown away by how many critics have missed the camp in it."

When asked if Taylor minded the avalanche of personal scrutiny that followed its release, Antonoff replied: "That was what it was designed for. That's the whole point of the song."

The song interpolates the melody of the 2007 chart-topping song 'I'm Too Sexy' by British band Right Said Fred. According to band member Fred Fairbrass, he and his brother Richard were contacted just a week before 'Look What You Made Me Do' was released and were asked whether a "big, contemporary female artist who hasn't released anything for a while" could use a portion of the song for her latest single. They agreed to the deal, despite not knowing who the singer was until the morning after the song was released. Fred Fairbrass later told *Rolling Stone*, "I like the cynical aspect of the lyric, because 'I'm Too Sexy' is a cynical song, and I think she channelled that quite well."

The song went on to break chart records. Not only was it Taylor's fifth chart-topper on the Hot 100, remaining there for three consecutive weeks, it was the most streamed track in a single day on Spotify. Topping the digital chart, it was downloaded 353,000 times. It also beat the record for the most streamed track in one week by a female artist (84.4 million).

The record-breaking music video, her most successful to date, was directed by Joseph Kahn and filmed in May 2017. According to Taylor, part of the premise for the video was the idea that "if everything you write about me was true, this is how ridiculous it would look." True to form, the video contains numerous references, far too many to unravel here, but among the many scenes we find Taylor as a zombie crawling out of a grave that has a headstone reading 'Here Lies Taylor Swift's Reputation'; lying in a bathtub filled with diamonds (apparently $10 million worth of the real thing); seated on a throne surrounded by writing snakes and being served tea; crashing an expensive Bugatti car; holding a Grammy up in front of the paparazzi; swinging in a golden cage; robbing a streaming company while wearing a cat mask; standing on the wing of a plane before sawing it in half; and, for the climax, standing on a T-shaped throne while white clones of herself from past videos begin to bicker, with taunts of being "so fake" and "playing the victim".

The video was premiered at the MTV Video Music Awards on August 27th 2017, and broke the record for the most-watched video within 24 hours with some 43.2 million views on YouTube. It also broke the same record for Vevo, with 27.7 million views. It also went on to be ranked by PopSugar as the most iconic pop video of the 2010s and amassed a total of more than 1.23 billion views (and counting).

The song inevitably received polarised reviews:

Variety - "'Look What You Made Me Do' makes the superstar sound like a tougher chick than the tougher chick we were already getting to know, but there's also the undeniable element of Swift being a girl who just wants to have fun... the fun, that is, of playing around with her own fury"; **Spin** - "[A song] about inner turmoil that feels like it's fighting itself, with ugly parts fused together searching for a compromise that is never found"; **Los Angeles Times** - "The reverberating crescendo builds and ever more delicious is the wickedness of Swift's menacing protagonist"; **Slant** - "The song, self-critical or not, is still explicitly meant as a diss track directed at an arguably mentally unstable black artist"; **USA Today** - "It cheapens the work of an artist who was once among her generation's best songwriters"; **People** - "Swift chose to usher in this new era with a song that molts every thought you've ever had about Taylor Swift over the past decade, every prom queen dress she's ever worn on the red carpet...every critic who's ever oversimplified her catalog based on her dating life"; **NME** - "Feels like a bit of a misstep"; **Seattle Times** - "It's campy, pulpy garbage and it's also bloody brilliant. If you're going to blame your public controversies on everyone but yourself, at least have fun with it"; **Vulture** - "The villain costume sits uneasy on Swift's shoulders, and even worse, the songwriting just isn't there"; **Rolling Stone** - "This just sounds like a trivial time-waster by her standards - Swift's celebrity feuds are not really one of the hundred most interesting things about her".

So it Goes... **

Taylor Swift - Max Martin - Shellback - Oscar Gorres)
Produced - Max Martin, Shellback & Oscar Gorres
Released - November 10 2017

A song about Joe Alwyn? The song certainly seems to relate to Taylor falling in love with someone. Whoever it is referring to, she finds him attractive and feels deeply connected. Taylor manages to balance just how sexual she and her lover are being by giving each a verse to describe their separate roles. With "scratches down your back", Taylor unapologetically embraces her sexuality with her lyrics.

One theory surrounding *Reputation* is that the album is split into two parts, with the first seven songs about how her reputation has been formed by the media, and the remaining eight about her actual life. This could explain the "three-dot" ellipses surrounding the opening track, "...Ready for It?" and this, the seventh track, "So it Goes..."

Sometimes these Swifties can be so clever...

Vulture - "This one comes and goes without making much of an impact"; **Rolling Stone** - "A great moment that lets you know Swift - like the rest of us - has been listening to Lorde"; **NME** - "An ethereal synth-pop moment laced with EDM and trap".

Gorgeous ***

(Taylor Swift - Max Martin - Shellback)
Promo Single
Produced - Max Martin & Shellback
Released - October 20 2017
Chart peak positions

Hot 100 #13; Digital Songs #1; Alternative Streaming Songs #2; UK #15; Canada #9; Australia #9; NZ #19; Japan #52
RIAA Certification - Gold

Taylor describes an infatuation for a seemingly unrequited love, a guy so attractive that she feels compelled to be with him despite her already having a boyfriend. Of course, she does let the cat out of the bag and tells fans at her Secret Session that this song and all the other positive love songs on the album are about Joe Alwyn. There had also been rumours that it could have referred to her allegedly cheating on ex-boyfriend Calvin Harris with Tom Hiddleston.

In October, Taylor had given a preview of the song on Instagram which featured a baby voice saying "gorgeous" over an electropop production. The baby was James, the daughter of Blake Lively and Ryan Reynolds. Taylor decided to feature James' voice after while playing an acoustic demo to the couple, James kept saying "gorgeous".

The song shows Taylor taking a more assertive role, no longer being heartbroken over unrequited love or hopeless romances.

Although the song was not released to radio, it still managed to draw 3.6 million with an all-format airplay audience. On the digital chart, it extended Taylor's record as the artist with the most chart-topping debuts (13), and also made *Reputation* the first album since Drake's *Views* in 2016 to spawn three or more digital number ones, and the first by a female artist since her own *1989*.

Variety - "'Gorgeous' finally provides some of the conventional pleasure that only a pop song about falling deeply in crush can"; **Billboard** - "With its oh-so-breathless delivery and obsession with always being right, 'Gorgeous' could pass for a parody of a Taylor Swift song - in fact, the joke's already gone over some people's heads. But Swift's never been wittier"; **Glamour** - "[Taylor] single handedly saving pop music in 2017"; **People** - "It's pleasant, and it grows on you with each listen, much because the lyrics - while not exactly poetry - perfectly capture that smitten feeling everyone's experienced"; **Vulture** - "The melody is a little too horizontal to stick, and the lyrics have a touch of first draft about them"; **Rolling Stone** - "This song could rate higher, except she basically did an even better version with 'You Need to Calm Down'"; **NME** - "It's about seeing somebody who is unbelievably hot that you develop a massive rush, existing partner be damned".

Getaway Car **
(*Taylor Swift - Jack Antonoff*)
6th Single (Australia)
Produced - Jack Antonoff & Taylor Swift
Released - September 27 2018
Chart peak positions
Australia Digital Tracks #33; NZ #9

Taylor uses the imagery of criminals and a speeding car as the central metaphor for her efforts to run away from a relationship to be with someone else, only to find out that the new relationship will also come to an end. Although the inspiration for the song is not clear, the name Tom Hiddleston has frequently been discussed on social media. The lyrics add weight to the theory, suggesting a quick transition between relationships, as was the case with the high-profile breakup with Calvin Harris and the sudden debut of Hiddleston.

The lyrics "think about the place you first met me" and how "the ties were black, the lies were white" are no doubt a reference to when Taylor first encountered Hiddleston at the Met Gala.

In September 2018, it was announced that 'Getaway Car' would be released as an exclusive single in Australia and New Zealand, in support of the upcoming Australian shows of the *Reputation* tour.

It was lauded by many critics as one of the highlights of the album for both the cinematic quality of the lyrics and its reference to popular culture figures.

Irish Times - "It's one of the best songs on the album. Again, showing her storytelling prowess, this song could be about anyone's love life, and not just her specific billionaire boyfriends. You see, relatability is important sometimes"; **Pop Sugar** - "While Taylor admits that she and Tom were like Bonnie and Clyde playing games with the media, she seems to allude that she was the one who ended up playing Tom in the end. Is this Taylor's way of confirming that their relationship really was all for show?"; **Rolling Stone** - "Noir Tay makes her big entrance…a femme fatale playing two fall guys against each other".

King of My Heart ***
(Taylor Swift - Max Martin - Shellback)
Produced - Max Martin & Shellback
Released – November 10 2017

Seen by many fans to be an out and out love letter to her boyfriend Joe Alwyn. Where certain songs on the album reference the loss of various kingdoms and castles, it appears that she has found a more personal kingdom in which a new love interest is now ruling her "heart, body and soul", and the crown she has to offer means more to her than ever before.

During the album's release party, Taylor explained: "I think it's really interesting when people talk about their love stories…there seems to be these definitive phases, and it doesn't matter how long that phase lasts, there seems to be a moment when you knew it transitioned into the next phase... And what I find interesting are the moments where it switches, because you always hope that that switch is going to move you forward and not backward. Because, it can happen both ways. It can happen either way."

Taylor had first teased her fans on the music video of 'Ready for It', in which she hints at the song's title with a red graffiti crowned heart on a wall in the background. She also revealed to *Entertainment Weekly* that, like other songs on the album, inspiration had come from *Game of Thrones* and the relationship between the characters Deanerys and Khal Drogo.

Vulture - "Swift is writing about a relationship from inside of it, instead of with hindsight. It's a different skill, which could explain why the boyfriend character here is less vividly sketched than some of her other ones"; **NME** - "This electro-pop moment has a sweet sentiment: that the extravagance of past relationships isn't what Swift wants anymore, and now this new love interest could be The One".

Dancing with Our Hands Tied ****

(Taylor Swift - Max Martin - Shellback - Oscar Holter)
Produced - Max Martin, Shellback & Oscar Holter
Released - November 10 2017

According to a fan who attended the album's Secret Session party, Taylor revealed the inspiration for the song came when she spent several months out of the public gaze in Los Angeles, only to be hounded by the paparazzi while coming out of a gym. Overwhelmed by the experience, she realised just how impossible it was to have a normal life, and now fears that the relationship she is in is doomed to die due to outside pressure.

Despite the constant strain that is threatening to tear their world apart, they are still able to temporarily enjoy their relationship as though they are dancing together for the first time. "I loved you in secret" is a line from the song which is featured in the 'Ready for It' music video as graffiti on the walls.

The song was co-written and co-produced by Swedish songwriter and producer Oscar Holter, who had previously worked with Pink and Katy Perry. In the last chorus of the song, Taylor's voice hits notes never been heard before in her career.

Vulture - "*Reputation* sags a bit in the middle, never more than on this forgettable 80s-inspired track"; **Rolling Stone** - "She slips away in secret with a forbidden lover who paints her blue heart gold"; **NME** - "This electronic, beat-heavy song...is basically as close as we've ever come to a Swiftie club remix".

Dress ***

(Taylor Swift - Jack Antonoff)
Produced - Taylor Swift & Jack Antonoff
Released - November 10 2017
Chart peak position
 Alternative Streaming Songs #7

A sexually-charged ballad detailing Taylor's craving and lusting over another lover, and reputed to be about Joe Alwyn, although Karlie Kloss, Tom Hiddleston, Drake, and even Ed Sheeran have been in the frame. But if this is one of the "positive" love songs that Taylor mentions to her fans, it has to be about Alwyn, and references in the song also point his way. In addition to this, Taylor told fans that the tracks on the album are in some sort of chronological order which makes their relationship fit the timescale.

As the name suggests, many of the sexual references in the song pertain to dresses.

Apparently, when played at the Secret Sessions, certain fans tweeted that Taylor's parents either left the room or seemed uncomfortable with the lyrics about bedpost notches, stripped off clothes, and wine-fuelled sexy baths.

This Antonoff collaboration was not far removed from Taylor's duet with Zayn on 'I Don't Wanna Live Forever', and should have been released as a single.

Talking to iHeartRadio, Taylor said: "This song is one of those things where almost every line is something that I came up with like a year before, and then when I was writing the song, I just cherry picked...And I was really proud of the hook of this because it sounds like a pickup line, and yet it is a love song about deep and tender feelings."

Billboard - "If you think Swift's recent submerging in pop and even hip-hop has you prepped for this one, you're mistaken. Because 'Dress' is a *slow jam*. As in spilled wine and hands that can't stop shaking..."; **Vulture** - "An appropriately slinky track that gives us an unexpected payoff for years of lyrics about party dresses"; **NME** - "By a mile the steamiest cut from *Reputation*; this slinking song details the pang of secret lust in breathy falsetto".

This is Why We Can't Have Nice Things ***
(Taylor Swift - Jack Antonoff)
Produced - Taylor Swift & Jack Antonoff
Released - November 10 2017

In this anthemic and sometimes comical song, Taylor throws some shade at her haters. Where several songs on the album appear to take digs at Kanye West, none cut deeper than this one. With lyrics that talk about giving someone a second chance, having her back stabbed, and then getting "mind-twisted" on the phone by them, it wouldn't have taken the naivest Swiftie long to figure out who she's referring to. Near the end of the song, Taylor appears to give an apology, even though she can't go through with it.

Taylor told iHeartRadio: "It's about when people take nice things for granted. Like friendship, or trusting people, or being like open or whatever. Letting people in on your life, trusting people, respect - those are all really nice things."

Elite Daily - "It's clear that this is a new Swift, one who is over what people think of her. If you consider how Swift is portrayed in the press - boy-crazy, narcissistic, manipulative, even empty-headed at times - *Reputation* is taking Swift's, uh, reputation and turning it on its head. Swift is writing her own narrative, being boy-crazy and revenge-thirsty on her own terms"; **Rolling Stone** - "The most 'therein' moment on *Reputation*"; **NME** - "A powerful sentiment, but an acquired taste".

Call It What You Want ****
(Taylor Swift - Jack Antonoff)
Promo Single
Produced - Taylor Swift & Jack Antonoff
Released - November 3 2017
Chart peak positions
 Hot 100 #27; Digital Songs #1; UK #29; Australia #16; NZ #34
RIAA Certification - Gold

With a nice change of pace, Taylor gives a warm message to a lover that supported her through a tough time, leading some reviewers to cite this song as the perfect transition track from *1989* to *Reputation*, with its familiar edgy lyrics.

In a later interview for *Rolling Stone*, Taylor said that it was about her "newly quiet, cozy world that was happening on [her] own terms for the first time." In a sombre, reflective mood, she looks back at the tumultuous public scrutiny of the past few years and realises that it's no longer important. All that matters now is the strength of her relationship, so the media can see it however they want to.

During the Secret Session release party, Taylor explained: "The way I feel the album is, as far as a storyline, is I feel like it starts with just getting out any kind of rebellion, or anger, or angst, or whatever. And then, like, falling in love, and realising that you kind of settle into what your priorities are, and your life changes, but you welcome it because it's something that matters to you. And this last part of the album feels like settling into where I am now. So, it started with where I was when I started making the album, and ends with kind of my emotional state now. And this song, I think, really reflects that probably the best on the album."

The song topped the Digital Songs chart with 68,000 copies, making Taylor the first artist to have 15 entries reach number one, and also extended her record for the most debuts on the top spot with 14.

Vulture - "[The song] deals in gossamer and light; its spare, airy production evokes, or attempts to evoke, a sense of radiant, protective romance in the wake of a devastating social debacle"; **USA Today** - "When it comes down to it [the song] is unlikely to change the minds of fans who think Swift's *Reputation* output so far has been lacklustre, but for a love song that nimbly toes the line between sincere and saccharine, it's a surprisingly effective and grown-up new effort"; **Redbrick** - "Melodically, it lacks the strength of past singles such as 'Blank Space' or 'You Belong with Me'. It offers little variation between the choruses and the verses and is yet to get stuck in my head. The lyrics are far from masterful... being a poor attempt for such an experienced and clever songwriter"; **Rolling Stone** - "The warmest Rep electro-ballad, about how exotic it feels to give up worrying about judgy strangers and start living a damn life"; **NME** - "She doesn't care what people think anymore".

New Year's Day *****
(Taylor Swift - Jack Antonoff)
4th Single
Recorded - Rough Customer Studio, Brooklyn
Produced - Taylor Swift & Jack Antonoff
Released - November 27 2017
Chart peak positions
  Hot Country Songs #33; Country Airplay #41; Digital Song Sales #44

Saving the best for last, we have one of Taylor's finest ballads, in which she reflects on the aftermath of a party-fuelled romance, and how her feelings for her partner will live on even after the moment has ended. She uses the title as a metaphor, as she explained it to her fans at the Secret Sessions party: "We threw a big New Year's Eve party in London this year, and I was thinking about how everybody talks and thinks about who you kiss at midnight. Like it's this big romantic idea ... But I think there's something even more romantic about who's gonna deal with you on New Year's Day. Who's willing to give you Advil and clean up the house? I think that states more of a permanence."

Another great Swift-Antonoff collaboration, it was also the quickest song to record. In an interview for *Entertainment Weekly*, Antonoff revealed how he had encouraged Taylor to capture emotions at a particular time when "you can feel like you can conquer the world, or you can feel like the biggest piece of garbage that ever existed." He also stated that the recording session was inspired by Joni Mitchell's ability to capture emotional honesty: "You don't want to get the absolute perfect vocal take or the perfect panning or compression...It has nothing to do with genre, or how loud or soft it is. You just want the song to feel like itself. You want to feel like you're home within the song...I don't know what we would be thinking if we tried to f*ck with it. I'm so proud of it because, personally, I think it's some sort of hint at the future."

Antonoff had nailed it on the head. This was a prime example of Taylor's artistic maturity, and the perfect way to close what was an album full of vengeful drama with a song of reflective spirit. Breaking away from the synth-heavy, aggressive production at the core of the album, it stood in stark contrast with its stripped-down, sombre instrumentation, allowing the intricate lyrics (on a par with 'All Too Well') to perfectly capture that emotional moment in time.

Prior to its release on country radio on November 27th, Taylor had premiered the song with an airing of her Secret Sessions performance during the ABC series *Scandal* on November 9th, and then performed the song live four days later on Jimmy Fallon's late-night show, with what would be an emotional time for the host.

'New Year's Day' became her first chart entry on Hot Country Songs since her collaboration with Tim McGraw on 'Highway Don't Care' in 2013. Critics were almost unanimous in their praise:

Glamour - "We've had it wrong this whole time: 'New Taylor' isn't on *Reputation* - not on the first 14 songs, at least. Nope, that's 'Old Taylor', addressing her past issues one last time as a form of catharsis. It's only on 'New Year's Day' where we catch a glimpse of 'New Taylor'; a woman who, finally, is done with the drama - the sentimentalist who valued songwriting above all else"; **Spin** - "There is more to life, and certainly to pop stardom, than good songwriting. But how telling that, to conclude the album at greatest risk of violating her own aesthetic judgements, Swift has come back to what she does best"; **Newsweek** - "Fire up the high school graduation playlists. This one is a keeper"; **Vulture** - "Like a prestige cable drama, Swift likes to use her final track as a kind of quiet summing-up of all that's come before. Here, she saves the album's most convincing love song for last, an appreciation for the everyday pleasures of a healthy relationship"; **Rolling Stone** - "The one-time poet laureate of teen crushdom turns out to be even sharper at adult love songs…This is the kind of song she should keep writing into her forties and fifties"; **NME** - "The groggy clear up that takes place after a raucous New Year's house party has never sounded so idyllic".

"The gatekeeper to her own heart"

The day after the album's release, Taylor went on SiriusXM radio at their New York glass-walled "fishbowl" studio to perform stripped-down versions of the album's last two tracks, 'Call It What You Want' and 'New Year's Day', and a haunting acoustic rendition of Tom Petty's 'American Girl', arguably her finest cover. *Billboard* recorded: "Rocking the coolest dark plaid trousers and button-adorned heels, Swift first sat toward the front of the fishbowl, pointing out that she was basically on the set of her 'Ready for It' music video, ready to break through the glass. Then, in a single sentence she confirmed many fan theories, and explained that the album was representative of her life, beginning at the first track with where she was and how she felt when starting the album, and followed the drama through to the present time with track 15."

The following day she guested on *Saturday Night Live* for the first time in eight years, and, introduced by host Tiffany Haddish, performed 'Ready for It' and an acoustic 'Call It What You Want'. In describing the performance of the first song, one reviewer commented how "she did her best to buck the usually clean image that the world had come to know her as. Notable here was the moment where Taylor combined the lyric about touching her with a sensual movement toward her pelvis. This was about as polar opposite of clean-cut, and another proclamation that she's not the Taylor of old." Even with the more mellow second song, she was seen to be getting her point across: "This is a new Taylor, one that not everyone is going to like or take seriously. She doesn't care though, and neither do her fans who are ready to go on this journey with her into this new era."

A more emotional night came on November 13th when Taylor was asked to appear on *The Tonight Show with Jimmy Fallon.* The host had recently lost his mother and had cancelled all shows for that week. The show's producer knew they wanted someone special for the first show back, and when it was known that Taylor was in town, he reached out to her: "She was not scheduled to do our show today. But we wanted something special for this first show back, so we asked her on a complete whim, since she had been in town doing *SNL*. She said yes with zero hesitation."

During the show, Fallon recalled his childhood: "When we were little, my mom would walk us to this store, me and my sister, and she would squeeze my hand three times and say, 'I love you', and I would squeeze back, 'I love you too'…Last week, I was in the hospital and I grabbed her hand and squeezed, 'I love you'."

Serendipitously, the lyrics of 'New Year's Day', the song Taylor had chosen to perform, referred back to Fallon's story: "You squeeze my hand three times in the back of the taxi/I can tell that it's gonna be a long road."

According to the producer, "I nearly gasped. Tears. I think everyone in the audience started sobbing. I could see Jimmy silhouetted at his desk dabbing his eyes with a tissue. We all lost it." The show's resident drummer later tweeted: "I'm just realising Taylor didn't readjust the song's lyrics for tonight's performance. But the narrative literally applies to the words Jimmy spoke of his mother. Wow. You can't plan these things."

That same day, Taylor's management announced the first 27 dates for the *Reputation* Tour jointly with Ticketmaster, with the first concert in Glendale, Arizona on May 8th. Tickets would be going on sale to the general public on December 13th, Taylor's birthday. On her Taylor Nation Twitter account, she captioned the list of dates, "We'll see you soon!"

The following month came the usual string of festive appearances. On December 1st, Taylor performed a six-song set at the KISS FM Jingle Ball in Inglewood, as part of iHeartRadio's Jingle Ball Tour. It included a duet with Ed Sheeran on 'End Game', the first time the pair had sung together since 2013.

That same day, Taylor announced a series of new dates for next year's world tour, with additional concerts in Manchester, Dublin and London, following an overwhelming demand for tickets. Fortunately, none of the dates would clash with Katy Perry's tour schedule booked for around the same time. Three days later it was announced that an Australian leg of the tour would kick off in Perth in October.

On December 2nd, Taylor was in San Diego for a "fierce and feisty" performance at Poptopia, the newly-named holiday show hosted by local radio station 99.7-FM KMVQ. In one of the biggest-ever music line-ups in the Bay Area, the bill also included Ed Sheeran, Dua Lipa, Niall Horan, Khalid and Fifth Harmony. A week later, she was in the Windy City for the B96 Chicago and Pepsi Jingle Bash, this time without Sheeran, but they were reunited the next day for the Z100 Jingle Ball in New York. *Billboard* wrote: "Swift certainly didn't disappoint. Donning a sequinned black shirt embellished with a Santa hat-wearing snake, Swift brought the house down with *Reputation* banger 'Ready for It' before throwing in a couple of *1989* jams…"

Taylor's final performance of the year came on the 10th with the second night at Capital FM's Jingle Bell Ball in London in front of 16,000 screaming fans. The radio station reported: "To showcase exactly why she's one of the most loved artists on the entire planet, she owned the stage from start to finish. London's O2 was lit up with smartphones filming the pop legend and combined with the voices of thousands of her fans singing every word to her biggest and best hits, it made for one seriously magical atmosphere…It's clear that the old Taylor isn't dead, she's just new and improved with a fierce attitude - and ready to claim her now serpent-wrapped throne."

Meanwhile, *Reputation* was making waves in the charts. On its release, it became Taylor's fourth consecutive album to debut atop the Hot 200 chart, with first-week sales of over a million copies. It would go on to be the best-selling album of 2017 by a female, and the second-best by any artist (behind Ed Sheeran's *Divide*), with total worldwide sales which would eventually amount to 4.5 million.

In the main, the reviews were positive and gave a nod to Taylor's maturity and grown-up impulses. But there were others accusing her of giving in to her personal dramas.

Rolling Stone - "A song cycle about how it feels when you stop chasing romance and start letting your life happen…. [It showed] the dark, deeper side of the pop mastermind"; **The Independent** - "Swift's old palette of virginal white and pale blue is gone, replaced by reds and shimmering gold"; **The Guardian** - "[The songs] may be mired in bitterness and gossip, but the pop star's songwriting smarts and lyrical prowess are impossible to deny…"; **NME** - "Is this a relatable record? If you've ever wanted to exact revenge on someone, the answer is yes"; **New York Times** - "[The album] is a public renegotiation, engaging pop music on its terms, not hers"; **USA Today** - "Swift takes ownership of her narrative in a way listeners haven't heard before. She's the predator, the person holding all the control, the gatekeeper to her own heart…And that private reputation, she proves, is more important to her than all the headlines in the world".

Reputation would be Taylor's last album under her contract with Big Machine Records.

Reputation Intact

"There are two ways you can get through pain. You can let it destroy you, or you can use it as fuel to drive you: to dream bigger, work harder"

Friendships lost and regained

2018 started with what seemed like some positive news. During an appearance on Bravo's late-night talk show *Watch What Happens Live* on January 14th, Kim Kardashian told host Andy Cohen that her feud with Taylor was now over, saying, "I feel like we've all moved on." A little while later she indicated that she was "making peace" with the singer by sharing a video of her listening to her song 'Delicate' on Snapchat.

If that was true, the media hounds could probably now put that to bed, and focus on what appeared to be a new development in Taylor's personal life.

After months of speculation, the year began with reports that Taylor Swift and best friend Karlie Kloss were no longer the partners in crime they once were, especially when fans detected the model's lack of support on Instagram for Taylor's new single, 'Look What You Made Me Do', but did notice her reference to liking Katy Perry's 'Swish Swish' track. Rumours of a rift circulated in February when Kloss and Perry were reported by *People* magazine having dinner together in LA with *Vanity Fair* writer Derek Blasberg and jewellery designer Jennifer Meyer. Even actress Jennifer Lawrence, a mutual friend, was becoming concerned, and in an interview for her new movie *Red Sparrow,* revealed that if she was really a spy, she would "like to know what's going on...that's the honest to God truth", as it was keeping her awake at night.

Taylor's friendship with the supermodel had begun in 2012 with the singer's *Vogue* cover interview, when she had noticed a photo of her and said, "I love Karlie Kloss. I want to bake cookies with her!" Kloss read the article and tweeted Taylor, "Hey, love the @voguemagazine cover! Your kitchen or mine?" From that moment the two of them presumably became friends privately, no doubt over cookies and wine, but they would not be spotted together in public until the Victoria's Secret Fashion Show in November 2013, where Taylor performed as Kloss was on the catwalk.

In March the following year, the two of them went on a road trip together and Kloss documented it on Instagram with a caption to one of the pictures reading "Karlie ♡'s @taylorswift". They were seen together at the pre-Oscars party and then spent the summer out and about in New York, with Kloss staying in Taylor's guest room. After a repeat of their performance at the next VS Fashion Show in December, they appeared on the cover of *Vogue* together, and, in May 2015, Kloss was one of the squad members featured in the music video for 'Bad Blood'.

In the summer of 2016, after the Kanye-Kim feud had reared its snake-like head, Kloss was asked by *Sunday Times'* style magazine if she thought Kim was a good person, and although, at first, appearing a little reticent to answer, said she had been "a lovely person to me in the past...I really don't know her that well." Kloss later went on Instagram: "I will not allow the media to misconstrue my words. Taylor had always had my back and I will always have hers."

In one of the pair's last public sightings in October 2016, they were snapped exiting the Bowery Ballroom, and for Taylor's 27th birthday in December, Kloss tweeted: "Happiest of Birthdays to my ride and die @taylorswift... I feel blessed to count you as my friend, sister and partner in crime. Can't wait to celebrate together very soon."

A few days later she would be spotted entering Taylor's Tribeca apartment in New York.

Now, in March 2018, the *New York Times* had run an article on Kloss, listing Taylor as one of her "closest friends" and suggesting that, despite all the rumours, the pair remained good friends "and talk frequently." Kloss made a point of saying, "Don't believe everything you read."

With that particular rumour seemingly dispelled for now, it was only a matter of time before Katy Perry's name cropped up in the media once more. Although things between them seemed to have been put on the back burner, it was never too far away from the backs of media minds, and anything that was said or done by either party would light up the internet. During a March edition of *American Idol,* for which Perry was a celebrity judge, one of the contestants confessed to her that Taylor Swift was his idol, not Perry. When he apologised, Perry told him, "Oh, you don't have to say sorry, I love her as a songwriter as well."

In February, the *New York Post* reported that Taylor had "drastically overpaid" $.9.8 million for a second-floor Tribeca apartment at 155 Franklin Street from financier Jeremy Phillips in an off-market deal. Taylor already owned two top-floor units that she had combined into a gigantic penthouse complex of some 8,000 square feet, as well as the townhouse next door at 153 Franklin that she had bought for $18 million in September 2017. This brought her total spending spree on the block to $47.7 million.

According to reports, Taylor was in the process of turning all four Tribeca properties into one giant compound, with plans to add a driveway in front of the townhouse leading to an indoor garage that would allow her to enter the next-door apartment from inside.

At the beginning of March, Taylor announced the opening acts for the *Reputation* Tour. Camila Cabello was a Cuban-born American singer-songwriter who had risen to fame as a member of the girl group Fifth Harmony, which had come third in *The X Factor* in 2012. After going solo, her debut album *Camila* had topped the Hot 200 in January. Cabello had been previously speculated to be the opening act because her own *Never Be the Same* tour did not clash with Taylor's schedule. Joining her on the tour was Charli XCX (aka Charlotte Aitchison), an English singer-songwriter, whose collaboration with Swedish electro-pop duo Icona Pop on 'I Love It' had topped the UK charts in 2012. Also joining the Agency for the tour was guitarist and keyboard player Max Bernstein.

On the last day of the month, Taylor made a surprise appearance in the documentary *The Bluebird Café Easter Eve Concert*, celebrating the 35th anniversary of the legendary Nashville music venue, the very place where Taylor had been "discovered" by Scott Borchetta 14 years ago. Sharing the stage with her old singer-songwriter friend Craig Wiseman, who she had met at a charity show as a teenager, she received a standing ovation. Addressing the audience, she said: "I think any songwriter in town would echo my sentiments and say that this is kind of the only place where this exists - this particular place where you get to come and hear the writer's take on the songs they've put out into the world."

Taylor then explained that one of her earliest lessons in songwriting was that all a song needed was three chords and simplicity: "If there's truth in it, don't overthink it. It can be the same three chords over and over again." As a way of illustrating her point, she then sang 'Shake It Off'. Before performing the next song, Taylor recalled the time she had given 'Better Man' to the band Little Big Town, and how great it was to hear one of her own compositions being performed by another artist for the first time. She also revealed how, when she was 17, she had invited Wiseman to co-write a song with her, but he declined the offer. "I couldn't stop thinking about the idea," she said, "I thought there was something to it. I really liked it." There certainly was something to it - it was called 'Love Story', and she then performed the song, with what must have been a slightly embarrassed Wiseman looking on.

Sugarland's Babe

April saw the release of the single 'Babe' by country duo Sugarland, consisting of singer-songwriters Kristian Bush and Jennifer Nettles. The song was originally written by Taylor and Patrick Monahan, the lead singer of the band Train. According to Monahan, in an interview with ABC News Radio, Taylor had asked him to co-write a song for her 2012 album *Red*, and when it failed to make the cut, it was hoped it would be on the deluxe release. At the time, Monahan said: "It's a song called 'Babe'. So, it's her song; I was just lucky enough to be a part of it with her, and I'm gonna ask the same of her in the future. She's very talented, she's a no-nonsense young kid. I'm not going through different relationships and breakups and all that stuff that young people do, so her perspective is very fresh. And I think that's what I admire the most." Unfortunately, the song was never recorded.

Six years later Taylor, being a fan of Sugarland's music, got in touch with them and said she would like to work with them. After a spell of solo projects with his partner, Sugarland's Kristian Bush told *Entertainment Tonight*: "[Taylor] was gracious enough to reach out to us when she heard we were coming back together and doing a record. She said, 'I have a song, would you like to do it?' And we said, 'Uh, yeah.' I was a little anxious. I didn't want to mess it up." Jennifer Nettles added: "But she loved it and wanted [us] to be a part of it, which is exciting."

It would be an unusual experience for the duo, as they had never featured anyone else on their previous albums. With Taylor providing backing vocals, it was recorded and released on the Big Machine label on April 20th.

Delighted with the result, Taylor told her fans on Instagram: "I'm so happy that it gets its own life. I'm so happy that Sugarland wanted to record it and has done such a great job with it, and I'm so stoked I get to sing on it too."

The song peaked at #2 on Billboard's Digital Songs chart; #8 on Hot Country Songs, and #72 on the Hot 100. *Rolling Stone* called it a "foot-stomping song", and said it was reminiscent of the music of the *Speak Now* days.

It was only the second song Taylor had written for another country act, following on from 2014's 'Better Man', and it was also the first country song on which she was credited as an artist since the time she made her full transition to pop.

Taylor not only collaborated on the idea for the music video, but featured in it too. Directed by Anthony Mandler, it presents Jennifer Nettles and actor Brandon Routh as a married couple, with Taylor playing the role of the secretary who is having an affair with her married boss, played by Routh. Kristian Bush plays the neighbour who witnesses the events as they unravel.

'Babe' would be included on Sugarland's album *Bigger*, when released in June, and they would get the chance to perform the song with Taylor during the *Reputation* tour in Arlington.

"A masterclass in pop"

The day before the tour commenced in Glendale, Taylor invited 2,000 fostered and adopted children to a private two-hour dress rehearsal. According to *Teen Vogue*, an email had gone out a few days before the show encouraging families to sign up. As it was also National Foster Care Month, it was perfect timing. Although cameras were banned during the performance, the "gracious and generous hostess" stayed on after the show for a couple of hours for pizza, photos and hugs.

On May 8th, the day the tour was set to begin, Taylor posted to her Instagram Stories a photo of an olive branch and a handwritten note that Katy Perry had just sent her. There was a dog on the envelope and, what was legible of the writing, read: "Hey old friend - I've been doing some reflecting on past miscommunications and the feelings between us. I really want to clear the air..." The words "deeply sorry" could also be made out in the letter. Taylor replied with the caption, "Thank you, Katy" with a double pink heart emoji.

During the opening night of the tour at the University of Phoenix Stadium, Taylor briefly opened up about her feud with Kanye West and Kim Kardashian, but used her words to empower the 60,000 fans: "A couple of years ago, someone called me a snake on social media, and it caught on. I went through some times when I didn't know if I was going to get to do this anymore. I wanted to send a message to you guys that if someone uses name-calling to bully you on social media, and even if a lot of people jump on board with it, that doesn't have to defeat you. It can strengthen you instead." Once again, Taylor had managed to say just the right thing at just the right time.

Rolling Stone was there to review the opening show, saying that, "for the most part she went epic, with giant inflatable cobras, pyro, multiple stages and hordes of dancers...This might be her most outstanding tour yet - even when she's aiming for maximum stadium-rock razzle-dazzle bombast, she gives it all the vibe of a mass communion... No pop star goes to such absurd extremes to avoid repeating herself, even when repeating herself would be more than good enough. The girl just likes a challenge, even if that means she wants to stand under a surreal inflatable snake to sing her heartfelt confessions about autumn leaves and maple lattes."

The *New York Times* wrote: "Since the release of *Reputation* in November, the snake has become Ms Swift's spirit animal, but also the symbol that's gotten in the way of her spirit."

Following the show in Denver on May 25th, Taylor flew to the UK to appear in BBC Music's Biggest Weekend in Swansea two days later. In front of an audience of 26,000, she told them: "You're not just singing along but you're screaming along…which is the best. It kind of took my breath away a little when I first came out here."

BBC News reviewed the six-song performance: "If her set was ruthless in its efficiency, it was nonetheless a masterclass in pop - from Swift's effortless vocals and shape-throwing choreography to her adorable between-song banter."

Returning to the States, Taylor completed the first leg of the North American tour with two shows in Chicago at the beginning of June. The first seven shows of the tour had grossed $54 million with some 390,000 tickets sold. The sell-out shows in Glendale and Santa Clara has grossed $7.21 million and $14 million respectively, while the Pasadena shows grossed nearly $16.3 million.

Reviewing the concerts at the Rose Bowl, the *Los Angeles Times* called them "a master class in the constructive use of the modern technology that's allowed her to establish and nurture an exceptionally powerful connection with a massive audience."

The European leg of the tour commenced on June 8th with concerts in Manchester, Dublin and London. At London's Wembley Stadium, Taylor performed two shows in front of over 143,000 fans on both nights. Reviewing the shows, *The Guardian* wrote: "As stadium-sized pop shows go, it's something of a triumph: for a woman who keeps complaining that she's damaged goods, she seems to be doing just fine." The *Evening Standard* was also impressed: "[It] was a moment when pop's innocent princess took control of her own story. Once upon a time, things happened to her that seemed beyond her control: John Mayer dumped her; a radio DJ groped her at a backstage meet and greet, Kim Kardashian called her a snake on social media, and Kanye West did all manner of horrible things. Now, the DJ has been beaten in court, Mayer was exposed in one of her songs, West's genius is faltering, and as for snakes, they belong to Swift now."

Taking a break from the tour, Taylor performed a secret acoustic gig in Chicago on June 27th in front of a modest 200 fans. The show was recorded for *Taylor Swift NOW*, as part of Taylor's big deal with AT&T and DirecTV. Taylor only sang five songs, explaining that she was trying to rest her voice for the rest of the tour, but after the show she posed for photos with all the audience to make up for it.

The second North American leg kicked off in Louisville three days later and culminated in Arlington on October 6th. During that time, Taylor performed in front of a record 174,000 fans at Foxborough for two consecutive nights, and also did two shows in Toronto, her only Canadian dates. At the Atlanta show on August 11th, she made another impassioned speech before singing 'Clean': "Looking back, a year ago I was not playing in a stadium in Tampa, I was in a courtroom in Denver, Colorado. This is the day the jury sided in my favour and said that they believed in me…I guess I just think about all the people that weren't believed and the people who haven't been believed, and the people who are afraid to speak up because they are afraid to speak up because they think they won't be believed." Some of those

236

in the audience held up dollar bills as a gesture to mark the dollar that Mueller was court-ordered to give her after the ruling.

In September, Joe Alwyn was interviewed by *Vogue* and spoke about his relationship with Taylor for the first time, only to say he didn't want to talk about her! - "I'm aware people want to know about that side of things. I think we have been successfully very private and that has now sunk in for people - but I really prefer to talk about work."

Early the following month, he spoke briefly about Taylor's newfound political activism. After what had been a career-long silence, she had finally waded into the world of politics to endorse a couple of Tennessee congressional candidates. When interviewed about it, Alwyn said briefly: "I think it's great, and I think it's important."

Supporting the Tennessee two

On October 7th, Taylor had indeed raised her political flag for the first time when she threw her support behind Tennessee Democrat politicians Phil Bredesen, for the Senate, and Jim Cooper, for the US House, in advance of the mid-term elections in November.

Taking to Instagram, she wrote: "In the past I've been reluctant to publicly voice my political opinions. I feel very differently about that now. I always have and always will cast my vote based on which candidate will protect and fight for the human rights I believe we all deserve in this country. I believe in the fight for LGBTQ rights, and that any form of discrimination based on sexual orientation or gender is WRONG. I believe that the systemic racism we still see in this country towards people of colour is terrifying, sickening and prevalent. I cannot vote for someone who will not be willing to fight for dignity for ALL Americans, no matter their skin colour, gender or who they love... So many intelligent, thoughtful, self-possessed people have turned 18 in the past two years and now have the right and privilege to make their vote count..."

Taylor also criticised Tennessee Republican candidate and US representative Marsha Blackburn for her opposition to certain LGBTQ rights: "As much as I have in the past and would like to continue voting for women in office, I cannot support Marsha Blackburn. Her voting record in Congress appals and terrifies me. She voted against equal pay for women. She voted against the re-authorisation of the Violence Against Women Act, which attempts to protect women from domestic violence, stalking, and date rape. She believes businesses have a right to refuse service to gay couples. She also believes they should not have the right to marry. These are not MY Tennessee values."

Responding to the claim that Bredesen had endorsed Brett Kavanaugh's appointment to the Supreme Court, despite accusations of sexual assault against him, Taylor said: "For a lot of us, we may never find a candidate or party with whom we agree 100% on every issue, but we have to vote anyway."

Taylor's years of political silence had drawn just as much vitriol as her decision to speak out, and it came as no surprise that she would now receive both praise and a fierce backlash from both fans and the media alike. Six years before she had told *Time* magazine: "I don't talk about politics because it might influence other people, and I don't think that I know enough yet in life to be telling people who to vote for."

This public neutrality would see fans projecting their views on to her, and before long she had developed an almost-cult following among white nationalist groups who dubbed her their queen and their ideal of white femininity, and some critics began to wonder why she wouldn't denounce them. Then on the day of the Presidential election in 2016, Taylor had urged her fans to vote without revealing how she would cast her own ballot, naturally prompting a frenzy of curious tweets.

In an interview for *The Guardian* three years later, she admitted she was totally broken by the experience: "Every domino fell. It became really terrifying for anyone to even know where I was. And I felt completely incapable of doing or saying anything publicly, at all. Even about my music. I always said I wouldn't talk about what was happening personally, because that was a personal time...I just need some things that are mine. Just *some* things."

Speaking to *Variety*, she explained: "As a country musician, I was always told it's better to stay out of politics. The Trump presidency forced me to lean in and educate myself ...I started talking to my family and friends about politics and learning as much as I could about where I stand. I'm proud to have moved past fear and self-doubt, and to endorse and support leadership that moves us beyond this divisive, heartbreaking moment in time."

In 2017, she moved a little closer to revealing a more liberal tendency when she tweeted support for Women's March: "So much love, pride, and respect for those who marched. I'm proud to be a woman today, and every day." However, the fact that she didn't attend the march led to some criticism, with one writer judging her comments a craven way of "reducing what was a political protest to a girl power party." On her birthday that year, she posted a short message on Instagram saying she "couldn't have asked for a better year", leading those who saw little to celebrate in Trump's first year in office begging to differ.

Now with her endorsement of the Tennessee two, white supremacists felt betrayed, telling her to stick to her music. Even President Trump chimed in, telling reporters: "Marsha Blackburn is doing a very good job in Tennessee. She's leading now substantially, which she should. She's a tremendous woman. I'm sure Taylor Swift doesn't know anything about her. Let's say that I like Taylor's music about 25% less now, OK?"

The criticism came with its fair share of support, too. Film director Rob Reiner tweeted: "A big shout out to Taylor Swift for speaking out. You can single handedly change this country. Impress on your fans how critical and powerful their voices are. If you get them to the polls on Nov 6, everything you care about will be protected."

What had finally politicised Taylor? Many commentators say it was the assault trial, watching the rights of her LGBTQ friends being "eroded", and Trump in the White House that did it. Speaking later to the *Guardian*, she confessed: "The things that happen to you in your life are what develop your political opinions. I was living in this Obama eight-year paradise of, you go, you cast your vote, the person you vote for wins, everyone's happy! This whole thing, the last three, four years, it completely blindsided a lot of us, me included."

"The next chapter..."

On October 9th, Taylor performed 'I Did Something Bad' at the AMAs in Los Angeles, and was also presented with the award for Favourite Pop/Rock Album for *Reputation.* During her acceptance speech, she teased her fans by giving a little hint: "I always look at albums as chapters in my life. And to the fans, I'm so happy that you like this one... But I have to be really honest with you about something: I'm even more excited about the next chapter." This coy little teaser once again sent Taylor's fans into a frenzy. Was she talking about a new album, or maybe an interesting development in her relationship with Joe Alwyn?

In a later interview for *Entertainment Weekly*, Taylor spoke about the genesis of the new album, calling it an epiphany she had experienced during the tour. She saw that, despite the caricature that she thought had been created of her, there were so many people who saw what others could not bring themselves to see: "I would look out in the audience and I see these amazing, thoughtful, caring, wonderful, empathetic people. So often with our takedown culture, talking shit about a celebrity is basically the same as talking shit about the new iPhone. So, when I go and I meet the fans, I see that they actually see me as a flesh-and-blood human being. That - as contrived as it may sound - changed [me] completely, assigning humanity to my life."

Those positive thoughts and energy would form the basis of her next album.

On October 19th, the final leg of the *Reputation* tour began in Perth, followed by several more dates in Australia and New Zealand, before finally coming to an end in Tokyo on November 21st. Stuff.co.nz reviewed the Auckland concert: "Her Friday night performance in the rain...was polished, pristine and perfected - but what else would you expect from the biggest star in the English-speaking world? To be honest, her show was near perfect. Too perfect, perhaps. But there was no way I could write that Swift disappointed her fans. To do so, I would have had to ignore the small child screaming like clockwork every two seconds next to me. She was very, very excited. A lot of the crowd was."

The *Reputation* Stadium Tour had been a record-breaker at almost every venue. The debut show at Glendale had set new venue records for both gross and attendance, beating Metallica's gross earnings the previous year by nearly $2 million, and One Direction's attendance record in 2014 by over 2,600 seats. At the Levi Stadium in Santa Clara, Taylor beat her own gross and attendance records set by the *1989* Tour. The two-show run at the Rose Bowl in Pasadena earned $16.2 million, a venue record for a solo headliner, beating U2's 2017 *Joshua Tree* record by nearly $5 million. The Irish band's grossing records were also surpassed at several other venues.

By the time of the concert in Miami in mid-August, the tour had grossed $202.3 million in North America alone, beating Taylor's own record set with *1989,* and achieved with fewer dates. Ultimately, *Reputation* achieved a total gross of $266.1 million, making it the highest grossing tour in US and North American history, beating the Rolling Stones' $245 million for their *A Bigger Bang Tour* of 2005-2006, and doing it with just 38 shows compared to their 70. Remarkable as this was, the record would soon be smashed by none other than Ed Sheeran, whose ÷ Tour went on to gross $775 million from 255 shows just two years later.

Signing with Universal Music Group

"Talk about your blank spaces: Taylor Swift is about to have one in the spot where her label affiliation goes. In less than three months' time she'll be a free agent..." So claimed *Variety* magazine back in August 2018. Taylor was already free to negotiate a new record deal with rival companies, although she couldn't sign any new deal before November, the anniversary of the release of *Reputation*, and the official expiration of her obligation to Scott Borchetta and Big Machine Records.

According to reports, Taylor's reps were already having preliminary discussions with the major label groups, as well as talks about the possibility of returning to Nashville-based Big Machine as their flagship artist. For someone whose first five albums had been certified multi-platinum, a feat no other artist could claim, Taylor was now the hottest property in music, and she could not be in a better position to attract suitors.

It was expected that whatever the deal, Taylor would retain the rights to her masters, the essential key to her future career, and also negotiate ownership of her previous albums, currently in the hands of Big Machine, from which a reported 80% of its revenue had derived in recent years.

Not that often would artists as big as Taylor come up for grabs, and it was speculated that she could secure a deal for as much as $20 million per album. Doug Davis, a top lawyer in the music industry, said: "There's no precedent to look to regarding the top-selling artist of the digital era becoming a total free agent. Taylor Swift is at an extraordinary point in her career where she can write her own ticket in regards to the commercial terms and deal structure. If she is seeking to break financial records and extend with a major, she could have the biggest artistic deal of the century so far. If she wants to be creative and choose an alternative structure for capitalisation, she could create her own business model."

Signing up to one of the major labels would be one obvious attraction. Although at Sony-owned Columbia she would be stablemates with fellow giant artists like Adele and Beyoncé, she would certainly be the top dog at the Warner Music Group. A high-ranking spokesperson for Sony indicated that getting a deal with them would depend largely on what Scott Borchetta was willing to do

240

at Big Machine, and that it would be a non-starter if he decided to give in on the masters.

Then there was the Universal Music Group (UMG), the last of the "big three" record labels, and the company which distributed both the Big Machine and Republic labels. For those in the business, this looked her likeliest choice. A source for the label divulged: "Lucian Grainge [chairman of UMG] will do everything in his power to make sure she doesn't get away. Bear in mind, UMG is looking to sell 50 percent of the company. If someone offers her $100 million, he'll go to $120 million."

To move away from UMG midstream was seen to be a risk, and it was generally felt that it would be better for Taylor to remain with the company that had made her one of the biggest artists on the planet. But it was also suggested she might go with their imprint Republic label, not Big Machine, as it had enjoyed a lucrative relationship with the singer since the success of her "pop" albums, *1989* and *Reputation*. What's more, unlike Big Machine, Republic had the advantage of having its own Top 40 radio promotion department.

If Taylor did decide to stick with Big Machine, there was the question of the masters. The master is the name given to the first recording of a song or piece of music from which copies are made for sales and distribution; the owner of the master owns all copies, such as digital versions for download or streaming, and physical versions available on cd and vinyl.

Scott Borchetta had long signalled that he would not surrender what was considered his company's biggest asset. With no apparent breakthrough in sight, it would leave Borchetta's label, as *Variety* suggested, "in the position of giving up a piece of Swift's future in order to hold on to a bigger piece of her past." Holding on to the masters of an artist's lucrative back catalogue could be seen as a priority for any label, but there was a catch. To licence synch rights to her previous music would not be possible without Taylor and her publishing company agreeing to it, as she was within her rights as the songwriter. Without that, Borchetta could do little with the music other than stream it.

Whether Taylor and the man who had discovered her "and made her Queen" could reach an agreement in those three months remained to be seen. The decision, when made, would affect the rest of her career in a way she never thought possible.

On November 19th, just over a year since her last album under contact to Big Machine Records was released, it was announced that Taylor had signed a new multi-year, multi-album global recording agreement with Universal Music Group. According to the contract, UMG would serve as the exclusive worldwide recorded music partner for Taylor, while UMG's imprint label Republic would serve as her label partner in the US.

Taylor stated on Tumblr that not only would she own her masters going forward, but that UMG would share with its artists the proceeds from the sale of its Spotify equity and make them non-recoupable against the artists' earnings, as Sony had done with its $750 million profit collected from the April sale of 50% of its 5.7% share in the streaming company.

Back in March, UMG had been the last of the "big three" to commit to sharing proceeds from the sale of its Spotify equity with its artists, a move seen to be contentious, given the streaming service's drop in value.

241

According to *Rolling Stone*, the deal with Taylor also specified that the hypothetical equity sale would result in payments to UMG artists regardless of their account status, which meant that they would receive money even if they were in the red with the company for unrecovered advances.

Taylor was quick to praise the working relationship with UMG and Republic over the years: "It's so thrilling to me that they, and the UMG team, will be my label family moving forward. It's also incredibly exciting to know that I own all of my master recordings that I make from now on. It's really important to me to see eye to eye with a label regarding the future of our industry. I feel so motivated by new opportunities created by the streaming world and the ever-changing landscape of our industry."

She also pointed out there was one important condition that meant more to her than any other: "I asked that any sale of their Spotify shares result in a distribution of money to their artists, non-recoupable. They have generously agreed to this, at what they believe will be much better terms than paid out previously by other major labels. I see this is a sign that we are headed toward positive change for creators - a goal I'm never going to stop trying to help achieve, in whatever way I can..."

UMG's head Lucian Grainge paid tribute to his new acquisition: "Few artists in history approach Taylor Swift's combination of massive global hits and creative brilliance. She is so multi-talented she can achieve anything. I have such enormous respect for Taylor, in particular for her use of her hard-earned influence to promote positive change. Because of her commitment to her fellow artists, not only did she want to partner with a company that understood her creative vision and had the resources and expertise to execute globally on her behalf, she also sought a partner whose approach to artists was aligned to hers. With these shared beliefs, there is so much we can accomplish together..."

A few hours after the deal was announced, Borchetta tweeted Taylor: "I had the time of my life fighting dragons with you! Best wishes for what's next." Thus ended their remarkable 13-year road trip together that had taken Taylor from being another Nashville country wannabe to unimaginable worldwide fame far beyond her wildest dreams.

The lure of *Cats*

As far as Taylor's wildest dreams were concerned, it came as quite a surprise when film director Tom Hooper, the very one who had passed her by four years ago for a role in *Les Misérables*, offered her a part in his forthcoming movie version of the Andrew Lloyd Webber musical *Cats*. An animated film adaptation based on the musical had initially been on the cards in the 1990s, but was abandoned with the studio's closure. Lloyd Webber then surprised Universal Pictures, who owned the film rights to *Cats*, with news that he was in the process of putting a new project together. By May 2016, Hooper was confirmed as the director.

While still considering the technical aspects of whether the movie would be computer-generated or entirely live-action, casting began in January

2018. Anne Hathaway was considered for a role but was involved in other projects, as was Hugh Jackman, who turned it down. By July, it was announced that Jennifer Hudson, James Corden and Ian McKellen had been cast for the movie, and, what's more, to the surprise of both media and fans alike, Taylor Swift had been offered an as-yet-unnamed role, even without having to audition. It seemed as if she was not going to be denied this time, and would dig her claws in to keep the role.

Speaking to Vulture.com, Lloyd Webber hinted that Taylor would play either the flirty Bombalurina or the skittish Demeter, and that the duo would perform the song 'Macavity the Mystery Cat'. Although admitting he wasn't sure yet, he said she would be playing one of the "Macavity girls". Asked why Taylor had been chosen, he said: "Well, basically, Tom Hooper thought it was a really good idea, and of course, she loves cats. We'll see. I mean, I haven't met her, so I'm looking forward to meeting her and seeing her [at work]."

After almost two years of speculation about her relationship with Joe Alwyn, Taylor finally acknowledged his existence on November 23rd, with a post on Instagram of a clipped trailer for his new movie, the future-Oscar-winning *The Favourite,* along with a caption describing the film as "phenomenal" and imploring her fans to go see it. Two days later, the actor reiterated that he wanted to keep his private life private in an interview for *GQ*. Skirting around the topic of their relationship, he said, "No one is obliged to share their personal life." When asked to choose his favourite Swift song, he said: "I'm just not even going into that side of the world."

Toward the end of November, Taylor began recording her new album. With the role of executive producer, she brought in another fine team. As well as retaining Jack Antonoff, she snagged Joel Little, the Kiwi songwriter and producer who had co-written the Grammy-winning 'Royals' for Lorde. Then there was Louis Bell, who had recently produced for Shawn Mendes, Jess Glyne, Camila Cabello, and Rita Ora; and Canadian producer Frank Dukes (aka Adam King Feeney), best known for his work with Cabello.

Most of the recording was done at Electric Lady Studios in New York, with other work carried out in Los Angeles, New Zealand and London. According to Taylor, she approached the recordings as if she was doing a live performance and most of the album was done in single takes. Of the songs originally chosen for the album, 'Only the Young' failed to make the final cut.

The end of a troublesome year

On December 5th, Taylor appeared at the Ally Coalition Talent Show at the Town Hall in New York, an event which raised funds for homeless and at-risk LGBTQ youth. She was invited by singer-songwriter Hayley Kiyoko to duet with her on an acoustic version of 'Delicate'. Taylor had previously invited Kiyoko to perform with her on stage at the Gillette Stadium in Foxborough back in July.

The following day, *Time* magazine recognised Taylor as being one of the Silence Breakers who inspired women to speak out about harassment, and named her their Person of the Year. In an interview she granted the magazine, her first since last year's trial, she said: "I think that this moment is important for awareness, for how parents are talking to their children, and how victims are processing their trauma, whether it be new or old. The brave women and men who have come forward this year have all moved the needle in terms of letting people know that this abuse of power shouldn't be tolerated. Going to court to confront this type of behaviour is a lonely and draining experience, even when you win, even when you have the financial ability to defend yourself."

In the weeks leading up to Christmas, Alwyn opened up a little about his relationship with Taylor. Talking to *Esquire*, he was asked if he had sought guidance from friends before he started dating the singer, and replied: "I didn't seek out advice on that, because I know what I feel about it. I think there's a very clear line as to what somebody should share, or feel like they have to share, and what they don't want to and shouldn't have to."

Work started on *Cats* in London on December 12th. For her role as Bombalurina, the mischievous, rebel-rousing outsider who sprinkles catnip over the Jellicle Ball, Taylor joined her co-stars in "cat school", to master the feline movements of their four-legged characters. Speaking to Variety, she said: "We would literally do hours on end of barefoot crawling on the floor, hissing at each other. We learned about cat instincts and the way they carry themselves and the way they process information, the way they see the world, the way they move... And it just was so funny because of what the end result is, there's just never been a movie made like this, which is why it was so fun to be a part of."

On her 28th birthday, Taylor was spotted at Cineworld in London's Leicester Square to see Alwyn in the premiere of the movie *Mary Queen of Scots,* in which he played Queen Elizabeth's lover, and then attend the after-party.

For Taylor, the turbulent and troublesome year had ended on a positive note. Despite the on-off feuds with fellow artists, losing some friendships and regaining others, and having the most intimate and sensitive details of her personal life played out in a courtroom, it had seen her complete the most successful world tour of her career, sign a lucrative deal with a record label that she felt was the right one to further her career, and begin another exciting adventure into the world of movies.

Behind everything that was going on in her life, whether good or bad, there was the continuing presence of someone in the background who would be with her on every step of her journey. Not only was Taylor deeply in love; she had found for herself an everlasting soulmate.

The Worst-Case Scenario

"This is what happens when you sign a deal at fifteen to someone for whom the term 'loyalty' is clearly just a contractual concept"

A basketful of Easter eggs

On January 6th, Taylor Swift and Joe Alwyn both attended the Golden Globe Awards in Beverly Hills, although separately. Alwyn was there to see whether his latest movie *The Favourite* would win Best Picture (although it would go to *Green Book*). Taylor was invited to present the awards, along with Idris Elba, for Best Original Score and Best Original Song to the eventual winners, Justin Hurwitz, for *First Man*, and 'Shallow' from *A Star is Born*.

According to a source for *Us Weekly*, Taylor and Alwyn never walked the red carpet together, but it was noted that while Taylor presented the award to Lady Gaga, Alwyn, who was watching on a teleprompter, "shifted his gaze to the stage near Taylor" and she gave him "a sassy cute little smile at his table's direction."

Just over a week later, and after years of silence between the two, Kim Kardashian appeared on Andy Cohen's *Watch What Happens Live*, and, during the show's "Squash the Beef!" segment, was asked by the host if there was "still a beef with Taylor after all that went down." She replied, "Over it. I feel like we've moved on," and later added that she would rather be stuck in an elevator with Taylor over Drake, the Canadian rapper.

When the Grammys came around the following month, Taylor opted instead to attend the Brit Awards after-show party in London with Alwyn, despite *Reputation* being nominated for Best Pop Vocal Album (it lost out to Ariana Grande, anyway). The two of them were spotted and photographed walking together hand-in-hand, with Taylor looking stunning in a pale blue Stella McCartney gown, giving off "major Cinderella vibes" alongside her beau.

On February 24th, speculation began on "TS7", the unofficial name given to Taylor's next album, with a photo posted by the singer on Instagram of seven palm trees on a turquoise starry sky backdrop. Fans zeroed in on the accompanying caption which was simply seven palm tree emojis, suggesting to many that she was referring to what would be her seventh album. Others counted the number of stars and deduced that it could be the number of days until the album's release (February 24th was actually the day the album was finished). Taylor later said: "I couldn't expect [my fans] to know that. I figured they'd figure it out later, but a lot of their theories were actually correct. Those Easter eggs were trying to establish that tone."

In an interview for *Elle* in March, Taylor revealed that her mother Andrea was once more facing a battle with cancer: "I've had to learn how to handle serious illness in my family. Both of my parents have had cancer, and my mom is now fighting her battle with it again. It's taught me that there are real problems and then there's everything else. My mom's cancer is a real problem. I used to be so anxious about daily ups and downs. I give all of my worry, stress, and prayers to real

245

problems now." Many of Taylor's fans had assumed that Andrea had won her battle.

At The iHeartRadio Music Awards in Los Angeles on March 14th, Taylor won Best Music Video for 'Delicate' and Tour of the Year. While filming of *Cats* continued in London, there were reports that Taylor and Joe Alwyn were about to get engaged. A source for *Us Weekly* said: "Taylor's friends are all talking about a proposal and how she really wants to marry Joe. He's her dream guy", while another source for *People* echoed the revelation: "Taylor really got lucky to meet Joe, and she is the first one to say it. Joe really is one of a kind."

On April 13th, Taylor hatched more Easter eggs. On her official website she released a countdown that ended at midnight on the 26th. On April 25th there was news of a mural of a butterfly in a neighbourhood of Nashville, painted by street artist Kelsey Montague. *USA Today* reported: "Rumours had drawn hundreds of Taylor Swift fans to Nashville's Gulch neighbourhood…after a mural linked to Swift was debuted last week got an update, potentially linked to Swift's mysterious social media countdown teasing a surprise coming Friday, April 26."

Sure enough, around midnight on that day, Taylor turned up in front of the mural to have photos taken with fans and thanking them for their "FBI detective skills".

Montague had been commissioned by ABC at the last minute to a do the mural for the NFL draft with "butterfly wings, stars, rainbows, cats, etc" and had no idea that she was actually working on something for Taylor.

At the stroke of midnight, Taylor released 'ME!' as her new single, featuring Brendon Urie. The music video was also released at the same time.

On April 23rd, Taylor performed at the *Time* 100 Gala in New York, celebrating the magazine's annual list of the World's 100 Most Influential People. In a tribute to Taylor for the *Time* 100 issue, fellow artist Shawn Mendes wrote: "Taylor makes the job of creating music for millions of people look easy. It all comes from her - her belief in magic and love, and her ability to be as honest and warm as possible. She's the master of putting the perfect amount of thought into not overthinking, and that's why her music connects so well."

During the gala, Taylor performed 'Style', 'Delicate', 'Love Story', 'New Year's Day' and 'Shake It Off'.

At the start of May, Taylor was at the Billboard Music Awards in Las Vegas, where she received nominations for Top Female Artist and Top Touring Artist. During the show, she performed her new single, 'ME!' along with co-writer Brendon Urie. Three weeks later they performed the song together on the finale of *The Voice* in Los Angeles. *Hollywood Life* wrote: "It was definitely a party! Taylor looked absolutely gorgeous in a long-sleeved pink dress, which featured a fringed hemline. She had her hair pulled back into a ponytail and wore pink lipstick and eyeshadow to really embrace the bubblegum look."

"We need to stand together"

Later that month, there was more inside news on the Perry front. *Entertainment Tonight* revealed: "Katy planned a very personal, sweet apology and took time to write a kind of note in hopes Taylor would see how much she cared about putting this behind them. Katy told friends if Taylor didn't accept this apology, she would keep trying because she is done holding on to the past and wants to be part of the change in today's society. She wants to set a good example for women, so she planned to never give up, if that is what it took."

In what looked like another step toward rekindling their friendship, they began to support each other on social media. Taylor added Perry's new single 'Never Really Over' to her Apple Music playlist, while Perry liked Taylor's post on Instagram, announcing to the world she had a new ragdoll cat called Benjamin Button (named after the Brad Pitt movie), to join her two Scottish folds, Olivia Benson (named after a character in *Law & Order: SVU*) and Meredith Grey (after a character in *Grey's Anatomy*).

While these seemingly affectionate little touches were warming the hearts of fans of both artists, Taylor's own love life was never far away from the media spotlight. During May, she made a rare public outing with Alwyn in Paris where they were seen having breakfast at Café de Flore and then strolling through the city, and later in the month were seen dining at San Vicente Bungalows in Hollywood with another celebrity couple, Robert Pattinson and Suki Waterhouse. *Us Weekly* reported that according to a witness the two couples had spent the night laughing and chatting.

Meanwhile, Taylor had been encouraging her fans to try and find the forthcoming album's title in the 'ME!' music video. Asked about the clues in an interview for *The Independent*, she said: "I think you see it once, and you hear it twice." This led many fans to deduce that the word "lover" was in the title, as it appears once in the video (on a neon sign) and twice in the lyrics of 'ME!'

On June 1st, Taylor performed a career-spanning set for her first iHeartRadio Wango Tango in Carson. Dressed in tie-dyed rainbow shorts, with matching jacket and sneakers, she kicked off the evening by calling attention to the petition for the Equality Act she had posted on Instagram the day before: "A lot of my songs are about love, and who you love, how you identify, you should be able to live your life however you want to live your life, and you should have the same exact rights as everybody else. So started this petition....So if you sign it, it would really mean a lot to me, because I think we need to stand up for each other, we need to stand together. Don't you?"

Taylor closed the set with another performance of her latest single 'ME!', with Brendan Urie as the surprise guest.

On June 13th Taylor finally confirmed in an Instagram live-stream that the new album's title was indeed *Lover* and that it would be released on August 23rd. She also announced the next single, 'You Need to Calm Down', would be out the next day, June 14th, with its music video three days later. The song addresses internet trolls and voices Taylor's continuing support for the LGBTQ+ community.

A few days later, Taylor attended a Pride event at the Stonewall Inn in Greenwich Village to celebrate the 50th anniversary of the Stonewall Riots of June 1969, when an early morning police raid on the Stonewall Inn sparked a series of spontaneous demonstrations by the city's gay community. Their decision to fight back served as a catalyst for a new generation of political activism, and was instrumental in launching the Gay Pride movement in the city.

In front of an intimate, shrieking audience, Taylor was introduced by *Modern Family* star Jesse Tyler Ferguson. Having heard that 'Shake It Off' was his favourite karaoke song, Taylor launched into it and even let the host join in at the end.

After what had been a most enjoyable six months, Taylor was now looking forward to the remainder of the year and the release of her next album.

No one could have predicted what happened next.

Braun to break her heart

On June 30th, it was announced that Scooter Braun's Ithaca Holdings had agreed to acquire Scott Borchetta's Big Machine Label Group in a blockbuster deal backed by Carlyle Group, the giant global investment firm, and several other private equity firms. The $300 million-plus deal meant that Braun would not only own Taylor's six-album back catalogue, but also those of fellow artists on Big Machine's roster, including Reba McIntire, Rascal Flatts, Lady Antebellum, Cheap Trick, Thomas Rhett, Sugarland, Florida Georgia Line, Jennifer Nettles and Brantley Gilbert. The deal would also include Big Machine Music, the music publishing operation.

As part of the deal, Borchetta would acquire a minority interest in Ithaca and join its board while remaining president and CEO of BMLG. After a shareholders' meeting on June 25th, Braun went on to buy out other minority stakeholders, including Scott Swift's 4%.

39-year-old New Yorker Braun was a talent manager, investor, and entrepreneurial record executive, widely known in the business as the manager of artists such as Ariana Grande and Justin Bieber, and founder of the record label Schoolboy Records and the entertainment marketing company SB Ventures. In 2010, Ithaca Holdings had raised £120 million for venture capital which included investments in Uber, Spotify and Editorialist, and in 2018 it was reported by media outlets that Ithaca, with $500 million under management, would be collaborating with J D Roth's GoodStory Entertainment in acquisitions for unscripted, live event, and documentary films.

According to a source, *Billboard* claimed that Taylor's team knew about Braun's acquisition at the time of the shareholders' meeting, although Taylor herself admitted she only knew about it when it had been officially announced five days later. With that, she turned straight to Tumblr and expressed her views the only way she could:

"For years I asked, pleaded for a chance to own my work. Instead, I was given an opportunity to sign back up to Big Machine Records and 'earn' one album back at a time, one for every new one I turned in. I walked away because I knew once I signed that contract, Scott Borchetta would sell the label, thereby selling me and my future. I had to make the excruciating choice to leave behind my past. Music I wrote on my bedroom floor and videos I dreamed up and paid for from the money I earned playing in bars, then clubs, then arenas, then stadiums.

"Some fun facts about today's news: I learned about Scooter Braun's purchase of my masters as it was announced to the world. All I could think about was the incessant, manipulative bullying I've received at his hands for years.

"Like when Kim Kardashian orchestrated an illegally recorded snippet of a phone call to be leaked and then Scooter got his two clients together to bully me online about it. Or when his client, Kanye West, organized a revenge porn music video which strips my body naked. Now Scooter has stripped me of my life's work, that I wasn't given an opportunity to buy. Essentially, my musical legacy is about to lie in the hands of someone who tried to dismantle it.

"This is my worst-case scenario. This is what happens when you sign a deal at fifteen to someone for whom the term 'loyalty' is clearly just a contractual concept. And when that man says 'Music has value', he means its value is beholden to men who had no part in creating it. When I left my masters in Scott's hands, I made peace with the fact that eventually he would sell them. Never in my worst nightmares did I imagine the buyer would be Scooter. Any time Scott Borchetta has heard the words 'Scooter Braun' escape my lips, it was when I was either crying or trying not to. He knew what he was doing; they both did. Controlling a woman who didn't want to be associated with them. In perpetuity. That means forever.

"Thankfully, I am now signed to a label that believes I should own anything I create. Thankfully, I left my past in Scott's hands and not my future. And hopefully, young artists or kids with musical dreams will read this and learn about how to better protect themselves in a negotiation. You deserve to own the art you make.

"I will always be proud of my past work. But for a healthier option, *Lover* will be out August 23."

Taylor signed off, "Sad and grossed out."

Later that same night, Borchetta posted a statement entitled "So, It's Time for Some Truth", and explained that Taylor may not have read the text he sent her the night before the deal went public, and also that it was possible that her father, being a shareholder, would have known but may not have had the chance to tell her. But he found it hard to believe she hadn't heard about it from someone. Later, a spokesperson for Taylor told *People* magazine that Scott Swift did not know of the deal in advance, as he was not on the board of directors, and that he did not take part in a shareholder phone call on the 25th due to the strict ruling that bound all shareholders and prohibited any discussion at all "without risk of severe penalty."

In Taylor's Tumblr post, she mentioned Braun getting two of his clients together to bully her. This goes back to 2016, when KanyeGate was in the headlines. Braun had managed West on and off the previous year, and also had the likes of Ariana Grande and Justin Bieber as clients. The incident Taylor referred to was a photo Bieber had posted on Instagram showing himself facetiming with three men, including Braun and West, with the caption: "Taylor Swift what up". Taylor then used the image in her recent Tumblr post, with a red circle drawn around Braun and the message: "This is Scooter Braun, bullying me on social media when I was at my lowest point. He's about to own all the music I've ever made."

When Bieber saw this, he posted on Instagram an old image taken of him with Taylor on Instagram and apologised for his "distasteful and unfair" actions of three years ago. He also claimed Braun had not been part of the facetiming joke and had even told the Canadian singer not to behave that way. However, he took a dislike to the way Taylor had now got her fans charged up to bully Braun: "For you to take it to social media and get people to hate on Scooter isn't fair. Scooter has your back since the days you graciously let me open up for you! What were you trying to accomplish by posting that blog? Seems to be like it was to get sympathy. You also knew that in posting that your fans would go bully Scooter…Neither Scooter or I have anything negative to say about you. We truly want the best for you. I usually don't rebuttal things like this, but when you try and deface someone I love's character, that's crossing the line."

Meanwhile, a number of artists were coming to Taylor's defence. On June 30th rapper Todrick Hall posted: "For those asking, I left Scooter Braun a long time ago…I am saddened by this news, but not shocked. He is an evil person whose only concern is his wealth and feeding his disgusting ego. I believe he is homophobic & I know from his own mouth that he is not a Swift fan."

Film and music video director Joseph Kahn wrote: "I feel terrible for Taylor. This is the record business at its most ruthless and shady. She is genuinely one of the nicest people ever and does not deserve this. She should own her work. These people are soulless." Taylor's friend Cara Delevingne responded to Bieber's post: "I wish you spent less time sticking up for men and more time trying to understand women and respecting their valid reactions."

Braun also had his fair share of support. His wife, Yael Cohen, took to Instagram to have a swipe at Taylor: "Your dad is a shareholder and was notified, and Borchetta personally told you this before it came out. So no, you didn't find out with the world… Girl, who are you to talk about bullying? The world has watched you collect and drop friends like wilted flowers. My husband is anything but a bully, he's spent his life standing up to people and causes he believes in."

Braun also defended himself: "The idea of Scott and I working together is nothing new, we've been talking about it since the beginning of our friendship. I reached out to him when I saw an opportunity and, after many conversations, realized our visions were aligned. He's built a brilliant company full of iconic songs and artists. Who wouldn't want to be a part of that? By joining together, we will create more opportunities for artists than ever before, by giving them the support and tools to go after whatever dreams they wish to pursue."

On July 2nd, Don Passman, Taylor's attorney, made the unusual move of issuing a statement: "Scott Borchetta never gave Taylor Swift an opportunity to purchase her masters, or the label, outright with a check in the way he is now apparently doing for others."

A number of fellow artists including Cher, Halsey and Iggy Azalea had shown support for Taylor on social media over the Scooter Braun deal. Back on July 13th, singer Kelly Clarkson had sent her a thought-provoking tweet: "Just a thought. U should go in & re-record all the songs that u don't own the masters on exactly how you did them, but put brand new art & some kind of incentive so fans will no longer buy the old versions. I'd buy all of the new versions just to prove a point."

That certainly gave Taylor food for thought.

A love letter to love itself

While Taylor tried to make sense out of what had happened, she still had schedules to keep. On July 10th she performed for VIP guests at the live-streamed Amazon Prime Day Concert at the Hammerstein Ballroom in New York, which also featured sets from Dua Lipa, SZA and Becky G. According to *Hollywood Reporter*, Taylor avoided blatantly calling out Scooter Braun, but did so in a more subtle way with the line from 'Shake It Off' and its reference to the "lying, dirty, dirty cheats of the world". Meanwhile, on July 22nd, 'The Archer' was released, the only promotional single from the new album.

On August 11th, Taylor was at Hermosa Beach, California, for the Teen Choice Awards and came away with their first-ever surfboard-shaped Icon Award, specially adorned with images of her cats, and presented to her by her great friend Alex Morgan, one of the stars of the US World Cup-winning soccer team. Ten days later she promoted her new album on *Good Morning America* with a live performance from Central Park, even ordering pizza for the fans who had camped out all night to see her. For the show she performed 'You Need to Calm Down', 'ME!' and 'Shake It Off', and during the interview with Robin Roberts revealed more details about her plan to re-record songs from her past albums: "Something that's very special to me about this album [*Lover*] is it's the first one that I will own". Asked about the re-recordings, she said: "Yeh, that's true and it's something I'm very excited about. My contract says starting from November 2020 I can start recording albums 1-5. I think artists deserve to own their work. It's next year. I'm gonna be busy."

That same day, Taylor appeared on a *Lovers Lounge* YouTube Live stream and performed an acoustic version of 'The Archer'. Talking about the theme of the new album compared to previous ones, she said: "I wrote this from a perspective from a much more open, free, romantic, whimsical place, and I'm so happy to share that with you soon." During the show, Taylor introduced her friend Stella McCartney to the stage. In collaboration with the singer, and in keeping with the colourful, aesthetic feel of the album, McCartney had designed a line of sustainable merchandise, with each piece costing less than $100.

The album's title track 'Lover' was released on August 16th as the third official single, along with details of the album's tracklist placed on social media. On the 23rd, the day of the album's release, Taylor performed a small acoustic set of *Lover* songs for SiriusXM from the Town Hall in New York. It included a first live performance of 'Daylight', the last track on the album.

During the show, Taylor imparted words of wisdom she wished she had known when she was younger: "I treated life like a report card, like I was being graded on every single moment of every single day. And if I got less than an A minus, I pretty much felt worthless. I still struggle with that every day. But what I would like to say is that life is not a report card. You're not being graded on this moment to moment. Go easy on yourselves, kids. Be kind to yourselves."

In a promotional interview for a YouTube live stream on August 22nd, Taylor revealed that the original title for the album had been *Daylight*, and it was only when she wrote 'Lover' that she changed her mind: "I decide an album title based on something that has a nice theme to it and a ring." After writing 'Lover', Taylor revealed that she knew it would be the album's title and that it would "depict the tone for the record", and how the song came to be "a real catalyst for what this album has become."

In an exclusive interview for *Entertainment Weekly*, Taylor gave her thoughts on the new album: "There's a lot of a lot on this album. I'm trying to convey an emotional spectrum. I definitely don't wanna have too much of one thing…You got some joyful songs and you get the bops, as they say. [There's also] some really, really, really, really sad songs…but not enough to where you need to worry about me…This time around I feel more comfortable being brave enough to be vulnerable, because my fans are brave enough to be vulnerable with me. Once people delve into the album, it'll become pretty clear that that's more of the fingerprint of this - that it's much more of a singer-songwriter, personal journey than the last one."

Speaking to *Rolling Stone*, Taylor admitted the album was far removed from what she had previously done: "*Lover* feels like a return to the fundamental songwriting pillars that I usually build my house on. It's really honest; it's not me playing a character. It's really just how I feel, undistilled. And there's a lot of very personal admissions in it…I love building on the metaphor for a very long time. You know, the whole of *Reputation* was just a metaphor, but this is a very personal record."

As an added bonus for fans, the deluxe edition of the album would include a treasure trove of Taylor's journal entries going back to when she was at school.

In the liner notes to the album, with words as inspiring and captivating as the lyrics within, Taylor wrote: "This album is a love letter to love itself - all the captivating, spellbinding, maddening, devastating, red, blue, gray, golden aspects of it…In honour of fever dreams, bad boys, confessions of love on a drunken night out, Christmas lights still hanging in January, guitar string scars on my hands, false gods and blind faith, memories of jumping into an icy outdoor pool, creaks in floorboards and ultraviolet morning light, finally finding a friend, and opening the curtains to see the clearest, brightest daylight after the darkest night. We are what we love."

LOVER
Label - Republic
Recorded - Electric Lady Studios, NY, Golden Age West, Auckland NZ;
  Golden Age, LA; Electric Feel, LA; Metropolis, London
Produced - Taylor Swift, Jack Antonoff, Joel Little, Louis Bell & Frank
  Dukes (Adam King Feeney)
Released - August 23 2019
Singles - 4
Chart peak positions
  Hot 200 #1; UK #1; Canada #1; Australia #1; New Zealand #1; Japan #3
RIAA Certification - 2 x Platinum
Selected awards and nominations
2019 People's Choice Awards - Favourite Album of the Year (won)
2019 AMA Awards - Favourite Pop/Rock Album (won)
2020 Grammys - Best Pop Vocal Album (nominated)
2020 iHeart Radio Music Awards - Pop Album of the Year (won)
2020 Billboard Music Awards - Top 200 Album (nominated)

I Forgot That You Existed ***
(Taylor Swift - Louis Bell - Adam King Feeney)
Recorded - Electric Feel Studio LA
Produced - Taylor Swift, Louis Bell & Frank Dukes
Released - August 23 2019
Chart peak positions
  Hot 100 #28; UK Streaming # 39; Canada #29; Australia #24; NZ #3

On an album in which Taylor lets go of all the drama she described throughout *Reputation,* this catchy opening song serves as the perfect introduction to its warmer, more inviting theme of love in all its complexities. She explained:

"*Reputation* for me was about grieving the loss of your reputation and all the phases you go through."

The song was co-written with producer Louis Bell and Adam King Feeney (aka Frank Dukes), the Grammy award-winning Canadian producer, songwriter and DJ, whose samples had been used by many major artists. Taylor recalled: "I was writing with two writers I hadn't even worked with before, so I wanted to come in with an idea that was pretty much all there, melody and lyrics. So, I had this idea called 'I Forgot You Existed', and I wanted it to be really simple. I thought it might a really fun way to open the album, like, basically kind of shrugging off a lot of things that you've been through that have been causing a lot of struggle and pain. And just, one day you wake up and you realise you're indifferent to whatever caused you that pain."

Within hours of the song's existence, the media became alive with suggestions that it was referring to either Kanye West or Calvin Harris. We'd like to think not, as Taylor was surely in a better place now, distancing herself from all the dark drama that had gone before and stepping into the daylight.

PopMatters - "It's the perfect combination of polished and casual - the smooth, minimal production contrasts with Swift's voice slipping from singing to speaking mis-line, punctuated with bubbly giggles"; **The Guardian** - "Presumably aimed at Kanye West, a track that slightly defeats its premise by existing, but it sweeps aside old dramas to confront Swift's real nemesis, herself"; **Vulture** - "Probably too noncommittal to be a first single, but man, imagine how different the buzz for *Lover* would have been had this winning song been our introduction to the era"; **NME** - "Tay Tay rejoicing in the peace and quiet brought on by not giving a shit about the haters".

Cruel Summer ****
(Taylor Swift - Jack Antonoff - Annie Clark (St Vincent))
Recorded - Electric Lady Studios, NY
Produced - Taylor Swift & Jack Antonoff
Released - August 23 2019
Chart peak positions
  Hot 100 #29; UK #27; Canada #28; Australia #22; NZ #28

Taylor sings about falling in love with current boyfriend Joe Alwyn while her public life was in shambles. Speaking to iHeartRadio, she explained: "I wrote about the feeling of a summer romance, and how often a summer romance can be layered with all these feelings of, like, pining away and sometimes even secrecy. It deals with the ideas of being in a relationship where there's some element of desperation and pain in it, where you're yearning for something that you don't quite have yet, it's just right there, and you just, like, can't reach it."

In one of the journal entries that accompanied the album's release, Taylor referred to the summer of 2016 as "the apocalypse", highlighting just how painful it had been for her. That was the year in which Taylor had first met Alwyn at a Met Gala while still dating Calvin Harris and then seeing Tom Hiddleston shortly after. It might well be that Taylor had secretly fallen for Alwyn at the same time.

The song was a collaboration with Jack Antonoff and Annie Clark, the Grammy award-winning American singer-songwriter and producer, known professionally as

St Vincent, of whom Taylor was a huge fan. She also plays guitar on the track, with Antonoff on keyboards.

Before its release, Taylor had teased fans with the music video for 'You Need to Calm Down', in which Adam Lambert is shown giving a 'Cruel Summer' tattoo to Ellen De Generes. Also, in the video for 'Lover', there are lyrical clues to the song in board game titles.

Rolling Stone - "It's vintage Swift, a burst of mischief and desire, messy drama with a wink, yet it hits at fresh power, the thrill of hearing one of pop's most underestimated chameleons daring you to wonder what she can't do"; **PopMatters** - "Incredibly moody and cinematic, soaked in pink-red beach sunsets and swept along in the wind like palm tree leaves".

Lover *****
(Taylor Swift)
3rd Single
Recorded - Electric Lady Studios, NY
Produced - Taylor Swift & Jack Antonoff
Released - August 16 2019
Chart peak positions
  Hot 100 #10; AC #10; Adult Top 40 #6; Mainstream Top 40 #16; UK #14;
  Canada #7; Australia #3, NZ #3
RIAA Certification - 2 x Platinum
Selected awards & nominations
2020 Grammys - Song of the Year (nominated)
2020 MTV Video Music Awards - Best Pop Video (nominated)
2020 MTV Video Music Awards - Best Art Direction (nominated)

Taylor's dedication to her partner of three years has been cited by some fans as being the singer's favourite composition at the time. It may have been the case, as she told *Good Morning America*, that the song was her proudest lyrical moment on the album: "That song is a cozy, warm blanket for me, like I'm really proud of that one. I just think lyrically top to bottom that song is the one that, of the things that people have heard so far, that's the one that I'm just like, 'ah', really proud of."

This was a solo effort by Taylor, one of three on the album: "I wanted to make music that in a lot of ways feels timeless and is really confessional." In an interview for *Rolling Stone*, Taylor recalled: "I was sitting up at the piano in my loft, and I had the chorus. It just kind of happened immediately. It was one of those ones that I wrote very, very, very quickly; and I was working out the cadence of the first verse and it just sort of fell together."

Apparently, all the instruments used on the track were made before 1970, giving the song a timeless feel. According to producer Jack Antonoff, the track was recorded entirely at New York's Electric Lady Studios with just Taylor and engineer Laura Sisk in the room: "Taylor wrote every stitch of this song and came in and played it for me - just a perfect moment to hear what she had done alone the night before."

On its day of release, 'Lover' topped the US iTunes chart, her 35th song to do so, thereby extending her record as the female with the most number one singles in iTunes history. The song also debuted at #10 on the Hot 100, tying with Madonna for the most top 20 hits in the chart's history with 20 each.

The Independent - "The title track…is poignant and unfussy, a reminder of Swift's ability to distil infatuation into something specific and universal"; **PopMatters** - "Sweetly romantic, earnest, and sprinkled with those little nuggets of narrative detail that distinguish Swift's lyrics; **Time** - "'Lover' shows off Swift at the intersection of sing-song acoustic pop and folksy storytelling"; **Toronto Star** - "The first real standout. The lady can sing and, as has often been the case on recent Swift recordings, that fact comes through best when she casts away the state-of-the-art bells and whistles and plays it stripped down"; **Vulture** - "A self-consciously muted ballad about slowing down and settling down into an adult relationship"; **Rolling Stone** - "This bombshell is the kind of twangy guitar ballad people thought she didn't feel like writing anymore, except she's celebrating the kind of adult passion people assumed wasn't melodramatic enough for her to bother singing about"; **NME** - "A celebration of being smugly, head-over-heels in love…this enchanting, romantic tune is a sepia-tinged dream".

The Man ***
(Taylor Swift - Joel Little)
4th Single
Produced - Taylor Swift & Joel Little
Released - January 28 2020
Chart peak positions
  Hot 100 #23; AC #21; Adult Top 40 #9; Mainstream Top 40 #20; UK #21;
  Canada #21; Australia #17; NZ #15
Selected awards & nominations
2020 MTV Video Music Awards - Best Direction (won)
2020 MTV Video Music Awards - Video of the Year (nominated)
2020 MTV Video Music Awards - Video for Good (nominated)
2020 MTV Video Music Awards - Best Video (nominated)
2021 BMI Pop Awards - Award-winning song (won)
2021 BMI Pop Awards - Publisher of the Year (won)

According to *Vogue*, Taylor "has often wondered how she would be written and spoken about if she were a man". During her *Lover Enhanced* Spotify campaign she revealed: "It's not 'what would I do if I were a man?' It's about how I would be seen if I'd done exactly the same stuff…If I had made all the same choices, all the same mistakes, all the same accomplishments, how would it read?"

Interviewed by *Billboard*, Taylor spoke about the inspiration for the song: "We [women] have to curate and cater everything, but we have to make it look like an accident. Because if we make a mistake, that's our fault, but if we strategise so that we won't make a mistake, we're calculating. There is a bit of a damned-if-we-do, damned-if-we-don't thing happening in music."

The satirical music video saw Taylor making her solo directorial debut. With the planning taking several months, Taylor told YouTube: "I wanted to show a heightened reaction of how the world reacts to someone who's male, hot, rich, young and cocky. I wanted to show how there's immediate approval and benefit of the doubt given, in a ridiculous way." The video has Taylor playing her theoretical male counterpart and alter-ego, Tyler Swift, which involved hours of prosthetic makeup, and portrays examples of the sexualisation and objectification of women in the workplace. The video makes visual references to the movie *The Wolf of Wall Street*.

Among those appearing in cameos were Tik-Tok stars Loren Gray and Dominic Toliver, actress Jayden Bartels, Scott Swift, and a brief appearance by Dwayne Johnson. The video was released on YouTube on February 27th 2020, and would later earn Taylor the award for Best Direction at the MTV Video Music Awards.

With lyrics that even namecheck Leo Di Caprio and his habit of vacationing in St Tropez with much younger girlfriends, the critics couldn't help but be generally on her side: **The Atlantic** - "Her most explicit musical statement on sexism"; **New York Times** - "A stern synth-pop take on sexism that's also Swift at her funniest"; **Teen Vogue** - "[The song] gives women permission to keep challenging sexist double standards, and fans are here for it": **Vulture** - "It feels a bit like an op-ed that goes viral for one day"; **Rolling Stone** - "'The Man' is the sharpest feminist anthem she's written (so far)"; **NME** - "A searing take-down of sexist double standards wrapped up in a synth bow".

The Archer *****
(Taylor Swift - Jack Antonoff)
Promo Single
Recorded - Electric Lady Studios, NY
Produced - Taylor Swift & Jack Antonoff
Released - July 23 2019
Chart peak positions
  Hot 100 #38; UK #43; Canada #41; Australia #19; NZ #28

In one of her most delicate and gut-wrenching songs, Taylor describes the self-destruction that she's experienced in trying to hold on to past relationships and asks her partner to help her hold on to what is beautiful about them. She declares herself "ready for combat" before contemplating just how interested in confrontation she might really be.

With Taylor's tendency to make track five on her albums the most vulnerable song on the record, she certainly delivers with this one. In the lead-up to its release, Taylor teased her fans with the music video for 'ME!', which features Cupid-like figures, and again in the video for 'You Need to Calm Down', which has singer Hayley Kiyoko shooting an arrow at the number five.

In what is one of the best Swift-Antonoff collaborations, the song is centred around the metaphor of the archer, which is also the zodiac symbol for the Sagittarius-born singer, and features her as both "hunter and the hunted", reflecting how she's been cast in different lights at various stages of her career. As the song builds to a climax, Taylor employs lyrics from the nursery rhyme 'Humpty Dumpty' to describe her "emotional anguish", to remind us how her life has been marked by both haters and betrayal.

Vulture - "Once Swift got all the kiddie shit out of her system, she gave us this cathartic self-examination, the first gem of the inescapable *Lover* rollout"; **Rolling Stone** - "The ultimate Goth Tay powerhouse: obsessed with revenge and guilt, shooting poison arrows into her own heart, still trying to settle the score after the battle's over"; **NME** - "Swift discloses her own insecurities in a remarkably vulnerable way".

I Think He Knows ***

(Taylor Swift - Jack Antonoff)
Produced - Taylor Swift & Jack Antonoff
Released - August 23 2019
Chart peak positions
Hot 100 #51; UK Streaming #65; Canada #48; Australia #38

Another love letter to Joe Alwyn, in which Taylor describes what attracts her to him, with several small details about his mannerisms. Unlike the vulnerability found in the previous track, this one exudes confidence. The song is reminiscent of Prince's 'Kiss' with its falsetto chorus and finger clicks, and should have been a single.

Time - "There's a refreshing self-awareness and sense of humour to this first-crush love song, which is laced with references to Nashville and descriptions of infatuation. But more than anything, Swift gets to play with her attitude"; **Entertainment Weekly** - "Swift has a crush that makes her feel young, and therefore is taking listeners back to a familiar place when she was a teen becoming famous for writing songs like this"; **Vulture** - "Not, as the title might imply, a slinky cheating ballad. Instead, it's a straightforward love song. The stripped-down production in the verses makes a fun contrast with the bubbly chorus, but otherwise there's not much here".

Miss Americana & the Heartbreak Prince ***

(Taylor Swift - Joel Little)
Produced - Taylor Swift & Joel Little
Released - August 23 2019
Chart Peak Positions
 Hot 100 #49; UK Streaming #63; Canada #47; Australia #32

Taylor goes full metaphor in a song which at first may seem like another high school-based love story, but is, in fact, a strong political statement and confirmation of her liberal stance. The song would inspire the 2020 documentary *Miss Americana,* in which the singer details how revelations in her personal life led her to become politically vocal.

Written a couple of months after the US midterm elections, Taylor takes the subject of politics and finds a metaphorical place for it to exist: "I was thinking about a traditional American high school, where there's all these kinds of social events that could make someone feel completely alienated. And I think a lot of people in our political landscape are just feeling like we need to huddle up under the bleachers and figure out a plan to make things better."

Great protest songs are not usually soaked in metaphor, but more straight to the point. Here Taylor was breaking away from her usual tendency toward the literal and encouraging her fans to listen more closely and delve beneath the symbolism of a high school narrative and equate it to what was really going in government and its effect on America's values.

Speaking during her *Lover Enhanced* Spotify campaign, she said: "This song is about disillusionment with our crazy world of politics and inequality, set in a metaphorical high school. I wanted it to be about finding one person who really sees you and cares about you through all the noise. The cheerleader chants are actually my voice doing a twist on the 'Go! Fight! Win' chant."

The song of course is largely aimed at the Trump administration. Speaking on iHeart Radio after the album's release, Taylor said: "We're a democracy - at least, we're supposed to be - where you're allowed to disagree, dissent, debate. I really think that [Trump] thinks this is an autocracy." In an interview for *The Guardian*, she claimed: "All the dirtiest tricks in the book were used and it worked... [he was] gaslighting the American public into being like, 'if you hate the president, you hate America'."

In answer to why she didn't endorse Hilary Clinton in the election, she said: "I was just trying to protect my mental health. I just knew what I could handle and what I couldn't. I was literally about to break...I felt useless. And maybe even like a hindrance. [I feel] really remorseful for not saying anything."

The song was another collaboration with Joel Little and is reminiscent of Lorde's 2013 album *Pure Heroine,* which Little also produced.

Spin - "By turns personal and political, propulsive and slow-burning, 'Miss Americana & the Heartbreak Prince' feels like a perfect fantasia of old and new. A conceptual evolution, and a love story for increasingly precarious times"; **The Guardian** - "It takes a classic Swift lyrical trope - the Springsteen-y one in which two young sweethearts vow to leave their small town - and retools it to reflect the abandon-ship despair engendered by Trump's America"; **Vulture** - "After years of being dinged for staying apolitical in her art, Swift here takes her first step into the arena, reframing the most recent presidential election through the high-school environment that provided so much of her early inspiration"; **Rolling Stone** - "She wrote this Lana-esque tale as a political allegory - looking at the whole country as one big high school where the damsels are depressed, and the mean cheerleaders leer at bad, bad girls".

Paper Rings *
(Taylor Swift - Jack Antonoff)
Produced - Taylor Swift & Jack Antonoff
Released - August 23 2019
Chart peak positions
  Hot 100 #45; UK Streaming #53; Canada #40; Australia #28; NZ #4

Toe-tapping song in which Taylor reaffirms her commitment with Joe Alwyn by recounting the story of their relationship and declaring she would even marry him with homemade paper rings. A chance for Taylor to let her hair down and have a bit of rollicking fun.

At the Secret Sessions party, she said: "The whole song is just basically reminiscing on fun memories. And then in the chorus, it talks about how...your whole life you talk with your friends about how, like, 'Oh my God. Do you wanna get married? What do you want your ring to look like? What kind of ring do you want?' I don't know, I just feel like if you really love someone, love someone, you'd be like, 'I don't care.' And so, it talks about that concept as the hook."

As a tease for her fans, a paper ring appeared in the upper left corner on certain shots on the music video for 'ME!'

Vulture - "Had Swift never moved to Nashville, this pop-punk confection sounds like something she might have released in the late naughts": **Rolling Stone** - "A girl-group tribute with a pop-punk surge"; **NME** - "This fidgety cut from *Lover* is Swifty's big jitterbug moment".

258

Cornelia Street ****
(Taylor Swift)
Produced - Taylor Swift & Jack Antonoff
Chart peak positions
  Hot 100 #57; UK Streaming #73; Canada #51; Australia #40

A relatable and bittersweet song in which Taylor reminiscences about an earlier relationship which had taken place some three to four years ago, when she was renting a townhouse on the Greenwich Village street while renovation work was carried out on her Tribeca apartment.

According to the singer: "It's about the things that took place, the memories that were made on that street. I rented an apartment there, and just wanted to write a song about all the nostalgia of, you know, sometimes in our lives we assign, you know, we kind of bond our memories to those places where those memories happened, it's just something we do if we romanticise life, which I tend to do."

With its wonderful acoustic details, Taylor has cited this solo effort as one of her most personal songs on the album. Add a star for her live performance at the *City of Lover* concert in Paris.

Pitchfork - "A lovely, understated tribute to memory and nostalgia with the power to make one rarefied block of Manhattan feel universal"; **The Music** - "There is a sound of thunder here amongst a chaotic collision of music. The most beautiful parts of this song are when the music dulls and it's just Swift and her piano"; **Vulture** - "She's looking back at their past, hoping her memories won't be poisoned by whatever comes next. It's as powerfully observed as all her best work - love makes nostalgists of us all"; **Rolling Stone** - "A ballad about how scary it is to realise how much you have to lose - how the brand-new-crush tingle of 'Holy Ground' eventually turns into the place where you have to build a life".

Death by a Thousand Cuts ***
(Taylor Swift - Jack Antonoff)
Produced - Taylor Swift & Jack Antonoff
Released - August 23 2019
Chart peak positions
  Hot 100 #67; UK Streaming #81; Canada #64; Australia #48

Taking inspiration from a Netflix documentary, Taylor compares the possibility of a breakup to a slow and painful death. Although not related to a personal relationship, she imagines what it would be like if it happened: "I watched this movie on Netflix called *Someone Great.* It's this amazing like well-done romantic comedy with a heart and just like depth to it, because it's about this relationship that ends after like eight or nine years...I cried watching the movie, and so, for like a week, I start waking up from dreams that I'm living out that scenario, that that's happened to me."

Jennifer Robinson, the documentary's director and lifelong fan of Taylor, posted a response on Instagram: "I was a certified basket case wandering around LA in pyjamas, heartbroken over a boy I'd left behind in New York. *1989* was there like a best friend with a bottle of tequila and a bear hung. I found the most comfort in 'Clean', a song about rebirth after lost love. It inspired me and *Someone Great.* And now, in the most surreal, what the f**k is even happening, full circle situation I find myself with a new song that will help me through heartbreak."

259

In turn, Swift commented on iHeart Radio: "I just wrote a song based on something she made, which she made while listening to something I made, which is the most meta thing that's ever happened to me".

Bustle - "Clearly, artists don't have to be sad to write a good breakup track. They just have to have access to good breakup stories. And that means that Swift should be under no pressure to hold onto heartache just to write more songs"; **Rolling Stone** - "The saddest breakup song ever inspired by a movie".

London Boy **

(Taylor Swift - Jack Antonoff - Cautious Clay - Mark Anthony Spears)
Produced - Taylor Swift & Jack Antonoff
Released - August 23 2019
Chart peak positions
Hot 100 #62; UK Streaming #47; Canada #54; Australia #42

With this undoubtedly being another ode to Joe Alwyn, a lad raised in London's Tufnell Park, Taylor finally shares with fans some of their most memorable times together. On BBC's *Live Lounge*, she said: "This is supposed to be over the course of three years. Like, somebody told me, 'they think that you're talking about one day', and I was like, 'oh no, you'd never make it. You wouldn't make it. You'd make it in three years'."

In the song, Taylor namechecks London locations and some of the British traditions she has discovered, and has her *Cats* co-stars Idris Elba and James Corden doing a soundbite in patented Cockney drawl, most likely a recording of their conversation on Corden's late night show in 2017.

Another Swift-Antonoff collaboration, 'London Boy' also has songwriting credits for American producers Mark Anthony Spears (aka Sounwave) and Cautious Clay (whose single 'Cold Play' has its rhythm on the song).

Taylor's London-based fans also questioned her choice of afternoon walking spots, which are in fact some of the busiest areas of the capital. Some even wondered how she would have managed to travel to all the places she mentions, in order, and in just one afternoon. Taylor would never cut it as a London tourist guide, and she probably never went to half the places she mentions, but if it's just because she liked the sound of their names, that's good enough for me.

The Gryphon - "It's the lazy lyrics and cringey generalisations that make this song an unbearable listen"; **Vulture** - "The song that gave the entire United Kingdom a chance to clown on Taylor Swift, which is the best gift the nation has received from an American since FDR's Lend-Lease program": **Rolling Stone** - "The best part of this song is its wide-eyed enthusiasm, the least London of emotions"; **NME** - "Cringe and weirdly entertaining in equal measures".

Soon You'll Get Better (featuring the Dixie Chicks) ****

(Taylor Swift - Jack Antonoff)
Produced - Taylor Swift & Jack Antonoff
Released - August 23 2019
Chart peak positions
Hot 100 #63; Hot Country Songs #10; UK Streaming #98; Canada #71;
Australia #54

In Taylor's own words, the hardest song on the album to write. To attempt to compose a song about her mother's continuing battle with cancer was one thing, but to record it and place it on the album was something that had to be discussed with her family. On her *Lover's Lounge* livestream before the album's release, she admitted: "I think songs like that are really hard for you to write emotionally, maybe they are really hard to write and hard to sing because they are really true."

In arguably her most heartbreaking song since 'Ronan', Taylor produces more of a prayer than a song, and one that echoes the sentiments of her previous mother-inspired song, 'The Best Day', written nine years before in much happier times. Both are the twelfth track on their respective albums.

For this song, Taylor teamed up with her longtime music idols, the Dixie Chicks, to supply background vocals. Lead vocalist Natalie Maines described how Taylor was showing "that vulnerable place of figuring this shit out for herself", while fellow band member Emily Strayer added: "The power she has right now to change things is way beyond any power we ever had. She's in a different position than we ever were."

Taylor would go on to perform the song just the one time for One World: Together at Home, in order to help raise money for Covid-19 relief the following April.

Rolling Stone - "The most vulnerable lyrics Swift has written in her entire career"; **Consequence of Sound** – "The most heavenly harmonies of her career"; **Vulture** - "The song is simple, sincere, and affecting, and Swift's vocals infuse the heartbreaking details with just the right amount of childish vulnerability"; **Rolling Stone** - "It's definitely heavy to hear the teenager who sang 'The Best Day' and 'Never Grow Up', once so mortified her mom was dropping her off at the movies, now an adult driving her mom to the hospital"; **NME** - "It's a difficult listen precisely because it's so incredibly honest".

False God ***
(Taylor Swift - Jack Antonoff)
Produced - Taylor Swift & Jack Antonoff
Released - August 23 2019
Chart peak positions
 Hot 100 #77; Canada #77; Australia #59

In what is a rather soulful and sensual song, Taylor compares her relationship with Joe Alwyn to something greater than themselves by using religious imagery, at the same time noting how New York has an important part to play. At the time, Perez Hilton and others suggested the song could be related to Donald Trump.

Hollywood Life - "This appears to be another track about Taylor's relationship with Joe and how they've gotten through some hard times, even when others didn't believe they would. It also explored the physical side of their romance with some sexy lyrics"; **The Spinoff** - "Even though Swift has grown as a vocalist, she doesn't quite bring enough vocal weight to give this slow-burn blasphemous jam and kind of sensuality"; **Vulture** - "A woozy r&b track livened up by an undaunted vocal performance and a saxophonist really making the most of their time in the spotlight"; **Rolling Stone** - "Her wintry tribute to Eighties r&b...She's showing off, but it's all right".

You Need to Calm Down ***

(Taylor Swift - Joel Little)
2nd Single
Produced - Taylor Swift & Joel Little
Released - June 13 2019
Chart peak positions
  Hot 100 #2; AC #11; Adult Top 40 #3; Dance/Mix Show Airplay #16; Dance Club
  Songs #50; Mainstream Top 40 #9; UK #5; Canada #4; Australia #3; NZ #5; Japan #23
RIAA Certification - 3 x Platinum
Selected awards & nominations
2019 MTV Video Music Awards - Video of the Year (won)
2019 MTV Video Music Awards - Video for Good (won)
2019 MTV Video Music Awards - Best Pop (nominated)
2019 MTV Video Music Awards - Best Direction (nominated)
2019 MTV Video Music Awards - Best Art Direction (nominated)
2019 MTV Video Music Awards - Best Editing (nominated)
2020 Grammys - Best Pop Solo Performance (nominated)
2020 BMI Pop Awards - Award-winning song (won)
2020 BMI Pop Awards - Publisher of the Year (won)

In one of her most controversial songs and music videos, Taylor addresses those detractors who post hurtful comments on social media. Taylor explained to Beat 1: "It's about how I've observed a lot of different people in our society who just put so much energy and effort into negativity, and it just made me feel like, 'You need to calm down, like you're stressing yourself out. This seems like it's more about you than what you're going off about. Like, just calm down'."

In an interview for *Vogue*, Taylor explained: "The first verse is about trolls and cancel culture. The second (and most controversial) verse is about homophobes and the people picketing outside our concerts. The third verse is about successful women being pitted against each other."

Following its release during Pride Month, voices around the internet raised concern about Taylor using gay rights as a fashion statement and equating the online hate she had been receiving to the violence that the LGBTQ community had been facing. In the song, co-written with Joel Little, Taylor namechecks GLAAD (Gay & Lesbian Alliance Against Defamation), to which she had made a generous donation at the start of Pride month, leading to the organisation seeing an influx of online donations of $13, perhaps a nod to Taylor's favourite number. In return, they plugged Taylor's song on Twitter and sold limited edition stickers with the song's lyrics.

Some critics suggested that Taylor should have made the song just about the LBBTQ community without inserted herself into it, while others said she shouldn't even be telling people how to act or feel as allies, and as a presumed heterosexual she shouldn't be "queerbaiting".

Taylor strongly denied having any intention of queerbaiting her fans, and, in a Tumblr post, said: "To be an ally is to understand the difference between advocating and baiting. Anyone trying to twist this positivity into something it isn't needs to calm down."

In an emailed statement, GLAAD President Sarah Ellis said: "Taylor Swift continues to use her platform to speak out against discrimination and create a world where everyone can live the life they love. In today's divisive political and cultural

262

climate, we need more allies like Taylor, who send positive and uplifting messages to LGBTQ people everywhere."

The song became Taylor's 16th top-ten debut on the Hot 100 (the second best-ever behind Drake's 20), making her the first and only female artist with 16 top-ten debuts in chart history.

In what some referred to as Taylor's most political move yet, the music video, directed by Taylor and Drew Kirsch, was shot in a mock-up of a trailer park in Santa Clarita, California, and features a host of celebrity cameos, including a number who are LGBTQ, including Ellen de Generes, Todrick Hall, Jesse Tyler Ferguson, Adam Lambert, and RuPaul. A collection of drag queens also impersonate real-life singers, including Adele, Lady Gaga, Nicki Minaj, and Ariana Grande, but perhaps the most surprising appearance comes from Katy Perry, confirmation that her feud with Taylor had indeed come to an end.

Esquire - "[The song] misses the point of being an LGBTQ ally by equating online haters with the personal societal struggle of LGBTQ people"; **Spin** - "From the sarcastic plod of the chorus to the political treasure hunt of the lyric video, 'You Need to Calm Down' itself feels a little like a 'cop out'. Swift remains one of the decade's most important pop stars - it's just a shame *Lover* is shaping up to be so safe"; **NME** - "Withering in its measured response"; **Pitchfork** - "Bewildering and underwhelming at the same time".

Afterglow **
(Taylor Swift - Louis Bell - Adam King Feeney)
Produced - Taylor Swift, Louis Bell & Frank Dukes (Adam King Feeney)
Released - August 23 2019
Chart peak positions
 Hot 100 #75; Canada #72; Australia #57

In a song that has Taylor returning to the production team of 'I Forgot You Existed', she asks her partner for forgiveness for overreacting to a misunderstanding, blaming herself for almost being the one that "burned us down". Her solution - to meet each other in the "afterglow". The song title had been teased in the music video for 'Lover' where a hand is seen playing the words "After" and "Glow" in a game of scrabble.

With its compelling chorus and prominent drums, commentators suggest the production was seemingly inspired by Lana Del Rey's *Born to Die*.

The Music - "Swift has never sounded as awe-inspiring. We're at the point in the album - after the shock of track 13 - that you just have to sit back and appreciate every ounce of warmth and honesty Swift provides"; **Vulture** - The airy vibe and heavy drums recall Swift's 2017 output with the fear and paranoia swapped out for honesty and accountability"; **Rolling Stone** - "In a good old-fashioned Taylor metaphor party, she compares herself to an arsonist, a wrestler, an island, a prison warden and an ambulance siren"; **NME** - "There's little that lives long in the memory about this drum-driven number".

ME! (featuring Brendon Urie of Panic! At the Disco) **
(Taylor Swift - Joel Little - Brendon Urie)
1st Single
Recorded - Electric Lady Studios, NY & Golden Age West, Auckland NZ

Produced - Joel Little
Released - April 26 2019 (single version); August 26 2019 (album version)
Chart peak positions
 Hot 100 #2; AC #6; Adult Top 40 #5; Dance/Mix Show Airplay #19; Dance Club Songs #8;
 Mainstream Top 40 #7; Digital Song Sales #1; UK #3; Canada #2; Australia; #2; NZ #3;
 Japan #6
RIAA Certification - 2 x Platinum
Selected awards & nominations
2019 MTV Europe Music Awards - Best Video (won)
2019 MTV Video Music Awards - Best Collaboration (nominated)
2019 MTV Video Music Awards - Best Visual Effects (won)
2019 MTV Video Music Awards - Best Cinematography (nominated)
2020 BMI Pop Awards - Award-winning song (won)
2020 BMI Pop Awards - Publisher of the Year (won)

Just hours before its release as a single, Taylor appeared on *Good Morning America* to describe it: "ME! is a song about embracing your individuality and really celebrating it, and owning it. I think that with a pop song, we have the ability to get a melody stuck in people's heads, and I want it to be one that makes them feel better about themselves."

Taylor continued the trend of teasing her fans by posting an image of a diamond heart with the caption "4.26", but after a YouTube credits leak the day before its release, the collaboration was confirmed by Taylor herself when she appeared during ABC's NFL Draft with a mural that she had specially commissioned.

Deciding that this needed to be duet, Taylor invited Brendon Urie, lead vocalist of the band Panic! At the Disco, who was also given a writing credit. They began working together in New York in January.

In a YouTube live chat, Taylor spoke about working with him: "Brendon has always been one of my favourite performers and I've always had it in the back of my mind that it would be INSANE to find the right thing to collab on and when I wrote this chorus I KNEW." In another interview on Instagram, she added: "As soon as I thought of the chorus, melody…I was like this is definitely a duet because it feels like you would want both sides. It's kinda about individuality and also confidence in a relationship where you're like 'you're irreplaceable, I'm irreplaceable, let's just not be insecure about this'."

Taylor chose the song to be the first single because, "it's just sort of a celebration and it kind of bursts open this new world that I see as this new album. It's very flamboyant and colourful and sort of playful and mischievous." In an interview for the *Independent* she added: "I wanted [fans] to see that I'm heading in a different direction musically than they've seen in the past few years…a bit of a palette cleanser before they hear more of this new project."

'ME!' attained the record for the highest-ever jump on the Hot 100, with 98 spots jumped from its debut to the consecutive week. Released on April 26th, the music video gained 65.2 million views on YouTube in its first 24 hours, making it the biggest 24-hour debut for a female or solo artist on the platform, and also broke her own record set by 'Look What You Made Me Do' for the biggest 24-hour VEVO debut.

The music video was directed by Taylor Swift and Dave Meyers and included the customary batch of Easter eggs, this time apparently giving hints to her next single, album, and tour. It features Taylor and Brendon Urie as a couple who get into a fight, after which Taylor storms out into a colourful wonderland.

Time - "The star is Swift's celebratory confidence. Sugar-sweet and destined for school sing-a-longs…Swift veers away from her normally specific songwriting to instead offer up an anthem of self-love"; **The Independent** - "Swift once again proves her mastery of the infectious pop hook in one of the most drastic reinventions of her career to date"; **The Atlantic** - "The only thing Swift reveals with this song is that she really, really wants a hit"; **Vulture** - "When it comes to reclaiming a sense of carefree innocence, the song is probably too successful - the we're-all-just-kids-having-fun vibe aims for *cheesy* and lands at *grating*"; **Rolling Stone** - "For the second time in a row, it's the weakest track by a mile".

It's Nice to Have a Friend ****
(Taylor Swift - Louis Bell - Adam King Feeney)
Produced - Taylor Swift, Louis Bell & Frank Dukes (Adam King Feeney)
Released - August 23 2019
Chart peak positions
 Hot 100 #92; Canada #97# Australia #72

In the most unassuming and captivating track on the album, Taylor describes a childhood relationship that ends in marriage. Not only is it the shortest track of her entire catalogue (2:30), it is quite unlike anything she has done, leading *Billboard* to describe it as "a song that could say more but chooses not to". The misleading title points to a platonic relationship but isn't revealed as something much more until midway through the song.

Both production and writing are shared with Louis Bell and Adam King Feeney, and its gentle steel drums and ghost-like harps complement the wonderful lyrics. Then, for a finishing touch, there are samples from Toronto's Regent Park School of Music Youth Choir. Not only do the children sing on the track, but all proceeds go toward the youth program itself.

Many Swifties were quick to see the song as an updated retake of Taylor's similar 'Mary's Song (Oh My My My)', which was based on her neighbours who had married after knowing each other since childhood.

In an interview for *Billboard*, Taylor said: "…we all want love, we all want to find somebody to set our sights with and hear things with and experience things with. But at the end of the day, we've been searching for that since we were kids! When you had a friend when you were nine years old, and that friend was all you talked about, and you wanted to have sleepovers and you wanted to walk down the street together and sit there drawing pictures together or be silent together, or be talking all night. We're just looking for that, but endless sparks, as adults."

Billboard - "[The song] is the most captivating song on *Lover*. It's the rare Swift song that suggests more than it implies, that punctuates with commas and ellipses rather than exclamation marks and hard periods, and its delicate, crystalline beauty is unlike anything we've heard from Swift before"; **Rolling Stone** - "Love how this story starts with a lost glove - seven years after the lost scarf in 'All Too Well'.

Daylight *****
(Taylor Swift)
Produced - Taylor Swift & Jack Antonoff

Released - August 23 2019
Chart peak positions
 Hot 100 #89; Canada #87; Australia #70

To close the album, Taylor chooses a gorgeous self-penned song about how she was unlucky in love with past relationships, but now has met someone who brightens up her life in so many ways. In an interview for *Elle*, she explained: "I've come to the realisation that I need to forgive myself for making the wrong choice, trusting the wrong person, or figuratively falling on my face in front of everyone. Step into the daylight and let it go."

In selecting the track to be the last song, she said in her Spotify campaign that "it recognises past damage and pain, but shows that it doesn't have to define you. For me, the *Reputation* album seemed like nighttime. The *Lover* album feels completely sunlit."

Taylor considered making this the title track for the album, but thought it would be too sentimental, and that *Lover* was "more of an accurate theme in my head."

Rolling Stone - "The finale of *Lover*, and a passionate sequel to 'Clean'; **Vulture** - "I do love a good spoken-word mission statement"; **The Music** - "If after listening to that lyric, and the entirety of this record, you still have reason to drop slander on the popstar, we want answers because we just don't get it"; **Entertainment Weekly** - "A great bookend to her twenties"; **Medium** - "It is a poignant declaration and reveals the truth that is hiding in plain sight throughout the album - that the lover of the title isn't a man she's infatuated with, it's her".

Not so much of a wistful romantic love song; this, for Taylor, is the dawn of a new consciousness.

"Never cared less...never been happier"

Like *Reputation*, *Lover* went on to be another record-breaker. For the second time since 2014, Taylor became the top selling female artist of the year. The album shifted 3.2 million copies around the world in its first week of release, and was first international album in China to reach first-week sales of a million via all platforms, joining *1989* and *Reputation* as the country's top-selling international digital album.

On the first day of its US release, the album sold 450,000 copies alone, making it the biggest sales week of the year, beating the record set by the Jonas Brothers' *Happiness Begins*. Debuting at number one on the Hot 200, it became Taylor's sixth chart-topper (only her debut album had failed to make it), and she became the first female artist to have six albums sell more than half a million copies in a single week, also equalling Beyoncé's record of having the most consecutive chart-topping album debuts on the Hot 200 by a female artist. It was also Taylor's fourth album to become the best-seller of the year in the US, following on from *Fearless*, *1989* and *Reputation*.

It also became her fourth chart-topper in the UK, her fifth in Australia, and her sixth in Canada.

And the records kept coming. *Lover* was streamed 226 million times in its first week alone, only the second female artist in the US to achieve this for an album. It also became the world's biggest-selling album of 2019 by a solo artist, with an

266

estimated 3.2 million copies, just missing out on the overall record set by the Japanese vocal group Arashi's album *5x 20 All the Best 1999-2019,* which sold 3.3 million.

With every track on the album charting simultaneously on the Hot 100, it beat Billie Eilish's record set earlier in the year. In September Taylor returned to the top spot of the Billboard Artist 100 chart for a 37th week, extending her all-time record as the longest-running number-one act on the chart.

Reviews were once again generally positive: **Esquire** - "When Taylor eases up on the self-mythologising, *Lover* is pretty damn good...There are a few too many songs and too much Jack Antonoff, but Swift remains one of her generation's greatest songwriters"; **Variety** - "It's not even a contradiction to say that *Lover* is Swift's most mature album and her most fun one, all at once"; **USA Today** - "As for what Swift thinks of other people's perceptions, however, *Lover* makes her feelings clear: She's never cared less, and perhaps, as a result, has never been happier"; **The Atlantic** - "She's now claiming transcendence with *Lover,* but it's the hard-earned, hard-kept kind, with musical wobbles - in sonic character and in quality - to match"; **Washington Post** - "Every melody sounds expertly prim; every lyric feels completely literal. You know what you're in for, which seems to be the entire point"; **The Guardian** - "*Lover* offers plenty of evidence that Swift is just a better songwriter than any of her competitors in the upper echelons of pop"; **New York Times** - "Being a pop star, she's learned, is different from being yourself - except when it isn't"; **Rolling Stone** - "Whatever there is to be read into these songs, they are for one person and one person alone: Taylor Swift, Finally"; **Cosmopolitan** - "*Lover* should have been a goddamn work of art. Instead, it's an entire album that feels recycled from everything Taylor has already created. That's not the worst thing in the world, but it also could have and should have been better"; **Pitchfork** - "Taylor Swift is a little wiser and a lot more in love. Though uneven, *Lover* is a bright, fun album with great emotional honesty... Heartbreak can strengthen you; love sustains you. If only all of *Lover* had the same heart".

With the album's release, Swifties began the time-honoured process of dissecting the songs' lyrics for hidden clues about relationships, or to be more precise about Joe Alwyn. They paid particular attention to 'Lover' and 'Paper Rings' as possible indications of an impending marriage announcement. In an interview for *The Guardian* on August 24th, Taylor laughingly explained why she avoided speaking about their relationship: "I've learned that if I do, people think it's up for discussion, and our relationship isn't up for discussion. If you and I were having a glass of wine right now, we'd be talking about it - but it's just that it goes out into the world. That's where the boundary is, and that's where my life has become manageable. I really want to keep it feeling manageable."

A source for *People* was reported to say: "Joe's personality is great for Taylor. He is very calm and always very supportive. He's sympathetic and understanding and supports her speaking out about things that she doesn't agree with...There's something refreshing and different about their relationship. Joe makes Taylor very happy, and it's hard to picture her not spending the rest of her life with him. Her family loves him. He seems older than he is and is a fantastic guy...Joe loves acting but doesn't want to be a celebrity. They both agree that for their relationship to keep working, they want to keep things more quiet. She's the happiest she's ever been."

In 1999, The Artist (formerly known as Prince), had announced he would re-record all of his back catalogue after failing in a bid to gain possession of it from Warner, and famously referred to the record company contracts as "slavery". In June, *Billboard* had learned from several music industry lawyers that standard recording contracts had a rerecording restriction prohibiting artists from remaking a song that had previously been released by the label (sometimes including non-releases during the duration of the contract), but it was only for a set period, in most cases three to five years.

In an exclusive interview for *Good Morning America* aired on the 25th, shortly before a live performance in New York, Taylor revealed: "My contract says that starting November 2020, so next year, I can record albums one through five all over again…It's next year. It's right around the corner. I'm going to be busy. I'm really excited…I just think that artists deserve to own their work. I just feel very passionately about that."

During the interview, Taylor also cast aspersions on Borchetta: "I knew he would sell my music, I knew he would do that. I couldn't believe who he sold it to. Because we've had endless conversations about Scooter Braun, and he has 300 million reasons to conveniently forgot those conversations."

The next day, Taylor attended the MTV Video Music Awards in Newark and, according to *Billboard*, opened the show with an "eye-popping, candy-coloured treatment" of 'You Need to Calm Down', and later performed 'Lover' on guitar, with the audience swaying along with their arms, making for a "surprisingly affecting throwback to the early part of her career".

Planning *Lover Fest*

On August 27th, four days after the release of the album, Taylor did a radio interview for *On Air with Ryan Seacrest* and spoke about plans for a *Lover* tour: "I'm not quite sure what we're doing with touring because with this album, I was so full-on planning this album release and directing the videos and putting all these different clues in these videos and trying to make this album release experience the most fun one for my fans, that I didn't wanna plan what we're gonna do in terms of live and I don't want to do the same thing every time because I don't want my life to feel like I'm on a treadmill. There's a lot that goes into touring that nobody knows like you have to reserve stadiums like a year and a half in advance and that to me is like a lot ... I definitely want to play this album live for a lot of people. I definitely want to give fans an opportunity and give me the opportunity to vibe with them on these songs in a live setting and see them sing the words back, but I don't really know exactly what way that's going to happen."

While plans for the tour were underway, Taylor celebrated the album's release on September 9th by holding the City of Lover Concert, a one-off event at the Olympia theatre in Paris. Tickets for the show had been reserved for fans from a select 37 countries who had bought the album and entered online contests. Although filmed at the time, it was held back until May 17th 2020, when an edited version was aired as a one-off primetime broadcast by ABC called *Taylor Swift: City of Lover.*

During the hour-long concert at the small venue, Taylor performed 16 songs, eight of which were from her new album, and explained to the die-hard Swifties in the audience: "There are a lot of the songs on this album that's just come out that I've never played live before, and I was thinking about how I'd really like to play some of these songs for the very first time...I was thinking the best way to do it would be playing the songs acoustic, the way I wrote them". Unfortunately, the televised broadcast only included the eight songs from *Lover.*

As always, the concert had that special Taylor touch of connecting with her fans. A giant screen showed messages her fans had written to her, and all were given wristbands that flickered and flashed in synch with the music to give it an amazing electric atmosphere.

NME had nothing but praise for the concert, saying "It's hard to imagine her sounding better." The highlight of the evening came midway through the performance when Taylor's band and dancers left the stage, and the backdrop of flashing graphics faded to black, leaving the singer alone in the spotlight to play an amazing acoustic set with just guitar and piano. The lyrics to each song, even the new ones, were blasted back at the singer by the 2,800 fans.

This was Taylor at her very best. Any concerns about the media negativity that had cast shadows on her personal and professional life over the past few months were laid to rest in one fell swoop with this triumphant performance. If this was a precursor of what her fans and the music world could expect with next year's Lover Fest Tour, the future for Taylor could not have looked any brighter.

A week later, on September 17th, Taylor announced to her 85 million followers on Twitter the news they had been waiting for: "The *Lover* album is open fields, sunsets, + SUMMER. I want to perform it in a way that feels authentic. I want to go to some places I haven't been and play festivals. Where we didn't have festivals, we made some. Introducing, Lover Fest East + West!"

But there was a twist. Taylor had been very open about not wanting to spend her whole life on tour, and felt now that she had found a way of touring that best suited her. Whereas typically she'd spend nine months in the year after an album release on the road, she planned to limit herself to four stadium dates in America in the summer and a trip around the festival circuit in Europe. Steering clear of the big capital cities that her tours were usually associated with, the tour would commence on June 20th and initially consist of smaller venues in seven European countries, beginning in Belgium, and followed by Germany, Norway, Denmark, Poland, France and Portugal (Spain was added later). It would be her first appearance in four of these countries since the *Speak Now* tour.

But not all the concerts would be on a smaller scale. On July 18th Taylor would hold her first-ever official concert in South America with a performance in Sao Paulo, Brazil. Tickets for the show would go on sale on October 25th, with an estimated 100,000 people queuing for tickets before selling out in just 12 hours. Due to the demand, a second date would be added. Lover Fest West would kick off the four US shows, with two nights at NFL's new SoFi stadium in Los Angeles on July 25th and 26th, where she became its inaugural performing artist. This would be followed by Lover Fest East and two shows at the giant Gillette Stadium in Foxborough, Massachusetts on July 31st and August 1st.

As a warm-up to the tour, Taylor was also set to appear at Capital One's JamFest at Atlanta's Centennial Olympic Park on April 5th, as part of the 2020 NCAA March Madness Music Festival.

On September 18th, Taylor did another interview for *Rolling Stone* in which she spoke in detail about her music and some of the events over the past few years. On the subject of KanyeGate, she divulged some new details about events that led up to the "phone call": "The world didn't understand the context and the events that led up to it. Because nothing ever just happens like that without some lead-up. Some events took place to cause me to be pissed off when he called me a bitch. That was not just a singular event. Basically, I got really sick of the dynamic between he and I. And that wasn't just based on what happened on that phone call and with that song - it was kind of a chain reaction of things."

Meanwhile, while in London with her boyfriend that autumn, Taylor was invited to gatecrash a recording of a special album being made to raise money for BBC's annual Children in Need charity appeal. A number of celebrities were performing songs, including three stars of the hit series *Broadchurch,* and when it was revealed that English actor Shaun Dooley had chosen her 'Never Grow Up' track from *Speak Now,* fellow actor Olivia Colman got in touch with Taylor via her *Favourite* co-star Joe Alwyn, and asked if she would come down to the studio and surprise Dooley as he was about to record the song.

Watching from the control room, Taylor interrupted the recording midway to tell Dooley: "Can you do it just a little bit more American? It's a bit Yorkshire..." Looking up, and realising it was Taylor, Dooley, already a massive fan, was overcome with emotion, and when she came down to hug him, he confessed how much the song meant to him as a father. In turn, Taylor confessed it was a song that she couldn't sing live, as it was "about moving out and realising that I wasn't going to be a kid anymore, and never have that again".

On October 5th, Taylor made her fifth appearance on *Saturday Night Live.* Introduced by guest-host Phoebe Waller-Bridge, she opened the show with an incredible version of 'Lover'. *Billboard* was equally impressed: "From her turtleneck to her hoop earrings to the piano and the stage behind her, everything popped in various shades of spearmint as she eased into slow burn of Lover...Sheets of music were suspended as if they were frozen mid-twirl in the air around the piano, and the performance threw to the whimsy and pops of colour from the romantic music video while keeping things sweet and spare - but just as potent as the original".

Her second song of the night was the darker 'False God', and, with a quick costume change into black sequinned slacks and an oversized ebony jacket, she once again delivered a snazzy performance, along with saxophonist Lenny Pickett. After the show, there was a rare glimpse of Taylor and Joe Alwyn hand-in-hand heading to the Zuma restaurant for the after-show party.

Ten days later, Taylor was in Washington to do a performance for the *NPR Music Tiny Desk Concert* series in front of over 300 employees and guests at the radio station's offices. In a chequered suit and burgundy velvet shirt, she told the audience: "I just decided to take this as an opportunity to show you guys how the songs sounded when I first wrote them." With a venue she described as her "favourite corner of the internet", she quipped, "It's just me. There's no dancers, unfortunately." Then, from behind the NPR Music chief's desk, she performed acoustic versions of 'The Man', 'Lover', 'Death by a Thousand Cuts' and 'All Too Well'.

During the performance, Taylor addressed the age-old question the press had been asking her - What will you write about if you ever get happy? Although she described *Lover* as a happy, romantic album, she revealed that by talking to friends about their breakups, watching movies and reading books about failing relationships, she always had her head full of woeful lyrics. "It's still here! Yes!" she replied.

It was another perfect, but all-too brief performance, and one showcasing just how incredible the singer is in stripped-down, solo-session mode. In hindsight, it was a portent of what was to come in the months ahead.

Four days later, Taylor joined fellow artists at the Hollywood Bowl for the annual We Can Survive concert, in aid of the American Cancer Society. Performing a five-song set of hits, Taylor described how the event was especially important to her, as her mother was once again fighting her own battle with cancer: "The night means a lot to me, it means a lot to my family, and I know some of you here tonight really personally relate to and appreciate the fact that this night benefits cancer research."

The making of *Miss Americana*

In the wake of the *Taylor Swift: Reputation Stadium Tour* concert film, released on Netflix in December 2018, Taylor had expressed an interest in them doing a documentary about her. It would later be described as "an unvarnished and emotionally revealing look at Swift, during a metamorphic phase in her life, as she learns to accept her role as not only a singer-songwriter and entertainer, but as an influential woman harnessing the full power of her voice".

To direct the film, Taylor chose Lana Wilson, best-known for her work on the Emmy-award-winning 2013 documentary *After Tiller*, which dealt with late-term abortion providers. Taylor told *Variety* that she was impressed by how Wilson's documentaries "look for nuance and subtlety in addressing subjects that do lend themselves to soapboxes", and that their first conversation was about their "mutual desire to avoid propaganda in any form".

Given the title *Miss Americana,* the documentary had taken the name from the song 'Miss Americana and the Heartbreak Prince', one of the tracks on *Lover* that was written by Taylor and Joel Little, highlighting her disillusionment with the current state of politics in the US. Wilson told *Variety* that the title was meant to refer to the less glamorous side of stardom: "Even if you don't know the song, I see the movie as looking at the flip side of being America's sweetheart, so I like how the title evokes that too."

Wilson followed Taylor through what was to be one of the most important phases of her life, beginning towards the end of the *Reputation* tour and ending with the making of *Lover*. Along the way, the film covered several years of the singer's life through flashbacks, interviews, home and cellphone videos, as well as studio and concert footage. Also, there were sensitive topics covered that Taylor had often avoided while being interviewed: she now spoke more candidly than ever before about media scrutiny, her lack of self-esteem, her mother's cancer diagnosis, her newfound political voice, and even body image issues that led to eating disorders.

She revealed that she couldn't look at pictures of herself too often as she thought she looked fat and would then see comments made on social media "that'll just trigger me to starve a little bit, just stop eating... I thought that I was just, like, supposed to feel like I was gonna pass out at the end of a show or in the middle of it." Although not revealing if she had sought treatment in the past, she confirmed she didn't do it anymore, admitting, "There's always some standard of beauty that you're not meeting."

On the subject of self-esteem, Taylor admitted that the negative perception some people had of her had done some serious damage: "[Celebrities are] people who got into this line of work because we wanted people to like us, because we were intrinsically insecure, because we liked the sound of people clapping 'cause it made us forget about how much we feel like we're not good enough. So, when people weren't clapping anymore, it hurt." Of the negativity she was facing, she replied, through tears, "It just gets loud sometimes."

The 85-minute documentary would have its world premiere at the Sundance Film Festival in January 2020, and was shown in selected cinemas eight days later.

In the interview for *Variety*, Taylor said: "The bigger your career gets, the more you struggle with the idea that a lot of people see you the same way they see an iPhone or a Starbucks. They've been inundated with your name in the media, and you become a brand. That's inevitable for me, but I do think that it's really necessary to feel like I can still communicate with people. And as a songwriter, it's really important to still feel human and process things in a human way. The through line of all that is humanity, and reaching out and talking to people and having them see things that aren't cute. There's a lot that's not cute in this documentary."

A song for Victoria

With filming of Tom Hooper's movie *Cats* now almost completed, Taylor was aware that Andrew Lloyd Webber was looking for a new song to be performed by the Royal Ballet's principal ballerina, Francesca Hayward, who plays the lead role as the graceful white cat, Victoria. The movie follows her journey from being abandoned as a kitten to meeting up with a tribe of London cats called Jellicles preparing for their yearly Jellicle Ball.

Lloyd Webber recalled: "When I read the screenplay, I said, 'This is really interesting, but there's nothing that this character [Victoria] sings.' Seems to me, if we're going to use her as the eyes through which everything is seen, at some point we have to hear something from her point of view."

For inspiration, one cat-lover turned to another. The role of Victoria had primarily been a ballet role in the original stage production, performed solely through gestures and dance and without lyrics. Now that role had been elevated to lead, there was a need for a new song for her to perform.

Taylor recalled: "I had heard these rumblings and rumours, like, 'They want a song. Andrew's going to write an original song for Victoria, the lead cat', and I was just like, 'Aw man. I so badly want to get in on that'. But I [also thought], 'I can't crash this…I really wish that I could write that with him'."

On October 24th, after days of getting a feel for Victoria's storyline by watching it being played out on set, Taylor was invited to Lloyd Webber's house for a rehearsal of 'Macavity', the song she performs in the movie. Pleased with the rehearsal, he then began to play a melody on the piano.

In an interview for Beat 1, Taylor recalled: "He played this, and I'm running through all the score of *Cats*, like, 'This is not in the original musical' …There's no top line. So, a top line on a song is the words and the melody that somebody sings. So, if you have a song stuck in your head, chances are you're singing the top line. What he has got is this beautiful instrumental piece. As soon as he starts playing it, I start singing the top line."

Taylor knew where the song would be put in the movie, immediately after Jennifer Hudson sang 'Memory' for the first time: "I thought, wouldn't it be interesting if you had this young kitten reflect off of what she just heard and give sort of her counter point of view? Because 'Memory' is Grizabella singing about how she had these beautiful, incredible moments in her past. She had these glittering occasions and she felt beautiful and she felt wanted and now she doesn't feel that way anymore. And I was just thinking, okay, so what if you've got this little kitten that's been deserted and kind of tossed out by her owners, and she's had to wander around the streets of London wondering where she's going to find a home. Wouldn't she be thinking, 'At least you had those amazing memories'?"

According to Taylor, the first line that came to her was, "And the memories were lost long ago/ but at least you have beautiful ghosts". It was like some sort of an epiphany. Her she was, in front of one of the world's greatest songwriters, and she had just given his leading cat a specific voice and something to say.

In a featurette done to promote the movie, the two of them make their collaboration seem easy, with Lloyd Webber saying, "This is a new song", and Taylor saying, "I'll do the lyric". According to him, "she did it then and there, more of less." Taylor once quipped: "If you can't get T S Eliot. Get T.S."

Lloyd Webber later said: "I feel this new song is a pretty integral part of this new version of *Cats*. Without the new song, the movie would hugely be the poorer." In an interview for *Hollywood Reporter*, he praised Taylor: "I think she's written lyrics that are first, dramatic, and secondly, it's almost as if she's read T S Eliot herself. Maybe she had, because she's so thorough and professional."

The film's director, Tom Hooper, was also impressed with Taylor's work, describing the "extraordinary beauty" of the lyrics, and adding that Taylor had a "profound understanding of what we're trying to do with the movie." What's more, the songs were recorded live on set, rather than in a recording studio.

In the movie the song is performed by Francesca Hayward, with Taylor's version played over the closing credits. Speaking to *Billboard*, Taylor described it as being sung "from a young voice who is wondering if she will ever have glory days. Longing for the sense of belonging, she sees everyone finding. Reaching for it, desperately afraid of never having beautiful ghosts of days gone by to cling to in her older years."

The song was released by Polydor as a digital single on November 15th, a month before the movie.

273

Beautiful Ghosts ****
(Taylor Swift - Andrew Lloyd Webber)
Label - Polydor
Promo single
Produced - Greg Wells, Tom Hooper & Andrew Lloyd Webber
Released - November 15 2019
Chart peak positions
  Digital Song Sales #14; UK Download #32; Canada Digital #31; Australia
  Digital #22; NZ #36
Selected awards and nominations
2020 Golden Globes - Best Original Song (nominated)
2021 Grammys - Best Song Written for Visual Media (nominated)

Even though Taylor's brief performance in the movie may have been questionable to some, her contribution to 'Beautiful Ghosts' would win well-deserved nominations at both the Golden Globes and the Grammys. Meanwhile, there was a mixed bag of reviews:

Variety - "Swift returns to a more youthful tonality in her voice in her reading of the song...In essence, we're hearing the return of the ghost of the younger Swift"; **Elite Daily** - "Swift definitely hit the nail on the head with this track. Every word is dripping with passion and, when you're done listening, you'll find yourself longing for the good old times you never even had"; **TimeOut** - "Beautiful Ghosts is a bad song... Swift's lyrics clank with banality at nearly every turn of phrase"; **New York Post** - "Her humdrum, factory-made lyrics don't quite match up to T S Eliot's eclectic poems used in the original musical ...Vapid and whiny, and lacking distinctiveness"; **Vulture** - "Ever the dutiful student, Swift follows all the parameters of the assignment, but ultimately, it feels like watching someone do homework".

#IStandWithTaylor

In an interview for Capital FM on November 1st, Taylor revealed: "I've got some pretty intense things happening with my family right now. I can't go on a long tour that I can't go home to my family for. Where there are question marks in my life and things that are really important to me and my family, I have to be able to have some breathing room in my touring schedule and I think they [the fans] kind of understand that."

In early November, Taylor flew out to the Far East to promote the new album. After appearing once again on the Japanese morning show *Sukkiri*, she went on to Shanghai to headline at the *Alibaba 11.11 Countdown Gala,* a live show leading up to the e-commerce company's annual Singles' Day shopping extravaganza. Taylor performed 'ME!', 'Lover' and 'You Need to Calm Down' in a show that was televised across the country on November 10th. Back in the States that same day, *Lover* won Album of the Year at the People's Choice Awards in Santa Monica.

In a couple of weeks, Taylor was due to be honoured at the AMA Awards as Artist of the Decade, and she was preparing to sing a medley of her hits for the show. However, this had now been thrown into doubt.

On the 15th she posted a statement on Tumblr accusing Scooter Braun of barring her from performing her old hits:

"Don't know what else to do... I've been planning to perform a medley of my hits throughout the decade on the show. Scott Borchetta and Scooter Braun have now said that I'm not allowed to perform my old songs on television because they claim that would be re-recording my music before I'm allowed to next year. Additionally - and this isn't the way I had planned on telling you this news - Netflix has created a documentary about my life for the past few years. Scott and Scooter have declined the use of my older music or performance footage for this project, even though there is no mention of either of them or Big Machine anywhere in the film. Scott Borchetta told my team that they'll allow me to use my music only if I do these things: if I agree to not re-record copycat versions of my song next year (which is something I'm both legally allowed to do and looking forward to) and also told my team that I need to stop talking about him and Scooter Braun.... The message being sent to me is very clear. Basically, be a good little girl and shut up. Or you'll be punished. This is WRONG. Neither of these men had a hand in the writing of those songs. They did nothing to create the relationship I have with my fans... Please let Scott Borchetta and Scooter Braun know how you feel about this...I just want to be able to perform MY OWN music. That's it. I've tried to work this out privately through my team but have not been able to resolve anything..."

In an unsigned press release posted to their website, Big Machine stated they had never barred Taylor from performing at the AMAs or blocking the Netflix documentary, although not directly addressing the use of her past hits in either. The statement also fired back an allegation that Taylor had "admitted to contractually owing millions of dollars and multiple assets to our company."

Taylor's team hit straight back, issuing a statement that confirmed Borchetta "flatly denied the request" for both the AMAs and Netflix, and claimed that Big Machine owed the singer $7.9 million in unpaid royalties over several years.

However, all this time, Braun had remained relatively quiet, apart from a tweet on November 19th which had a photo reading "Kindness is the only response", along with his own message, "Words to live by". Three days later, Braun posted on Instagram asking Taylor to discuss the situation with him and to put their differences aside. Apparently, according to Braun, as a result of Taylor's post, he had been receiving threats that he felt were putting the safety of his family in jeopardy.

Seemingly out of the blue, Taylor suddenly got the green light from Big Machine to perform her old songs at the AMAs. In a statement to *Billboard*, a representative of Big Machine said that the company had "agreed to grant all licences of their artists' performances to stream post show and for re-broadcast on mutually approved platforms. It should be noted that recording artists do not need label approval for live performances on television or any other live media. Record label's approval is only needed for contracted artist's audio and visual recordings and in determining how those works are distributed".

Strangely enough, Taylor's name was never mentioned in the statement, but it had to be seen as one more battle won by the singer.

Miss Americana's director Lana Wilson explained why Taylor's issues with Borchetta and Braun were not covered in the documentary: "The Big Machine stuff happened pretty late in our process. We weren't that far from picture lock. But there's also not much to say that isn't publicly known. I feel like Taylor's put the story out there in her own words already, and it's been widely covered. I was interested in telling the story that hadn't been told before, that would be surprising and emotionally powerful to audiences whether they were music industry people or not."

"I'm so lucky to get to do this"

On a star-studded night at the AMAs in Los Angeles, with her parents looking on from the audience, Taylor was presented with the award for Artist of the Decade by none other than Carole King. The legendary songwriter commended Taylor for her lyrical strength and the reliability within her music. The prestigious award had only been won once before by Garth Brooks.

During her acceptance speech, Taylor said the honour celebrated ten years of "hard work and of art and of fun and memories...All that matters to me is the memories I have had with you guys, with you the fans, over the years...Thank you for being the reason why I am on this stage, from the very first day of my career until tonight, I love you with all of my heart...I'm so lucky to get to do this."

Taylor also won awards for Artist of the Year (for the fifth time), Favourite Pop/Rock Female Artist, Favourite Adult Contemporary Artist, Favourite Music Video (for 'You Need to Calm Down') and Favourite Pop/Rock Album (for *Lover*). Taylor's six-trophy haul took her career tally at the AMAs to 29, beating the previous record of 26 held by Michael Jackson.

Kicking off her set with the feminist anthem 'The Man', Taylor was dressed in a button-down white shirt adorned with all her album titles and she danced along with a group of kids. Revealing a sparkling gold leotard underneath, she then exploded on stage with a medley of hits, joined by Camila Cabello and Halsey for 'Shake It Off', and Misty Copeland and Craig Hall for 'Lover'.

According to E!News, Taylor spent Thanksgiving in London with Joe Alwyn after hosting a party for members of her squad. A source for *Us Weekly* reported: "Taylor has been spending a lot of down time in London. She doesn't go out much other than to take a walk with Joe or go to the local pub. They spend a lot of time with Joe's family and friends. All weekend, they had people come over or they went to family members' homes."

It was while in London that Taylor wrote 'Christmas Tree Farm', a nostalgic look back at growing up in Pennsylvania. It was written, recorded and released as a single in a matter of just six days. On December 2nd, the very day after writing the lyrics and melody, Taylor went to a local studio with co-producer Jimmy Napes, an English singer-songwriter (best known for collaborating with Grammy-award-winning singer Sam Smith), and recorded the song there and then, with some gospel backing added the following day.

The music video was directed and produced by Taylor and shot at Pine Ridge Farm in Cumru Township, Pennsylvania, where she grew up before moving to Wyomissing. It consists of home videos from her childhood, and was released on December 6th 2019. A second video about the making of the song was released on the 23rd.

276

Christmas Tree Farm ***
(Taylor Swift)
Label - Republic
Single
Recorded - London Lane Studios
Produced - Jimmy Napes & Taylor Swift
Released - December 6 2019
Chart peak positions
  Hot 100 #59; AC #3; Adult Top 40 #40; Holiday 100 #19; UK #71; Canada #55;
  Australia #96; NZ #9

In an interview with *Rolling Stone*, Taylor spoke about coming up with the idea for the song: "Because I grew up on one. It's about how you're in the city and you're stressed out and your life is feeling really low, but in your heart, it is a Christmas Tree farm."

Elle - "An infectious and personal pop holiday track"; **New York Post** - "Her new song additionally serves as a cheery love letter to an unseen soulmate who brings a sense of yearning to her heart"; **Rolling Stone** - "It took a few years, but she finally got to jingle all the way, with this impeccably cozy carol".

Returning to the States, Taylor guested on *Good Morning America* on December 5th, and announced that the song would be released at midnight the next day, along with a music video. In a message to her fans, Taylor explained why she decided to release it early: "When in doubt, ask the itty-bitty pretty kitty committee. When they shun you with silence, ambivalence, and judgmental brush offs... just put the song out anyway."

Two days later, Taylor was at the Capital FM Jingle Bell Ball at London's O2 Arena to perform a nine-song set which included the new song, complete with digital snowflakes, a Santa hat, and the music video as a backdrop.

At a lavish ceremony on December 12th, she became the first-ever recipient of Billboard's Woman of the Decade Award at the Hollywood Palladium. Rounding off a long acceptance speech, she said: "Thank you for a magnificent, happy-free, confused, sometimes lonely but mostly golden decade. I'm honoured to be here tonight. I feel very lucky to be with you, thank you so much."

During the month, it was also announced that Taylor would once again be headlining the British Summertime Music Festival in London's Hyde Park on July 11th. Also, following much speculation in the press, she would be making her debut at Glastonbury, the legendary British music festival, to help celebrate its 50th Anniversary in June, becoming only the sixth solo female artist to headline.

In an interview for *Variety*, Taylor explained: "I wanted to be able to perform in places that that I hadn't performed in as much, and to do things I hadn't done before, like Glastonbury. I feel like I haven't done festivals, really, since early in my career - they're fun and bring people together in a really cool way. But I also wanted to be able to work as much as I can handle right now, with everything that's going on at home. And I wanted to figure out a way that I could do both those things."

It was beyond question that her mother's illness was the main concern: "We don't know what is going to happen. We don't know what treatment we're going to choose. It just was the decision to make at the time, for right now, for what's going on." Taylor revealed that it was during the filming of *Miss Americana* that her

277

mother had been diagnosed with breast cancer for the second time: "She was going through chemo, and that's a hard enough thing for a person to go through…While she was going through treatment, they found a brain tumour. And the symptoms of what a person goes through when they have a brain tumour is nothing like what we've ever been through with her cancer before. So, it's just been a really hard time for us as a family."

Meanwhile, Taylor confirmed that she was blocking sync uses of her classic hits, refusing to give the green light as she did not own the masters. Speaking to *Billboard* in December, she suggested that "every week, we get a dozen sync requests to use 'Shake It Off' in some ad, or 'Blank Space' in some move trailer, and we say no to every single one of them." Taylor added: "The reason I'm re-recording my music next year is because I do want my music to live on. I do want it to be in movies, I do want it to be in commercials, but I only want that if I own it."

During the interview, Taylor reiterated her claim that she was never given the opportunity to purchase her masters: "I spent ten years of my life trying rigorously to purchase my masters outright and was then denied that opportunity, and I just don't want that to happen to another artist if I can help it. I want to at least raise my hand and say, 'This is something that an artist should be able to earn back over the course of their deal - not as a renegotiation ploy - and something that artists should maybe have the first right of refusal to buy. God, I would have paid so much for them! Anything to own my work that was an actual sale option, but it wasn't given to me."

The day before her 30th birthday, Taylor performed once again at the annual Z100 iHeartRadio Jungle Ball at Madison Square Garden, along with fellow artists that included Halsey, Lewis Capaldi, Lizzo and the Jonas Brothers. During her set she told the crowd: "For me lately, I've been focusing less on doing what they say I can't do and more on doing whatever the hell I want."

Rolling Stone wrote later: "If you thought there was any chance Taylor was going to surrender the stage before midnight and miss the opportunity to turn the entire event into her own personal birthday bash, you've probably never heard of Taylor Swift. This girl likes to make a scene, which is why she rules the pop world."

Christmastime in London

The following day she flew out to London to guest on BBC's *Strictly Come Dancing* and perform 'Lover' amidst a graceful dance routine. Three days later she was back in New York for the premiere of *Cats,* with Alwyn there to give her some subtle support, and then guested on *The Tonight Show with Jimmy Fallon,* for a pre-recorded performance of 'Memory'. Along with the host, the Roots, and her *Cats* co-stars Jennifer Hudson, James Corden, Jason Derulo and Francesca Hayward, they recreated the show's "classroom instruments" segment in an ornate ballroom, with various instruments presumably scavenged from a nearby alley.

According to a source for E!News, Taylor spent her Christmas holiday in London with Alwyn, with some of her family flying in to spend some time with them. Pagesix.com had reported that summer that Taylor had been looking to spend up to $30 million on a new London "love nest" for the couple. A source close to the singer reported: "Taylor is looking for a grand home in London with two kitchens, so she and Joe can live in privacy and entertain properly. They've been splitting their time between London and Nashville - and she keeps sending her jet for him so they can be together. She has three private jets and even her own hanger."

The source also added: "This is just another sign of how close they are. She's the happiest she's ever been."

In an interview for *People* in December, Alwyn was asked whether he minded his girlfriend writing about him, and he responded, "No, not at all. No. It's flattering", adding that he never pays attention to things not worth his time (such as all the negative stuff), explaining, "I turn everything else down on a dial. I don't have any interest in tabloids. I know what I want to do, and that's this, and that's what I am doing."

Taylor was now 30 years old and had been in the public eye for half her life. Although on a personal level it had been another rollercoaster year, her career status had reached new heights. According to *Forbes*, she had topped the Celebrity 100 list of highest-paid entertainers of 2019, with earnings of $185 million for the 12-month period from June 2018 to June 2019, bettering her own record takings of $170 million for 2015-2016, and, as of September 7th 2019, her incredible 95 career chart entries on the Hot 100 was second only to Nicki Minaj's 104 among female artists, but still a long way behind The Glee Cast's 207 and Drake's 204.

All seemed to be on course for an exciting new year for Taylor, both personally and professionally.

Meanwhile, governments around the world were finally awakened to what had been going on for weeks out in the Far East. 2020 would be the year that no one could have foreseen, and its deadly impact one that would never be forgotten.

Out of the Woods

*"When lockdown happened, I just found myself completely listless
and purposeless - and that was the first three days of it"*

A clarion call for change

On January 9th, the World Health Organisation announced a mysterious coronavirus-related pneumonia in the city of Wuhan, China, with a reported 59 deaths. Ten days later, as cases were being reported in Japan and Thailand, the US took the precaution of screening passengers coming in from Wuhan at three of its major international airports. The very next day a Washington resident became the first person in the US with a confirmed case, having returned from Wuhan on January 15th. At the end of the month, WHO declared a Global Heath Emergency, with a reported death toll of more than 200 and some 9,800 confirmed cases from human-to-human transmission. By March 11th, it would be officially declared a pandemic and quarantine measures put in place.

That was still two months away. In the meantime, life as normal went on.

Following its world premiere on January 23rd, *Miss Americana* received high praise: **The Sundance Institute** - "Director Lana Wilson offers a multifaceted window into Swift, her creative process, and her singular experience of being one of the brightest lights on the world's global stage. Showcasing Swift's trademark vulnerability and her fierce intelligence and wit, Wilson captures moments both tender and exhilarating as the superstar embarks on the latest chapter of her already extraordinary career"; **New York Times** - "85 minutes of translucence… [Swift is] self-critical, grown up and ready, perhaps, to deliver a message beyond the music"; **Salt Lake Tribune** - "An eye-opening look at Taylor Swift finding a new voice… [and] shows Swift as an artist and activist just warming up for the next act"; **New York Post** - "Wilson and her team captured moments that felt personal, vulnerable, and deeply authentic, and they did so with a skill and artistry that Instagram Live stories just can't match"; **The Guardian** - "too stage-managed… brand management dressed up as insight"; **Variety** - "Controlled and sanded-off confection of pop-diva image management"; **Empire** - "Nothing new seems to break through her barriers".

At the Critics' Choice Documentary Awards in November, *Miss Americana* would win the award for The Most Compelling Living Subjects of a Documentary.

To coincide with the documentary's release, the song 'Only the Young' was also released as a promotional single. Featured toward the end of the film, and played over the end credits, it was written by Taylor and Joel Little, but had been held back from being included on *Lover*.

Only the Young ****
(Taylor Swift - Joel Little)
Label - Republic
Promo single

Produced - Joel Little & Taylor Swift
Released - January 31 2020
Chart peak positions
  Hot 100 #50; UK #57; Canada #57; Australia #31; NZ #2
Selected awards and nominations
2020 People's Choice Awards - Soundtrack Song of 2020 (won)
2021 Hollywood Music in Media Awards - Best Original Song - Documentary
  (nominated)

With Little's daughters Emmie and Lila supplying the backing vocals for this rousing anthem, the song had been inspired by the US midterm elections of 2018, for which Taylor had broken her political silence. The lyrics dealt with President Trump, vote-tampering and school shootings, and was a clarion call for the youth of America to get involved in politics and make changes, with the *Los Angeles Times* reaffirming Taylor's status as a "significant cultural figure". Four days ahead of the 2020 election in October, Taylor would allow Joe Biden to use the song in a campaign ad, the first time she'd ever had her music used to support political candidates.

Variety - "An anthem for millennials who might've come away disillusioned with the political process"; **Rolling Stone** - "A clever Swiftian fake-out, giving everyone a totally wrong idea of where she was heading musically"; **Vulture** - "An admirable stance, certainly, but as the doc's closing number makes clear, creatively it remains an awkward fit. Swift is not a natural polemicist outside the realm of interpersonal relationships"; **NME** - "Tackling gun violence and providing a message of hope for the next generation, Taylor emerged as the activist we all need right now".

Lover Fest postponed

With the Lover Fest warmup concert in Atlanta on April 5th already cancelled due to the pandemic, Taylor took to Instagram on April 17th to tell her fans: "I'm so sad I won't be able to see you guys in concert this year, but I know this is the right decision. Please, please, stay healthy and safe. I'll see you on stage as soon as I can but right now what's important is committing to this quarantine, for the sake of all of us."

A statement from her team read: "Fighting COVID-19 is an unprecedented challenge for our global community and the safety and wellbeing of fans should always be the top priority. Health organizations and governments around the world have strongly discouraged large public gatherings for an undetermined period of time. With many events throughout the world already cancelled, and upon direction from health officials in an effort to keep fans safe and help prevent the spread of COVID-19, sadly the decision has been made to cancel all Taylor Swift live appearances and performances this year."

Revised dates for 2021 were still to be decided, and refunds would be made available from May 1st.

The day after the announcement, Taylor made what would be her last live performance for many months for the NBC special *One World: Together at Home,* a historic global event launched by Lady Gaga in collaboration with Global Citizen and aimed at "celebrating and supporting" health care and essential workers all over the world. The show, hosted by Jimmy Fallon, Jimmy Kimmel and Stephen Colbert, featured some 70 artists performing songs from their homes. The list included Lady Gaga, Paul McCartney, the Rolling Stones, Celine Dion, Billie Eilish and Stevie Wonder.

Taylor performed 'Soon You'll Get Better', the song she had written about her mother's illness; she had previously said she wouldn't perform it because of how difficult it was for her to "emotionally deal" with. It was just one of many poignant performances that evening that helped raise almost $128 million in response to the pandemic. *Variety* summed up her remarkable performance: "It was up to Swift - not usually thought of as a bracingly downbeat figure - who emerged as a sober truth-teller at nearly the last minute, appearing alone, mirrored by her piano top, to perform a song she may be unlikely to sing under any other circumstance outside the studio", adding: "With verses so distraught they threaten to betray the deceptively optimist title as magical thinking."

Billboard commended Taylor's performance, writing that she "effectively ripped our hearts out and reminded us of the power of music to both reflect and ease our pain. It was a tough, lovely and cathartic moment".

Of course, Taylor knew it was only a matter of time before Scooter Braun put another fly in the ointment. Just a week after the show, she informed her fans on Instagram: "I want to thank my fans for making me aware that my former record label is putting out an 'album' of live performances of mine tonight. This recording is from a 2008 radio show performance I did when I was 18. Big Machine has listed the date as a 2017 release, but they're actually releasing it at midnight. This release is not approved by me. It looks to me like Scooter Braun and his financial backers, 23 Capital, Alex Soros and the Soros family and the Carlyle Group have seen the latest balance sheets and realised that paying $330 million wasn't exactly a wise choice and they need money. In my opinion ... just another case of shameless greed in the time of coronavirus. So tasteless, but very transparent."

The album *Taylor Swift - Live from Clear Channel Stripped 2008* was released on the Big Machine label. According to Taylor, the eight-track radio recording had been made during a 2008 Clear Channel affiliates' internet-only performance when she was 18.

Her mentioning of the Soros family in her tweet apparently drew allegations of associating Soros and Braun, who were both Jewish, with "greed and profiting off the pandemic". In response, Bend the Arc, a Jewish progressive political advocacy group, with which Soros was closely involved, tweeted Taylor: "You have every right to be upset about others profiting off your music. But please don't share antisemitic conspiracy theories about the Soros family. 'Shameless greed' is a dog-whistle used against Jews. Your Jewish fans deserve better."

The album received the criticism it deserved. *Pitchfork* wrote "it feels like the unauthorised cash grab it is" and referred to it as "a cheap bootleg". It was reported to have sold just 33 copies in the US.

Katy, Kanye and Kim – the final word?

In the meantime, with little going on in the music world due to lockdowns, it seemed that any development in the relationship between Taylor and her old adversary Katy Perry would serve to satisfy the media's attention. In March, Perry had told *Stellar* magazine that, although they were on good terms, they weren't exactly hanging out all the time: "Well, we don't have a very close relationship because we are very busy, but we text a lot". She went on to say how impressed she was with the *Miss Americana* documentary, "because I saw some self-awareness starting to happen, and I saw a lot of vulnerability."

However, there was soon something from Taylor's past to nourish the news-starved music press. On March 21st, *People* published a newly-leaked transcript of the 2016 phone conversation between Taylor and Kanye West, which exonerated her long-standing claim that West did not tell her that he planned to rap "I made that bitch famous" about her in his new single, 'Famous'. An article in *The Guardian* on the 24th highlighted the fact that the line did not appear anywhere in the 20-minute tape of the call, which previously had only been seen in edited snippets leaked by Kim in 2016. In the new clip, Taylor and West were seen debating whether he should sing "I feel like Taylor Swift might owe me sex" or "I feel like me and Taylor might still have sex". After he repeats the lyrics, Taylor expressed her relief: "I thought it was going to be like, 'That stupid, dumb bitch'. But it's not."

Immediately, Swifties took over Twitter in a rage against West and his wife.

On March 23rd, Taylor posted a response on Instagram: "Instead of answering those who are asking how I feel about the video footage that was leaked, proving that I was telling the truth the whole time about *that call* (you know, the one that was illegally recorded, that *somebody* edited and manipulated in order to frame me and put me, my family and fans through hell for 4 years) … SWIPE UP to see what really matters". Taylor then shared a link to WHO and Feeding America, calling on her fans to join her in donating money to them during the pandemic.

Kim responded by accusing Taylor of lying about West not calling to ask for permission: "The lie was never about the word 'bitch'. It was always whether there was a call or not and the tone of the conversation. I never edited the footage (another lie) - I only posted a few clips on Snapchat to make my point and the full video that recently leaked doesn't change the narrative".

It all boiled down to the different interpretations of events. Tree Paine, Taylor's publicist, responded by re-posting the statement she released in 2016 after West had released the song: "Kanye West did not call for approval, but to ask Taylor to release his single 'Famous' on her Twitter account. She declined and cautioned him about releasing a song with such a strong misogynistic message. Taylor was never made aware of the actual lyric 'I made that bitch famous'." Paine added a PS - "Who did you guys piss off to leak that video?"

Later that night and into the morning, Kim brewed up the #KimKarsashainIsOverParty storm with a long Twitter thread calling Taylor out, saying that she "had chosen to reignite an old exchange - that at this point in time feels very self-serving given the suffering millions of real victims are facing right now".

This was followed, one after the other, with tweets in defence of her husband: "I didn't feel the need to comment a few days ago, and I'm actually really embarrassed and mortified to be doing it right now, but because she continues to speak on it, I feel I'm left without a choice but to respond because she is actually lying.

"To be clear, the only issue I ever had around the situation was that Taylor lied through her publicist who stated that 'Kanye never called to ask for permission...' They clearly spoke so I let you all see that. Nobody ever denied the word 'bitch' was used without her permission.

"At the time when they spoke the song had not been fully written yet, but as everyone can see in the video, she manipulated the truth of their actual conversation in her statement when her team said she 'declined and cautioned him about releasing a song with such a strong misogynistic message.' The lie was never about the word bitch, it was always whether there was a call or not and the tone of the conversation.

"I never edited the footage (another lie) - I only posted a few clips on Snapchat to make my point and the full video that recently leaked doesn't change the narrative.

"To add, Kanye as an artist has every right to document his musical journey and process, just like she recently did through her documentary.

"Kanye has documented the making of all of his albums for his personal archive, however has never released any of it for public consumption & the call between the two of them would have remained private or would have gone in the trash had she not lied & forced me to defend him."

And finally, "This will be the last time I speak on this because honestly, nobody cares. Sorry to bore you all with this. I know you are all dealing with more serious and important matters."

As far as Taylor was concerned, she had been vindicated. The saga of KanyeGate was over. For many of her fans, what had happened on the night of VMAs, twelve years ago, had only made West famous, not her. Her music, once again, would now be the focus.

"It started with imagery..."

Taylor had never planned to record a new album so early in the year, as she explained in an interview for *Entertainment Weekly*: "Early on in quarantine I started watching lots of films. We would watch a different movie every night. I'm ashamed to say I hadn't seen *Pan's Labyrinth* before. One night I'd watch that, then I'd watch *LA Confidential*, then we'd watch *Rear Window,* then we'd watch *Jane Eyre*. I feel like consuming other people's art and storytelling sort of opened this portal in my imagination and made me feel like, 'Well, why have I never done this before? Why have I never created characters and intersecting storylines? And why haven't I ever sort of freed myself up to do that from a narrative standpoint?'"

It would be a complete change of artistic direction for Taylor. Virtually every song on her seven previous studio albums had been related to events in her own life. This would be different. These songs would be stories about characters or places that she had made up, and as a result, it would necessitate a different kind of

284

storytelling. Speaking to *Variety*, Taylor said: "My world felt opened up creatively. There was a point that I got as a writer who only wrote very diarist songs that I felt was unsustainable for my future moving forward."

In late April, Taylor reached out to Aaron Dessner, the 44-year-old musician and producer, best known as being the founding member of the indie-rock band The National, along with his brother Bryce. He had first met Taylor on *Saturday Night Live* in 2014, and she had gone to see the band play in the summer of 2019. In an interview with *Pitchfork*, he recalled: "She talked a lot with my brother and me. That's when we realised how much of a fan she was, and how lovely and down to earth. I don't know how many people who have that sort of success, so it's a nice feeling to realise they're cool. That left a good impression."

Taylor heard from Dessner that the band members lived in different parts of the world and that he made the tracks and then sent them to his lead singer Matt Berninger. Taylor thought to herself that was a "really efficient" method of making music, and maybe she could do something similar for a project.

When lockdown happened and she had already been stuck in Los Angeles for four months, Taylor decided to get in touch with Dessner. In the text she wrote: "Hey, it's Taylor. Would you ever be up for writing songs with me?" Dessner replied, "Wow, of course." The timing couldn't have better for both of them, as everything they had planned for the year had been cancelled. What's more, they both had a head full of ideas.

Taylor told *Rolling Stone*: "When lockdown happened, I just found myself completely listless and purposeless - and that was the first three days of it."

Dessner had been living with his family in France when the pandemic broke out and had just managed fly back home before the borders were closed. At his Long Pond Studio in the beautiful Hudson Valley area of upstate New York, he settled down, aiming to write music for The National or even The Big Red Machine, his recent collaboration with Justin Vernon of the band Bon Iver. That was until he got the call from Taylor.

Working remotely with her, Dessner at first thought it would take a while for song ideas to come along. In his interview for *Pitchfork*, he recalled: "She was very clear that she didn't want me to edit any of my ideas; she wanted to hear everything that was interesting to me at this moment, including really odd, experimental noise. So, I made a folder of stuff, including some pretty out-there sketches." Within a matter of hours, Taylor had sent him the song 'Cardigan', fully written in a voice memo. "That's when I realised that this was unusual - just the focus and clarity of her ideas. It was pretty astonishing."

He told *Rolling Stone*, "It was like a lightning bolt had struck the house." As time went on, it happened just like that, with sudden voice memos being sent to him: "It was so inspiring that I wrote more ideas that were specifically in response to what she was writing."

With a song like 'Peace', Dessner recalled: "I realised she can do anything. She is so versatile. It's just a harmonised bassline with a pulse and a drone, and she basically wrote a Joni Mitchell love song to it. She only did one vocal take, and that's what's on the record."

The two writers were in touch with one another almost every day for three or four months by text and phone calls. Dessner would mail her folders of instrumentals, while in return she sent him the "entire top line" - melody and lyrics. Dessner admitted he didn't know "what the song would be about, what it was going to be called, or where [she] was going to put the chorus."

Then there was the collaboration with Jack Antonoff, who had worked closely with her on *Lover*, and would co-write four of the tracks on *folklore*: speaking to Newsbreak, he recalled: "Working with Taylor is a full connection to all of the wonder of making music. Knowing her and making work with her gives me faith in the ability for people to grow, to actually grow. It has been one of the most deeply important personal and creative relationships in my life."

Like Dessner, Antonoff had to get used to working remotely: "Feels almost a shock that this all was even real. Sending tracks back and forth. Laura [Sisk] recording Taylor's vocals in another room in CA - me patched in from NY. Maybe it was conditions that we had to make it under, but I've never heard Taylor sing better in my life or write better. All of it." Taylor named her home studio "Kitty Committee Studios", due to her cats Benjamin and Olivia having fights in the background while they were recording: "It really was bizarre, but at the same time, it was my favourite recording experience."

According to Dessner, there was no outside influence at all. Apart from Taylor's boyfriend, family, and management team, nobody knew about the album, not even the label, until hours before it was launched: "For someone who's been in this glaring spotlight for 15 years, it's really liberating to have some privacy and work on her own terms. She deserves that. At times, if I wanted friends to play on the record, it was a little difficult because you can't send a file with her vocals. But everyone was cool. At the end, I reached out to some wizards just to add bits, and that was nice."

Dessner managed to reach out to regular collaborators to provide instrumentation and vocals remotely, including Justin Vernon (of Bon Iver) and his National bandmates. Bryce Dessner also wrote some of the instrumentation, while drummer Bryan Devendorf performed drums on 'Seven'.

On July 23rd Taylor uploaded nine photos on social media, all forming an image of the singer standing alone in a forest. None of the photos had a caption or any explanation. A second message was then posted on all her social media accounts:

"Most of the things I had planned this summer didn't end up happening, but there is something I hadn't planned on that DID happen. And that thing is my 8th studio album, *folklore*. Surprise, tonight at midnight I'll be releasing my entire brand-new album of songs I've poured all of my whims, dreams, fears, and musings into. I wrote and recorded this music in isolation but got to collaborate with some musical heroes of mine…Before this year I probably would've overthought when to release this music at the 'perfect' time, but the times we're living in keep reminding me that nothing is guaranteed. My gut is telling me that if you make something you love, you should just put it out into the world. That's the side of uncertainty I can get on board with. Love you guys so much ♥□"

A second post quickly followed, revealing the cover artwork and the tracklist, and announcing there would also be a deluxe edition. As it was her eighth studio album, Taylor announced she had made eight deluxe cd editions and eight deluxe vinyl editions that would be available for just one week, exclusively on her website.

A third and final post announced that the music video for 'Cardigan' would also be released at midnight.

This had taken both her fans and the music world by complete surprise. Unlike previous albums, there had been no Easter eggs, no publicity campaign, nothing. Just the fact that Taylor had managed to pull this off in such a short space of time, and in such trying circumstances, was beyond belief.

With the album title, the imagery and the song names, everyone knew that there was something very different here, compared to her previous albums. Just how different they were about to discover.

In the introduction to the album, Taylor writes:

"It started with imagery. Visuals that popped into my mind and piqued my curiosity. Stars drawn around scars. A cardigan that still bears the scent of loss twenty years later. Battleships sinking into the ocean, down, down, down. The tree swing in the woods of my childhood. Hushed tones of 'let's run away' and never doing it. The sun-drenched month of August, sipped away like a bottle of wine. A mirrored disco ball hovering above a dance floor. A whiskey bottle beckoning. Hands held through plastic. A single thread that, for better or for worse, ties you to your fate. Pretty soon these images in my head grew faces or names and became characters. I found myself not only writing my own stories, but also writing about or from the perspective of people I've never met, people I've known, or those I wish I hadn't."

FOLKLORE

Label - Republic (UK - EMI)
Recorded - Long Pond Studio, NY; Kitty Committee Studio, LA; Rough Customer
   Studio, Brooklyn; Electric Lady Studios, NY; Conway Recording, LA, April Base,
   Fall Creek, WI.
Produced - Aaron Dessner, Jack Antonoff & Taylor Swift
Released - July 24 2020
Singles - 4
Chart peak positions
   Hot 200 #1#; Top Alternative #1; UK #1; Canada #1; Australia #1; NZ #1;
   Japan #10
RIAA Certification - Platinum
Selected awards and nominations
2020 People's Choice Awards - Album of the Year (nominated)
2020 AMA Awards - Favourite Po/Rock Album (nominated)
2020 Apple Music Awards - Songwriter of the Year (won)
2021 Grammys - Album of the Year (won)
2021 iHeartRadio Music Awards - Pop Album of the Year (won)
2021 Billboard Music Awards - Top Billboard 200 Album (nominated)
2021 Gold Derby Music Awards - Album of the Year (won)

The 1****

(Taylor Swift - Aaron Dessner)
4th single
Recorded - Long Pond Studio NY; Kitty Committee Studio, LA (vocals)
Produced - Aaron Dessner
Released - October 9 2020
Chart peak positions
   Hot 100 #4; UK #10; Canada #7; Australia #4; NZ #7

A song in which the narrator in a conversional tone ponders over how different her life might have been if any of her past lovers had turned out to be "the one". Instead, it ends in heartbreak and disappointment. Swifties had fun speculating that this was about boyfriend Joe Alwyn, but co-writer Aaron Dessner points out that it was written from the perspective of one of Taylor's friends and, like 'Hoax', was one of the last tracks to be recorded.

'The 1' provides the fitting transition from the effervescence of *Lover* and shows the singer with a much more mature and candid approach to love and relationships, and her innate ability to tell the whole story in just two sentences is never more evident than it is here.

With this one song, the listener knows that this album is going to be very different to all that's gone before. Much of the credit goes to Dessner, who not only plays all the instruments here, but has a penchant for writing and producing songs for female folky voices, while still retaining Taylor's signature melodic pop.

It wouldn't be a Taylor Swift album if it didn't break records, and the opening track began the tradition by becoming Spotify's biggest-ever debut by a female artist in the US, and also the second biggest globally with 7.4 million streams (behind her own 'Cardigan'). Taylor also became the first ever artist in Hot 100 history to debut two songs in the top four and three songs in the top six, simultaneously, with the track becoming not only the highest-peaking non-single in the chart's history, but also the longest-charting, with seven consecutive weeks.

The Guardian - "Swift is known for her vocal directness…but the demands of pop processing mean her voice has never been heard as it is here: the acceptance that colours it on 'The 1', a bouncy reminiscence of a lost lover from her 'roaring twenties'"; **Rolling Stone** - "The one folklore track that sounds like a continuation of *Lover*, with its languid finger-snapping Motown slink"; **Vulture** - "An easy, breezy intro destined to end up in Spotify's Favorite Coffeehouse playlist", **NME** - "Whatever 'new shit' Tay Tay is on, if it means she makes songs as good as this, we back it".

Cardigan *(Taylor Swift - Aaron Dessner)* *****
1st single
Recorded - Long Pond Studio, NY; Kitty Committee Studio, LA (vocals)
Produced - Aaron Dessner
Released - July 27 2020
Chart peak positions
  Hot 100 #1; Alternative Streaming Songs #1; AC #12; UK #6; Canada #3;
  Australia #1; NZ #2; Japan #94
Selected awards & nominations
2020 MTV Video Music Awards - Song of the Summer (nominated)
2020 UK Music Video Awards - Best Visual Effects in a Video (nominated)
2020 AMA Awards - Favourite Music Video (won)
2021 Grammys - Song of the Year (nominated)
2021 Grammys - Best Pop Solo Performance (nominated)
2021 iHeart Radio Music Awards - Best Lyrics (nominated)
2021 Gold Derby Music Awards - Song of the Year (won)
2021 Gold Derby Music Awards - Record of the Year (won)
2021 Gold Derby Music Awards – Best Music Video (nominated)

Although no names are mentioned, the general consensus is that Taylor is referring to a fictional character called Betty who is hoping that a past relationship with someone called James can be rekindled, and references a cardigan as a symbolic "lingering physical memento" of that long-lost love.

During a live Q&A ahead of its release, Taylor explained: "The song is about a lost romance and why young love is often fixed so permanently within our memories. Why it leaves such an indelible mark." Speaking later to BBC Radio 1, she added that by looking back, "how special it made you feel, all the good things it made you feel, all the pain that it made you feel."

According to the singer, the song is the first part of the album's "teenage love triangle", which continues with the later tracks 'August' and 'Betty'. In a live chat on the eve of the album's release, she revealed: "These three songs explore a love triangle from all three people's perspectives at different times of their lives."

The lyrics are arguably some of the finest of her career, with their mixture of heartbreak, loss, and hope. But the song also highlights one of her most underrated skills – her singing. Every descriptive word seems to fit perfectly into place, like an actress reading from a script, allowing you to not just hear the emotion in her sultry, quivering voice, but to feel it too.

According to Aaron Dessner, he sent the melody to Taylor who then sent the lyrics back to him an hour later. No one can deny that is a mark of songwriting genius, and that this lyrical collage she has conjured up is among her finest work.

'Cardigan' became Taylor's sixth number one in the US and second chart-topping debut since 'Shake it Off' in 2014. It also made her the first artist to debut at number one on both the Hot 100 and Hot 200 in the same week. With the single being joined in the top ten by 'The 1' and 'Exile', it increased her record number of top ten debuts for a female artist to 18.

The dream-like music video was a solo effort by Taylor, who wrote, directed and styled it. Brimming with metaphors, the story begins with Taylor in a candlelit cabin in the woods, dressed in a nightgown, and playing an upright piano. She climbs into it and is transported to a moss-covered forest and a grand piano that produces a waterfall. Climbing into the piano seat, the scene changes to a dark, stormy sea, where she keeps afloat by holding onto the piano, before once more climbing inside and returning to the cabin, where she puts on a cardigan.

According to *Rolling Stone*, "she had the whole storyline - the whole notion of going into the piano and coming out into a forest, the water, going back into the piano", and was inspired by watching fantasy and period movies during lockdown. Due to Covid restrictions, the whole crew had to abide by necessary safety guidelines, wearing masks and social distancing. Only those wearing certain wristbands were allowed to come within close contact of Taylor, and the video was filmed with a camera mounted on a robotic arm and operated remotely.

The video was released at the same time as the single. Replica cardigans would be at the centre of the album's successful cottagecore-centred merchandise.

Slate - 'Cardigan' represents a bit of a chart comeback for Swift. And the crazy thing is, if critical consensus around her new album folklore is to be believed, she pulled this off by not trying to have hits anymore"; **The Guardian** - "As cavernous and shimmering as a rock pool in a cave"; **NME** - "A swirling amalgam of glittering production, swooning strings with flickering piano, and lyrics that evoke the pain of young love"; **Rolling Stone** - "Swift sorts through the memories that go with breathing in the scent of a remembered lover".

The Last Great American Dynasty *****
(Taylor Swift - Aaron Dessner)
Recorded - Long Pond Studio, NY; Kitty Committee Studio, LA (vocals)
Produced - Aaron Dessner
Released - July 24 2020
Chart peak positions
 Hot 100 #13; UK Streaming #18; Canada #13; Australia #7; NZ #13

In a song that connects two women from different times, Taylor relates the story of St Louis socialite Rebekah (Betty) Harkness (nee West) (1915-1982), a divorcee who married William Harkness, heir to the Standard Oil Company. On his death in 1954, Rebekah inherited his fortune. They had been the owners of the mansion 'Holiday House', the Rhode Island property that Taylor had purchased back in 2013.

As a wealthy widow, Rebekah soon became the owner of a vast number of properties and indulged in many luxuries, especially her passion for dance and music. The tabloids became fascinated with her eccentric lifestyle, and neighbours at the Holiday House complained about her staging extravagant star-studded parties held on her front lawn. Known for having a string of lovers throughout her life, the final one was a self-identified gay dancer 25 years her junior. Despite receiving harsh criticism from the press, Rebekah was a patron of the arts and supported both ballet and dance organisations, as well as research into Parkinson's disease.

In the cleverly-crafted song, Taylor draws comparisons between herself and Rebekah, as they both enjoyed lavish parties at the house and were also targets of harsh criticism from both tabloids and individuals.

In an interview for *People*, she said: "It's about what happens when women step out of their cages and run. It can be a real pearl-clutching moment for society when a woman owns her desires and wildness. And I love the idea that the woman in question would be too joyful in her freedom to even care that she's ruffling feathers, raising eyebrows or becoming the talk of the town. The idea that she decided there were marvellous times to be had, and that was more important."

According to Taylor's research, Rebekah cleaned out her pool with Dom Perignon, and, after a feud with a neighbour, dyed their dog "key lime green", although according to the *Times* it was actually a cat.

Speaking to *Entertainment Weekly*, Taylor explained: "As soon as I found out about her, I wanted to know everything I could. So I started reading. I found her so interesting. And then as more parallels began to develop between our lives - being the lady that lives in that house on the hill that everybody gets to gossip about - I was always looking for an opportunity to write about her."

Taylor finally found the chance when she heard the instrumental track Dessner had sent to her.

Pitchfork - "With the intrigue of a story song and the intimacy of a biography, Swift delves into socialite anthropology and returns with an epitaph for a woman she'll never meet. The real magic is the winking humility of the image in the mirror: a woman criticised endlessly for being too rich and too gauche who knows that living well is still the best revenge"; **PopMatters** - Swift invokes the real-life story…through the prism of a whole community as a Greek chorus commentating on the action. It's an astute conceit that elevates a lyrical tale of small-town life to towering myth"; **Rolling Stone** - "Initially seemed more a gimmick than a song, with a clever twist that would wear off fast. But the intricate details just grow over time - melodically, production-wise, most of all vocally"; **Vulture** - "It's a crucial dose of levity on *folklore*, and a chance for Swift to show off her storytelling chops"; **NME** - "It's an impressive song, managing to communicate a huge amount of Harkness' life across in only a few minutes".

Exile (featuring Bon Iver) *****
(Taylor Swift - William Bowery - Justin Vernon)
2nd Single
Recorded - Long Pond Studio, NY; Kitty Committee Studio, LA (Taylor's vocals);
  April Base, Fall Creek, WI (Vernon's vocals)
Produced - Aaron Dessner & Joe Alwyn
Released - August 3 2020
Chart peak positions
Hot 100 #6; Adult Alternative Songs #9; Hot Rock & Alternative Songs #2; UK #8;
  Canada #6; Australia #3; NZ #5

Taylor describes two ex-lovers seeing each other following a breakup and telling different sides of the story. In a gripping vocal exchange with Justin Vernon of Bon Iver, he describes his feelings of confusion and betrayal about how soon his lover moved on, while she, in turn, tells him of the repeated warning signs that their relationship was not working, and that she now feels she doesn't owe him anything. Their different voices perfectly echo their conflicting views.

In a clip sent to radio stations, Taylor said: "Exile is a song that was written about miscommunications in relationships, and in the case of this song, I imagined that the miscommunications ended the relationship. They led to the demise of this love affair, and now these two people are seeing each other for the first time, and they keep miscommunicating with each other."

Under the pseudonym of William Bowery, Taylor's boyfriend Joe Alwyn wrote the song's piano melody and the first verse sung by Vernon, and they developed the song into a rough demo of a duet, with Taylor singing both male and female parts. Although Alwyn played the original piano part, the recording had some difficulties, and, in the end, it was Vernon who got to play on the finished track.

It came as no surprise that William Bowery was in fact Joe Alwyn, as the clues had always been there. His great-grandfather was a composer called William, and Taylor and Joe had been seen hanging out at the Bowery Hotel in New York at the start of their relationship. Some fans also noted that there was a bar called the Bowery at the intersection of Sunset Boulevard and Vine Street in LA, and the words "Sunset and Vine" were used in the lyrics of 'Gorgeous', her not-so-subtle love letter to Joe.

In the *Long Pond Sessions* special, Taylor confirmed the fan speculation by saying, "So, William Bowery is Joe, as we know. Joe plays piano beautifully...He's always just playing and making things up and kind of creating things. Joe had written that entire piano part...He was singing the Bon Iver part...and I was entranced, and asked if we could keep writing that one." After hearing him sing, Taylor knew it had to be a duet. As they were both fans of Vernon's work with Bon Iver and Big Red Machine, when his name cropped up in a discussion with producer Dessner over who should sing on the track, they agreed to send him a copy of the demo, and he readily agreed to do it.

Dessner recalled: "He tweaked some parts and added parts as well…At some point I felt like a superfan, hearing two of my favourite singers. This was all being done remotely, but it was one of those moments where your head hits the back of the wall and you're like, f**k. Okay."

Eonline - "This duet with Justin Vernon is a devastating dream. We're not sure what crumbling relationship inspired the track, but whatever it was must've hurt because this stunner - with its swirling strings and plodding piano - hits like a punch to the gut"; **Consequence of Sound** - "The song acts as a contrapuntal of a dissolving romance, the two voices alternating while remaining separate, harmonising only with themselves. Like most of these songs, 'Exile' marks maturity: The lyrics are clever but restrained, and the emotions are not only high-pitched but possess complex, shifting depths"; **Rolling Stone** - "She and Justin Vernon blend their very different voices…At first it sounded like their vocals just don't fit together - yet that's what the song is about"; **Vulture** - "The first sign that folklore would not be an album you put on in the background while doing something else", **NME** - "It's an emotive cut, and one of Swift's most impressive collaborations".

My Tears Ricochet *****
(Taylor Swift)
Recorded - Kitty Committee Studio, LA (vocals); Rough Customer Studios, Brooklyn;
  Electric Lady Studios, NY; Conway Recording, LA
Produced - Taylor Swift, Jack Antonoff & Joe Alwyn
Released - July 24 2020
Chart peak positions
  Hot 100 #16; Hot Rock & Alternative Songs #3; Alternative Digital Songs #10;
  UK Streaming #20; Canada #14; Australia #8

In Taylor's words, a song about an "embittered tormentor showing up at a funeral of his fallen object of obsession". This glorious self-penned song by Taylor was the first to be written for the album, and the perfect choice for track #5, which since *Red* had become the honorary slot for the most emotional and vulnerable song of the album. Jack Antonoff was quoted as saying it was one of the best songs she had written, and that this and 'August' were the favourite songs they'd done together.

Taylor told *Entertainment Weekly* that the sale of her masters to Scooter Braun had motivated her to develop narratives around the subject of divorce. Watching the recent divorce-themed movie *Marriage Story* also gave her the inspiration to write the first lines of the song.

Some Swifties can see the song as a connection to Taylor's personal life, and in particular, Scott Borchetta's betrayal when she left Big Machine, while others have linked it to the song 'Look What You Made Me Do' in which she proclaims "the old Taylor is dead", thereby making the funeral imagery of this new song look like she's in mourning for her own metaphorical death.

Staged Haze - "Taylor is super self-deprecating in this song - one of my favourite songwriting traits of hers - and the relationship between admitting her failure to 'go with grace', while simultaneously embracing and accepting her anger is fascinating"; **The Forward** - "Each lyric is a bullet that tears apart the stories Borchetta tells to discredit Swift. The song builds and crescendos and dies down, leaving the listener well aware that this exhausting fight for her masters is never what Swift wanted. She just wants the art that made her who she is - her stolen lullabies - where they belong"; **Rolling Stone** - "One of her spookiest Goth Tay ballads"; **Vulture** - "A dramatic breakup anthem worthy of the years they spent together. She concocts a ghostly fantasy about watching your enemies wail at your funeral".

Mirrorball ***
(Taylor Swift - Jack Antonoff)
Recorded - Kitty Committee Studio, LA; (vocals); Rough Customer Studio, Brooklyn.
Produced - Jack Antonoff & Taylor Swift
Released - July 24 2020
Chart peak positions
  Hot 100 #26; Hot Rock & Alternative Songs #6; Alternative Digital Songs #20; UK
  Streaming #30; Canada #22; Australia #14

Taylor compares herself to a disco ball, reflecting all the different personalities around her, and how she shatters like glass when her heart gets broken. Written after Lover Fest was cancelled due to the pandemic, she confessed: "I realised, here I am, writing all this music, still trying, and I know I have an excuse to sit back and not do something, but I can't".

As a result, the lyrics directly reference the effects of the pandemic: "I think that, you know, the pandemic and the lockdown, and all that, runs through this album like a thread because it's an album that allows you to feel your feelings, and it's a product of isolation."

Esquire - "This is a woman who has seen *Eyes Wide Shut* and gotten right on the horn with a party planner. To know her must be exhausting, but to listen is a treat"; **Billboard** - "A swaying, deceptively simple indie-folk song about personal contortion for the sake of romantic fulfilment... Packed with harmonies and live drums, the song keeps Swift's voice as a breathy resignation, and the result is devastatingly pretty"; **Rolling Stone** - "A seething ballad about a loner feeling a little too loud and a little too bright, afraid everyone's staring at her flaws yet feeling invisible anyway".

Seven ****
(Taylor Swift - Aaron Dessner)
Recorded - Long Pond Studio, NY
Produced - Aaron Dessner
Released - July 24 2020
Chart peak positions
  Hot 100 #35#; Hot Rock & Alternative Songs #7; Alternative Digital Songs #19;
  UK Streaming #32; Canada #26; Australia #16

Intentionally placed as track #7, this is a harrowing song about seven-year-old Taylor witnessing a friend who is having a more challenging childhood, apparently suffering physical abuse from her parents, and the two of them making a pledge to run away together. Speaking to *Vulture*, Dessner recalled: "This is the second song we wrote. It's kind of looking back at childhood and those childhood feelings, recounting memories and memorialising them…That's what this album is doing. It's passing down. It's memorialising love, childhood, and memories. It's a folkloric way of processing."

PopMatters - "The painful epiphany that a childhood friend was being abused by her parents and Swift lacked both the knowledge and wherewithal to protect her. The result is heartbreaking"; **Rolling Stone** - "The little girls dream of escaping, running away to be pirate twins, but there's no resolution - just a mystery that gets more confusing that she tries to live with it", **Vulture** - "The folkiest track on *folklore* serves up a Southern Gothic vision of childhood, where wild innocence brushes past darkness that's only apparent in retrospect"; **NME** - "It's a snapshot of being young and carefree while real life gradually creeps into the picture".

August *****
(Taylor Swift - Jack Antonoff)
Recorded - Kitty Committee Studio, LA (vocals); Rough Customer Studio, Brooklyn.
Produced - Jack Antonoff, Taylor Swift & Joe Alwyn
Released - July 24 2020
Chart peak positions
  Hot 100 #23; Hot Rock & Alternative Songs #5; Alternative Digital Songs #8; UK
  Streaming #29; Canada #19; Australia #13

The second track of the teenage love triangle, following on from 'Cardigan', and one that has had Swifties theorising over for months. Although no name is mentioned, the general consensus is that the song relates to the "other" woman in the triangle, who has a fling with James, the boyfriend of 'Cardigan's Betty character. Although realising that it's not meant to last, she lives in hope and recounts the exhilaration and endless potential of their summer romance.

Describing the protagonist of the song, Taylor said: "She seems like she's a bad girl, but really she's not a bad girl. She's really a sensitive person who really fell for him, and she was trying to seem cool and seem like she didn't care because that's what girls have to do."

According to co-writer Jack Antonoff, he produced the instrumental first and sent it over to Taylor who then wrote the lyrics "on the spot", describing it as "just an intuitive thing". Taylor actually came up with the bridge for the song while she was in the middle of recording the track in the vocal booth.

During the *Long Pond Sessions* documentary, Taylor explained the Betty/James love triangle and added a fresh twist: "I've been in my head calling the girl from 'August' Augusta, or Augustine."

Once again, track placement was intentional, with it being #8 on Taylor's eighth album and its eight deluxe versions, and, of course, August being the eighth month.

Rolling Stone - "One of the album's most amazing moments"; **The Interns** - "Together they've crafted something spectacular. The way the instrumentation on this slowly takes flight is a stroke of genius, matched by Swift's gently undulating songwriting... This may actually be the best thing Antonoff and Swift have ever made together. The album's true centrepiece and the best song so far"; **Chicago Tribune** - "While the whole world was hunkered down this spring, somewhere in the woods, Taylor Swift was astral-projecting into the 90s...and she came back down to Earth with August"; **Vulture** - "Even in fiction, Swift's ability to capture the wistful ache of nostalgia remains unmatched"; **NME** - "A melancholic dream-pop ballad".

This Is Me Trying *****

(Taylor Swift - Jack Antonoff)
Recorded - Kitty Committee Studio, LA (vocals); Rough Customer Studio, Brooklyn;
 Electric Lady Studios, NY; Conway Recording, LA
Produced - Jack Antonoff, Taylor Swift & Joe Alwyn
Released - July 24 2020
Chart peak positions
 Hot 100 #39; Hot Rock & Alternative Songs #9; Alternative Digital Songs #13;
 Alternative Streaming Songs #8; UK Streaming #39; Canada #30; Australia #18

Taylor revealed that one of the songs on the album is told from the perspective of "a 17-year-old standing on a porch, learning to apologise." This is most certainly that song, and would tie in nicely as an addition to the teenage love triangle as a dramatic retelling of James' apology for cheating on Betty.

Reminiscent in sentiment to 2011's 'Back to December', this sees the alcoholic narrator having the humility to admit fault for a damaged relationship and making efforts to repair it, although the healing process has its complications.

With another superbly crafted collaboration with Antonoff, Taylor wrote: "I've been thinking about people who, if they're either suffering through mental illness or they're suffering through addiction, they have an everyday struggle. No one pats them on the back every day, but every day they are actively fighting something."

Insider - "A cinematic study of regret and accountability... 'This Is Me Trying' quickly strikes a more sinister tone than its predecessors - still nostalgic and wistful, but carrying an edge, like a threatening secret"; **Rolling Stone** - "The easiest *folklore* song to underrate, because it seems so deceptively straight-ahead"; **Vulture** - "This unguarded track surfs along with its heart on its sleeve, plus a languid saxophone and a few great turns of phrase... The climax sneaks up on you like a moment of clarity"; **Los Angeles Times** - "Swift seems off her metaphor game in the ungainly 'Cardigan', but she's utterly on point in this mournful orchestral-pop dirge...as sharp a rendering of regret as any we've heard from her".

Illicit Affairs *****

(Taylor Swift - Jack Antonoff)
Recorded - Kitty Committee Studio, LA (vocals); Rough Customer Studio, Brooklyn,
Produced - Jack Antonoff, Taylor Swift & Joe Alwyn
Released - July 24 2020
Chart peak positions
 Hot 100 #44; UK Streaming #41; Canada #33; Australia #21

In what is perhaps the most overlooked track on the album, Taylor tackles the subject of infidelity. Whether it's about the narrator who's feeling wronged by a cheating partner, or whether it's the "other woman" character who had wanted more, seems irrelevant. This is arguably one of Taylor's greatest writing accomplishments, with lyrics that are breathtaking in their emotive description, and, in an album of standout songs, should be celebrated for its songwriting perfection.

In the twelve years since 'Should've Said No' on her debut album, Taylor's concept of infidelity seems to have changed from one of outright condemnation to one that now recognises it can lead to both a "mercurial high" as well as the inevitability of heartbreak.

295

The highlight of the song is the bridge toward the end, where she finally vents her built-up anger at her lover, before quietly admitting that, despite how he's made her feel, she will still "ruin" herself for him, time and time again. In an interview with *Rolling Stone*, Taylor seemed to be describing the song: "When I was making *folklore*, I went lyrically in a total direction of escapism and romanticism. And I wrote songs imagining I was like, a pioneer woman in a forbidden love affair."

Affinity - "This song has some of the most nuanced songwriting in Taylor Swift's discography. If you ever want to understand what sets her apart from the rest of her peers, listen to this song"; **Vogue UK** - "How Swift can make a clandestine romance seem so film noir...'Illicit Affairs' goes into the gritty details and heartache of infidelity, like meeting in parking lots and buying perfume for a lover who doesn't care"; **Variety** - "The best cheating song since, well, *Reputation's* hard-to-top 'Getaway Car'. There's less catharsis in this one, but just as much pungent wisdom, as Swift describes the more mundane details of maintaining an affair with the soul-destroying ones"; **Insider** - "Illicit Affairs has growing power and will likely become one of those tracks than fans form a strong emotional attachment to over time"; **Rolling Stone** - "A cheating ballad that can turn me into a godforsaken mess any time...the muted regret boils over in the bridge"; **NME** - "A heart-wrenching story of complicated infidelity...Swift manages to spin a whole tale of secret meetings, lies and clandestine romance, and the emotional impacts it can have".

Invisible String ****
(Taylor Swift - Aaron Dessner)
Recorded - Long Pond Studio, NY
Produced - Aaron Dessner
Released - July 24 2020
Chart peak positions
  Hot 100 #37; UK Streaming #43; Canada #29; Australia #19

Taylor explains the song's imagery in the album's prologue: "A single thread that, for better or worse, ties you to your fate". This is a reference to a Far East Asian folk myth about a "red thread of fate" tied around the fingers of two soulmates, connecting them by either end. In the song, Taylor shows gratitude for her string of failed relationships for paving the way for her current, solid relationship with Joe Alwyn.

There are a number of hidden messages found in the lyrics and nods to previous songs. Joe Alwyn figures in references to Nashville, London, and the English Lake District; while there are links to 'Bad Blood' and the feud with Katy Perry. There are also references to 'Delicate' and 'Daylight', both widely believed to be written about Alwyn, and it appears that even Joe Jonas and his infamous breakup phone call gets a nod.

Taylor wrote: "I remember I wrote it right after I sent an ex a baby gift. And I was just like 'Man, life is great'."

Washington Post - "She sings over the sound of cherubs plucking harps, tracing a years-long relationship back to its start...Providing those garish narrative details ...in her mildest voice makes her testimony feel totally real and a little sad"; **Staged Haze** - "Is there anything more quintessentially Taylor Swift than imagining her as a teenager in the park reading a book, dreaming about the day where she finally meets the person she's been waiting for?"; **Dallas Observer** - "If fans were in doubt about Swift's development...this song proves that the teenaged girl with whom we fell in love has now grown up – and with her, so has an entire generation of fans"; **Vulture** - "*Folklore* finds Swift replaying memories over and over, trying to mine them for meaning that might not have been apparent in the moment. She does that most literally in the album's best track"; **NME** - "A sweet ode to Swift's past relationships, and how they led her to where she currently is".

Mad Woman ****
(Taylor Swift - Aaron Dessner)
Recorded - Long Pond Studio, NY
Produced - Aaron Dessner
Released - July 24 2020
Chart peak positions
  Hot 100 #37; Hot Rock & Alternative Songs #10; Alternative Digital Songs #9;
  Alternative Streaming Songs #9; UK Streaming #50; Canada #38; Australia #25

Taylor's strong feminist message about the social taboo that surrounds female anger, surely inspired by the drama concerning Braun, Borchetta and the lost masters, in which she was perceived to be a delusional, crazy woman in her arguments with the two men.

Although not mentioning them by name in the song, she told producer Dessner in the *Long Pond Sessions:* "I was thinking the most rage-provoking element of being a female is the gaslighting. There have been instances of this recently with someone who is very guilty of this in my life, and it's a person who tries to make me feel like I'm the offender by having any kind of defense. I feel like I have no right to respond, or I'm crazy, or I'm angry. How do I say why this feels so bad?"

This is Taylor displaying her customary energy in a subject so dear to her heart - the fine line that women are expected to tread with their emotions.

The Guardian - "Swift's longest lyrical obsession is the loss of innocence, a theme she makes fairly devastating here...The tense, slippery 'Mad Woman' traces the self-perpetuating cycle of women being angered by being labelled angry"; **Vulture** - "A haunting evocation of female rage. It gives us the unrepentant knife-twisting that *Reputation* only gestured at"; **NME** - "Skewers the sexist trope of angry women being branded hysterical".

Epiphany ***
(Taylor Swift - Aaron Dessner)
Recorded - Long Pond Studio, NY; Kitty Committee Studio, LA (vocals).
Produced - Aaron Dessner
Released - July 24 2020
Chart peak positions
  Hot 100 #57; Hot Rock & Alternative Songs #11; Alternative Digital Songs #23;
  Alternative Streaming Songs #10; UK Streaming #58; Canada #44; Australia #29

In a hymnal song Taylor references her grandfather's military service, and uses war metaphors to pay tribute to medical workers risking their lives helping patients during the Covid-19 pandemic. Archie Dean Swift served in the Pacific during World War II and had fought at Guadalcanal in 1942 where he attended to an injured comrade. Taylor describes someone hoping to find peace in their dreams amidst a chaotic and violent world.

In an interview for *Vulture*, Aaron Dessner said: "In the past, heroes were just soldiers. Now they're also medical professionals. To me, that's the underlying mission of the song. There are some things that you see that are hard to talk about. You can't talk about it. You just bear witness to them."

Esquire - "This is where Swift goes full chamber-pop, where she earns the "alternative" categorization this album falls under on the streaming services. If you can get yourself to a field of wheat and slowly run your hand over the top of it while listening, I'd recommend that"; **The Interns** - "Epiphany is the first moment on the album that truly looks for peace. It's a sprawling atmospheric beast that has Swift like you've never heard her before"; **The Atlantic** - "Swift sings of him on a 1942 battlefield, attending to a comrade bleeding out. Her voice is a translucent beam; her syllables fall slowly like ash. But by verse two, she's singing from somewhere else: a 2020 medical ward of plastic sheaths and labored breathing"; **NME** - "Warm, unpretentious…it sees Swift go full-on indie".

Betty *****
(Taylor Swift - William Bowery)
3rd Single
Recorded - Kitty Committee Studio, LA (vocals); Rough Customer Studio, Brooklyn.
Produced - Aaron Dessner, Jack Antonoff, Taylor Swift & Joe Alwyn
Released - August 17 2020
Chart peak positions
 Hot 100 #42; Hot Country Songs #6; UK Download #92; UK Streaming #46;
 Canada #32; Australia #22

The final part of the teenage love triangle sees cheating James apologising to Betty for his fling with the female narrator of 'August', although not exactly fully owning up to it. Although all three songs are connected by a common theme and lyrics, each had a different sound to make each narrative unique, and nowhere is it more unique than on this wonderfully upbeat song which echoes Taylor's country roots.

In the song, a female character called Inez appears to have been the one to tell Betty of the affair. (Betty, James and Inez are named after the daughters of Ryan Reynolds and Blake Lively). With its feminist approach, Taylor has Betty flourishing on her own with the cheating James still unable to own up to his mistakes. James' gender is never explicitly stated in the lyrics, which led some to wonder if James could be a girl and that the love triangle story could in fact be one of sapphic love. When asked about this, Dessner replied: "I can't speak to what it's about. I have my own ideas. I also know where Taylor's heart is, and I think that's great anytime a song takes on greater meaning for anyone."

However, the gender was soon revealed in an interview Taylor did for *Billboard*: "[James] has lost the love of his life basically and doesn't understand how to get it back. I think we all have situations in our lives where we learn to really, really give a heartfelt apology for the first time. Everybody makes mistakes, everybody really messes up sometimes, and this is a song that I wrote from the perspective of a 17-year-old boy." Taylor also cited Patty Griffin's 'Top of the World' as being the inspiration to write the song from a male perspective.

Joe Alwyn wrote the chorus of the song, again under a pseudonym, as Taylor explained in the *Long Pond Sessions*: "I just heard Joe singing the entire fully formed chorus of 'Betty' from another room. And I was just like, 'Hello'. It was a step that we would never have taken, because why would we have ever written a song together? So, this was the first time we had a conversation where I came in and I was like, 'Hey, this could be really weird, and we could hate this, so because we're in quarantine and there's nothing else going on, could we just try to see what it's like if we write this song together?'.…We decided to make it from a teenage boy's perspective apologising after he loses the love of his life because he's been foolish."

'Betty' gave Taylor a welcome return to the Country Songs chart, the first time since 'Soon You'll Get Better'.

Time - "The web of perspectives and emotions outlined in the track trio presents Swift fans with plenty of material to parse through as they unravel the mystery of Swift's feelings and her new album's connotations"; **Pitchfork** - "'Betty', a story of fraught young love, showcases the maturity and nuance that Swift has gained since she was a teenager herself. In the past, she had sung about regretting a breakup and unfairly blowing fights out of proportion. But 'Betty' is the rare truly apologetic Swift song"; **Vulture** - "A song about a love triangle which, depending on how you listen to it, could be about three women and absolutely zero men. To arrive at that interpretation, you need to know that, like much of Swift's best songwriting, it's all coded…"; **Rolling Stone** - "Every aspect of 'Betty' sounds designed to explode when she finally gets the chance to take it to the stage"; **NME** - "With it woozy harmonica riffs and chiming vocals, it's a beaut".

Peace ***
(Taylor Swift - Aaron Dessner)
Recorded - Long Pond Studio, NY; Kitty Committee Studio, LA (vocals)
Produced - Aaron Dessner
Released - August 17 2020
Chart peak positions
 Hot 100 #58; Hot Rock & Alternative Songs #12; Alternative Digital Songs
 #18; Alternative Streaming Songs #11; UK Streaming #62; Canada #46; Australia #33

Taylor worries what affect her "crazy" celebrity life and her shortcomings could have on her partner and whether the lack of privacy could jeopardise their relationship. In an interview for *Rolling Stone*, she revealed: "'Peace' is actually more rooted in my personal life. [It comes after] carving out a human life within a public life, and how scary that can be when you do fall in love and you meet someone, especially if you've met someone who has a very grounded, normal way of living…The idea of privacy feels so strange to try to explain, but it's really just trying to find bits of normalcy."

In the lyric video for the song, some commentators have suggested the words "robbers to the east/Clowns to the West" are references to Scooter Braun "stealing" her masters, and, with the W capitalised in West, a swipe at Kanye West - two individuals who have had an effect on her personal life.

Variety - "If you like your love ballads realistic, it's a bit of candor that renders all the compensatory vows of fidelity and courage all the more credible and deeply lovely"; **The Guardian** - "She tentatively asserts what's at the core: the deep dedication she sings about on the resonant, minimalist 'Peace'"; **Washington Post** - "Swift finally appears to be wrestling with the riddle of her existence: being the most 'normal' superstar alive. For someone like her, a quiet, peaceful, ordinary happily-after-after kind of life is clearly impossible"; **Rolling Stone** - "The most stripped-down confession on *folklore*, just her solo voice and a few guarded hopes for the future"; **Vulture** - "Her unassuming authenticity keeps it far from humblebrag territory"; **NME** - "Celebrates a partnership strong enough to withstand the soaring highs and painful lows alike".

Hoax ***
(Taylor Swift - Aaron Dessner)
Recorded - Long Pond Studio, NY; Kitty Committee Studio, LA (vocals)
Produced - Aaron Dessner
Released - July 24 2020
Chart peak positions
  Hot 100 #71; Hot Rock & Alternative Songs #14; UK Streaming #70; Canada
  #51; Alternative Streaming Songs #12; Australia #43

A surprisingly darker edge for the final track on the album, in which Taylor describes having to endure a toxic relationship and being driven to despair, unable to let go. According to co-writer Dessner, 'Hoax' and 'The 1' were the final songs written after the album was completed: "We thought it was complete, but Taylor then went back into the folder of ideas. She wrote 'The 1', and then she wrote 'Hoax' a couple of hours later and sent them in the middle of the night. When I woke up in the morning, I wrote her before she woke up in LA and said, 'I agree. These are the bookends, you know?'"

Working with Dessner, Taylor admitted that this song was the first time she had explored multiple themes: "What if not all of these feelings are about the same person? What if I'm writing about several different, very fractured situations? Like one is about love, and one is about a business thing that really hurt, and one is about a sort of relationship I considered family, but that really hurt?...I definitely had those moments of doubt... and I was really happy when you kind of pushed me forward, like, 'Nope, do the things that make you uncomfortable'."

Speaking to *Vulture*, Dessner said: "After writing all these songs, this one felt the most emotional and, in a way, the rawest. It's one of my favourites. There's sadness, but it's a kind of hopeful sadness. It's a recognition that you take on the burden of your partners, your loved ones, and their ups and downs...That's part of how I feel about those songs ['Peace' and 'Hoax'] because I think that's life. There's a reality, the gravity or an understanding of the human condition."

Slate - "These late moments of *folklore* are those it perhaps nudges closest to the naked intimacy of peak Joni Mitchell"; **Mill Valley News** - "Hoax reflects on a situation in which someone can't let go of a person who's hurt them and all of the conflicting emotions that accompany it. Almost perfectly, Swift translates these feelings to lyrics"; **The New Nine** - "Well, if there was ever a song to give you one final feeling of closure, this is most definitely it. This is the ultimate breakup track. Fin. Done"; **Rolling Stone** - "A desolate break-up lament, lifted by Aaron Dessner's melancholy piano"; **Vulture** - "So intimate it's almost uncomfortable: Just Swift, a piano, and quiet strings, bathed in religious imagery and nods to private tragedies we'll probably never know about"; **NME** - "The least memorable moment from the fantastic *folklore*, this slow waltzing tune is inoffensive, but lacks excitement".

The Lakes ****
(Taylor Swift - Jack Antonoff)
Folklore Deluxe Editions
Recorded - Kitty Committee Studio, LA (vocals); Rough Customer, Brooklyn.
Produced - Jack Antonoff & Taylor Swift
Released - August 18 2020
Chart peak positions
  Digital Song Sales #5; Bubbling Under Hot 100 #18; UK Download #21;
  Canada Digital #9; Australia Digital #7; NZ Hot Singles #13

Inspired by Joe Alwyn taking Taylor to the English Lake District National Park for a vacation. The area was home and inspiration for a group of celebrated poets in the first half of the 19th century, most notably Samuel Taylor Coleridge, John Keats, and William Wordsworth.

Taylor had already referenced her trip to the Lakes in 'Invisible String' and was well versed in poetry, soaking up the romanticism of treading in the footsteps of some of her favourite poets. Talking to *Billboard*, she recalled: "There was a poet district, these artists that moved there. They were kind of heckled for it and made fun of for it as being eccentrics…I remember when we went, I thought, Man I could see this. You live in a cottage; you've got wisteria growing up the side of it. Of course, they would escape like that."

Dessner told *Vulture*: "That's Jack's song. It's a beautiful kind of garden, or like you're lost in a beautiful garden. There's a kind of Greek poetry to it. Tragic poetry, I guess."

Although the focus of the song is on the natural beauty of the Lakes, the lure of escapism, and, of course, her "muse" Joe Alwyn, it still features one of Taylor's signature lyric daggers aimed at "namedropping sleaze" - unnamed people who have upset her in the past. Braun, Kanye and Kim are no doubt front runners.

Taylor explained: "It's kind of the overarching theme of the whole album, of trying to escape, having something you want to protect, trying to protect your own sanity, and saying, 'Look, they did this hundreds of years ago. I'm not the first person who's felt this way'." Jack Antonoff added: "I think the idea of getting away and figuring out how to remove the things that are not working in one's life is the story of this [pandemic]."

'The Lakes' was featured as a bonus track on the eight physical deluxe editions of the album released on August 7th, and was made available on digital and streaming platforms on August 18th, along with a lyric video on Taylor's YouTube channel.

Pop Juice - "The Lakes is Swift's cry for a getaway from the watchful eyes of the public, for an escape to somewhere obscure where she can't be found. She's found love, and maybe that's all she needs. And given that she's marketed this place as the 'perfect place to cry', we'd really love to know how to get there, too"; **Sputnik Music** - "Instead of making past drama the focal point of 'The Lakes'…she wisely sidesteps it early on and hones in on isolation and self-care. She sings about the natural beauty…and specifically about how isolating herself from the toxicity of celebrity and internet culture is helping to heal her"; **Vulture** - "An attempt at channelling the naturalistic imagery of the Lake Poets winds up overwrought and overwritten".

On August 20th Taylor released a subdivision of *folklore* in thematic chapters, each comprising six tracks:

The Escapism Chapter EP
The Lakes, Seven, Epiphany, Cardigan, Mirrorball, Exile
The Sleepless Nights Chapter EP
Exile, Hoax, My Tears Ricochet, Illicit Affairs, This Is Me Trying, Mad Woman
The Saltbox House Chapter EP
The Last Great American Dynasty, August, The 1, Seven, Peace, Betty
The Yeah, I Showed Up at Your Party Chapter EP
Betty (live from the ACMs), *The 1, Mirrorball, The Last Great American Dynasty, Invisible String, Cardigan*

A natural progression

Taylor reflected on the album for *Billboard*: "This is the first album that I've ever let go of that need to be 100% autobiographical. Because I think I felt like I needed to do that. I felt like fans needed to hear a stripped from the headlines account of my life and it actually ended up being a bit confining. That's been my favorite thing about this album. It's allowed to exist on its own merit without it just being 'oh, people are listening to this because it tells them something they could read in a tabloid'."

Like many of Taylor's albums, *folklore* would prove to be a record-breaker. On the first day of its release, it amassed over 80.6 million global streams on Spotify, earning it the Guinness World Record for the most opening-day streams for an album by a female artist, beating the former record held by Ariana Grande's album, *Thank U, Next*. The first single, 'Cardigan', scored 7.7 million first-day global plays on Spotify, the highest figure of 2020 for a female artist. It also beat Apple Music's record for the most-streamed pop album in 24 hours with 35.5 million streams. Taylor became the year's second-most streamed woman on Spotify (after Billie Eilish), while also becoming Amazon Music's top streamed artist of the year.

On its release, it was reported that the album had sold over 2 million copies in its first week, with over 1.3 million of those within the first 24 hours of its release. By year's end, Taylor was the best-selling soloist and best-selling female artist of the year. *folklore* also became the first album since Taylor's own *Lover* to move half a million units in a week. Its first-week sales alone were enough to make it the best-selling album of the year. Debuting at #1 on the Hot 200, it became the longest-reigning chart-topper of the year at eight weeks.

Taylor also became the first artist to have the best-selling album of a calendar year for five times, following *Fearless, 1989, Reputation*, and *Lover*. She also became the first woman to have seven albums debut at #1 on the Hot 200, and tied with Janet Jackson for the third-most chart-topping albums on the Hot 200, and was the first female since Barbra Streisand to have six albums spend more than one week at #1.

Taylor also beat her own *Reputation* record for the longest-running number one album by a woman, became the first solo female artist to have five albums each top the charts for six weeks or more, and surpassed Whitney Houston's record as the woman with the most weeks atop the Hot 200 (47). She also trumped her own *Lover* as the woman with the most simultaneous Hot 100 debuts (16), and beat Nicki Minaj's record as the woman with the most Hot 100 entries (113).

The reviews were as impressive as the records that had been broken.

Esquire - "She's been a precocious country star, an awards-show over-actress, a Max Martin muse, a pop queen, a good girl, a bad guy, a villain, a victim, a tabloid fixture, and a real estate speculator. Now she guides us through the darkest American moment we've ever lived through. *folklore* is the sound of exploration and confidence, searching and serenity, joy and uncertainty. It's the therapy session you need, the story that manages to hold your interest, the scented candle you could afford back in February"; **Rolling Stone** - *folklore* is yet another mesmerising musical score from Swift – a shift toward a broad Indie-folk sound (à la, of course, the National) that still feels distinctly Swift-ian, as if she's been making music like this her whole career. Lyrically too, the record finds Swift playing with character and myth in new ways that – befitting the album's title – recall the great American folk tradition"; **US Magazine** - "The quality of *folklore* indicates that Swift is thriving in isolation, something not everyone can say. At one point, the album was a sunken treasure chest, filled with gems but closely guarded within the walls of the artist's home. But now, it has floated to shore, and, boy, is it a saving grace for 2020"; **The Independent** - "exquisite, piano-based poetry... Swift has always had a particular talent for describing secret behaviour in exquisite detail - on *folklore* she's outdone herself... Maybe there wasn't a perfect time to release *folklore*. But it's a near-perfect album"; **The Times** - "The pop megastar has turned to sweet folk and it suits her"; **Variety**: "What keeps you locked in, as always, is the notion of Swift as truth-teller, barred or unbarred, in a world of pop spin. She's celebrating the masked era by taking hers off again"; **Washington Post** - "She still falls back on her most reliable lyrical tactics: fairy-tale analogies, teenage memories and rom-com dialogue that give the formless confusion of love a nifty shape. But now her devices tangle and collide in new ways, creating blue sparks".

Folklore had completed Taylor's transformation. It was sonically different from anything she had done before, and only 'Safe & Sound' and 'The Archer' came anywhere near to the style of songwriting we were now seeing. Although the transition came as a complete surprise to both fans and the music world in general, in reality it was just a natural progression.

Over the last few years, her public persona had taken a beating with KanyeGate, resulting in a period of self-imposed isolation prior to the release of *Reputation*. Then came the documentary *Miss Americana* and her self-realisation that her "good girl" image might not be there anymore: "When people decided I was wicked and evil and conniving and not a good person, that was the one thing I couldn't really bounce back from. My whole life was centred around it. The reason why that backlash hurt so much was because that used to be all I had."

It was the beginning of the reinvention of Taylor Swift. Now involved in politics and standing up against those that had done her wrong, the once-upon-a-time kitten had become a lioness, with fans who had matured with her still hanging on to every word she said like the modern-day philosopher and beacon of inspiration she had become.

But it was her songs and her storytelling that now took centre stage, and rightly so, and with *folklore* and the album soon to follow hot on its heels, the music world would finally come to acknowledge that Taylor was one of the most talented songwriters of her generation.

On September 16th Taylor was at the ACM Awards for her first performance there in seven years. Held at the legendary Grand Ole Opry in Nashville, she debuted 'Betty', playing a guitar that had rainbow strings while seated on a stool. For the performance, she wore a sustainable Stella McCartney wardrobe from top to bottom, with a turtleneck covered in maroon sequins, khaki pants with short, pink stripes on each shin, and strappy black kitten heels with gold chains around each ankle. According to *People*, she "wore a curly bun with bangs, and minimal makeup that included rosy cheeks and peach-coloured lipstick", which was seen to replicate her character in the video for 'Cardigan'.

A month later came the Billboard Music Awards in Los Angeles, at which Taylor lost out in the nominations for Top Artist, Top Female Artist, Top Billboard 200 Artist, Top Billboard 200 Album (for *Lover*), Top Song Sales Artist, and the Billboard Chart Achievement.

The Long Pond Sessions

It would be one of the most intimate performances of Taylor's career and the perfect way to showcase the songs from her new album. With Covid restrictions making it impossible to conduct live performances, Taylor and her team of musician/producers came up with the perfect solution.

In September Taylor got together with brothers Aaron and Bryce Dessner, Jack Antonoff and Justin Vernon at the Dessners' secluded Long Pond Studio, a rustic cabin in the woods of the Hudson Valley of upstate New York, and the same studio where *folklore* had been engineered. The studio was on a waterfront estate and had been converted from a barn into a rustic cabin beside an elongated pond.

After isolating themselves separately for several months, the plan was to come together in the same room and make a documentary of recording the complete album live. There would be stripped-down renditions of all 17 songs, performed in album order, with "cozy chats" on the creative process and inspiration behind each song, all done in the tranquil surroundings of a wooden cabin, complete with wine and a blazing fire. Apart from some shots of Taylor in her home studio, the complete film was shot at the cabin.

Dessner recalled: "We played all night and drank a lot of wine after the fireside chat - and we were all pretty drunk, to be honest."

The setting could not have been more perfect, easily evoking the nostalgic, wistful feel of the album. Taylor performed the songs seated on a couch with headphones and wearing an oversized plaid shirt-dress. Aaron Dessner and Jack Antonoff played instruments that included a piano, drum machine, and a variety of guitars and keyboards, with an engineer in the background.

With the absence of a film crew, due to the restrictions, the filming was done with cameras embedded in the studio together with a robotic camera mounted on a curved track. For the duet with Taylor on the song 'Exile', Justin Vernon of Bon Iver appeared from his studio thousands of miles away in Wisconsin via a video stream. Throughout the whole recordings, they would never get to meet in person.

Another detail revealed in the film, and one that came as no real surprise to the Swifties, was that the anonymous songwriter William Bowery, who wrote parts of 'Betty' and 'Exile', was indeed boyfriend Joe Alwyn.

Like the original album, the 106-minute-long film, *folklore: The Long Pond Sessions,* was also a surprise for fans when its release was only announced just hours before its US launch on the Disney+ Channel at midnight on November 25th. As her debut as a film director, this was the perfect example of Taylor at the peak of her creative power. At the same time, the two-disc album *folklore: The Long Pond Studio Sessions (From the Disney+ Special)* was also released to streaming and digital platforms. Disc One was the original deluxe album, while the second disc consisted of the live Long Pond recordings.

Rolling Stone - "On a Thanksgiving weekend where most of us will be too far away from the ones we love the best; this is a gift to be grateful for"; **NME** - "An early Christmas present"; **New York Times** - "A musical experience".

"The most natural thing in the world"

Maybe the biggest surprise of the year for Swifties and the music world in general was the revelation that while *folklore* was being made, there was also a planned second "sister" album under way for release later in the year. For Taylor, it was a spontaneous decision to continue the creative chemistry with Aaron Dessner and Jack Antonoff and make a thematic sequel.

In an interview for *Rolling Stone,* Dessner described how the new album *evermore* (like *folklore*, stylised in lower case) came to be: "It was after we'd written several [songs], seven or eight or nine. Each one would happen, and we would both be in this sort of disbelief of this weird alchemy that we had unleashed. The ideas were coming fast and furiously and were just as compelling as anything on *folklore*, and it felt like the most natural thing in the world."

Speaking to Apple Music, Taylor also described how the album came about: "Even the day after releasing *folklore*, Aaron and I were still bouncing ideas back and forth and we just knew we were gonna keep writing music. With this one I have this feeling of sort of quiet conclusion and sort of this weird serenity of we did what we set out to do and we're all really proud of it, and that feels really, really nice."

The writing process remained the same, with Dessner sending Taylor the instrumental tracks to which she would write lyrics. Dessner recalled that he "didn't need to talk [to her] much about structure or ideas or anything."

After the release of *folklore*, Taylor and Dessner wrote two songs, 'Closure' and 'Dorothea', for Dessner's and Justin Vernon's band Big Red Machine, but, instead, they ended up on *evermore*.

In his interview with *Rolling Stone,* Dessner described his working relationship with Taylor: "I've rarely had this kind of chemistry with anyone in my life - to be able to write together, to make so many beautiful songs together in such a short period of time. Inevitably, I think we will continue to be in each other's artistic and personal lives. I don't know exactly what the next form that will take, but certainly, it will continue. I do think this story, this era, has concluded, and I think in such a beautiful way with these sister records."

Taylor told Dessner that *folklore* felt like spring and summer to her, while *evermore* was fall and winter. From a temporal standpoint, it does feel like an album "set in autumn... with winter chills setting in", with Dessner adding what he called a "wintry nostalgia" to most of the music.

Stolen Lullabies

On November 16th *Variety* reported that Scooter Braun had sold Taylor's master recordings to the private equity firm Shamrock Capital in October, in a deal reported to be worth $300 million. That same day, Taylor posted a statement on Instagram:

"A few weeks ago, my team received a letter from a Disney-owned private equity company called Shamrock Holdings, letting us know that they had bought 100% of my music, videos and album art from Scooter Braun. This was the second time my music has been sold without my knowledge. The letter told me that they wanted to reach out before the sale to let me know, but that Scooter Braun had required that they make no contact with me or my team, or the deal would be off. As soon as we started communication with Shamrock, I learned that under their terms Scooter Braun will continue to profit off my old musical catalog for many years. I was hopeful and open to the possibility of a partnership with Shamrock, but Scooter's participation is a non-starter for me."

The sale of Taylor's artwork to Shamrock would mean it could use the art from her albums, or re-issues of albums (Big Machine had already re-issued all her albums in vinyl), for future merchandise, clothing, and accessories, which Taylor would be unable to block, profit from, or duplicate. As songwriter on all of her songs she had the power to block synchronisation licence requests for films, television, and advertisements, which she had publicly acknowledged she would be "doing with abandon".

However, it was reported by the RIAA that in 2019 the music industry had generated over $11 billion in gross revenues, but only 2.5% was from synchronisation licence fees. The remaining income generated came from physical music sales, digital downloads and streaming, which Taylor was unable to prevent Shamrock (and, for that matter, Braun) from profiting from. As songwriter, however, she still profited from the publishing rights on her masters, and would not be losing out with her old albums being streamed (but neither would Shamrock or Braun, for that matter).

Although it was another bitter pill to swallow, Taylor showed her customary measure of dignity by not disparaging Braun, and finished the statement by saying to her fans: "I have recently begun re-recording my older music and it has already proven to be both exciting and creatively fulfilling. I have plenty of surprises in store. I want to thank you guys for supporting me through this ongoing saga, and I can't wait for you to hear what I've been dreaming up..."

Taylor also claimed that, prior to the sale, she had discussed with Braun the possibility of negotiating control of the masters, but Braun's team wanted her to sign an NDA (non-disclosure contract) preventing her from saying anything about Braun "unless it was positive". Taylor said: "I would have to sign a document that would silence me forever before I could even have a chance to bid for on my own work…He would never even quote my team a price. These master recordings were not for sale to me."

Along with the statement, Taylor also shared a letter she had sent to Shamrock on October 28th in which she said that following the sale, she had had "a great deal of hope for my musical legacy and our possible future [working] together", but now she could not "in good conscience bring myself to be involved in benefiting Scooter Braun's interests directly or indirectly".

Acknowledging the fact that re-recording her old albums would diminish the value of the old masters, she explained to them that it was "my only way of regaining the sense of pride I once had when hearing songs from my first six albums without feelings of guilt for benefiting Scooter".

In a statement obtained by *Billboard*, Shamrock commented on the deal: "Taylor Swift is a transcendent artist with a timeless catalogue. We made this investment because we believe in the immense value and opportunity that comes with her work. We fully respect and support her decision and, while we hope to formally partner, we also knew this was a possible outcome that we considered. We appreciate Taylor's open communication and professionalism with us these last three weeks. We hope to partner with her in new ways moving forward and remain committed to investing with artists in their work".

Although approached for a response by a number of sources, Braun refused to comment.

The good news was that with the coming of November, Taylor was officially "free" to re-record her first six albums as per contract. She told *Good Morning America*: "I'm very excited about it. I just think that artists deserve to own their own work. I just feel very passionately about that."

She celebrated by taking to social media with the hashtag #TaylorisFree. But there was a catch. With the streaming platforms, Taylor was in effect competing with herself. Thousands of Swifties already had her back catalogue in their music libraries, and it was deemed unlikely that they would be willing to fork out for the re-recorded versions, no matter how good they might sound. Only time would tell.

Winter in the forest

In November, Taylor received Apple Music's award for Songwriter of the Year. In her acceptance speech she said: "Winning songwriter of the year in any capacity in any year would be so exciting but I think it's really special because this particular year was a year where I really feel like songwriting was the one thing that was able to keep me connected to fans that I wasn't able to see in concert." That same month she also won Artist of the Year for the third time at the AMA Awards in Los Angeles, and picked up trophies for Favourite Pop/Rock Female Artist and Favourite Music Video (for 'Cardigan'), although *folklore* was pipped for Favourite Pop/Rock Album by Harry Styles' *Fine Line*. Taylor accepted the awards from a Nashville studio where she was working on the re-recording of her album *Fearless*.

Three days short of her birthday, on December 10th, Taylor once again uploaded nine photos on her Twitter account, which put together formed a grid image of the

307

singer's back. Shortly afterward, she dropped a bombshell by announcing, on all social media platforms, the release of a new album:

"I'm elated to tell you that my 9th studio album, and *folklore's* sister record, will be out tonight at midnight eastern. It's called *evermore*. To put it plainly, we just couldn't stop writing songs. To try and put it more poetically, it feels like we were standing on the edge of the folklorian woods and had a choice: to turn and go back or to travel further into the forest of this music. We chose to wander deeper in. I've never done this before. In the past I've always treated albums as one-off eras and moved onto planning the next one after an album was released. There was something different with *folklore*. In making it, I felt less like I was departing and more like I was returning. I loved the escapism I found in these imaginary/not imaginary tales. I loved the ways you welcomed the dreamscapes and tragedies and epic tales of love lost and found into your lives. So, I just kept writing them…"

The post also revealed the track list for the album, and that the single 'Willow' would also be released at the same time as the first single, together with its music video.

In a following message she wrote: "Ever since I was 13, I've been excited about turning 31 because it's my lucky number backwards, which is why I wanted to surprise you with this now. You've all been so caring, supportive and thoughtful on my birthdays, and so this time I thought I would give you something!"

In the liner notes to the album, Taylor described how some of the songs mirrored or intersected with one another:

"The one about two young con artists who fall in love while hanging out at fancy resorts trying to score rich romantic beneficiaries. The one where longtime college sweethearts had very different plans for the same night, one to end it and one who brought a ring. Dorothea, the girl who left her small town to chase down Hollywood dreams - and what happens when she comes back for the holidays and rediscovers an old flame. The 'unhappy ever after' anthology of marriages gone bad that includes infidelity, ambivalent toleration, and even murder. The realisation that maybe the only path to healing is to wish happiness on the one who took it away from you. One starring my grandmother, who still visits me sometimes…if only in my dreams."

The album was release at the stroke of midnight on December 11th, which was also the birthday of Emily Dickinson, the famous poet who had ended her love poem to her partner Sue with the word 'evermore'.

EVERMORE
Label - Republic (UK - EMI)
Recorded - Long Pond Studio, NY; Scarlet Pimpernel UK; Ariel Rechtshaid's house, LA
Produced - Aaron Dessner, Taylor Swift, Bryce Dessner & Jack Antonoff
Released - December 11 2020
Singles - 3
Chart peak positions
  Hot 100 #1; Top Alternative Albums #1UK #1; Canada #1; Australia #1; New Zealand #1;
  Japan #16

Willow *****
(Taylor Swift - Aaron Dessner)
1st Single

Recorded - Long Pond Studio, NY
Produced - Aaron Dessner
Released - December 11 2020
Chart peak positions
  Hot 100 #1; AC #6; Adult To 40 #1; Hot Rock & Alternative Songs #1; UK #3;
  Canada #1; Australia #1; NZ #3

The opening track, which strategically sums up the songs' storytelling style. According to Taylor, it's "about intrigue, desire, and the complexity that goes into wanting someone. I think it sounds like casting a spell to make somebody fall in love with you." Of course, fans are convinced this is about Joe Alwyn.

Following the release of *folklore*, producer Aaron Dessner composed an instrumental he called 'Westerly' (the name given to Taylor's Rhode Island home), and sent it to Taylor. Within an hour, she had written lyrics and sent it back to him with the title 'Willow'. In an interview for Apple Music, she said she chose this for the opening song because Dessner's instrumental felt "witchy" and "magical" and the perfect vibe for the album. While he played most of the instruments on the track, his twin brother Bryce handled the orchestration.

Taylor conveys her romantic state of mind using metaphors such as the willow tree. On November 22nd she had posted on Instagram a photo of her sitting in a wooden cabin, with the caption "Not a lot going on at the moment." Eagle eyes would have noticed a framed picture of a willow tree hanging on the wall. And in a later tweet in which she thanked *Rolling Stone* for ranking *folklore* as the best album of the year, she wrote the comment, "throws self to the base of a willow tree by a reflection pool at midnight."

'Willow' went straight to the top of the charts on its release, becoming Taylor's seventh number one on the Hot 100, and making her the first artist in chart history to debut an album and a single at number one simultaneously on two separate occasions, having already achieved it with *folklore* and 'Cardigan'. This also extended her record for the most debuts in the top ten by a female artist.

The music video was again directed by Taylor, her third, and describes life's twists and turns in finding the right partner. It picks up where the 'Cardigan' video left off, and now back in the cabin, a golden thread in her hands leads her back inside the magical piano which then opens into a rabbit hole underneath a willow tree, from where the thread leads her on a mysterious journey.

Shot under the same safety measures as 'Cardigan', it was released at the same time as the single.

Insider - "Swift can take a deeply tangled human experience - here, the web of desire and admiration and possessiveness, to the point where you'd let the person ruin you - and put it down on paper as if it's the simplest thing to explain"; **Variety** - "'Willow' is a cousin to the previous record's 'Invisible String' and 'Peace', even if it doesn't offer quite as many clearly corroborating details about her current relationship as those did"; **Billboard** - "'Willow' marries the power of Swift's songwriting with the type of careful production details that fans can explore and eventually wrap themselves in"; **Spin** - "A traipsing earworm not unlike *Reputation's* surprise hit "'Delicate'", perhaps better suited for beach bonfires than a trek through Tennessee forests"; **Vulture** - "A love song, but it's so prickly and suspicious it doesn't always sound like one".

Champagne Problems ***
(Taylor Swift - William Bowery)
Recorded - Long Pond Studio, NY
Produced - Taylor Swift & Aaron Dessner
Released - December 11 2020
Chart peak positions
 Hot 100 #21; Hot Rock & Alternative Songs #3; Alternative Digital Songs #6;
 UK #15; Canada #6; Australia #12; NZ #24

A song in which a would-be fiancé with personal issues turns down her boyfriend's earnest marriage proposal right before Christmas, and then accepts responsibility for the heartache that follows.

Taylor describes the story as "longtime college sweethearts [who] had very different plans for the same night, one to end it and one who brought a ring."

Co-written with Joe Alwyn, the song also implies the narrator of the song has a history of mental illness, something Taylor relates to in an interview on the Zach Sang show: "I definitely don't feel good all the time, and I don't think anybody does...there have been times where I needed to take years off because I just felt exhausted, or I felt, like, really low or really bad." Like a number of songs on *evermore*, 'Champagne Problems' feeds into the same aesthetic of its sister album, with a conclusion that hints to the social topics of 'Mad Woman'.

PopMatters - "'Champagne Problems', which describes a relationship dashed by the narrator rejecting a proposal, likely had Swifties clutching their pearls even as Swift explicitly described *evermore* as a set of 'tales' - to be taken seriously but not literally"; **Variety** - "A superb example of her abilities as a storyteller who doesn't always tell all: She's playing the role of a woman who quickly ruins a relationship by balking at a marriage proposal the guy had assumed was an easy enough yes that he'd tipped off his nearby family"; **Iowa State Daily** - "'Champagne Problems' is devastating and leaves listeners reeling in thought and secondhand heartbreak long after the last note. This by far is the best song on the album and arguably in her entire discography".

Gold Rush ***
(Taylor Swift - Jack Antonoff)
Recorded - Rough Customer Studio, Brooklyn; Electric Lady Studios, NY;
 Long Pond Studio, NY
Produced - Taylor Swift & Jack Antonoff
Released - December 11 2020
Chart peak positions
 Hot 100 #40; Hot Rock & Alternative Songs #7; Alternative Digital Songs #12;
 UK Streaming #48; Canada #14; Australia #21

Another fine Swift-Antonoff collaboration in which the narrator daydreams about someone that everybody else wants, but due to her dislike of jealousy and anxiety, and maybe even lack of self-esteem, her fantasy of them being together remains just that - a dream. Some reviews criticise the songwriting for its repetition (it only has six lines that are not repeated), but the instrumentation and the way it changes and shifts the mood is breathtaking.

Slate - "It's where a subdued take on the spirit of *1989*-style pop resurges with necessary energy. Swift is singing about having a crush on someone who's too attractive, too in-demand, and relishing the fantasy, but also enjoying passing it up"; **Hub Pages** - "With a richer instrumental background than the previous two songs and vocal dubbing throughout the track, the gold rush is more about that person who everybody wants."

Tis the Damn Season ***
(Taylor Swift - Aaron Dessner)
Recorded - Long Pond Studio, NY
Produced - Aaron Dessner
Released - December 11 2020
Chart peak positions
  Hot 100 #39; Hot Rock & Alternative Songs #6; Alternative Digital Songs #14;
  UK Streaming #52; Canada #13; Australia #25

Taylor captures the complex and emotional processes of a woman returning to her hometown for the lonely holidays, hoping to rekindle a relationship with her ex "for weekends", while leaving her actual lover behind. With the misleading title and its December release, a "jingle bells" holiday tune was expected, not this tale of seasonal infidelity. Instead, it's a punch to the gut.

The woman in question is Dorothea, who will appear again later in the album. In the liner notes, Taylor describes one of the songs being about "what happens when [Dorothea] comes back [from Hollywood] for the holidays and rediscovers an old flame." Confirmation that she's referring to this track comes with references in the lyrics to both Los Angeles and the winter holidays.

A day before the album's release, Taylor teased her fans: "I also know this holiday season will be a lonely one for most of us and if there are any of you out there who turn to music to cope with missing loved ones the way I do, this is for you." Aaron Dessner recalled that it was written overnight during the *Long Pond Studio Sessions*: "That song, for me, has always felt nostalgic or like some sort of longing. And the song that Taylor wrote is so instantly relatable, you know..."

Slate - "Full of things none of us ought to do this year – go home to visit our parents, hook up with an ex, spend the weekend in their bedroom and their truck, then break their hearts again when we leave. But it's done with such yuletide affection..."; **Utah Statesman** - "From what I can tell, there are no Christmas connections here, unless being drawn back to your hometown love is your type of Christmas song"; **Vulture** - "Blue-Christmas anthem, which is all about the somber ritual of hooking up with your hometown ex over the holidays".

Tolerate It ****
(Taylor Swift - Aaron Dessner)
Recorded - Long Pond Studio, NY
Produced - Aaron Dessner
Released - December 11 2020
Chart peak positions
  Hot 100 #45; Hot Rock & Alternative Songs #8; Alternative Digital Songs #13;
  Alternative Streaming Songs #5; UK Streaming #59; Canada #18; Australia #33

Poignant song about a woman trapped in a relationship with an emotionally withholding, unappreciative man. Reserved for track #5, as the most vulnerable song on the album, the hurt and anger in Taylor's voice leaves many listeners reaching for the tissues. Taylor explained: "I decided on track five because of the lyrics...and how it's so visual, and conveys such a specific kind of hurt." Like many that are both a blessing and a curse, it's another of her gut-wrenching ballads - one has no choice but to feel the emotions being drawn out.

During an interview for Apple Music, Taylor revealed that the song was inspired by reading *Rebecca* by Daphne Du Maurier: "I was thinking, wow, her husband just tolerates her. She's doing all these things and she's trying so hard to impress him, and he's just tolerating her the whole time. There was a part of me that was relating to that, because at some point in my life, I felt that way."

Co-writer Dessner told *Rolling Stone* that after he wrote the piano track, he deemed it "too intense" and initially thought Taylor wouldn't like it: "But I sent it to her, and it conjured a scene in her mind, and she wrote this crushingly beautiful song to it and sent it back. I think I cried when I first heard it."

Renowned for Sound - "'Tolerate It' offers a more melodic piano intro, which makes it a shame this song about unappreciated love is somewhat lyrically weak"; **MTV** - "When you're feeling gaslit or ignored in a relationship, this one is here with a nice warm hug and soul-crushing bridge"; **Consequence of Sound** - "Swift's narrative storytelling is on full display... a quietly devastating domestic portrait of a relationship that has dissolved into ruins"; **The Franklin Post** - "The song begins with an unassuming piano sequence and evolves into something sweeping as Swift enters. Shifting between ice-cold and pleading, her voice tells a story of trying so hard for someone, of giving everything, and receiving only shallow appreciation in return."

No Body, No Crime (featuring Haim) ****
(Taylor Swift)
2nd Single
Recorded – Long Pond Studio, NY; Ariel Rechtshaid's House, LA (Haim's vocals)
Produced - Taylor Swift & Aaron Dessner
Released - January 11 2021
Chart peak positions
  Hot 100 #34; UK #19; Canada #11; Australia #16; New Zealand #29

After eight albums, Taylor's obsession with true crime stories is finally revealed with this murder-and-disposing-of-the body song. It was inspired by the famous real-life disappearance of five-year-old Marjorie West in Pennsylvania in 1938, which, although heavily covered by the media, still remains unsolved. While the family were picnicking to celebrate Mother's Day, Marjorie's 11-year-old sister Dorothea left her alone for a few minutes, and when she returned, she had disappeared and was never seen again.

In Taylor's crime story, we learn that the narrator's best friend Este has a husband who is acting very differently and smells of infidelity. When Este fails to show up to Olive Garden one day, her best friend and her sister set out to get revenge on the person they suspect is involved in her disappearance - the same person whose mistress just happens to be sleeping in Este's bed. Taylor's twist is that the narrator isn't after revenge on her own husband, but on her best friend's husband and framing the husband's mistress for the murder.

For this delightfully twisted track, Taylor invited along her longtime friends Este and Danielle Haim to provide backing vocals, her first collaboration with them. Returning to her country roots, Taylor wrote the song on a rubber-bridge guitar and forwarded it on a voice memo to Dessner to do the instrumentation. The Haim sisters then recorded their vocals at the home studio of engineer Ariel Rechtshaid in Los Angeles, which were then sent on to Taylor at Long Pond, who at the time was filming the *Long Pond Sessions* special.

Talking to *Entertainment Weekly*, Taylor recalled working with Este Haim: "I had finished the song and was nailing down some lyric details and texted her, 'You're not going to understand this text for a few days but – which chain restaurant do you like best?' And I named a few. She chose Olive Garden and a few days later I sent her the song and asked if they would sing on it. It was an immediate 'Yes'."

Slate - "A straight-up contemporary country song, specifically a twist on and a tribute to the wronged-woman vengeance songs that were so popular more than a decade ago"; **The Ringer** - "Somehow both an *evermore* highlight and one of the record's gravest disappointments. It's a semi-cheeky murder ballad in the grand tradition of the Chick's 'Goodbye Earl'. But it's just not cheeky or that matter camp enough"; **Hellgate Lance** - "Inspired by a mix of old film noir films, true crime documentaries, and a long-standing tradition of female revenge songs in country music"; **Vulture** - "More like a musical costume party than a genuine attempt at embodying darkness".

Happiness ****
(Taylor Swift - Aaron Dessner)
Recorded - Long Pond Studio, NY; Scarlet Pimpernel Studios, London (vocals)
Produced - Aaron Dessner
Released - December 11 2020
Chart peak positions
  Hot 100 #52, Hot Rock & Alternative Songs #9; Alternative Digital Songs #8;
  Alternative Streaming Songs #7; UK Streaming #66; Canada #24; Australia #37

Taylor mourns a crumbling relationship, but looks to the future and tries to see the good in even the worst days. According to Dessner, he had been working on the instrumental for 'Happiness' for over a year, and believed it would be a Big Red Machine song. But Taylor loved the music so much it was decided to include it on the album with quickly-penned lyrics.

This, and the bonus track 'Right Where You Left Me', were the last two tracks written for the album, according to Dessner: "I walked into the studio and Jon Low, our engineer here, was mixing and had been working the whole time toward this. And I came in and he's in the middle of mixing and I was like, 'There are two more songs'. And he looked at me, like …'We're not gonna make it.' Because it does take a lot of time to work out how to finish them. But she sang them remotely." The track was completed just a week before release.

In describing the song on a live chat, Taylor said: "Happiness is a very deceptive title. That's all I'll I say."

Definitely a song to make one feel acceptance and peace.

Just Random Things - "Taylor thinks he wants to apologise for dragging this relationship to the grave. But is she willing to forgive? The old Taylor might have"; **MSN** - "Seemingly named for Daisy's first words in the F Scott Fitzgerald novel [*The Great Gatsby*], "I'm p-paralysed with happiness", the soothing ballad finds Swift stepping into the character's lovelorn shoes."

313

Dorothea ****
(Taylor Swift - Aaron Dessner)
Recorded - Long Pond Studios, NY; Kitty Committee Studio, LA (vocals)
Produced - Aaron Dessner
Released - December 11 2020
Chart peak positions
 Hot 100 #67; Hot Rock & Alternative Songs #13; Alternative Streaming Songs #10;
 UK Streaming #74; Canada #34; Australia #47

The first song Taylor wrote for the album, about the small-town lover who the ambitious LA actress, Dorothea, (from the song 'Tis the Damn Season'), has left behind in Tupelo, perhaps years after their Christmas tryst. In full, old high school-romance mode, Taylor conjures up a song that could easily be seen as another extension to the teenage love triangle.

Taylor referred to the song as a "girl who left her small town to chase down Hollywood dreams", but then clarified that the narrative is "not a direct continuation of the Betty/James/August storyline, but in [her] mind Dorothea went to the same school as Betty, James and Inez."

The song sparked off speculation that it was about none other than Selena Gomez, with the name referring to Selena's favourite movie, *The Wizard of Oz*, and since "Dorothy" was also the name of a character she played in *The Fundamentals of Caring*. Taylor also sings about "mom and her pageant schemes" on the track, potentially referencing the pageants Selena took part in as a child.

Grazia - "She writes to an old friend that she is no longer close with, letting them know she only has 'well wishes' and wondering if she's still the same person she knew growing up...You would think people would be more concerned with figuring out who of the men that have caused her heartbreak she's wrote about this time around"; **Vulture** - "A wistful recollection of the narrator's high-school relationship with the title character, who skipped town, became a big star, and never looked back."

Coney Island (featuring The National) ***
(Taylor Swift - William Bowery - Aaron Dessner - Bryce Dessner)
3rd Single
Recorded - Long Pond Studio, NY; Scarlet Pimpernel Studios, London (vocals)
Produced - Aaron Dessner & Bryce Dessner
Released - January 18 2021
Chart peak positions
 Hot 100 #63; Hot Rock & Alternative Songs #12; Alternative Digital Songs
 #23; Alternative Streaming Songs #9; UK #75; Canada #31; Australia #42

Taylor duets with the National's wistful lead vocalist Matt Berninger in a melancholic song about a couple sharing memories of their past relationship, and evoking feelings of both loss and nostalgia in the settings of Brooklyn's famous seafront playground.

After working for months with the National's Aaron Dessner on both *folklore* and *evermore*, this is Taylor's first collaboration with the entire band. Dessner recalled in an interview with *Rolling Stone* how he and his brother Bryce were working on a bunch of music, some of which they had sent to Taylor: "Taylor and [Joe Alwyn] wrote this incredible song, and we first recorded it with just her vocals. It has this really beautiful arc to the story, and I think it's one of the strongest, lyrically and musically...We started talking about how it would be cool to get the band, and I called Matt [Berninger] and he was excited for it. We got Bryan [Devendorf] to play drums and we got Scott [Devendorf] to play bass and a pocket piano, and Bryce helped produce it. It's weird, because it does really feel like Taylor, obviously, since she and [Joe] wrote all the words, but it feels like a National song in a good way."

Berninger described working with Taylor as "like dancing with Gene Kelly. She made [him] look good and didn't drop [him] once". Taylor's vocals were recorded in both Los Angeles and London studios.

Iowa State Daily - "Swift is not successful because of her voice or musical talents, but her songwriting capabilities and her expert lyricism, and that is further displayed by this song"; **Contact Music** - "An acoustic indie rock number whereby the gravelly tone of Matt Berninger's voice adds a certain depth, contrasting beautifully with Taylor's sweet, airy vocal"; **Spin** - "A lonely waltz down a Brooklyn boardwalk. The merger of Swift's wispy head voice and Berninger's bass is sinfully good".

Ivy ***
(Taylor Swift - Aron Dessner- Jack Antonoff)
Recorded - Long Pond Studio, NY
Produced - Aaron Dessner
Released - December 11 2020
Chart peak positions
  Hot 100 #61; Hot Rock & Alternative Songs #11; Alternative Digital Songs #16;
  Alternative Streaming Songs #8; UK Streaming #77; Canada #28; Australia #43

Taylor writes about a married woman being drawn into a clandestine affair. The subject of infidelity had recently been covered on *folklore* with the excellent songs 'Illicit Affairs' and 'August', and Taylor wrote on Twitter: "The 'unhappy after' anthology of marriages gone bad that includes infidelity, ambivalent toleration, and even murder."

Once more, it is a song overrun with metaphors and brimming with good Swiftian dark-fairytale grist that fans have to puzzle over. Unlike other songs, where the perspective is of the person being cheated on, this shows an understanding rather than blame. According to *Hollywood Life*, the track is part of a three-song trilogy "inspired by stories she's heard, movies she's seen and more", and follows on from 'Tolerate It' and 'No Body, No Crime'.

Iowa State Daily - "The lyrics paint a more complicated story of infidelity and desire…The song is similar to 'Dorothea' in the sense that on the surface, the songs are enjoyable to listen to yet are more than just skin deep upon more attentive listening"; **Insider** - "'Ivy' is a member of the album's 'anthology of marriage gone bad', telling the story of a woman who's falling in love without her husband. But Swift knits whimsy and intimacy into this would-be story of traditional failure"; **Vulture** - "Swift play a woman who's fallen head over heels for a man who's not her husband. A tragic setup, but there's an ecstasy in her voice".

Cowboy Like Me *****
(Taylor Swift - Aaron Dessner)
Recorded - Long Pond Studio, NY
Produced - Aaron Dessner
Released - December 11 2020

Chart peak positions

Hot 100 #71; Hot Rock & Alternative Songs #15; Alternative Digital Songs #24;
Alternative Streaming Songs #13; UK Streaming #91; Canada #43; Australia #55

A song about two gold-digging con artists whose cat-and-mouse fling of scamming people comes undone when they fall in love with each other. Some compare the plot similarities to the 1931 romantic comedy *Blonde Crazy,* starring James Cagney and Joan Blondell.

Taylor described the song as "two young con artists who fall in love while hanging out at fancy resorts trying to score rich romantic beneficiaries". Backing vocals are provided by Marcus Munford, lead singer of English band Munford & Sons. Taylor wrote on Twitter: "I loved creating these songs with Aaron Dessner, Jack Antonoff, WB, and Justin Vernon. We've also welcomed some new (and longtime) friends to our kitchen table this time around."

Billboard - "On a song that finds Swift circling around thoughts of love, independence and commitment in the context of another with a similar mindset, she and Dessner offer an ambitious mix of folk, sun-kissed alternative and a whiff of country music that Swift was once rooted in"; **Vulture** - "This twangy ballad about con artists who fall in love feels like the work of that alternate-reality Swift. Fortunately, the lived-in cynicism of the lyrics belies the tune's anonymous qualities".

Long Story Short ***
(Taylor Swift - Aaron Dessner)
Recorded - Long Pond Studio, NY
Produced - Aaron Dessner
Released - December 11 2020
Chart peak position

Hot 100 #68; Hot Rock & Alternative position #14; Alternative Digital Songs #17;
Alternative Streaming Songs #12; UK Streaming #84; Canada #39; Australia #49

Taylor sums up her own four-year journey with Joe Alwyn, with references to some of the turmoil she had to experience along the way (like West and Hiddleston), and how, by having him as her "safe place", she has finally found resolution and peace.

In an interview with Paul McCartney for *Time* magazine, Taylor spoke about how Alwyn had changed her life: "I think that in knowing him and being in the relationship I am in now, I have definitely made decisions that have made my life feel more like a real life and less like just a storyline to be commented on in tabloids. Whether that's deciding where to live, who to hang out with, when to not take a picture - the idea of privacy feels so strange to try to explain, but it's really just trying to find bits of normalcy."

Vulture - "*Reputation* found Swift playing at being over it while clearly not being over it; here, the sentiment finally feels genuine. I think I speak for everyone, though, when I say we'd be fine with this being her final word on the subject".

Marjorie *****
(Taylor Swift - Aaron Dessner)
Recorded - Long Pond Studio, NY
Produced - Aaron Dessner
Released - December 11 2020
Chart peak positions

Hot 100 #75; Hot Rock & Alternative Songs #16; Alternative Digital Songs #18; Alternative Streaming Songs #14; UK Streaming #94; Canada #48; Australia #57

Taylor drops another emotional bombshell with this tribute to her late grandmother Marjorie Finlay, who died in 2003, and was the one who inspired her to pursue a career in music. In one of her most evocative songs, Taylor thanks her for life-lessons given, even quoting her special words of wisdom, "Never be so kind you forget to be clever...Never be so clever you forget to be kind", and wishing she could have learned much more from her had she lived.

Seen as the companion song to *folklore's* 'Epiphany', and *Lover's* 'Soon You'll Get Better', this is as personal as it gets for Taylor. Toward the end of the song, Taylor uses old recordings of Marjorie's operatic voice behind the lines in which she imagines her grandmother is singing to her.

In an interview for *Rolling Stone*, Dessner revealed: "I collect a lot of rhythmic elements like that, and all kinds of other sounds, and I give them to my friend Ryan Olson, who's a producer from Minnesota and has been developing this crazy software called Allovers Hi-Hat Generator. It can take sounds, any sounds, and split them into identifiable sound samples, and then regenerate them in randomised patterns that are weirdly very musical...That's how I made the backing rhythm for 'Marjorie'. Then I wrote a song on it, and Taylor wrote to that. In a weird way, it's one of the most experimental songs of the album."

By what may be a coincidence, 'Marjorie' and 'Epiphany', the two songs about her grandparents, are both track #13 of their respective albums.

Rolling Stone - "A heart-shredding masterpiece...It's not just the centrepiece of a stunning album, it's a song that ties up all her favourite obsessions into a story of love, death, and grief. It's one of the best things she's ever done. It's a new peak for her as a story-teller"; **Iowa State Daily** - "This song is for Swift, and if other people are just so happy to enjoy it, that's a happy coincidence"; **The Franklin Post** - "Grandmotherly advice, lovely tales, and ghostly occurrences make this song as memorable as the woman it commemorates - a comfort for anyone who has lost a family member".

Closure ***
(Taylor Swift - Aaron Dessner)
Recorded - Long Pond Studio, NY
Produced - Aaron Dessner, B J Burton & James McAlister
Released - December 11 2020
Chart peak positions
Hot 100 #82; Hot Rock & Alternative Songs #17; Alternative Streaming Songs 15; Canada #57

A curious track in which the narrator is frustrated when a past enemy reaches out to her and expects there to be no animosity left between them, and also one of those songs that Swifties have found hard to decode. Names like Harry Styles, Tom Hiddleston, and even former longtime friend Karlie Kloss have been suggested as the subject.

Kloss seems to be the front runner, as they were no longer being seen together. The fallout seems to go back to 2016 when Kloss referred to Kim Kardashian as a "lovely person". This was followed with the music video for 'Look What You

Made Me Do' in which Taylor wore a t-shirt with all her friends' names on - except that of Kloss, who at the time had become friends with both Katy Perry and Scooter Braun.

If that wasn't evidence enough, when Kloss married Joshua Kushner in 2019, with Scooter Braun among the guests, Taylor was conspicuous by her absence. The marriage to Kushner also made Kloss the sister-in-law to Jared Kushner and Ivanka Trump. Even when Taylor was involved in the harrowing legal dispute with Braun, Kloss was content to spend her "new life" in the company of new friends, including Braun.

In an interview with *Elle* in 2019, Taylor said: "It's sad, but sometimes when you grow, you outgrow relationships. You may leave behind friendships along the way, but you'll always keep the memories." Of course, this remains speculation, and one that still keeps her fans' fingers busy on social media.

Although Taylor has never revealed who it's about, she did make the comment: "*evermore* deals a lot in endings of all sorts, shapes, and sizes, all the kind of ways we can end a relationship, a friendship, something toxic, and the pain that goes along with that."

The song was also co-produced by Brandon "BJ" Burton, who had worked extensively with Justin Vernon and Bon Iver, and drummer James McAlister, who had previously worked on *folklore*. Dessner recalled working with Vernon at his Wisconsin studio where they processed Taylor's vocals for the song through his Messina chain: "He was really deeply involved in this record, even more so than the last record."

The Cowl - "The narrator addresses someone attempting to neatly end a relationship with them, frustrated that the addressee insincerely wants to wash their hands of the failed connection"; **Vulture** - "Features one of the bigger production swings of Swift's quarantine era, an industrial drum track that sparks up a song that otherwise remains subdued".

Evermore (featuring Bon Iver) ****
(Taylor Swift - William Bowery - Justin Vernon)
Recorded – Long Pond Studio, NY; April Base, Fall Creek WI (Vernon's vocals)
Produced - Taylor Swift & Aaron Dessner
Released - December 11 2020
Chart peak positions
  Hot 100 #57; Hot Rock & Alternative Songs #10, Alternative Digital Songs
  #5; Alternative Streaming Songs #11; UK Streaming #85; Canada #26;
  Australia #45

For the title track, we have another fine Taylor-Alwyn collaboration and another duet with Bon Iver (Justin Vernon). Taylor relates the emotive story of someone who is suffering from a long period of low mental state before realising that the pain will not be permanent, concluding the album with a hopeful "this too will pass" sentiment.

For Taylor's remarkable vocal exchange with Vernon, Dessner pointed out the contrast between this performance and that of 'Exile', for which Vernon's voice remains on his lower register, while Taylor counters with her higher range; on 'Evermore', she sings in her lower range against Vernon's full multitracked upper register.

Joe Alwyn also plays piano on the track and recorded it remotely.

With vaccines now finally being approved and distributed in the fight against the Covid-19 pandemic, this message of hope serves as the perfect song to complete the album and bring an end to the most difficult of years.

Affinity - "Providing a hopeful and satisfying end to two albums that were born out of the devastation that has been this year"; **Lamar Life** - "Every single lyric in this song is so powerful and it ends with a message of hope, which is so eloquent and something that we all need to hear"; **NME** - "It's a sentiment of hope for the future to finish a pair of albums created in the mess that has been this year"; **Spin** - "The piano blueprint jarringly shifts from Vernon's section and the grand call and response that follows. There will be some argument as to whether the passage is experimental magic or they just barely pulled it off"; **Vulture** - "If the duo's vocal parts feel uncomfortably stitched together at times, at least they come together for a rousing back-and-forth climax".

Right Where You Left Me ***
(Taylor Swift - Aaron Dessner)
Evermore Deluxe Editions
Recorded - Long Pond Studios, NY; Scarlet Pimpernel Studios, London (vocals)
Produced - Aaron Dessner
Released - January 7 2021
Chart peak positions
  Hot 100 Bubbling Under #12; Hot Rock & Alternative Songs #10; Alternative
  Digital Songs #2; UK Streaming #22; Canada Digital #20; Australia Digital #7

The narrator is sitting on her own in the dim light of a restaurant, her heart broken after the breakup of a relationship, and, as a result, remains stuck in the loss, while she sees everybody else moving forward in life, and in time. Taylor described the song's subject on Instagram, as someone "who stayed forever in the exact spot where her heart was broken, completely frozen in time."

Along with 'Happiness', these were the last tracks written for the album. Seemingly reflecting on what it's like to be abandoned by someone close and the devastating experience of then being frozen out, it has been speculated that this is another song that relates to her breakup with Karlie Kloss, as does the following track, only with a little more conviction.

Vulture - "Swift sings from the perspective of a woman who's been frozen at the time and place she got dumped".

It's Time to Go ****
(Taylor Swift - Aaron Dessner)
Evermore Deluxe Editions
Produced - Aaron Dessner
Released - January 7 2021
Chart peak positions
  Hot 100 Bubbling Under #4; Hot Rock & Alternative Songs #9; Alternative
  Digital Songs #1; UK Streaming #20; Canada #86; Australia Digital #5

While the previous track is about dwelling on the past, this song is about having the courage to let go. Taylor describes it as "listening to your gut when it tells you to leave. How you always know before you know, you know?" With Taylor's experience of when to exit a relationship, Swifties were furiously sifting through the lyrics to find out who this was about, speculating that it could refer to either the highly publicised legal battle with Scooter Braun or former best friend Karlie Kloss.

Dessner commented on the song on Twitter: "The moment that the slide guitar and drums hit when Taylor sings 'that will find you the right thing'…and the whole arc of the song after…to me feels like such a beautiful, cathartic ending to *folklore* and *evermore*".

The song was apparently left off the standard album in favour of 'Happiness'.

Vulture - "Another post-breakup catharsis song".

The Woodvale mystery

The day after *evermore* was released, the *Daily Mail* published an article about Taylor and Joe Alwyn being married and reached out to Alwyn's family for comment: "They refused to dispel speculation about any secret union between the love-up pair, who have dating since the summer of 2016. A member of Joe's family laughed and told MailOnline: I'm sorry, I'm not going to say anything." That same day, Taylor went on social media and shared photos of the two of them on vacation in Utah, taken earlier in the year.

Meanwhile Swifties were once again getting in a flap over what seemed like the likelihood of a third album to follow shortly, completing what they thought was always intended to be a trilogy. Eagle-eyes had already noticed that the name "Woodvale" was carefully hidden on the cover of the hide-and-seek version of the *folklore* art. Not only did the word contain eight letters like the other two album titles, but Woodville was also the name of an estate in the English Lake District, the very place where Taylor and Alwyn had spent a vacation and which inspired her to write 'The Lakes'. When word got round that the Woodville estate had just been purchased, fans suspected that maybe the lovebirds had finally found their idyllic getaway cottage, in the romantic place where "all the poets went to die".

The day after celebrating her 31st birthday, Taylor guested on *Jimmy Kimmel Live* to talk about *evermore*, an album that the host described as like the "third season of *Lost*", due to the number of clues to be unravelled. Kimmel quizzed her about the "Woodvale" rumour, and Taylor replied: "I tend to be sort of annoyingly secret agent-y about dropping hints and clues and Easter eggs. It's very annoying but it's fun, and it's fun for me, because they like to pick up on things, and they'll notice lots of things in music videos, or whatever. And sometimes I take it too far and I made a mistake."

She then explained that while making *folklore*, she was "too afraid to even unveil the title to even my closest team mates and management. I didn't tell anyone the album title until it came out." She admitted that she came up with a "fake name" for folklore that had the same number of letters, and chose "Woodvale". "I wanted to see how they would look on the album covers, mocked them up, then decided I don't actually want to have a title on the album cover. And we forgot to take the fake code name off one of them."

There was no reason not to believe her, but, hey, this is Taylor Swift.

"The free-wheeling younger sibling"

On its release, *evermore* sold one million copies worldwide in its first week alone, Taylor's third album in 16 months to achieve that figure, and her the eighth consecutive studio album to do so. With the sales of *folklore* and *evermore*, she became the best-selling solo and female artist of the year, and second overall after BTS.

Although not available in physical copies during its first week of release, *evermore* beat the record held by its sister album for the biggest sales week and biggest streaming week in the US for a non-r&b/hip-hop album. It also made Taylor the third female artist to have eight number one albums, behind Barbra Streisand with eleven and Madonna with nine. With *folklore* reaching #3 on the Hot 200, Taylor became the first female artist to simultaneously have two albums in the top three in the chart's history.

With the two sister albums debuting within 140 days of each other, they achieved a world record for the shortest-ever gap between two chart-topping albums by a woman on the Hot 200. Taylor also extended her record as the female artist with the most weeks at number one on the Hot 200, tying with Michael Jackson for fourth overall.

All 15 tracks on the standard edition of *evermore* debuted simultaneously on the Hot 100, which made the album Taylor's third to chart all its standard tracks in the same week, and she also regained the record from Nicki Minaj for the female artist with the greatest number of Hot 100 hits in chart history with 128.

With eight tracks from *folklore* sitting on the Hot 100 alongside 14 from *evermore*, Taylor occupied 22 of the chart's fifty positions - the second most simultaneous entries in chart history since Linkin Park's 23.

In the UK, Taylor became the fastest female artist to have six number one albums in the chart (in the eight years 2012-2020), beating Madonna's record, for the period 1997-2008. She also became the first female artist to score six UK chart-topping albums in the 21st century.

Evermore also became her eighth chart-topper in Canada with all of the tracks debuting simultaneously, and 'Willow' becoming her seventh number-one single there, a feat also achieved in Australia. What's more, it went on to achieve the largest vinyl sales week in Nielsen history, with 102,000 copies, easily beating the record held by Jack White's *Lazaretto.*

In June 2021, *evermore* rose 73 places to #1 on the Hot 200 as a result of its vinyl release. It also marked the 53rd chart-topping week of her career, thus extending her record as the female act with the most weeks at #1 in Hot 200 history, and the third-most weeks overall, behind The Beatles and Elvis Presley.

The reviews for *evermore* were as expected:

American Songwriter - "Birth order matters here. If *folklore* is the archetypal older sister - a careful, yet hopeless romantic - then *evermore* is the bold, scrappy younger one. The record throws caution to the wind, baring secrets with little shame. Yet, its soundscape reflects the imitative patterns a younger sister can't help but follow faithfully....July's *folklore* was bound into a lush woodland fairytale, establishing a phantasmal motif. Her latest, *evermore*, is a Yuletided extension of the wistful wonderland. Except here, golden hour is cut short and wintery weather looms overhead"; **Evening Standard** - "Swift has morphed seamlessly from stadium superstar to woodland wanderer, crafting restrained ballads ideal for holed-up winter listening"; **Buzzfeed**: "In 2020, for those who wanted or needed it, Taylor Swift delivered what used to be normal: last-minute plans, something to talk about, something to enjoy, something to stay up for, something that will endure, a good surprise"; **PopMatters** - "On *folklore* and *evermore*, she, and her listeners, have turned her life into *folklore*, a blend of reality and fiction, lost in those deep woods of quarantine where she sits and writes arguably the best music of her career"; **New York Times** - "The sonic details of *evermore* are radiant and meticulous; the songwriting is poised and careful. It's an album to respect. But with all its constructions and conceits, it also keeps a certain emotional distance"; **The Independent -** " Swift has said she has no idea where she's going from here. She doesn't need to. But it's a Christmas treat to hear her enjoy creating a whole magical, mystical world away from the spotlight. No reinvention required"; **NME** - "If *folklore* is an introspective, romantic older sister, *evermore* is the freewheeling younger sibling. *folklore* was Swift's masterful songwriting spun through a very specific sonic palette; *evermore* feels looser, with more experimentation, charm and musical shades at play"; **Chicago Tribune** - "Too many of the remaining songs on *evermore* feel like leftovers from *folklore*, with recycled vocal cadences and melodic phrases or lyrical scenarios that seem unfinished"; **The Guardian** - "It's unclear where the stylistic shift of *folklore* and *evermore* is heading, whether it's a momentary diversion or a path Swift intends to continue down…Not everything here works, but taken together *folklore* and *evermore* make a convincing case for Swift's ability to shift shape and for her songs' ability to travel between genres: as lockdown overachievements go, it's pretty impressive"; **Rolling Stone** - "Granted, none of these stories are executed with more or less finesse than the ones on *folklore*. Whether by design, or simply by which songs she decided to put on which album, *evermore's* most revelatory moments come when Swift turns the mythmaking back around to herself"; **Spin** - "*evermore* is undeniable in about a half-dozen exciting ways, most of which defy all unwritten rules handcuffing many of Swift's constituents…At the top of her game and riding her greatest songwriting wave to date, Swift will write and release what she wants, when she wants".

In an interview for *NME*, Taylor reflected on the songwriting for the two albums: "There was a point that I got to as a writer who only wrote very diaristic songs that I felt it was unsustainable for my future moving forward. It felt too hot of a microscope. On my bad days, I would feel like I was loading a cannon of clickbait, when that's not what I want for in my life. I think when I put out *folklore*, I felt like if I can do this thing where I get to create characters in this mythological American town or wherever I imagine them, and I can reflect my own emotions onto what I think they might be feeling and I can create stories and characters and arcs, I don't have it feel like when I put out an album, I'm just giving tabloids ammunition and stuff."

Taylor explained that this new style of songwriting enabled her to feel that she was able to "maintain a place of good mental health and emotional health and all that. I saw a lane for my future and that was a real breakthrough moment of excitement and happiness." With *evermore*, she had a "feeling of quiet conclusion and this weird serenity of we did what we set out to do."

The Best is Still to Come

"These songs were once about my life. Now they are about yours"

Evermore vs *evermore*

In a world that had been changed forever by the pandemic, it would seem trivial and even shallow to talk about its impact on music. But with the great human desire to return to some kind of normalcy, it had a part to play.

With an ironic twist of fate, being locked down had unlocked the best music of Taylor's career, and, in doing so, had surprised millions of her fans by giving them something to talk about, to savour, and, as it turned out, something to help them endure what for many was their worst time.

With three albums completed in a little over 18 months (including *Lover*), there had been no chance to test them out on tour, and it would remain a frustrating time for both Taylor and her fans worldwide. What would a tour have looked like, anyway, with four or more hours of material to sift through?

In the meantime, Taylor had been subtly donating money and offering financial help to families struggling during the crisis. In March she joined her mother to combine their donations of $50,000 to make up the GoFundMe goal of a mother of five daughters widowed after her husband had died of Covid a week before Christmas. In December, Taylor had also donated $13,000 each to two Nashville mothers struggling financially, and helped others who had lost their jobs and owed money and faced eviction. She also donated thousands of dollars to fans who had tweeted her after taking financial hits.

Taylor had also quietly kept a Nashville record store afloat after it was forced to close through Covid, and had paid the staff salaries and healthcare for the next three months.

In February 2021, Taylor's legal team was faced with yet another challenge, and it came from the most unlikely source. A fantasy theme park in Pleasant Grove, Utah, called Evermore Park, filed a lawsuit against Taylor and her team for allegedly infringing its trademark name, and sought to prevent further use of the word. They demanded "statutory damages of $2 million per counterfeit mark per type of goods or services sold" or a part of the revenues from the use of the title, including all legal fees.

Back on December 29th, the park's counsel had delivered a cease-and-desist letter to Taylor's legal team, to which they declined to abide and hit back at with the claim: "If anything, your client's website traffic has actually increased as a result of the release of Ms Swift's recent album which, in turn, could only serve to enhance your client's mark."

The park then came back with the claim that the title of the album was confusing their customers and "negatively affects the park's searchability", and that their staff were being asked by customers if the album was a collaboration between Taylor and the park. What's more, their official website had seen a 330.4% surge in comparison to the previous day which, according to them, was affecting their "Google footprint". The lawsuit also pointed out that their merchandise and original music under the "Evermore" trademark had become "harder to find" since the day of the album's release.

Team Taylor denied all accusations and called the lawsuit "baseless", claiming that it was "inconceivable" that each party's merchandise could cause confusion. According to *Billboard*, they also revealed that the park's founder and CEO, Ken Bretschneider, already had five lawsuits filed against him and his group by major construction companies claiming they were owned between $28,000 and $400,000 in unpaid fees for work on the park.

On February 24th Swift's team countersued the park for allegedly infringing Taylor's songs 'Love Story', 'You Belong to Me' and 'Bad Blood' by continually using them in performances without a licence, "blatantly" ignoring numerous notices from the publishing company BMI, and also revealed that Bretschneider, after anticipating a lawsuit, had sought a retroactive licence from BMI that would cover all performances dating as far back as 2018.

In March, it was reported by a spokesperson for Taylor's team that, by way of a resolution, both parties had decided to "drop and dismiss their respective suits without monetary settlement."

There was also an issue with the name *folklore*, when it was revealed that the African clothing company The Folklore had got their lawyers involved after finding out that the official album merchandise was using their name in a similar style logo. CEO Amira Rasool, speaking to *InStyle*, said: "Clearly Taylor didn't find The Folklore and make this sketch, but at the end of the day, Taylor is the one who's profiting off of it. This is her team, so it's up to her to make it right." And Taylor did make it right, smoothly and swiftly, and had the logo altered. She then personally tweeted Rasool to make a pledge: "Amira, I admire the work you're doing and I'm happy to make a contribution to your company and to support the Black in Fashion Council with a donation."

The calculated risk

In light of the current surge in Covid cases, it came as no surprise when, on February 26th, Taylor took to Twitter to tell her millions of fans that Lover Fest had now been cancelled and would not be rescheduled:

"I love coming on her to tell you good news, or to share a new project with you. It's not my favourite thing in the world to have to tell you news I'm sad about. I'm so sorry, but I cannot reschedule the shows that we've postponed. Although refunds have been available since we first postponed the *Lover Fest* shows, many of you hung onto your tickets and I too hung onto the idea that we could reschedule. This is an unprecedented pandemic that has changed everyone's plans and no one knows what the touring landscape is going to look like in the near future. I'm so disappointed that I won't be able to see you in person as soon as I wanted to. I miss you terribly and can't wait til we can all safely be at shows together again."

Despite this disappointment, Taylor was far from being at a loss for something to do musically. Ever since the hidden messages surrounding the release of *folklore* and *evermore*, Swifties had been speculating that there was a third album in the pipeline. On February 11th she had posted a message on social media: "I'm thrilled to tell you that my new version of *Fearless (Taylor's Version)* is done and will be with you soon. It has 26 songs including 6 never before released songs from the vault. 'Love Story (Taylor's Version)' will be out tonight. Pre-order now…"

Although she didn't announce the release date for the album, she hinted it in a long coded essay on social media that was written entirely in lower case except for the letters APRIL NINTH.

In the message Taylor reflected on the original groundbreaking album:

"*Fearless* was an album full of magic and curiosity, the bliss and devastation of youth. It was the diary of the adventures and explorations of a teenage girl who was learning tiny lessons with every new crack in the façade of the fairytale ending she'd been shown in the movies."

Taylor then reiterated why she was re-recording it: "Artists should own their own work for so many reasons, but the most screamingly obvious one is that the artist is the one who really *knows* that body of work, for example, only I know which songs I wrote that almost made it to the *Fearless* album. Songs I absolutely adored, but were held back for different reasons (don't want too many breakup songs, don't want too many down-tempo songs, can't fit that many songs on a physical cd). Those reasons seem unnecessary now. I've decided I want you to have the whole story, see the entire vivid picture, and let you into the entire dreamscape that is my *Fearless* album…"

According to *The Guardian* on February 11th, it was assumed that Taylor's hardcore fanbase, by showing support for her battle to own her own music, would forsake the original recordings of her first six albums in favour of the new versions. Recording began in late November 2020, but it was a calculated risk. Only time would tell.

Just ahead of Valentine's Day, the single 'Love Story (Taylor's Version)' was released, along with a lyric video on YouTube, and followed a few weeks later by an electronic version, remixed by Swedish producer Elvira, and one of the previously unreleased tracks, 'You All Over Me'. Although the jury may have been out on the remix, hearing the song raised "from the vault" for the very first time had many of her fans in raptures.

In an interview on the *People* tv show in April, Taylor described the recreation process for *Fearless* and how she wanted to retain the essence of the Grammy-award-winning original: "In terms of production, I really wanted to stay very loyal to the initial melodies that I had thought of for these songs. And so, we really did go in and try to create a 'the same but better' version. We kept all the same parts that I initially dreamed up for these songs. But if there was any way that we could improve upon the sonic quality, we did. We just kind of took all the knowledge that we've acquired over decades of playing this music and applied that to it…But yeah, I did go in line by line and listen to every single vocal and think, you know, what are my inflections here. If I can improve upon it, I did. But I really did want this to be very true to what I initially thought of and what I had initially written, but better. *Obviously*."

Much of the production was handled by Taylor and Nashville-based Christopher Rowe, who had worked on the mixing of *Fearless* 13 years before. In a radio interview, Taylor spoke about the re-recording of 'Love Story': "I really wanted my touring band to get a chance to play on this version because a lot of them spent years playing this song over and over again. So, it was really important to me to have my band who have toured with and shared a stage with me for so many years playing on the record. But we also have Jonathan Yudkin, the original fiddle player, we've got Caitlin Evanson, the original backup vocalist, and I think it's really, really great that it's a combination of the originals and people who have been sweating on stages with me for over a decade playing on this album."

Among the other familiar names were Paul Sidoti (electric guitar), Matt Billingslea (drums), Mike Meadows (acoustic guitar, banjo and mandolin) and Amos Heller (bass). Colbie Caillat also returned as featured backing vocalist on the track 'Breathe'.

Jack Antonoff and Anton Dessner were brought in to produce the six previously unreleased tracks, and while Taylor's vocals were recorded remotely in Los Angeles, the music tracks were laid down in Nashville studios. One noticeable absentee was Nathan Chapman, the original producer of Taylor's first four albums, which led a number of fans to suspect there was bad blood between them. But he was still involved with producing records for artists on the Big Machine label; and whether he had been invited to participate or not, becoming involved in something that could dramatically impact on sales of the original versions now owned by Big Machine could be deemed an untenable conflict of interests.

Although the decision was taken to remain faithful to the original recordings as much as possible, there were some small alterations. In the songs 'You Belong to Me', 'Superstar' and the unreleased 'Bye Bye Baby', there were subtle lyric changes to make them more meaningful, and Taylor's re-recorded vocals seemed stronger and deeper in contrast to the original nasal tone of the 18-year-old teenager.

Included in the 27 tracks was the re-recorded version of 'Today Was a Fairytale', the song Taylor had written for the 2010 movie *Valentine's Day*.

The Grammys

With Taylor receiving six Grammy nominations in a virtual live stream on November 24th 2020, it remained to be seen if and what she would perform on the night. With the emphasis on safety due to the pandemic, the regular venue was switched to the LA Convention Center, and, of course, there would be no audience. To minimalise physical contact, artists would have their own backstage area and there would be multiple stages for presenters and live performances. Although the plan was to make it appear an entirely live show, some of the performances would be pre-recorded.

At the ceremony on March 14th, it was a night of mixed emotions for Taylor, losing out on five of the awards. 'Cardigan' missed out for both Song of the Year (won by the emotive 'I Can't Breathe'), and Best Pop Solo Performance, which went to Harry Styles for 'Watermelon Sugar'. 'Exile' was pipped for Best Pop Duo/Group Performance by Lady Gaga and Ariana Grande's 'Rain on Me'; while Dua Lipa's *Future Nostalgia* beat *folklore* for Best Pop Vocal Album. To complete the disappointment, 'Beautiful Ghosts' lost out to Billie Eilish's Bond theme, 'No Time to Die', for Best Song Written for Visual Media.

The most anticipated performance of the night came with Taylor's pre-recorded medley of three songs, two from *folklore* and one from *evermore*. After watching Taylor rehearse for it, the show's executive producer told *Entertainment Tonight*: "It's an amazing performance. It's genuinely, like, magical. I was grinning ear to ear…it's brilliant and it's beautiful, and I think it's gonna be one of the moments of the night, no doubt."

And, indeed, it was.

Taylor lay on the roof of a mossy cabin, in a faux forest setting, and sang 'Cardigan', wearing an Etro floor-length metallic blue chiffon dress, with gold accents throughout its floral pattern, and a Cathy Waterman braided hairpiece. With lighting effects creating the illusion of fireflies and even pixie dust hovering over the grass, she then switched into a full-length gold and blue floral print gown to join Aaron Dessner and Jack Antonoff inside the warm and cozy cabin to sing a shortened version of 'August', before finally stepping outside with them onto the lawn to perform 'Willow'.

It was her first Grammy performance in five years, and her seventh overall, and it conjured up images of what live performances of *folklore* and *evermore* might have looked like, had there been a chance for an intimate live concert.

In what turned out to be one of the pinnacles of her career, Taylor won the coveted award for Album of the Year for the third time (following on from *Fearless* and *1989*), thus becoming the first woman to do so, and only the fourth artist in Grammy history, following in the footsteps of Frank Sinatra, Paul Simon (including a Simon & Garfunkel album), and Stevie Wonder.

Taylor accepted the award along with her collaborators Aaron Dessner, Jack Antonoff, Jonathan Low and Laura Sisk. Dessner started off the acceptance speeches by paying tribute to Taylor, by "standing up here with one of the greatest living songwriters who somehow trusted me to collaborate in this crazy time we all lived through". Then, it was Taylor's turn. Wearing an amazingly ethereal long-sleeve custom Oscar de la Renta mini-dress, completely adorned with various flower appliqués, she made the briefest of speeches, giving boyfriend Joe Alwyn a direct shoutout for the first time at an awards show:

"I wanna thank all of my collaborators who are on the stage… I wanna thank Justin Vernon, I'm so excited to meet you someday. Joe, who is the first person that I play every single song that I write, and I had the best time writing songs with you in quarantine…I want to thank James, Inez, and Betty and their parents [Ryan Reynolds and Blake Lively] who are the second and third people that I play every new song that I write, but mostly, we just want to thank our fans. You guys met us in this imaginary world that we created, and we can't tell you how honoured we are forever by this. Thank you so much, and thank you to the Recording Academy. We will never forget that you did this for us. Thank you so much."

Also making history that night was Beyoncé, who set a new record with her 28th win, becoming the most awarded female artist in Grammy history, overtaking Alison Krauss.

Going Back to the Beginning

On April 2nd Taylor once again teased her fans on Instagram with the message: "The vault door is about to be as unhinged as you'll think I am after you watch this video. Expert Happy decoding!" The animated clip contained scrambled anagrams which, once unravelled, were - bye, fine, featuring, you, Maren, Mr, over, we, Keith, me, that's, were, baby, when, Morris, happy, all, you, don't, featuring, perfectly, Urban, and bye.

Swifties soon caught on by pulling out the words to the song 'You All Over Me', featuring Maren Morris, which had been released a week before, and then putting together possible song names from the remaining words. Another hint in the video was the bizarre and muffled background noise, which when played backward revealed snippets of what seemed like lyrics.

The following day, with many fans having already decoded the six track titles, Taylor revealed the full track listing for the album with the message: "You cracked the codes and guessed all the From the Vault titles. Here's the full track list, my friends."

Why start the re-recording with *Fearless*? The answer is simple. Not only is it still Taylor's best-selling album, but it felt like the right place for the musical makeover to kick off. These tracks are among her most personal stories and the tales of growing up, first loves, and female friendships now form the bedrock of what followed. This is quintessential teenage Taylor Swift, rooted in country, but with foundations of her pop auteurism plain to see.

FEARLESS (Taylor's version)
Label - Republic
Recorded - Blackbird Studios, Nashville; Conway Recording, LA
Produced - Taylor Swift, Christopher Rowe, Jack Antonoff & Aaron Dessner
Released - April 9 2021
Singles - 3
Chart peak positions
  Hot 200 #1# Top Country Albums #1; UK #1; Canada #1; Australia #1; NZ #1

Fearless (Taylor's Version)
Produced - Christopher Rowe & Taylor Swift
Released - April 9 2021
Chart peak positions
  Hot 100 #71; Hot Country Songs #14; Canada #46; UK Streaming #99; Australia #54; NZ Hot Singles #4

Fifteen (Taylor's Version)
Produced - Christopher Rowe & Taylor Swift
Released - April 9 2021
Chart peak positions
  Hot 100 #88; Hot Country Songs #20; Canada #56; Australia #72; NZ #7

Love Story (Taylor's version)
1st Single
Recorded - Conway Studios, LA; Blackbird Studios, Nashville TN
Produced - Christopher Rowe & Taylor Swift
Released - Feb 12 2021

Chart peak positions
Hot 100 #11; Hot Country Songs #1; AC #29; UK #12; Canada #7; Australia #21

Hey Stephen (Taylor's version)
Produced - Christopher Rowe & Taylor Swift
Released - April 9 2021
Chart Peak Positions
Hot 100 Bubbling Order #1; Hot Country Songs #20; Canada # 68; Australia #86; NZ
Hot Singles #7

White Horse (Taylor's version)
Produced - Christopher Rowe & Taylor Swift
Released - April 9 2021
Chart peak positions
Hot 100 Bubbling Under #2; Hot Country Songs #29; Canada #72; Australia #99

You Belong with Me (Taylor's version)
Produced - Christopher Rowe & Taylor Swift
Released - April 9 2021
Chart peak positions
Hot 100 #75; Hot Country Songs #16; UK #52; Canada #44; Australia #53; NZ
Hot Singles #5

Breathe (featuring Colbie Caillat) (Taylor's version)
Produced - Christopher Rowe & Taylor Swift
Released - April 9 2021
Chart peak positions
Hot 100 Bubbling Under #8; Hot Country Songs #34; Canada #78

Tell Me Why (Taylor's version)
Produced - Christopher Rowe & Taylor Swift
Released - April 9 2021
Chart peak positions
Hot 100 Bubbling Position #13; Hot Country Songs #41; Canada #92

You're Not Sorry (Taylor's version)
Produced - Christopher Rowe & Taylor Swift
Released - April 9 2021
Chart peak positions
Hot 100 Bubbling Under #11; Hot Country Songs #40; Canada #90

The Way I Loved You (Taylor's version)
Produced - Christopher Rowe & Taylor Swift
Released - April 9 2021
Chart peak positions
Hot 100 #94; Hot Country Songs #24; Canada #60; Australia #89

Forever & Always (Taylor's version)
Produced - Christopher Rowe & Taylor Swift
Released - April 9 2021
Chart peak positions
Hot 100 #65; Hot Country Songs #5; UK Streaming #83; Canada #37;
Australia #45

The Best Day (Taylor's version)
Produced - Christopher Rowe & Taylor Swift
Released - April 9 2021
Chart peak positions
  Hot 100 Bubbling Under #19; Hot Country Songs #45
Selected awards and nominations
2021 CMT Awards – Best Family Feature (nominated)

Change (Taylor's version)
Produced - Christopher Rowe & Taylor Swift
Released - April 9 2021

Jump Then Fall (Taylor's version)
Produced - Christopher Rowe & Taylor Swift
Released - April 9 2021

Untouchable (Taylor's version)
Produced - Christopher Rowe & Taylor Swift
Released - April 9 2021

Forever & Always (piano version) (Taylor's version)
Produced - Christopher Rowe & Taylor Swift
Released - April 9 2021

Come in with the Rain (Taylor's version)
Produced - Christopher Rowe & Taylor Swift
Released - April 9 2021

Superstar (Taylor's version)
Produced - Christopher Rowe & Taylor Swift
Released - April 9 2021

The Other Side of the Door (Taylor's version)
Produced - Christopher Rowe & Taylor Swift
Released - April 9 2021

Today Was a Fairytale (Taylor's version)
Produced - Christopher Rowe & Taylor Swift
Released - April 9 2021

Songs "from the Vault" -

You All Over Me (featuring Maren Morris) (Taylor's Version) ****
(Taylor Swift - Scooter Carusoe)
2nd Single
Released - March 26 2021
Produced - Aaron Dessner & Taylor Swift
Released - Mar 26 2021
Chart peak positions
  Hot 100 #51; Hot Country Songs #6; Country Digital #1; UK #52; Canada #29;
  Australia #34; NZ #3

Taylor writes about the feeling of still being connected to an ex-lover. Written in 2008, she invited Maren Morris as featured backing vocalist. Morris was twice-winner of Female Artist of the Year at the ACM Awards in 2020 and 2021 and Song of the Year for 'The Bones' in 2021. She had also appeared as a special guest at Arlington during the *Reputation* Tour. Sounding familiar to some Swifties, it had been leaked online in 2017.

Stylecaster - "Taylor is back in all her country twang glory, and we're so here for it. And it sounds like Taylor is, too".

Mr Perfectly Fine (Taylor's Version) ****
(Taylor Swift)
3rd Single
Produced - Jack Antonoff & Taylor Swift
Released - April 7 2021
Chart peak positions
  Hot 100 #30; Hot Country Songs #2; Country Digital #1; UK #30; Canada #23;
  Australia #19; NZ #25

Reported to be about ex-boyfriend Joe Jonas, this wonderful put-down of a song written in 2008 deals with a playboy who promises to stay with his girl and then ditches her when he gets bored. Taylor released this song as a surprise promotional single on April 7th, two days before the album.

Jonas went on to marry Sophie Turner, who later went on Instagram to show her admiration for the song.

Taylor described the song on Amazon Echo: "'Mr Perfectly Fine' is a song that I wrote alone. It was definitely an early indicator of me sort of creeping toward a pop sensibility. I've always listened to every type of music and even though *Fearless* is a country album, there were always these pop melodies creeping in. But I really love this song, and I love the bridge. I think the lyrics are just wonderfully scathing, and full of the teen angst that you would hope to hear on an album I wrote when I was 17 or 18, or you know, on that cusp."

People - "The upbeat track, which features both country and pop influences, finds Swift singing about a former lover who moved on with a new girl and has no qualms about his prior relationship"; **American Songwriter** - "Swift breathes new life into a timely classic. The reminiscent tune sends old-age feelings flooding back with the pop-country production that defined the *Fearless* era".

We Were Happy (Taylor's Version) ***
(Taylor Swift - Liz Rose)
Produced - Taylor Swift & Aaron Dessner
Released - April 9 2021
Chart peak positions
Hot 100 Bubbling Under #15; Hot Country Songs #43; Canada #95

One of the early Swift-Rose collaborations written in 2005, dealing with the feelings of guilt a girl has after falling out with her boyfriend. In a message on Twitter, Taylor described working with her old friend Keith Urban, who plays electric guitar and sings backing vocals: "I'm really honoured that Keith Urban is part of this project, duetting on 'That's When' and singing harmonies on 'We Were Happy'… His music has inspired me endlessly."

That's When (Taylor's Version) ***
(Taylor Swift - Brad Warren -Brett Warren)

Released - April 9 2021
Produced - Taylor Swift & Jack Antonoff
Chart peak positions
  Hot 100 Bubbling Under #3; Hot Country Songs #30; Canada #63; Australia #81

A duet with Keith Urban in which he contemplates taking someone back in the aftermath of a failed relationship. The original demo version of the song was sung only by Taylor with notably different lyrics.

The song was co-written by country music duo The Warren Brothers (Brett and Brad), who had a string of chart hits which culminated in a compilation album *Barely Famous Hits* in 2005. They also co-wrote songs for Tim McGraw, Faith Hill and Martina McBride.

Urban tweeted: "Jack Antonoff and Aaron Dessner asked if I'd join their band and I said, hell yes! They said you're gonna love our lead singer – she's fearless." Taylor also tweeted: "I'm counting down the minutes til we can all jump into this brave world together, filled with equal parts nostalgia and brand newness."

Don't You (Taylor's Version) ***
(Taylor Swift - Tommy Lee James)
Produced - Taylor Swift & Jack Antonoff
Released - April 9 2021
Chart peak positions
  Hot 100 Bubbling Under #14; Hot Country Songs #42; Canada #96

Cited as one of Taylor's rarest unreleased songs, this describes how she encounters an ex-boyfriend and remembers the pain of their time together. While he wishes to remain friends, the fact that he doesn't share the pain of what went before makes her decide to move on.

In an interview for Spotify, Taylor said: "[It's] a song I wrote with Tommy Lee James, who is a fantastic writer. We wrote it about the idea of seeing someone that you used to have a thing for, and seeing them out in public for the first time after you've heard that they've moved on and that, you know, your life is kind of in shambles, and they have moved on and they're really happy. And its's almost like, even them being nice to you hurts you, because you're like in such a state of pain and you haven't moved on yet."

Bye Bye Baby (Taylor's Version) ***
(Taylor Swift - Liz Rose)
Produced - Taylor Swift & Jack Antonoff
Released - April 9 2021
Chart peak position
  Hot Country Songs #49

Originally called 'The One Thing' according to an early tracklist, Taylor changed the lyrics of this collaboration with Liz Rose a number of times before final production. Fans have theorised why Taylor chose this for the last track on the album, with some believing it is her signal that she now owns the songs and is finally ready to move on, hopefully to her next recording.

Taylor seems to enjoy the mysterious effect of these songs and tweeted: "One thing I've been loving about these From the Vault songs is that they've never been heard, so I can experiment, play, and even include some of my favorite artists".

333

"A stroke of strategic genius"

Fearless (Taylor's Version) became Taylor's ninth consecutive album to debut at number one on the Hot 200 and achieved the biggest weekly streams ever for a country album by a female artist. It also became the first ever re-recorded album to reach number one in the US. Along with *folklore* and *evermore*, the album made Taylor the first female artist to have three number one albums in less than a year, breaking Donna Summer's previous record, and the four-month gap between *evermore* and *Fearless (Taylor's Version)* broke her own record for the shortest gap between number one albums by a woman.

The album also became Taylor's sixth chart-topper on the Top Country Albums chart, and her first number one since *Red*. Nine of the tracks on the album charted simultaneously on the Billboard Hot 100, thus extending her record to 136 for the biggest number of Hot 100 entries by a female artist.

In Canada, 16 of the tracks charted simultaneously on the Hot 100, increasing her total entries to an incredible 148, and in the UK the album debuted at number one, making it her seventh chart-topper and making her the only female artist with so many UK number one albums in the 21st century, and the third-most in history after Madonna's twelve and Kylie Minogue's eight. The album also broke The Beatles' 54-year-old record for the fastest accumulation of three number one albums (364 days between 1965-1966) by achieving it in 259 days, and by the middle of May she was the UK's best-selling artist of the year.

The reviews were highly supportive of Taylor's new project:

Marie Claire - "At this stage of her career, and with social media as the primary way of dispensing information to her fans, Swift finally gets to control the narrative - the 'crazy' element has been stripped away from her critically-acclaimed music, allowing her musical prowess to take center stage. In a way, the re-release is not *just* to take back ownership of her songs. It's to take back ownership of her story"; **NME** - "Swift never cringes away from her younger self. Instead, she revisits the songs with kindness and affection, celebrating the success of her teenage releases"; **Variety** - "The 18-year-old Taylor Swift is a great place to visit, but *folklore* and *evermore* are the places you'll want to return and live, unless you have an especially strong sentimental attachment to *Fearless*"; **Clash** - "Like a restored photograph brightening from black and white into colour, *Fearless (Taylor's Version)* is the same, but better"; **The Guardian** - "Swift has resisted any temptation to alter the song's pop-country arrangements or lyrics, even when the latter could have used a nip and tuck"; **Los Angeles Times** - "As for the lightweight bonus material - none of it argues that it deserves a place on *Fearless*, though 'Mr Perfectly Fine' comes close"; **The Telegraph** - "*Fearless* was always an exceptionally fine album of country-pop songs, detailing the romantic fixations of a wholesome teenage American girl on the verge of adulthood, and guess what? It still is".

According to the *New Yorker*, Taylor's re-recording was "a stroke of strategic genius". Designating the album and songs 'Taylor's Version' may have appeared straightforward enough, but it carried implications. Where it could just as easily have been described as "2020 version" or "new version", or even a different name altogether, this showed one significant difference - the album is not just the commercial asset of some "anonymous male industry entity, it has an explicit owner, and it's Taylor Swift."

Now the new name would give fans the clear-cut choice between the new and old versions, and Taylor was ultra-smart enough to understand that the short memory of the internet's algorithms and search engines would quickly favour 'Taylor's Version' over the original. And, to the sure dismay of Scooter Braun, that's exactly how it happened.

This was a significant moment in Taylor's career. Here she was, once again, turning fortune on its head and masterminding her very future, just like she did when she was an 18-year-old teenager, and securing a fairytale ending to years of uncertainty.

On April 13th, she guested on *The Late Show with Stephen Colbert* live from her studio, and immediately dismissed the host's claim that 'Hey Stephen' had been written about him.

The Brits

Next came the Brit Awards, already delayed three months due to Covid restrictions, and as Taylor was already quarantined in the country with Joe Alwyn, she was able to attend the ceremony at the O2 Arena on May 11th. Alwyn was unable to accompany her as he was busy shooting *Conversations with Friends* in Ireland.

Although not performing on the night, Taylor was there to receive their prestigious Global Icon Award, "in recognition of her immense impact on music across the world and incredible repertoire and achievements to date." She was not only the first female to be honoured, but the first non-British artist, the youngest, and only the fourth artist overall, following in the footsteps of Elton John, David Bowie and Robbie Williams.

The awards marked the first major live music event in the UK since the start of the pandemic and was part of the Government's scientific Events Research Programme, with enhanced testing for the 4,000 ticket holders, of which 2,500 were handed out free to NHS workers. As well as the special award, Taylor received her sixth nomination for International Female Solo Artist, but lost out to Billie Eilish.

Before she took to the stage for the special award, a video was shown which featured heartfelt tributes from longtime friends Selena Gomez and Ed Sheeran, and special messages from Annie Lennox and Zoë Kravitz. Gomez had high praise for her friend: "Taylor is the same girl I met when I was 15. And she cares so deeply for her fans. I wish I could be there and just support you and hang out with you. You deserve it and you're amazing."

For the special occasion, Taylor wore a beaded and rhinestone-embellished crop top and matching skirt from Miu Miu, paired with *Red*-era hair and red lipstick, and was presented with the award by *Game of Thrones* star Maisie Williams. Receiving the iconic award, she said: "I want to thank my friends and family who know exactly who they are. Whose opinion of me has never changed whether my stock was up or down. If there's one thing that I've learned, it's that you have to look around every day and take note of the people who have always believed in you and never stop appreciating them for it."

In true Taylor fashion, she then offered words of encouragement to the young artists in attendance: "I need you to hear me when I say that there is no clear path that comes free of negativity. If you're being met with resistance, that probably means that you're doing something new. If you're experiencing turbulence or pressure, that probably means that you're rising and there might be times when you put your whole heart and soul into something and it is met with cynicism or skepticism. You cannot let that crush you. You have to let it fuel you because we live in a world where anyone has the right to say anything they want about you anytime. But just please remember that you have the right to prove them wrong."

With there being no customary after-show party, Taylor chose to celebrate the night back at the hotel with her close friends and fellow award-winners Haim, and later went on Instagram with the message, "Spinning in my highest heels, luv #BRITS".

At the Billboard Music Awards in Los Angeles in May, Taylor won both Top Female Artist and Top Billboard 200 Artist, but lost out in the categories of Top Artist and Top Billboard 200 Album (for *folklore*). She also received another Guinness World Record (her fifth so far this year) for having the most number ones on the US Digital Songs chart, with 22 songs. A few weeks later came the iHeart Radio Music Awards at which Taylor won Best Pop Album of the Year for *folklore*, but lost in the nomination for Best Female Artist.

In her acceptance speech, Taylor described *folklore* as being "a sort of emotional life raft for me to put all my feelings into."

Later in the month, *Entertainment Tonight* released a story that confirmed the ongoing rumour of Taylor and Joe's engagement was still "alive and well". A source revealed: "They grew closer than ever during the quarantine and she really trusts him. They've been continuing to be pretty low-key about their relationship to the outside world to continue to protect it... They've discussed future plans and Taylor can see herself marrying Joe one day."

"She's worthy, Taylor Swift is worthy"

Back in 2019, just before legendary singer-songwriter Carole King took to the stage to present Taylor with AMAs award for Artist of the Decade, she was asked what it was about the singer that deserved the honour: "She's a really good songwriter. She writes actual songs with lyrics that touch the heart, and she's been doing it since she was 15 or something earlier. It's her heart. She's got a really good feeling for how people feel about love and life. She captures it. She's really good. She's worthy. Taylor Swift is worthy."

High praise, indeed, but, once on stage, Carole paid an even greater tribute: "Over the years, I've known some great songwriters, and I've also known some great singers and performers. It's rare to see all these talents in one person, but that defines Taylor Swift. Her lyrics resonate across the generations. Her songs touch everyone, and her impact around the world is extraordinary."

Since she was just 14 years old, Taylor had never known any other world than show business. Her parents had made her dream possible; but it was Taylor's extraordinary gift and supreme confidence that made that dream a reality.

With each successive album she continued to prove herself beyond doubt. Her debut album *Taylor Swift* had taken the country music world by storm with its expert lyricism and storytelling skills seemingly far beyond her years, while at the same time introducing her fabled "Easter eggs" as hidden meanings to the songs. Almost overnight she had become queen of the breakup anthem.

Her nine record-breaking albums had, in turn, made a huge impact on the charts, whether it be country or pop, and had subsequently sold in their millionsEach would make its mark in music history. *Taylor Swift* had earned her worldwide recognition, rubber-stamping her arrival as the newly-crowned Teen Queen of Country. With the sophomore *Fearless*, Taylor ventured more into country-pop stardom, becoming more adept with her tales of family life, love, and heartbreak, mixing both the painful and whimsical sides of relationships, often bursting with warmth and nostalgia. With this album, she created a whole Swiftian universe of fans of both country and pop, eager to deduce clues as to which lover songs referred to; and it also made her a very rich young lady.

Speak Now found the 20-year-old singer taking on more mature themes and writing all the songs herself, weaving stories that not only ventured outside of her own perspective, but also displayed a new level of girl power in relating personal experiences. While the subjects of songs became fuel for the tabloids, the growing interest in her celebrity status went well beyond her songwriting roots and became more complex. Fame and living in the public gaze brought a new layer to her songwriting, and, on future albums, it would inspire her to make bold lyrical shifts that would yield mixed reviews.

With the heartbreak and vulnerability found in *Red,* Taylor had well and truly bonded with fans old and new, taking a bigger step away from her county roots, and seeing things in a more adult and nuanced way, and writing with greater depth and passion. The wonderful *1989* saw a transition into pure pop and embodiment of the new era, with a versatility that produced some of the most gut-wrenching, powerful ballads and thumpingly-wild hits of her career. Then, after a three-year hiatus, the long-anticipated *Reputation* found Taylor fighting back at the media's misguided perception of her, reclaiming her own narrative, and breaking away from what had been her neutral, demure persona with highly emotive songs of love and betrayal.

Lover came next, a throwback to the wide-eyed teenage days, with songs reflecting much of her past work - the soft ballads and pop anthems - but now without that hard edge. On a personal level, Taylor was now more settled and totally loved-up, and it showed in the lyrics.

Then came the jewels, *folklore* and *evermore*, the "pandemic pair", which caught the music world completely off guard and gave her lockdowned fans a much-needed treat with a total shift away from the pop progression her last few albums had taken. Taylor created a whole new world for her listeners, with stories and characters that took her songwriting skills to the next level.

Here she was, not only having the confidence to push the envelope even further, but now doing exactly what *she* wanted to do, and totally revelling in the experience. It also gave the legions of Swifties a whole new mystical world to embrace and craving for more to follow.

In less than two decades, she has achieved more than what some established artists have managed to do in a lifetime, and, no doubt, students will be studying her lyrics in music class for decades to come.

Taylor has often been cited as one of the greatest songwriters of all time. *Rolling Stone* recently listed her at #97 (though I would place her in the top twenty, at least), but she has also been called a lazy songwriter. In a 2018 interview for *GQ*, producer Quincy Jones was asked his opinion of Taylor's songwriting. Pulling a face that was somewhere between "disapproval and disdain", he said: "We need more songs, man. F**king songs, not hooks."

When told she was considered by some to be one of the greatest songwriters of the era, Jones said: "Whatever crumbles your cookie." Referring to what was missing from Taylor's music, he said, "knowing what you're doing. Since I was a little kid, I've always heard the people that don't wanna do the work. It takes work, man. The only place you find success before work is in the dictionary, and that's alphabetical…A great song can make the worst singer in the world a star, but a bad song can't be saved by the three best singers in the world."

An interesting perspective about one of the hardest workers in the business. Maybe the legendary producer should be updated on how many Grammys Taylor has won for her songwriting.

Just her incredible ability to write amazing lyrics at the drop of a hat has always kept fellow songwriters fascinated. In an interview with *Harper's Bazaar*, Taylor gave an insight into how some of her songs are created:

"There are definitely moments when it's like this cloud of an idea comes and just lands in front of your face, and you reach up and grab it. A lot of songwriting is things you learn, structure, and cultivating that skill, and knowing how to craft a song. But there are mystical, magical moments, inexplicable moments when an idea that is fully formed just pops into your head. And that's the purest part of my job. It can get complicated on every other level, but the songwriting is still the same uncomplicated process it was when I was 12 years old writing songs in my room".

A leading British headmaster recently went on record to say that Taylor deserves to take her place in the canon of great philosophers, even admitting she had become a favourite source of inspiration, and he confessed to regularly sneaking her lyrics into school assemblies: "I think she's really quite amazing - the way she carries herself in an industry that is male dominated, the way that she says the things she wants to say. That her songwriting is telling her own stories and that they are gloriously the stories of a young woman negotiating the 21st century, is a great example for our young people."

But what of the future, once the re-recording of her old albums is complete? Although continuing popularity can never be assured, there is little doubt that whatever comes next with Taylor's music, it will not disappoint. At the time of writing, music fans throughout the world are only just beginning to get the chance to see their favourite artists live on stage again, and Taylor will no doubt be eager to return to something that is very close to her heart. With a backlog of three albums' worth of songs, many of which have never been performed live, and, of course, not forgetting those re-recorded *Fearless* gems, it remains to be seen what shape a concert or even a tour will take.

Taylor has had to suffer experiences that have shaken her to the core, not least her character and integrity being repeatedly called into question. She said it herself: "People throw rocks at things that shine." But she is no longer the naïve, wide-eyed teen with the long curly hair; she is now a dynamic and passionate woman and a constant force to be reckoned with in an industry that has dealt her curveballs over recent years.

Taylor has become one of the few artists that have enormous influence and the power to create changes in the music industry, and when she acts, people tend to listen. Of course, she's a multi-millionaire, but in doing what she has achieved, she has galvanised other, less-established artists to do the same and fight for better deals with the people who own their work.

She once told *Music Week*: "It always was and it always will be an interesting dance between a young woman and the music industry. We don't have a lot of female executives, we're working on getting more female engineers and producers, but, while we are such a drastic gender minority, it's interesting to try and figure out how to be."

According to Celebrity Net Worth, Taylor has amassed a fortune of $400 million and continues to make $150 million per year from her music and her various brand deals. Over the years, the bulk of the income has come from her mind-blowingly successful tours (*Reputation* had earned her around $9 million per show). And then there's her massive real estate portfolio, with some eight properties across the country, and, according to *Business Insider*, she's the owner of three private jets worth millions.

However, her philanthropy benefits millions of people at home and around the world and she will always be good to her word to always "pay it forward".

Looking back at a recording career of almost 15 years, the numbers don't lie. They are the result of all the hard work and time invested into becoming the very best she can be, and, with solid credibility, have given her the clout and opportunity to do things the way *she* wants it done.

In what can be a never-ending media circus, Taylor continues to maintain a sense of normalcy. She may still make mistakes, and the media will soon be quick to pick up on them. At the time of writing, she seems to have found a tranquillity in her personal life that will no doubt have some positive impact on her career. But with success always breeding some level of contempt, there will be the inevitable hawks out there circling, just waiting and maybe even hoping for this shining star to fall. But if that happens, there are those she can rely on for eternal support, and it's the millions of her devoted fans - no, her friends, as she prefers to call them - that will stand by her, as they've always done, now, tomorrow, and for evermore.

One thing's for sure, Taylor will continue to make music for decades to come - groundbreaking music that will surprise, astound, and inspire many, and add to what is already an undeniable long-lasting legacy.

Just sixteen years ago, Taylor Swift was a starry-eyed schoolgirl with a dream. Now she has become the brightest of stars.

Believe me when I tell you, the best is still to come...

SOURCES

Album liner notes
TV and radio interviews

Websites

taylorswift.com
taylorswiftfandom.com
allmusic.com
grammy.com
billboard.com
officialcharts.com
discogs.com
45.cat.com
Imdb.com

Books

Govan, Chloe, "Taylor Swift: The Rise of a Nashville Teen" *Omnibus* 2012
Jepson, Louisa, "Taylor Swift" *Simon & Shuster* 2013
Newkey-Burden, Chas, "Taylor Swift - The Whole Story" *Harper* 2014

Articles

Akers, Shelley, "Taylor Swift to Appear in Hanna Montana Movie" *People*
    Oct 27 2017
Beaumont-Thomas, Ben, "Taylor Criticises Scooter Braun after $300m Masters Sale"
    The Guardian Nov 17 2020
Blair, Olivia, "A Definitive Timeline Of Taylor Swift's Rise to Fame" *Cosmopolitan*
    Sept 14 2017
Caramanica, Jon, "A Young Outsider's Life Turned Inside Out" *New York Times*
    Sept 8 2014
Caramanica, Jon, "For Young Superstar Taylor, Big Wins Means Innocence Lost"
    New York Times Aug 28 2012
Caramanica, Jon, "OMG! Taylor Swift Does CSI!" *New York Times* Aug 14 2011
Caramanica, Jon, "Taylor Swift Angry, on Speak Now, *New York Times*
    Oct 21 2010
Carson, Sarah, "The Story of Taylor Swift: 10 Years at the Top in Her Own Lyrics"
    Daily Telegraph Nov 24 2016
CMT Insider Interview: Taylor Swift *CMT News* Nov 26 2008
Crane, Emily, "How Did Taylor Swift Lose Right to Her Six Best-Selling Albums?"
    Daily Mail July 1 2019
Dickey, Jack, "Taylor Swift Interview" *Time* Nov 24 2014
Donella, Leah, "Taylor Swift is the 21st Century's Most Disorienting Pop Star"
    NPR Sept 26 2018
Doyle, Patrick, "Musicians on Musicians: Paul McCartney & Taylor Swift" *Rolling
    Stone* Nov 13 2020
Dukes, Billy, "10 Things You Didn't Know About Taylor Swift" *Taste of Country*
    July 26 2020
Eells, Josh, "The Reinvention of Taylor Swift" *Rolling Stone* Sept 8 2014

Grady, Constance, "Newly Leaked Footage Shows Taylor Swift and Kanye West Talking Famous, *Vox* Mar 21 2020

Grigoriadis, Vanessa, "The Very Pink, Very Perfect Life of Taylor Swift" *Rolling Stone* Mar 5 2009

Hammel, Sara, "Taylor Swift & Jake Gyllenhaal Break Up: Source" *People* May 2012

Halperin, Shirley, "Scooter Braun Sells Taylor Swift's Big Machine Masters for Big Pay Day" *Variety* Nov 16 2020

Hatza, George, "Taylor Swift - Growing into Superstardom" *Reading Eagle* Dec 8 2008

Haylock, Zoe, "Who's In, Who's Out? An Exhaustive Timeline of Taylor Swift's Squad" *Vulture* Aug 21 2019

Hiatt, Brian, "Taylor Swift in Wonderland" *Rolling Stone* Oct 25 2012

Hiatt, Brian, "Taylor Swift: The Rolling Stone Interview" Sept 18 2019

Jo, Nancy, "Taylor Swift and the Growing of a Superstar: Her Men, Her Moods, Her Music" *Vanity Fair* Nov 10 2015

Jones, Nate, "All 179 Taylor Swift Songs Ranked" *Vulture* Jan 11 2021

Komonibo, Ineye, "Making Sense of the Flying Accusations Between Taylor Swift, Scooter Braun & Big Machine Records" *Refinery29* Nov 16 2019

Kosser, Michael, "Liz Rose: Co-writer to the Stars" *American Songwriter*, Dec 24 2011

Leahey, Andrew, "Songwriter Spotlight: Liz Rose" *Rolling Stone* Sept 26 2016

Marcus, Emily, "Taylor Swift Through the Years: From Nashville Upstart to Pop Superstar" *Us Weekly* May 11 2021

McPherson, Alex, "Taylor Swift: I Wanna Believe in Pretty Lies", *The Guardian* Oct 18 2012

Mansfield, Brian, "Taylor Swift Sees Red All Over" *USA Today* Dec 21 2012

Mylrea, Hannah, "Every Taylor Swift song ranked in order of greatness" *NME* Sept 8 2020

Neil, Chris, "Interview - Taylor Swift: Fan Fair in Nashville" *Country Weekly* June 2006

O'Connor, Roisin, "Full Version of Infamous Kanye West and Taylor Swift Phone Call Leaks" *The Independent* Mar 21 2020

Preston, John, "Taylor Swift: The 19-year-old Country Music Star Who Conquered America - and Now Britain" *Daily Telegraph* Jan 5 2012

Raab, Scott, "Why Taylor Swift Welcomed You to New York", *Esquire* Oct 2014

Shaw, Lucas, "The End of Taylor Swift's $300 Million Fight with Scooter Braun" *Bloomberg* Nov 22 2020

Snapes, Laura, "Taylor Swift: I Was Literally About to Break" *The Guardian* Aug 24 2019

Spanos, Brittany, "Taylor Swift vs Scooter Braun and Scott Borchetta: What the Hell Happened?" *Rolling Stone* July 1 2019

Tamarkin, Jeff, "Taylor Swift" *Allmusic* Feb 14 2021

Teti, Julia, "Taylor Swift's Romantic History: Every Man She's Loved & Lost from Joe Jonas to Joe Alwyn" *Hollywood Life* Oct 15 2020

Tiffany, Kaitlyn, "A History of Taylor Swift's odd, conflicting stances on streaming services" *The Verge* June 9 2017

Toomedy, Alyssa, "Taylor Swift and Conor Kennedy Breakup: Anatomy of a Split" *E!* Dec 4 2015

Various, "Taylor Swift and Joe Alwyn's Relationship Complete Timeline" *Elle* May 21 2021

Vatan, Kristin, "Breaking Down the Legal Terms in Taylor Swift's Music Ownership Dispute, *Entertainment Weekly* Nov 15 2019

Vincent, Alice, "Taylor Swift: The Rise, Fall, and Re-Invention of America's Sweetheart" *The Telegraph* Nov 3 2017

Widdicombe, Lizzie, "You Belong with Me", *New Yorker* Oct 10 2011

--The Unabridged Taylor Swift" *Rolling Stone*, Dec 2 2008

Willman, Chris, "Taylor Swift's Road to Fame" *Entertainment Weekly*, Feb 21 2015

Willman, Chris, "Taylor Swift: No Longer "Polite at All Costs" *Variety* Jan 21 2020

Woolcock, Nicola, "Head Praises Swift as great philosopher" *The Times* April 10 2021

Yahr, Emily, "Taylor Swift Explains Her Blunt Testimony During Her Sexual Assault Trial" *Washington Post* Dec 6 2017

- "Songwriter Taylor Swift Signs Publishing Deal with Sony/ATV" BMI May 12 2005

- "Taylor Swift vs Kanye West: A History of Their On-Off Feud" *BBC News* Oct 10 2018

- "A Complete Timeline of Kanye West & Taylor Swift's Relationship" *Billboard* Mar 23 2020

- "A Timeline of Taylor Swift's Feud with Kanye West and Kim Kardashian" *Cosmopolitan* Mar 24 2020

- "Taylor Swift - The Ultimate Guide" *Rolling Stone* May 11 2018

TAYLOR SWIFT

Bradley, Jonathan, "Why Taylor Swift's Self-Titled Debut is Her Best Album" *Billboard* Nov 7 2017

Christiano, Nick, "New Recordings: Taylor Swift" *Philadelphia Inquirer* Nov 12 2006

Dickinson, Chrissie, "Recordings: Taylor Swift" *Chicago Tribune* Nov 17 2006

Fontaine, James, "Taylor Swift Shows She's the Real Deal" *Palm Beach Post* Oct 30 2006

Hight, Jewly, "On Her Self-Titled Debut, Taylor Swift Captured the Dream of Young Love" *Vulture* Nov 10 2017

Holland, Roger, "Taylor Swift", *Pop Matters* Nov 9 2006

Johnston, Maura, "Taylor Swift" *Pitchfork* Aug 19 2019

Neal, Chris, "Taylor Swift Review" *Country Weekly* Dec 4 2006

Rosenbaum, Ken, "Taylor Swift: Taylor Swift Review" *Toledo Blade* Nov 12 2006

Rubin, Ronna, "Taylor Swift is a Veteran at 16" *GAC Music Beat* Oct 23 2006

Tamarkin, Jeff, "Taylor Swift" Album Review" *Allmusic*

- "Taylor Swift: Album Guide" *Rolling Stone* Dec 5 2012

FEARLESS

Caramanica, Jon, "My Music, My Space, My Life" *New York Times* Nov 7 2008

Cills, Hazel, "Taylor Swift: Fearless" *Pitchfork* Aug 19 2019

Christgau, Robert, "Consumer Guide" (Fearless)" *MSN Music* Mar 3 2016

Davis, Johnny, "Pop Review: Taylor Swift, Fearless" *The Observer* April 25 2016

Davies. Lucy, Fearless" *BBC Music* 2009

Gardner, Elysa, "Taylor Swift Hits All the Right Words" *USA Today* April 28 2016

Greenblatt, Leah, "Fearless" *Entertainment Weekly* Dec 5 2010

Keefe, Jonathan, "Taylor Swift: Fearless" *Slant Magazine* Mar 15 2011

Mylrea, Hannah, "Taylor Swift: Every Single Album Ranked and Rated" *NME* Dec 17 2020

Petridis, Alex, "Taylor Swift: Fearless" *The Guardian* Oct 16 2013

Reed, James, "Young Country Star's Fearless Proves She's Just That, and No More" *Boston Globe* Jan 13 2010

Richards, Chris, "Taylor Swift: Fearless and Full of Charm" *Washington Post* Nov 11 2008

Rosen, Jody, "Fearless" *Rolling Stone* Nov 13 2008

Roland, Tom, "Taylor Swift Fearless-ly Sets a New Precedent" *Great American Country* Dec 20 2009

Sheffield, Rob, "Taylor Swift: Fearless" *Blender* Dec 16 2008

Tucker, Ken, "Albums: Fearless" *Allmusic* Nov 15 2008

Wyland, Sarah, "Taylor Swift: Fearless" *Country Music Online* Jan 2009

--"Taylor Swift: Fearless" *Q Magazine* April 2009

SPEAK NOW

Caramanica, Jon, "Taylor Swift Angry on Speak Now" *New York Times* Oct 20 2010

Demarest, Abigail, "All of Taylor Swift's albums Ranked from Least to Most Iconic"

Insider Dec 11 2020

Deusner, Stephen, "Well Spoken: Taylor Swift, Speak Now" *Washington Post* Oct 26 2010

Heaton, Dave, "Taylor Swift; Speak Now" *Pop Matters* Nov 29 2010

Horton, Matthew, "Taylor Swift Speak Now Review" *BBC* 2010

Hyden, Steven, "Taylor Swift: Speak Now" *The A.V Club* Nov 2 2010

Keefe, Jonathan, "Review: Taylor Swift Speak Now, *Slant Magazine* Oct 25 2010

Johnston, Maura, "Revisiting Taylor Swift's Album Speak Now" *Vulture* Nov 10 2017

McPherson, Alex, "Taylor Swift Speak Now Review" *The Guardian* Sept 9 2010

Manning, Craig, "Taylor Swift: Speak Now" *Chorus.fm* Oct 22 2020

Moore, Rick, "Taylor Swift: Speak Now" *American Songwriter* Dec 15 2010

Powers, Ann, "Album Review: Taylor Swift's Speak Now" *Los Angeles Times* Oct 25 2010

Sheffield, Rob, "Speak Now: Taylor Swift" *Rolling Stone* Oct 26 2010

"Taylor Swift: Speak Now" *Pitchfork* Aug 19 2019

Stransky, Tanner, "Taylor Swift Tells EW About New Album Speak Now" *Entertainment Weekly* Dec 20 2019

Wede, Lydia, "10s of the 10s: Taylor Swift's Speak Now Speaks for Itself" *Iowa State Daily* Nov 19 2019

Willman, Chris, "Album Review: Taylor Swift's Speak Now" *Hollywood Reporter* Oct 19 2010

Wood, Mikael Wood, "Taylor Swift Speak Now" *Spin* Oct 26 2010

RED

Bernstein, Jon, "Taylor Swift's Red is Danceable, Dreamy – and Mature" *Time* Oct 24 2012

Bernstein, Jon, "Taylor Swift Looks Back on Her "Only True Breakup Album" Red" *Rolling Stone* Nov 18 2020

Caramanica, John, "No More Kids Stuff for Taylor Swift" *New York Times* Oct 24 2012

Coyne, Kevin, "Single Review: Taylor Swift's Red" *Country Universe* Aug 3 2013

Dolan, Jon, "Taylor Swift Red Album Review" *Rolling Stone* Oct 23 2012

Dukes, Billy, "Taylor Swift Red Album Review" *Taste of Country* Oct 19 2012

English, J, "Shocking Omissions: Taylor Swift's Red, a Canonical Coming-of-Age Album, *NPR* Aug 28 2017

Gallucci, Michael, "Taylor Swift: Red" *The A.V Club* Oct 24 2012

Keefe, Jonathan, "Review: Taylor Swift Red" *Slant* Oct 22 2012

Lachno, James, "Taylor Swift Red: Album Review" *Daily Telegraph* Oct 19 2012

Lansky, Sam, "Taylor Swift Red: Album Review" *Idolator* Oct 22 2012

McAlpine, Fraser, "Taylor Swift Red Review", *BBC Music* 2012

Maerz, Melissa, "Red Review – Taylor Swift" *Entertainment Weekly* Oct 26 2012

Mossman, Kate, "Taylor Swift Red Review" *The Guardian* Oct 18 2012

Mylrea, Hannah, "Taylor Swift: Every Single Album Ranked and Rated" *NME* Dec 17 2020

Nelson, Brad, "Taylor Swift: Red" *Pitchfork* Aug 19 2019

Pomarico, Nicole, "Fans Helped Change How Taylor Swift Feels About This Classic Red Ballad" *Bustle* Aug 30 2018

Sciarretto, Amy, "Taylor Swift, Red – Album Review" *Pop Crush* Oct 18 2012

Willman, Chris, "Taylor Swift's Red: Track by Track" *Hollywood Reporter* Oct 23 2012

Vena, Jocelyn, "Taylor Swift Red with Emotion on New Album" *MTV* Sept 3 2012

Yoshida, Emily, "Revisting Taylor Swift's Album Red" *Vulture* Nov 10 2017

- "Taylor Swift Red: Track by Track Review" *Billboard* Oct 19 2012

1989

Aswad, Jem, "Taylor Swift's Pop Curveball Pays Off with 1989 " *Billboard* Oct 24 2010

Beasley, Craig, "Taylor Swift: 1989" *Pop Matters* Oct 31 2014

Caramanica, John, "A Farewell to Twang" *New York Times* Oct 23 2014

Charlton, Laura, "Take a Breath - The Wildest Dream Video Isn't Racist - Now Exhale" *New York* Sept 4 2015

Eakin, Marah, "With 1989, Taylor Swift Finally Grows Up" *The A.V Club* Oct 28 2014

Frank, Alex, "The Simple Pleasures of Taylor Swift's New Album 1989" *Vogue* Oct 27 2014

Gill, Andy, "Taylor Swift 1989: Pop Star Shows Promising Signs of Maturity" *The Independent* Oct 27 2014

Hall, Scott, "Taylor Swift's 1989 Is a Classic of Sorts" *Utah Statesman* Nov 13 2014

Horton, Matthew, "Taylor Swift: 1989" *NME* Oct 27 2014

Jagota, Vrinda, "Taylor Swift 1989" *Pitchfork* Aug 19 2019

Kimberlin, Shane, "Taylor Swift - 1989" *Music OMH* Oct 27 2014

Lansky, Sam, "1989 Marks a Paradigm Swift" *Time* Oct 23 2014

Levine, Nick, "Taylor Swift 1989 Album Review" *Time Out* Oct 27 2014

Petridis, Alexis, "Taylor Swift: 1989 Review" *The Guardian* Oct 24 2014

Richards, Chris, "Taylor Swift's 1989: A Pivot into Pop, a Misstep into Conformity" *Washington Post* Oct 27 2014

Rutabingwa, Viviane & James Arinaitwe, "Taylor Swift is Dreaming of a Very White Africa" *NPR* Sept 1 2015

Sheffield, Rob, "1989 Review" *Rolling Stone* Oct 24 2014

Thompson, Eliza, "Taylor Swift's 1989: A Track-by-Track Review" *Cosmopolitan* Oct 27 2014

Unterberger, Andrew, "Taylor Swift Gets Clean, Hits Reset on New Album 1989" *Spin* Oct 28 2014

Wilson, Carl, "Contemplating Taylor Swift's Navel" *Slate* Oct 29 2014

- "Tayloe Swift's 1989 - Album Review" *New York Daily News* Oct 24 2014

- "Taylor Swift video director defends Wildest Dreams following "whitewash" claims" *The Guardian* Sept 3 2015

REPUTATION

Bassett, Jordan, "Taylor Swift: Reputation Review" *NME* Nov 10 2017

Battan, Carrie, "Taylor Swift's Confessions on Reputation" *The New Yorker* Nov 14 2017

Bebb, Louisa, "Album Review: Taylor Swift – Reputation" *Redbrick* Nov 19 2017

Bruton, Louise, "Reputation - Clever Songwriting, Beauty in Tiny Details" *Irish Times* Nov 10 2017

Caramanica, Jon, "Taylor Swift is a 2017 Pop Machine on Reputation, But at What Cost?" *New York Times* Nov 9 2017

Cinquemani, Sal, "Taylor Swift: Reputation" *Slant Magazine* Nov 10 2017

Dudley, Lauren, "The Verdict on Taylor Swift's Reputation Album" *Vogue* Nov 10 2017

Empire, Kitty, "Taylor Swift: Reputation Review - Lust, Loss and Revenge" *The Guardian* Nov 12 2017

Hodgkinson, Will, "Pop Review: Taylor Swift's Reputation" *The Times* Nov 10 2017

Jenkins, Craig, "Taylor Swift's Reputation Fixates on Big Enemies and Budding Romance" *Vulture* Nov 10 2017

Kornhaber, Spencer, "The Old Taylor Swift is Hiding Within Reputation" *The Atlantic* Nov 10 2017

Kranc, Lauren, "Three Years after Reputation It's Time to Accept It as Taylor Swift's Best Album" *Esquire* Nov 10 2020

Lynch, Joe, "Why Taylor Swift's Reputation is Her Best Album" *Billboard* Aug 22 2019

Lynskey, Dorian, "Reputation Review" *Q Magazine* Jan 2018

McDermott, Maeve, "Taylor Swift's Reputation: A Fully-formed Look at a Singer in Love, And in Control" *USA Today* Nov 9 2017

Mohammed, Sagal, "This Is What Everyone Is Saying About Taylor Swift's

Reputation" *Glamour* Nov 10 2017

Nied, Mike, "Taylor Swift's Reputation: Album Review" *Idolator* Nov 10 2017

O'Connor, Roisin, "Reputation by Taylor Swift – Album Review" *The Independent* Nov 10 2017

Powers, Ann, "The Old Taylor's Not Dead" *NPR* Nov 10 2017

Purdom, Clayton, "Taylor Swift Has a Big, Drunken Night Out on Reputation" *The A.V Club* Nov 11 2017

Rizzo, Laura, 2Reviews of Taylor Swift's Reputation Will Get You Pumped for the Drop" *Elite Daily* Nov 1 2017

Sargent, Jordan, "Embracing Evil on Reputation, Taylor Swift Has Never Sounded More Free" *Spin* Nov 14 2017

Sawdey, Evan, "Taylor Swift Reputation Review" *Pop Matters* Nov 13 2017

Schonfeld, Zach, "Reputation: A Track-by-Track Review" *Newsweek* Nov 14 2017

Schwartz, Alison, "Review: Why You Might Not Understand the Importance of Taylor Swift's New Song" *People* Aug 25 2017

Sheffield, Rob, "Reputation Review: Taylor Swift Ditches Tabloid Drama on Most Intimate LP Yet" *Rolling Stone* Nov 10 2017

Willman, Chris, "Album Review; Taylor Swift's Reputation" *Variety* Nov 9 2017

Wood, Mikael, "Taylor Swift's Privacy is a Public Act on Reputation" *Los Angeles Times* Nov 13 2017

Zoladz, Lindsay, "Taylor Swift Stakes her Reputation on Big Sounds and Petty Grievances" *The Ringer* Nov 10 2017

- "Taylor Swift Reputation Album Review" *Pop Sugar* Nov 12 2017

LOVER

Andriotis, Mary, "Taylor Swift's New Album Is Out and Here's All the Hidden References You Missed" *Teen Vogue* Aug 23 2019

Barr, Natalia, "Taylor Swift Takes the High Road on the More Mature Lover" *Consequence of Sound* Aug 26 2019

Baty, Emma, "Taylor Swift's New Album Lover is Good, But That's Not Good Enough Anymore" *Cosmopolitan* Aug 23 2019

Bruner, Raisa, "Let's Discuss the Lyrics to Every Song on Taylor Swift's Lover" *Time* Aug 23 2019

Burns, Alex, "Taylor Swift Lover Album Review" *Medium.com* Aug 26 2019

Caramanica, Jon, "Taylor Swift Emerges from the Darkness on Lover" *New York Times* Aug 23 2019

Catucci, Nick, "Taylor Swift Reaches for New Heights of Personal and Musical Liberation on Lover" *Rolling Stone* Aug 23 2019

Chiu, Melody, "On Lover, Taylor Swift - Self-Assured and Madly in Love - Revels in a Hard-Won Happy Ending" *People* Aug 23 2019

Empire, Kitty, "Taylor Swift Lover Review: A Return to Past Glories" *The Guardian* Aug 24 2019

Fitzmaurice, Larry, "Lover Is Pure Taylor Swift, at Her Most Content and Confident" *Entertainment Weekly* Aug 23 2019

Gaca, Anna, "Taylor Swift Lover" *Pitchfork* Aug 26 2019

Holmes, Dave, "When Taylor Swift Eases Up on the Self-Mythologising, Lover is Pretty Damn Good" *Esquire* Aug 23 2019

Harrison, Quentin, "Taylor Swift Constructs Another Masterclass of Pristine Pop Perfection with Lover" *Albumism.com* Sept 29 2019

Jenkins, Craig, "The Old Taylor is Back on Lover and the Best She's Been in Years" *Vulture* Aug 23 2019

Kornhaber, Spencer, "Taylor Swift Finds Her Faith on Lover" *The Atlantic* Aug 23 2019

Krieger, Deborah, "Creativity in a State of Romantic Bliss" *Pop Matters* Sept 3 2019

Larocca, Courteney, "Lover: All the Ways Taylor Swift's New Album Connects to Her Past 6" *Hollywood Life* Aug 23 2019

Leonard, Keira, "Track-by-Track: We Take You Through Taylor Swift's Brand-New

Album" *Music.com.au* Aug 23 2019

Levine, Nick, "Taylor Swift Lover Review" *NME* Aug 23 2019

McDermott, Maeve, "Taylor Swift is Kid Again on Lover, a Big, Messy Embrace of a New Album" *USA Today* Aug 23 2019

Moniuszko, Sara, "Taylor Swift Lover Reviews" *USA Today* Aug 23 2019

Pollard, Alexandra, "Taylor Swift, Lover Review: The Sound of an Artist Excited to Be Earnest Again" *The Independent* Aug 23 2019

Rayner, Ben, "Track-by-Track Review of Lover" *Toronto Star* Aug 23 2019

Richards, Chris, "The Pop Star Keeps Getting Older Without Growing Up" *Washington Post* Aug 23 2019

Sargent, Jordan, "Taylor Swift's Lover Shines in Its Quietest Moments" *Spin* Aug 26 2019

Willman, Chris, "Album Review; Taylor Swift's Lover" *Variety* Aug 22 2019

Zaleski, Annie, "Taylor Swift Is Done Proving Herself on the Resonant Lover" *The A.V Club* Aug 26 2019

- "The Spinoff Reviews All 18 Songs on Taylor Swift's Lover" *The Spinoff* Aug 26 2019

FOLKLORE

Caramanica, Jon, "Taylor Swift, a Pop Star Done with Pop" *New York Times* July 26 2020

Carras, Christi, "Reviews of Taylor Swift's folklore album Are In" *Los Angeles Times* July 24 2020

Empire, Kitty, "Folklore: Love and Loss in Lockdown" *The Guardian* Aug 1 2020

Erlewine, Stephen, "Taylor Swift; Folklore" *Allmusic* July 29 2020

Hann, Michael, "Taylor Swift's New Album Folklore Is Unlike Anything She's Done Before" *Financial Times* July 24 2020

Holmes, Dave, "With folklore, Taylor Swift Is Truly "On Some New Shit", And We Like It" *Esquire* July 24 2020

Jenkins, Craig, "Taylor Swift's folklore Isn't a Return to Her Roots, But Somewhere She's Never Been" *Vulture* July 27 2020

Keefe, Jonathan, "With Folklore, Taylor Swift Mines Pathos from a Widening Worldview" *Slant Magazine* July 27 2020

Kornhaber, Spencer, "Taylor Swift is No Longer Living in the Present" *The Atlantic* July 28 2020

Lipshutz, Jason, "Taylor Swift's Folklore: There's Nothing Quiet About This Songwriting Tour de Force" *Billboard* July 24 2020

Mapes, Jillian, "Taylor Swift Folklore" *Pitchfork* July 27 2020

Mylrea, Hannah, Folklore review: Pop Superstar Undergoes an Extraordinary Indie-Folk Makeover" *NME* July 24 2020

Nguyen, Giselle, "Taylor Swift's New Album Is a Fever Dream You Won't Want to Wake Up From" *Sydney Morning Herald* July 24 2020

O'Connor, Roisin, "Folklore: This Simmering Album is Exquisite, Piano-based Poetry" *The Independent* July 24 2020

Richards, Chris, "If a Taylor Swift Album Drops in a Pandemic, Does It Make a sound?" *Washington Post* July 24 2020

Schocket, Ryan, "Taylor Swift's Folklore Is a Personal Yet Vicarious Victory" *BuzzFeed* July 24 2020

Sheffield, Rob, "Taylor Swift Leaves Her Comfort Zones Behind on the Head-Spinning, Heartbreaking Folklore" *Rolling Stone* July 24 2020

Smyth, David, "Taylor Swift Folklore Review: A delicately Exquisite Indie Transformation" *Evening Standard* July 24 2020

Snapes, Laura, "Taylor Swift Folklore Review - Bombastic Pop Makes Way for Emotional Acuity" *The Guardian* July 24 2020

Sumsion, Michael, "Taylor Swift Abandons Stadium-Pop for a New Tonal Approach on Folklore" *Pop Matters* July 29 2020

Willman, Chris, "Taylor Swift's folklore: Album Review" *Variety* July 23 2020

Willman, Chris, "Taylor Swift's Folklore a Reflective Set Created in Covid-19 Isolation"

Chicago Tribune July 24 2020

EVERMORE
Bate, Ellie, "Evermore Is Taylor Swift's Least Autobiographical Album - Which Might Explain Why It's Her Best*" BuzzFeed* Dec 19 2020
Brown, Helen, "Evermore; Full of Haunting Tales That Transform Speakers into Campfires" *The Independent* Dec 11 2020
Empire, Kitty, "Taylor Swift: Evermore - A Songwriter for the Ages" *The Guardian* Dec 20 2020
Gardner, Abby, "Evermore Review: All the References and Easter Eggs You Need to Know" *Glamour* Dec 11 2020
Hodgkinson, Will, "Evermore Review: Second Surprise Album Chimes with the Mood of the Moment" *The Times* Dec 11 2020
Johnston, Maura, "Taylor Swift Levels Up on Evermore" *Entertainment Weekly* Dec 12 2020
Krieger, Deborah, "Taylor Swift Has Written the Best Music of Her Career with evermore and folklore" *Pop Matters* Dec 15 2020
Lancaster, Brodie, "Taylor Swift Is Back, Stronger Than Ever Before" *Sydney Morning Herald* Dec 11 2020
Mikael Wood, "Review: Taylor Swift's Surprise LP Evermore Is More - and Less - folklore" *Chicago Tribune* Dec 11 2020
Mylrea, Hannah, "Taylor Swift Evermore Review: The Freewheeling Younger Sibling to Folklore" *NME* Dec 11 2020
Parles, Jon, "Evermore, Taylor Swift's Folklore Sequel Is a Journey Deeper Inward" *New York Times* Dec 11 2020
Richards, Chris, "Taylor Swift Really Can't Help Herself" *Washington Post* Dec 11 2020
Shaffer, Claire, "Taylor Swift Deepens Her Goth-Folk Vision on the Excellent Evermore" *Rolling Stone* Dec 11 2020
Smyth, David, "Evermore Review: Restless Talent Conjures Another Brilliant Surprise" *Evening Standard* Dec 11 2020
Sodomsky, Sam, "Taylor Swift Evermore" *Pitchfork* Dec 15 2020
Zaleski, Annie, "Taylor Swift's Deeply Affecting Continues folklore's Rich Universal-building" *The A.V Club* Dec 14 2020

FEARLESS (TAYLOR'S VERSION)
Bernstein, Johnathan, "Taylor Swift Carefully Reimagines Her Past on Fearless (Taylor's Version)" *Rolling Stone* April 9 2021
Blum, Dani, "Fearless (Taylor's Version" *Pitchfork* April 20 2021
Dwyer, Kate, "Why Fearless (Taylor's Version) Hits Different in 2021" *Marie Claire* April 14 2021
Empire, Kitty, "Fearless (Taylor's Version) - A Labour of Revenge, But Also of Love" *The Guardian* April 10 2021
Goh, Katie, "I Made My Peace" - Fans Divided Over Taylor Swift's Re-recording Project" *The Guardian* April 15 2021
Harbron, Lucy, "Taylor Swift: Fearless (Taylor's Version)" *Clash* April 9 2021
Hodgkinson, Will, "Fearless (Taylor's Version) Review - Sweet, Nostalgic and as Wholesome as Apple Pie" *The Times* April 9 2021
Keefe, Jonathan, "Taylor Swift's New Fearless Gives Mature Voice to Her Insular Teen Musings" *Slant Magazine* April 13 2021
McCormick, Neil, "Taylor Swift Copies Her Younger Self - and she Sounds Even More Fearless Today" *Daily Telegraph* April 9 2021
Mylrea, Hannah, "Fearless (Taylor's Version) Review: A Celebration of the Star's Breakout Album" *NME* April 9 2021
Petridis, Alexis, "Fearless (Taylor's Version) Review - Old Wounds Take on New Resonances" *The Guardian* April 9 2021
Pollard, Alexandra, "Fearless (Taylor's Version) - Wisely trying Not to Rewrite History" *The Independent* April 9 2021
Smyth, David, "Fearless (Taylor's Version) - Now That's How to Win a War" *Evening*

Standard April 10 2021

Stewart, Allison, "Taylor Swift's New Take on Fearless Piles on the Nostalgia, Along with Some Revenge" *Washington Post* April 12 2021

Willman, Chris, "Taylor Swift Turns on a Facsimile Machine for Fearless (Taylor's Version) and It's Ingenious Recreations" *Variety* April 8 2021

Wood, Mikael, "A Principal Stand, a Bonanza for Swifties and a Shrug from Us: Taylor's Made-over Fearless" *Los Angeles Times* April 9 2021

Printed in the USA
CPSIA information can be obtained
at www.ICGtesting.com
LVHW012055061023
760367LV00003B/125

9 781912 587551